ALLAN MOSCOVITCH is a member of the School of Social Work at Carleton University.
GLENN DROVER is Director of the School of Social Work at Carleton University.

In contemporary society it is generally assumed that social welfare reforms overcome inequalities and injustices of society. This collection of thirteen critical essays on welfare in Canada tells a different story revealing inequality as endemic in our society.

With primary emphasis on the structuring of inequality rather than on inequality of condition, the essayists focus on the nature of capitalism and the political economy of social welfare. Their analysis reveals that social measures which have promoted reform have also served to reinforce capitalist relations of production. They consider the fundamental division between the owners of the bulk of capital and the non-owners or workers, and how social welfare reinforces the patterns of inequality through intervention at the fiscal level – income distribution, taxation, and social expenses – and at the social level – media, education, housing, health, and social services.

Stanley Ryerson's penetrating epilogue assesses the possibilities for a more equitable Canadian society.

This volume was planned to have broad academic appeal in the areas of politics, sociology, social work, Canadian studies, political economy, philosophy, history, and public administration.

Studies in the Political Economy of Canada

Close the 49th Parallel etc:
The Americanization of Canada
IAN LUMSDEN, editor
(in conjunction with the University League
for Social Reform)

Capitalism and the National Question in Canada
GARY TEEPLE, editor

The Canadian State:
Political economy and political power
LEO PANITCH, editor

Inequality:
Essays on the political economy of social welfare
ALLAN MOSCOVITCH and GLENN DROVER, editors

EDITED BY ALLAN MOSCOVITCH
AND GLENN DROVER

Inequality:
essays on the
political economy of
social welfare

UNIVERSITY OF TORONTO PRESS

Toronto Buffalo London

© University of Toronto Press 1981
Toronto Buffalo London
Printed in Canada

ISBN 0-8020-2403-3
  0-8020-6426-4 paperback

Canadian Cataloguing in Publication Data
Main entry under title:
Inequality : essays on the political economy of social
welfare

ISBN 0-8020-2403-3 (bound). – ISBN 0-8020-6426-4 (pbk.)

1. Equality – Addresses, essays, lectures. 2. Public
welfare – Canada – Addresses, essays, lectures.
3. Social service – Canada – Addresses, essays, lectures.
4. Canada – Social conditions – Addresses, essays,
lectures. I. Moscovitch, Allan, 1946-   II. Drover,
Glenn, 1935-
HV105.I53   361'.971   C81-094252-6

This book has been published with the assistance of block grants from the Canada
Council and the Ontario Arts Council.

Contents

Editors' preface

The essays in this book examine the political economy of social welfare in
Canada. In doing so, they are primarily concerned with the structuring of
inequality and only secondarily with inequality of conditions. We have
adopted this orientation in the essays and the book for two reasons. First,
while a growing body of literature has documented inequality of condition in
Canada (according to language, sex, ethnicity, race, age), considerably less
attention has been given to the relationship between the underlying structure of capitalism and the inequality of condition which is manifest. In making a choice to focus on the former, we are aware of the limitations of the
book in dealing with the latter. At the same time, the bias of the book is its
strength. By focusing on the nature of capitalism and the political economy
of social welfare we have sought to highlight the causes of inequality. Second, it is our view that the analysis of social welfare in Canada, as elsewhere,
is usually based on the assumptions that social welfare reforms are intended
to overcome or alleviate the inequalities and injustices of capitalist society;
and that these reforms have turned inequality into a marginal rather than
central question. The essays in this book tell a different story. Inequality is
again revealed as endemic to capitalism rather than marginal. Social welfare
measures which have promoted reform have at the same time maintained
and reinforced capitalist relations of production. It is the unfolding of
inequality, despite and because of social welfare, which is the major task of
this book.

The collection developed from seminars on poverty and wealth at Carleton and McGill universities. In those seminars, as in the essays which follow,
we set out to explore three interrelated issues: the peculiarities of capitalism
that reinforce inequality of condition, the contribution, if any, of social welfare measures to alleviate inequalities, and the exploration of strategies to

reduce inequalities. Our effort to explore these three interrelated issues stems from a commitment to equality as a socialist objective and an abiding interest in social welfare as a field of study.

The selection of essays in part I examines the debate which has occurred around inequality, the way in which inequality is structured into the division of social surplus between capital and labour, the distinctive features of Canadian capitalism and social class in the content of world-wide capitalism, and the dual role of the family as an institution for the reproduction of labour power and repression. These essays are united around the view that inequality is based on a fundamental division between those who own the bulk of capital – finance and machine – and those who do not own it but work for those who do. It is from this economic structural inequality that springs the inequality manifested in other realms and in the struggle over who gets what.

The essays in part II examine the ways in which social welfare reinforces the patterns of inequality. The significance of social welfare has received little systematic examination in Canada. Limited attention has been given, until recently, even to the specification of boundaries of social welfare. One of the few useful ways to specify the domain of study is to distinguish two types of collective welfare intervention: that which is mainly fiscal in nature and that which is essentially social. We have used this distinction in this book. Three essays are concerned with fiscal welfare (income distribution, taxation, and social expenses) while the others are concerned with social measures (media, education, housing, and social services).

To specify the boundaries of social welfare alone does not take us very far; it is also important to consider function. Social welfare measures, like other responses of the state, are closely tied to the social and material conditions of production. It follows, based on this proposition, that an understanding of social welfare must be predicated on an understanding of these conditions. By this we do not mean that economic conditions determine everything that we observe in society, but that the economic conditions in society are themselves in the last resort determining of social welfare measures in any period of time. Generally, therefore, fiscal welfare measures such as income redistribution, taxation, or social expenses will bolster, or at least not threaten, the accumulation of profits and capital. Secondly, and of equal importance, is the legitimation of the social order. Without acceptance of the capitalist mode of production by a majority of the population, private appropriation of capital would not be possible. Therefore, social welfare measures act to legitimate the social order in one of two ways: either by reinforcing the dominant ideology as in the case of media or education, or by improving and socializing the cost of, but not fundamentally changing, the social conditions of labour as in the case of housing and social services. In this way, social welfare measures come to be products of and integral to capitalism and thereby sustain and reinforce inequality.

The essays in part II also speculate on alternative strategies to current social welfare as ways of breaking down existing barriers to equality. As opposed to modifying existing social welfare measures, these proposed strategies suggest ways of transforming the structures of capitalism which underpin inequality.

There are many debts which we have incurred in the preparation of this manuscript which must be acknowledged. Friends and comrades with whom we work have provided, at many points, moral and intellectual support. In particular, here, we should mention assistance from Peter Findlay and Jim Albert. Pat Kerans, who figures also as a contributor, assisted in the organization of the conference which was the occasion for the preparation of early drafts of some of the essays published here. Lisa Hamlet, John Pyl, and Kathy Dunlop, all formerly graduate students in the School of Social Work at Carleton University, provided valuable assistance in the organization of that conference and in the preparation of several of the essays. A very rough draft of the articles was kindly and perceptively read by the Board Members of Studies in the Political Economy of Canada (SPEC), including Daniel Drache, Mel Watkins, Wallace Clement, and Leo Panitch, and by Rik Davidson of the University of Toronto Press. The valuable commentaries provided were used to effect revisions and editing, and the commissioning of several new articles. We should cite in particular the detailed review provided by Leo Panitch, whose trenchant criticisms assisted us immeasurably. Editorial assistance was provided by David Louden and by Anne Van Wyck, whose services were paid for by a grant from the Dean of Social Sciences and the Dean of Graduate Studies at Carleton University. In times of great stress additional editorial assistance was provided by Eleanor Drover. In addition, we received the unflagging and enthusiastic assistance of Bev Goold, who typed and retyped many portions of the manuscript. Typing assistance was also provided by Doreen Hallam, Jan Doherty, Lynn Gunn, Caroline Caiger, and Anne-Marie Pinhey. Finally, with the financial assistance of SPEC, David Louden spent many hours helping us to prepare the manuscript for publication.

INTRODUCTION

1
Inequality and social welfare

GLENN DROVER, ALLAN MOSCOVITCH

Social welfare is commonly understood by its students to refer to both a societal ideal and an array of social services or social reforms (usually associated with the welfare state).[1] When conceived of in the broader sense as an objective of society, social welfare implies, as a minimum, a social order in which equity and justice prevail.[2] The minimum criteria have been accepted by those who, like Marshall, equate welfare with the rights of citizenship.[3] The rights define membership in society. For Marshall the history of liberal democratic countries is simply one of a progressive extension of rights. He recognizes, however, the paradox that the extension of rights, based on equality, has coincided with the evolution of capitalism, based on inequality. For him, welfare, as rights, is compatible with capitalism and its class structure precisely because it is 'the foundation of equality on which the structure of inequality can be built.'[4] Rights make inequality more acceptable by promoting a sense of community and solidarity among citizens.

Ideologically, an approach to welfare based on minimum criteria can be divided into two paradigms: conservative welfarism and liberal welfarism.[5] In the conservative tradition, emphasis is placed on coalitions of individuals or consensus in decision making in order to achieve welfare. This perspective stems from a view of the individual as a maximizer of his own well-being. To judge whether welfare can be improved, the Pareto criterion is employed: any change can be made that will make one person better off without making any other person worse off. State action as a means of promoting welfare is considered unwarranted except under exceptional circumstances. Liberal welfarism, by contrast, places emphasis on collective or state intervention to secure rights. While acknowledging rational self-interest in obtaining rights, the liberal also acknowledges that rights can only be secured with mutual limitation. Collective intervention is warranted to provide for equality of opportunity, rarely for equality of outcome.

Socialists, in contrast to conservatives and liberals, have argued that social welfare as a societal objective is more than equity and justice. Social welfare presupposes substantive equality. A social welfare society is one in which rights, incentives, exchanges, regulations, and institutions are based on an egalitarian order. Tawney persuasively developed the social and moral case for equality in this way, not in the naïve sense of equality of talent or merit or personality, but rather in the sense of fundamental equalities, the provision of basic goods and services for everyone, the enlargement of personal liberties, and the mutual sharing of a common heritage.[6] Hence, Tawney associated social welfare with a society in which the planning of social and economic organization is established through institutions which meet common needs and share common resources.

Socialists, in other words, conceive of social welfare as a norm based on solidarity and co-operation but with a difference from the conservative or liberal. Social welfare is realized not only through the recognition of rights but in accordance with a system of organization of production and distribution based on a criterion of human need.[7] Welfare entails the regulation of work and living conditions as well as the distribution of output.[8] For Marx the social organization of capitalism constitutes the antithesis of social welfare. The capitalist mode of production, based as it is on private property, inheritance, production for private gains, and the allocation of resources through the market, assures not only the continuance of inequality but also the dominance of values such as competition and individualism over co-operation and solidarity. Consequently, welfare can only be realized as a norm after the means of production have been socialized.

While sharing a common vision of welfare as equality, however, socialists can also be divided ideologically. Social democrats rely upon state intervention in a capitalist order to achieve welfare. Marxists question whether state intervention fundamentally can change the basic structures of capitalism which prevent the achievement of social welfare. The social democrat, like the liberal, continues to be concerned with issues of rights and equality but places more emphasis on collective action.[9] Collective preference is presumed to lead to more equitable distribution, mainly, but not exclusively, through the state. In the Marxist framework, by contrast, social welfare is not separable from the mode of production, nor power from the division of labour.[10] A capitalist economic order is associated with the absence of welfare both because it atomizes individuals and because it creates a social division of labour in which the majority is dominated by a minority. The state, rather than being neutral to the process, as is often implied by social democrats, legitimizes existing patterns of rewards in accordance with the interests of private capital.

Aside from the conception of social welfare as an ideal, the term has another restricted meaning, namely, the collective provision of goods and services, status, and rights. This does not imply an egalitarian society; other values, such as efficiency, may prevail. Social welfare, in this sense, has become widely associated with the practice of social administration in England or social policy in Canada.[11] It presupposes intervention in society, increasingly in the form of state intervention, in order to tackle social problems. It involves gauging the nature and extent of these problems, evaluating current policies which supposedly respond to the problems, and developing alternative courses of action. While the definition of social policy or social administration varies widely, there is common consensus that it involves a range of public services or interventions related to areas such as education, social services, income redistribution, transfer payments, and housing. This does not mean that the state necessarily takes over in these areas (though that is sometimes true), but that state intervention acts either to offset inequalities that arise from the market or simply to assure universal access to services that are considered essential to individual well-being. As with the notion of societal welfare discussed above, social policy can be viewed from two vantage points. One way is to consider it as distinct from, but complementary to, economic policy. Since it is widely recognized in capitalist societies that the inequalities and injustices created by the market need to be offset, social policy is assumed to play an important role in enhancing equality. Social welfare therefore represents a form of state intervention intended to correct the perverse effects of the economic system. This idea of state intervention rests on the separation of the economic from the social and presupposes that social policies benefit those to whom they are addressed.[12]

In general, the degree of state intervention advanced from this perspective depends upon the extent to which the market is perceived as ineffectual in overcoming inequalities and injustices. Richard Titmuss distinguishes three approaches to social welfare that are pursued in contemporary capitalist societies.[13] They are restatements of the conservative, liberal, and social democratic traditions in micro. The first is a residual approach and is closely associated with a conservative philosophy of state intervention. It presupposes that individual needs are met primarily through two channels: the market and the family. Only when there is a breakdown in either does the state intervene, and then only minimally. The second is an industrial achievement model and approximates the liberal position. It incorporates an important role for welfare institutions as adjuncts of the market, primarily because the development of technology and industrialism creates social problems which are not easily resolved by the family or through other private institutions. The third is a redistributive model and corresponds to a social democratic perspective. It views 'social welfare as a major integrated institution in society providing universalist services outside the market on the basis of need.'[14] Unlike the liberal position, this model recognizes that not only equality of opportunity but also equality of outcome is necessary if individuals in society are to have a reasonable and equitable command over resources. It is this latter model that is usually associated with the welfare state. Hence students of welfare frequently assume that social welfare reforms are intended to overcome or alleviate many of the inequalities and injustices in society, a viewpoint stated most recently in a widely distributed book entitled *Social Welfare in Canada* by Andrew Armitage.[15]

The essays on social welfare in this book are based on an alternative perspective. We argue that social welfare reforms, while alleviating some inequalities and injustices, have not changed the fundamentals of capitalist society in any substantive way. The changes always remain within the bounds of the existing social order. This is not to deny that temporary benefits accrue to individuals in society in the process of reform, but to suggest that the reforms promote neither fundamental changes in the social structure of capitalism nor in class consciousness.[16] Instead of viewing social welfare policies as separate from economic activity or as necessarily beneficial, we hold that there is a dialectical relationship between reform and the maintenance of capitalist social relations. That is, while acknowledging that social reforms are instituted in order to offset injustices arising from the market, intervention is likely to leave untouched the political power of private capital or class relations. Ian Gough suggests that the state, when involved in social welfare reforms, is involved in a tightrope act,

balancing the concessions it can offer to its mass base on the one hand with the need to serve the political interests of capital on the other hand. So long as the concessions are there to be given it can walk quite a way along this tightrope without actually falling off; when the economy is in a downturn however its political survival is considerably more precarious. But all governments of whatever political complexion depend for their survival under bourgeois democracy on their ability to offer certain reforms and concessions to the struggles of the dominated classes.[17]

Post-war social policy in capitalist countries is considered by Gough to be part of a world-wide settlement between capital and labour brought about by militant class struggle. The extent of reform in various countries depends, he states, upon both the militancy of the working classes and their political influence. The greater the strength of the labour movement, the greater the concession.[18] In general, he considers the concessions to be more extensive in centralist states of Europe, where parties act in the interest of a particular class, than in federalist countries such as Canada, where political pressure is more diffused.

CAUSES OF INEQUALITY

Many studies have indicated that inequalities are characteristic of Canadian society. Indeed, they are pervasive throughout the developed world.[19] Why is this the case? A common answer given to this question is that goods and services are distributed according to desert or the value of work done.[20] This is an old theory but has been restated recently in an influential book by the American philosopher John Rawls, who argues that the significance of distributive measures, whether of goods and services, rights, or status, can be judged on the basis of two criteria.[21] First, each person in society has an equal right to the most extensive liberty compatible with like liberty for all; secondly, inequalities defined or fostered by institutional structures are arbitrary – unless one can assume that they will work to everyone's advantage.[22]

The importance of this theory for our purposes is that inequalities can be considered just if the conditions of the worse-off are improved over time. The presumption, as Rawls notes, is that 'inequality in expectation provides an incentive so that the economy is more efficient, industrial advance proceeds at a quicker pace and so on, the end result of which is that greater material and other benefits are distributed throughout the system.'[23] It follows that welfare state transfers or programs of equal opportunity can only be developed to the extent that 'they will not interfere with the efficiency and growth of the productive system.'[24] This approach, when applied to a capitalist society such as Canada, does not take into account the fact that inequality presupposes that one class will dominate another. While it acknowledges the concentration of wealth and power in capitalist societies, this is not considered to be a problem if government can prevent the concentration from exceeding a certain limit. The conception of government implied in Rawls' analysis assumes a neutrality between capital and labour, which, as we shall see shortly, is doubtful. More importantly, an explanation of 'just' inequalities based upon Rawlsian principles 'does not recognize that in a competitive market system where capital and labour are in separate hands, all capital, whatever its concentration, is power which controls and impedes the lives of others. Capital in that society is extractive power and the extractive power of the owners of capital diminishes the developmental powers of the non-owners.'[25]

INEQUALITY AND THE SOCIAL ORGANIZATION OF PRODUCTION

Rather than look at inequality as inherent in common characteristics of individuals, we posit that inequalities are primarily a consequence of the social organization of production. Under capitalism, production is owned and/or controlled by a relatively small group of people. The labour needed to keep production going is tied to a system of wages in which the worker has no ownership of the means of production. Within the labour-market, different occupational groups receive different wages from the highest to the lowest paid. The major sources of inequality lie in the distribution of material and symbolic resources among members of society, and the control over distribution is integrally linked to the underlying institutions of which it is a part. In capitalist societies, these can be defined as private property, capital accumulation, class, and sexism.

Private property
The misconception of property as a thing and as private property is, as Macpherson argues, a modern phenomenon.[26] Up to the sixteenth century, property was recognized as a right to the use of, or benefit of, something which included common resources as well as individual claims. Property as a right did not necessarily mean that an individual had exclusive control over the thing in question. It presupposed that individuals had enforceable claims, not unlimited claims, on land or capital. Rarely were the rights fully disposed of by a given owner because of multiple claims on resources.[27] The conception of property as a thing rather than a right came with the development of capitalism. With the full flowering of the market, as land and capital were exchanged, 'limited and not always saleable rights *in* things were being replaced by virtually unlimited and saleable rights *to* things.'[28] Property, in other words, became considered as an exclusive control over a commodity or thing which could be bought or sold on the market. This usage is still with us today although, as Macpherson argues, property is again being seen as a right in the twentieth century, more in the form of revenue than a material object.

More important than the association of property with a thing rather than a right, the identification of property almost exclusively with private property also arose in the early stages of capitalism.[29] Prior to the seventeenth century, rights in property were associated with common and private property. From that period on, land and other resources were converted into private possessions in which the owner had the perceived right to dispose of or alienate as he wished. Consequently, private property became 'an individual right unlimited in amount, unconditional on the performance of social functions, and freely transferable, as it substantially remains to the present day.'[30] It was the kind of property which was needed in order to enable the market to operate fully in the allocation of labour and resources, unrestrained by collective intervention. With that transformation, private property was increasingly justified by political and social apologists on the basis of just occupancy, social contract, or social utility.

When perceived as the exclusive possession of an individual or corporate entity, property is based on a principle of inequality. It allows the owner the almost unlimited power of excluding others from it, and of setting conditions for its use. The institution of individual property rights, therefore, fixes inequality as an immutable condition of life: the more property one owns, the more profit derived from it, the greater the ability to acquire more.[31] With substantial property a few individuals can live on the labour of others while the majority have little to sell except their own labour power.

In Canada recent studies illustrate the enormous concentration of private property in the past as well as in the present. Robert Chodos in his book *The CPR: A Century of Corporate Welfare* explains how Canada's largest private railway and some of its directors gained power through the procurement of land, mostly in the form of grants from the dominion government.[32] A different and more recent story of the power of private property has been told by Peter Spurr.[33] Writing about the concentration of urban land holdings in contemporary Canada, he concludes that 'in most of the largest centres in Ontario, Alberta, Saskatchewan, Manitoba, over 75% of residential lots are produced by a small minority of all developers.'[34]

Private property is, of course, more than ownership of land, even though land has always played an important part, at least historically, in the accumulation of wealth. Shareholders of the CPR were closely tied to ownership of commercial enterprises and the banks. The Hudson Bay Company, which preceded the CPR in terms of its influence in the west, is a case in point. The lucrative advantage of the company to its owners came from control over trade and commerce in an area larger than continental Europe, populated mainly by Indians and Metis.[35] This monopoly position gave the shareholders an enormous advantage. As one author suggests: 'The mark-up on merchandise sold to settlers and Indians was between 100 and 400 percent; private trading was outlawed and a capital offence. The Indians were then forced to rely exclusively on the company for gunpowder; and the few settlers that managed to squeeze into the territory ... depended on it as their sole market for agriculture produce.'[36]

The case of Canada's chartered banks is an even more intriguing story of power and control. Naylor has shown how a few chartered banks, such as the Bank of Montreal, came to dominate banking and finance in the period following Confederation.[37] Very often the same men who owned, or dominated the development of, the railways or trade also owned or dominated (usually by shared directorates) the banks. In addition, the power of banks was enhanced by close ties with the dominion government, a rapid series of mergers up to 1914, and strong linkages to other financial institutions. The result today is that Canada's banking system is one of the most centralized in the world, and boards of directors of these banks make up the 'who's who' throughout the country.

The concentration of property on this scale gives the owner extensive economic power. This applies whether the property is land, finance, capital, or ownership of the means of production. Wallace Clement has shown that economic enterprise is highly concentrated in Canada.[38] Contemporary Canadian society is dominated by a small number of corporations and their directors who constitute the corporate elite. Through a series of subsidiaries, affiliates, investments, and interlocking directorships, the power of these corporations is consolidated by control over the major sources of capital and 'over the paramount positions within most of the central economic sectors.'[39] The idea, then, that all Canadians enter into the market and compete equally for ownership of property in contemporary society simply is not true.

Moreover, what follows from the pre-eminence of private property – the right to possess – is the 'intergenerational transmission of the right to accumulate property.'[40] Inevitably this inheritance right leads to further inequalities by 'determining the vantage-ground upon which different groups and individuals will stand, the range of opportunities which shall be open to them, and the degree of economic stress which they shall undergo.'[41] The reason for this is simple. Inheritance causes an initial inequality, which is perpetuated through life. The result is a division of society into 'haves' and 'have-nots'; one engaging in the formulation of laws to protect its vantage position, the other struggling to obtain a portion of property to improve its lot. The unequal distribution of resources and power is consequently maintained not only by private property but by accidents of birth.

Capital accumulation and concentration
The tendency for capital to accumulate and to be concentrated in fewer and larger units is a central aspect of capitalist society.[42] This process dates back to

the early days of mercantile capitalism. As capitalism was transformed from the mercantile to the industrial form, the drive to accumulate took on new force. Increasingly, in nineteenth-century Canada, portfolio capital became important as investors from metropolitan nations, such as England and the United States, invested in the colonies and peripheral nations.[43] In this way they assured industrial production and the development of natural resources while maintaining control from the centre. Subsequently, as capitalism advanced from its entrepreneurial and corporate stage to the new phase of state monopoly capitalism, the process of centralized control and capital concentration through equity capital accelerated. At present, capitalism is a world-wide system of production and distribution, as well as a major force in world-wide inequality. It may be argued, in fact, that to the extent that capital accumulation is the major goal of free enterprise, inequality is its inescapable by-product. There are two reasons for this.

First, the later development of peripheral nations meant initially that industrialization lagged behind the metropolitan nations, partly because control of capital rested with the latter and partly because investment in the periphery was directed to the extraction of natural resources for use in manufacturing industries at the metropole. In addition, the larger markets were at the metropole. Consequently, capitalists in a country such as Canada did not build the necessary industrial enterprises and transportation infrastructure to compete with the metropolitan centres. Instead, they specialized in trade (functioning as intermediaries between Canadian staples and metropolitan markets) and later in finance and transportation (again to get staples to the markets), leaving industrial production to foreigners. In the twentieth century, control of productive capital shifted from Britain to the United States with the intensification of resource extraction and manufacturing in Canada. The modern consequences of this development are now well known: the emergence of the multinationals, foreign control, a staples economy, economic fragmentation, and political disintegration. The Watkins report, the Gray report, Walter Gordon, Eric Kierans, Abraham Rotstein, and Ian Lumsden – all have documented the increasing dependence of Canada on American capital.[44] Kari Levitt recounts dramatically the lengthening list of political and economic inequalities which have resulted.[45] In addition, Canada has consistently had a higher rate of unemployment and under-employment than most developed countries have had during the last thirty years.[46]

A second reason why inequality is an inescapable by-product of private capital accumulation is the uneven development inherent in growth. Uneven development stems from the fact that 'capitalism is a world system, based on an international division of labour and world-wide development of productive forces.'[47] In discussing the nature of capital we have already noted how uneven development on a world-wide scale leads to certain nations advancing at the expense of others because the surplus produced is controlled by dominant nations. Within a given economy, the same process is at work and is most evident in regional underdevelopment.

Traditional theory tends to view the problem of regional underdevelopment as resulting from the inability of regions to create self-sustaining growth due to distance from markets, lack of entrepreneurial initiative, poor infrastructure, low levels of education, or combinations of all four.[48] The idea that patterns of development are simply the result of anonymous market forces obscures the role of economic and political decisions made in the metropole which lead to the concentration of capital at the expense of the hinterland.[49] Within hinterland regions, independent commodity production, such as farming and craft industries, declines due to mechanization and migration to the urban industrialized areas. In contrast to central areas, modernization and industrialization do not take place except in selected capital-intensive resource extraction industries, which generate neither extensive employment opportunities nor alternative investments in associated manufacturing. What remains are primary sectors such as lumbering and fishing, but they are labour-intensive low wage industries. The structure of inequality which results from the uneven development in Canada has been documented most recently by Paul Phillips.[50] Average income in some regions falls behind that which is prevalent in central regions; unemployment and underemployment are intensified; manufacturing is concentrated in Ontario; migration is a way of life; public services are underdeveloped; and the Maritimes are economically stagnant.

Class
The idea of class, Tawney states, 'is among the most powerful of social categories.'[51] It is powerful because, as an objective reality, class has been widely observed in all societies, but as a subjective reality it is frequently denied. A group described as a class may not perceive itself as a class. Canadians, for example, can be divided by class according to their relationship to the means of production in the simplest of formulations – capitalists and workers. But the division of Canadian society according to these analytical concepts does not necessarily mean that all workers objectively defined will perceive themselves as workers. Rather, they will see themselves as white- or blue-collar workers, skilled or unskilled, civil servants or private producers. This distinction should not be used to confuse 'the fact of class with

the consciousness of class which is a different phenomenon. The former may exist without the latter.'[52] Within sociological circles, debates continue on the exact boundaries and causes of class, but most sociologists are agreed that class is, in many ways, synonymous with inequality.

In contemporary Canada, the class structure of the economy, and more particularly of a capitalist elite, has been documented by Wallace Clement. He suggests that inequality of opportunity is characteristic of Canada precisely because there is inequality of condition.[53] The accumulation of privilege which is associated with dominant positions is transmitted to those individuals who are most closely related by kinship to those in power. Through education, inheritance, careers, and informal associations, class differences are perpetuated in favour of a small and select group. Clement also examines the intricate relationship between the Canadian elite and its American counterpart – a relationship which, in many ways, shows the dominance of the multinational elite in the Canadian economy.[54] He draws on his findings to suggest that the Canadian elite are integrated into the world capitalist order in two ways – as mediators between core nations such as the United States and peripheral nations such as Latin America, and as hosts to extensive foreign investment.[55] An understanding of the go-between role of Canadian capital, he argues, is important to an appreciation of the peculiar structure of the capitalist class and, therefore, of the inequality which pervades Canadian society.

One consequence of Canadian economic development is the fragmentation of the elite within Canada and the increasing subordination of Canadian to foreign capitalists.[56] Another is an accentuation of the inequalities that were identified earlier, partly because Canadian capitalists have less say over wages and salaries than their American equivalents, and partly because the rapid growth of the comprador faction is simply a reflection of larger structural changes inherent in Canadian society – the concentration of capital and unequal development.

Sexism
Sexism is, by no means, exclusive to capitalism, but an understanding of inequality is not possible without consideration of sexism in capitalist societies. Increasingly, research seems to be indicating that except in terms of chromosomes, hormone production, and reproduction functions, there are no simple differences between the sexes that are not related to the socialization of individuals to societally accepted patterns of thought.[57] Consequently, one explanation of inequality between the sexes is that it results from socialization. Essentially this explanation assumes that inequalities between men

and women are passed on through the generations. Boys and girls are taught appropriate masculine and feminine behaviour from early life. This explanation is, of course, true to a degree but it fails to account for the source of the ideas and behaviour patterns which are part of the conventional wisdom. By positing the importance of ideas over structural factors the approach concentrates on examining and changing the transmission of ideas. An explanation of inequality, however, must consider not only how 'ideas are perpetuated and how they affect human behavior but also where these ideas originate.'[58]

According to Dorothy Smith the subordination of women came about, in part, because capitalism led to the separation of public and private spheres in the organization of production. The public sphere is where production takes place, where decisions count, where history is made. The private sphere is where service and support are given; it is outside the productive sphere. What is significant about this distinction is that the female in the private sphere is subordinate not simply or even primarily to the male but to the social organization of production (the public sphere).[59]

In contemporary capitalism, women also fulfil an increasingly important role in the labour force as well as for the labour force. Pat and Hugh Armstrong show the linkage between the home and the workplace as a subordinate relationship on two accounts.[60] Within the family a woman is subordinate because she is essentially dependent upon the male for income; within the labour force she is subordinate because she can only take on those jobs which do not interfere extensively with her maintenance and reproduction functions.

Beyond the relation between the family and production, however, women are also defined by their class positions. As Charnie Guettel states: 'Sex would be the primary contradiction if all males owned the means of production and all females worked for them. But almost all males and females, under capitalism, work for some males, not by virtue of the latter's maleness, but because they own property.'[61] If this is overlooked, one also overlooks that the oppression of women, determined in the first instance by the mode of production, would be less likely to exist if men were not in the first place providers in a class-based society. This is not to suggest, as noted earlier, that sexism exists only in capitalism, but it does imply that the form of sexism inherent in capitalism is integrally related to class structure in two ways. First, the class position of a woman influences her experience of sexism. In capitalism, for example, Smith argues that where middle- and working-class women had a productive role in the past in family maintenance, this is less the case today for bourgeois women.[62] Work for this class has become trivialized to the point where a woman functions primarily to keep up the image of what a house or household of good corporate standing should have. Secondly, it affects a woman's consciousness of herself as a woman. Because one woman has a superior position in society to another, not by virtue of her status as a woman but because of class, she is more likely to view existing structures as natural and inevitable. Class, in other words, helps to prevent women from being fully aware of their subordinate status as women.

The unequal position of women in the family and the workplace is widely acknowledged in Canada. In the family, two important tasks are housework and child care. In both of them inequality is pervasive. Housework, for example, has no place in the market; there are no wages, and women lack the independence which wages provide. In addition, the contribution they make to family enterprise is not necessarily recognized by law.[63]

Inequality in the home, however, is only one aspect of women's reality. Inequality in the workplace is even more pervasive. Women's increasing participation in the labour force has been attributed to a search for self-fulfilment, but for most, more income is the primary motivation. Some 64 per cent of the 1975 female labour force either were the sole support of their families or provided essential income to family maintenance.[64] On the other hand, while women have moved increasingly into the labour force, they have not moved into all occupations on an equal footing or obtained equal pay with men. Almost one-half of all working women are employed in organizations where they represent about two-thirds of all workers.[65] Over half of the female labour force works as stenographers, sales clerks, service workers, school teachers, garment workers, waitresses, nursing assistants, telephone operators, and janitors. Most of these occupations are low paid. By contrast, women represent less than 15 per cent of managerial, craft, production process, and related workers – most of whom are relatively highly paid.[66]

SOCIAL WELFARE, INEQUALITY, AND THE STATE

When we turn to the interrelationship between social welfare, inequality, and the state, it is important to recognize that in liberal democratic societies the state is popularly viewed as an institution which can and does alleviate injustices by moderating the inequalities generated by the market. The fact that inequalities persist in a capitalist market society is now widely accepted by people of all political persuasions. Some writers, of course, while acknowledging the existence of inequalities, are inclined to defend them or to suggest only marginal changes, while others propose more sweeping changes.[67] Both groups share the view that the state functions as a neutral arbiter between labour and capital or different classes within society, thereby being able to redistribute goods and services, rights, and statuses along more egalitarian lines.

We suggest that this view ignores the role which the state plays in the reproduction and reinforcement of social relations. Authors such as Miliband, O'Connor, Poulantzas, Panitch, and Gough vary in their interpretation of the role of the state, but agree that the capitalist state acts as an agent of dominant class interests.[68] This is done in three ways. The principal function is to support and expand the relations of production, since it is the continuing process of production of surplus, and accumulation of capital which is the basis of capitalist economies. The level of accumulation depends on the nature, availability, and cost of capital, as well as the level of skill, productivity, availability, and cost of labour. In relation to capital, the state attempts to establish a stable economic climate for the generation of surplus and capital accumulation through the use of a range of forms of state action, such as control of the money supply, provision of direct capital grants, marketing assistance, favourable terms of finance, and taxation.

The second function of the state is the maintenance of private property – an institution which, as we already noted, is itself the historical basis of inequality in capitalist societies. It is backed by the judicial system, the military, the police, and the courts. Because of the central importance of private property, this function is primarily coercive in nature and almost exclusively a public responsibility. It is the government of the day which sets the process in motion, creating the laws to be interpreted, using the judiciary or the police when particular forms of coercion are deemed necessary.

A third set of state actions (those which are of primary interest to us in this book) is geared to the maintenance and legitimation of the very inegalitarian social order which the other two functions of the state reinforce. State actions of this type have a two-fold character: they serve to maintain existing inegalitarian social relations of production in response to, or in anticipation of, working-class unrest or economic and political crises, while at the same time providing amelioration of the social conditions of labour. The state takes a major role in the provision of such essential services as education and housing, and in the provision of support services such as unemployment insurance, welfare, family allowances, family and child social services, all aimed at ensuring the continued availability of a relatively cheap and quiescent labour force.[69] It is important to note that unlike the coercive function, the legitimation function is not, as Althusser observes, an exclusive responsibility of the state.[70] Rather, it is a shared responsibility with institutions such as the church, the family, the schools, and the media. Thus inequalities are assured not only by the direct intervention of the state but by the support of allied institutions.

The growth of state-funded and state-administered programs in pursuit of legitimation represents a major change in the structure of state activity and in the social conditions prevalent in twentieth-century capitalist nations.[71] In this growth, Canada is no exception. If we date the early development of capitalism in Canada from the second third of the nineteenth century, then the period from the 1840s up until immediately before the outbreak of the First World War in 1914 is one in which the state and private welfare programs which are the precursors of the modern welfare state were established. This was the era of the rise of church-based, voluntary, charitable institutions, corporate welfarism, and limited state legislation.

In the inter-war period, there emerged from the economic and political turmoil a considerable number of state programs which now constitute integral parts of the Canadian 'welfare state.' Programs such as federally funded relief, unemployment insurance, pensions, mothers allowance, grants in aid of construction of housing, minimum wages, and limitations of hours of work laws all have their origins in this period. Near the end of and subsequent to the Second World War, additional social welfare programs were introduced into Canada both in order to aid economic reconstruction and to respond to anticipated and real working-class militancy which was being channelled into radical unions and political parties. The centralizing tendencies in Canadian capitalism and the reluctance of provincial governments to enter the field ensured that welfare programs were primarily initiated federally. External influences were also important. The (English) Beveridge report, released in 1942, was a Canadian best seller. Strikes, unionization, and the advance of the political fortunes of the CCF were all factors in influencing the government of the day to request Leonard Marsh, a prominent Canadian social researcher in the 1930s, to complete a report on social security early in 1943. Two years later, the re-elected government of Prime Minister Mackenzie King introduced legislation, based on one of the recommendations of Marsh's report, to establish a system of family allowances, a major expenditure at the time.[72]

The post-war compromise between labour and capital extracted at a high price in Britain and Europe appears to have required little more of the Canadian government than family allowances. The wartime apparatus which gave the state extensive involvement in most aspects of the economic sphere was systematically dismantled to be replaced again by private enterprise at public expense. Rent control, price and supply controls, and industrial relations regulations were transferred to provincial jurisdiction or ended. Wartime Housing Limited, a major state developer and landlord was replaced by Central Mortgage and Housing Corporation, a mortgage bank primarily for financial institutions, and the large stock of public housing was sold off.[73]

Ameliorative changes included revisions to the legislation providing for old-age and blind persons pensions, and to the Unemployment Insurance Act, and the establishment of federal grants-in-aid for the construction of hospitals, social assistance for the disabled, and the regulation of relief expenditures.

The first period of post-war federal Tory government saw few changes in the social welfare apparatus. A federal program for vocational rehabilitation and expansion of the availability of mortgage funds were the major changes occurring during the economic downturn which dominated the Diefenbaker years. A more important change took place in Saskatchewan in 1961 with the introduction of medicare by the CCF government of Tommy Douglas.

The change of federal government in 1963 established a period of five years of minority rule. The need for a formal political compromise to maintain the minority Pearson government, coupled with a political reawakening generated by the American civil rights movement, the international ban-the-bomb campaign, the Vietnam War, and the American war on poverty, and internalized in the first stirring in Canada of the war and post-war generation, were the political pressures for reform. In addition, national social legislation was viewed as a way of maintaining state structures (co-operative federalism) in response to the growing dissatisfaction of Quebec and the have-not provinces. The economic expansion of this period provided the base on which could be built a major reorganization and expansion of federal support for social welfare. The period also saw the renewal of liberal ideology through the belief that improved social conditions could be achieved by the introduction of equal opportunity programs.[74]

In the early Trudeau years, the same political and economic circumstances combined with majority government to generate even more optimism about the potential of the state to introduce social welfare reforms. However, by the mid-1970s, the tide had changed. Politically the federal government was increasingly faced with a legitimation crisis as English Canadians tired of a seemingly incessant struggle between Ottawa and Quebec. The provinces claimed that the federal government's centralist policies were infringing upon their constitutional responsibilties for social programs, and the constitutional conferences of 1968-71 broke down.[75] Economically the federal government was confronted with two issues. On the one hand, high rates of inflation and recession combined with the structural problems of a branch-plant economy to force it into a position of restraint.[76] On the other hand, there was the haunting realization, based upon a growing number of studies, that many of the equal opportunity programs simply had failed to achieve what they set out to do. Faced with these multiple pressures, the government cut out or cut back some of the social programs initiated in the early years of the Liberal regime, while others were reevaluated.

The Liberal years of 1963 to 1979 represented the rise and decline of post-war efforts to buttress equality of opportunity in Canada. From the early days of the Pearson administration to the middle years of Trudeau's, successive federal governments introduced a range of social welfare reforms that were intended ostensibly to promote equality among Canadians. They included the Canada Pension Plan (1965), the National Medical Care Insurance Act (1966), the Canada Assistance Plan (1966), the Department of Regional Economic Expansion (1969), the Unemployment Insurance Act (1971), Tax Reforms (1973), and a new Family Allowance Act (1973). They also included the institution since 1971 of a series of make-work programs, such as OFY, LIP, LEAP, and Canada Works, aimed at siphoning off the dissent generated by a youthful core of unemployed unable to find the jobs promised them in the resurgence of the myth of equality of opportunity in the 1960s.

Since 1973, the expansion of legitimation programs, put in place primarily during the previous ten years, has been a principal factor in the outstripping of the growth of state revenues by state expenditures. This squeeze of revenues by expenditures has been generated by an economic downturn, which has featured rising unemployment coupled with inflation and, consequently, a growth of union militancy in the face of the potential decline in real incomes. Wage controls, cut-backs in public (particularly social welfare) expenditures, changes in UIC, the eroding of health insurance, the expansion of the prison system, and the restatement of an ideology of blaming the victim for economic and political conditions less favourable for capital accumulation have taken the place of the high optimism of social welfare reform and equality of opportunity which dominated the 1960s. The new liberal ideology now in the process of formation stresses that capital accumulation is the basis of society. For the economy to grow, capital must grow. For capital to grow, there must be large profits. For profits to be large, there must be fewer wage demands, higher productivity, and fewer social welfare programs to drain off profits and capital. The myth that inequality can be eliminated is dying and being replaced again by inequality as necessity. While the process may result in more ideological clarity, it must be a source of concern and a cause for the renewal of working-class militancy in the face of the decline of hard-fought-for social programs. For the capitalist state, social welfare is a means of legitimation; the challenge for socialists and egalitarians is not to see social welfare programs disassembled but to renovate existing ones and to create new ones to serve different ends.

NOTES

1 The literature is extensive and growing. See, for example, Harold Wilensky and Charles Lebaux, *Industrial Society and Social Welfare* (New York 1965); Richard Titmuss, *Essays on the Welfare State* (London 1968); Gaston Rimlinger, *Welfare Policy and Industrialization in Europe, America and Russia* (New York 1971); David Gil, *Unravelling Social Policy* (Cambridge, Mass. 1973); Vic George and Paul Wilding, *Ideology and Social Welfare* (London 1976); Bill Jordan, *Freedom and the Welfare State* (London 1976); Ramesh Mishra, *Society and Social Policy: Theoretical Perspectives on Welfare* (London 1977).
2 Mishra, *Society and Social Policy*, 11
3 T.H. Marshall, *Social Policy* (London 1965)
4 T.H. Marshall, *Sociology at the Crossroads and Other Essays* (London 1963), 91, cited in Mishra, *Society and Social Policy*, 23
5 George and Wilding, *Ideology and Social Welfare*; the material in this paragraph is based on G. Drover and D. Woodsworth, 'Social Welfare Theory and Social Policy', *The Canadian Journal of Social Work Education*, IV, 3 (1978), 19-41.
6 R.H. Tawney, *Equality* (London 1964), 15 ('Introduction' by Titmuss)
7 Mishra, *Society and Social Policy*, 63
8 Ibid., 78
9 Drover and Woodsworth, 'Social Welfare Theory,' 24
10 Ibid., 26
11 For England, see the studies of Richard Titmuss, *Essays on the Welfare State* and *Social Policy: An Introduction* (London 1974). In Canada a recent book in this area is Shankar Yelaja, ed., *Canadian Social Policy* (Waterloo 1978).
12 Xavier Greffe, *La politique sociale* (Paris 1975), 15
13 Titmuss, *Social Policy*, chap. 2, and *Essays on the Welfare State*, chap. 2
14 Titmuss, *Social Policy*, 31
15 Andrew Armitage, *Social Welfare in Canada: Ideals and Realities* (Toronto 1975)
16 The distinction between reform and fundamental change has been made by Manuel Castells, *The Urban Question* (London 1979), 26 ff. For an application of the distinction, see Eric Shragge and Glenn Drover, 'Urban Struggle and Organizing Strategies,' *Our Generation*, XIII, 1 (Winter 1979), 61-76.
17 Ian Gough, 'State Expenditure in Advanced Capitalism,' *New Left Review*, 92 (July-Aug. 1975), 66
18 Ibid., 74
19 Frank Parkin, *Class, Inequality and Political Order* (St. Albans 1975); Walter Connor, *Socialism, Politics and Equality* (New York 1979)

20 This exploration of inequality is discussed in many texts. Two which are relevant to social welfare are W.G. Runciman, *Relative Deprivation and Social Justice* (London 1966); and Amartya Sen, *On Economic Inequality* (Oxford 1973).

21 J. Rawls, *A Theory of Justice* (Cambridge 1971), discussed in Albert Weale, *Equality and Social Policy* (London 1978), passim

22 Ibid., 33

23 John Rawls, 'Distributive Justice,' in Peter Laslett and W.G. Runciman, eds., *Philosophy, Politics and Society, Third Series* (Oxford 1967), 67, as cited in C.B. Macpherson, *Democratic Theory* (Oxford 1973), 91

24 Macpherson, ibid., 91

25 Ibid., 92

26 C.B. Macpherson, ed., *Property: Mainstream and Critical Positions* (Toronto 1978), chaps. 1 and 12

27 Ibid., 3 ff.

28 Ibid., 8 (emphasis in original)

29 Ibid., 9 f.

30 Ibid., 10

31 Bernice Shatz, 'The Defense of Socially Structured Inequality: A Theoretical Analysis,' PHD thesis, Brandeis University, Waltham, Mass., 1972, p. 43

32 Robert Chodos, *The CPR: A Century of Corporate Welfare* (Toronto 1973)

33 Peter Spurr, *Land and Urban Development* (Toronto 1976)

34 Ibid., 396

35 R.T. Naylor, 'The Rise and Fall of the Third Commerical Empire of the St. Lawrence,' in Gary Teeple, ed., *Capitalism and The National Question* (Toronto 1972)

36 Ibid., 16

37 R.T. Naylor, *The History of Canadian Business 1867-1914* (Toronto 1975), I, chap. 3

38 Wallace Clement, *The Canadian Corporate Elite*, Carleton Library Series, no. 89 (Ottawa 1975), 125

39 Ibid.

40 Shatz, 'Defence of Socially Structured Inequality,' 45

41 Tawney, *Equality*, 117, as cited in Shatz, ibid., 46

42 There is a great deal of literature on this subject; a very readable and well-known book is Paul Sweezy, *The Theory of Capitalist Development* (New York 1970).

43 The discussion in this section is based on Clement, *Canadian Corporate Elite*, chap. 2.

44 Summary statements of these reports are found in Abraham Rotstein and Gary Lax, *Independence: The Canadian Challenge* (Toronto 1972); see also Kari Levitt, *Silent Surrender* (Toronto 1970).

45 Levitt, ibid., 116-45

46 According to one report of the Organization for Economic Cooperation and Development, Canada had the highest average unemployment rate of seventeen developed countries from 1960 to 1975. See *Ministers of Labour and the Problems of Employment* (Paris 1976). In the *Labor Force Statistics* of OECD, Canada reported an unemployment rate in 1978 of 8.3 per cent, compared with 7.1 (U.S.); 2.2 (Japan); 6.4 (Australia); 7.4 (Finland); 5.2 (France); 3.8 (West Germany); 7.2 (Italy); 1.8 (Norway); 8.0 (Spain); 2.2 (Sweden); 5.5 (UK). See OECD, *Labor Force Statistics*, Quarterly Supplement (May 1979).

47 Gough, 'State Expenditure,' 68

48 See, for example, David Stager, *Economic Analysis and Canadian Policy* (Toronto 1973), chap. 15, 'Personal Income, Poverty and Regional Disparity.' Standard Canadian texts in this area are T.N. Brewis, *Regional Economic Policies in Canada* (Toronto 1968); and N.H. Lithwick, *Regional Economic Policy: The Canadian Experience* (Toronto 1978).

49 See, for example, B.B. Archibald, 'Altantic Regional Underdevelopment and Socialism,' in L. LaPierre, et al., eds., *Essays on the Left* (Toronto 1971); and Henry Veltmeyer, 'The Underdevelopment of Atlantic Canada,' *The Review of Radical Political Economics*, X, 3 (Fall 1978), 95-105.

50 Paul Phillips, *Regional Disparities* (Toronto 1978)

51 Tawney, *Equality*, 58

52 Ibid.

53 Clement, *Canadian Corporate Elite*, 71

54 Wallace Clement, *Continental Corporate Power* (Toronto 1977)

55 Ibid., 24

56 Ibid., chap. 10

57 Pat Armstrong and Hugh Armstrong, *The Double Ghetto* (Toronto 1978), chap. 4

58 Ibid., 132

59 Dorothy E. Smith, 'Women, The Family and Corporate Capitalism,' in Marylee Stephenson, ed., *Women In Canada* (Toronto 1973), 6 f.

60 Armstrong and Armstrong, *Double Ghetto*, 136

61 Charnie Guettel, *Marxism and Feminism* (Toronto 1974), 49

62 Smith, 'Women,' 25 f.

63 Armstrong and Armstrong, *Double Ghetto*, 61

64 Statistics Canada, Labour Force, Survey Division, *The Labour Force, 1976*, cat. no. 71-001

65 Stephenson, *Women in Canada*, 217

66 Ibid., 34

23 G. Drover, A. Moscovitch

67 For example, J. Rawls, *A Theory of Justice* (Oxford 1972); R. Nozick, *Anarchy, State and Utopia*, (Oxford 1974)

68 Ralph Miliband, *The State in Capitalist Society* (London 1974), *Marxism and Politics* (Oxford 1977); Gough, 'State Expenditure'; Leo Panitch, ed., *The Canadian State: Political Economy and Political Power* (Toronto 1977); James O'Connor, *The Fiscal Crisis of the State* (New York 1973); Nicos Poulantzas, 'The Problem of the Capitalist State,' in Robin Blackburn, ed., *Ideology in Social Science* (Glasgow 1977), 238-53

69 The discussion here relies on the 'Introduction' to *The Welfare State in Canada: A Select Bibliography*, prepared by Allan Moscovitch with Peter Findlay and Theresa Jennissen, forthcoming 1981.

70 Louis Althusser, 'Idéologies et appareils idéologiques d'état,' *La Pensée*, 151, (June 1970)

71 Moscovitch et al., *Bibliography*

72 See Elisabeth Wallace, 'The Changing Canadian State: A Study of the Changing Conception of the State as Revealed in Canadian Social Legislation, 1867-1948,' PHD thesis, Columbia University, 1950, chap. 13, pp. 331-50; J.R. Granatstein, 'MacKenzie King and the Turn to Social Welfare, 1943-45,' *Quarterly of Canadian Studies for the Secondary School*, II, 1 (Spring 1972); Alvin Finkel, 'Origins of the Welfare State in Canada,' in Panitch, *Canadian State*, chap. 12.

73 Allan Moscovitch, 'The State and Housing Policy: Origins to 1948,' unpublished, 1977

74 A good descriptive study of social welfare reform during the Diefenbaker and Pearson era is Dennis T. Guest, *The Emergence of Social Security in Canada* (Vancouver 1980).

75 See Richard Simeon, *Federal-Provincial Diplomacy: The Making of Recent Policy in Canada* (Toronto 1972), 116 ff; also Donald Smiley, *Canada In Question: Federalism in the Seventies* (Toronto 1976), 46 ff.

76 David Wolfe, 'The State and Economic Policy in Canada' in Panitch, *Canadian State*, chap. 9. There is also a good discussion of problems in James Laxer and Robert Laxer, *The Liberal Idea of Canada* (Toronto 1977), chaps. 1 and 8.

PART I
CAPITALISM AND INEQUALITY

2
Philosophic barriers to equality

PATRICK KERANS

This chapter is concerned with the ideological aspect of the struggle for equality. Moscovitch has argued in his essay that the basic assumptions of liberal economics constitute an ideological barrier to equality of outcomes.[1] The important assumption of liberal economics is that human liberty is characteristically exercised in a market situation, in an arm's length relation with other human beings, where strategies are shaped by suspicion (because of competition) and greed (because of profit maximization). The liberal contends that human creativity flowers best in competitive circumstances and would be severely dampened if the goal of social policy was primarily to assure equality of outcome.

In this paper my main task is philosophical: to argue that the liberal idea of equality is itself an ideological barrier to real equality. This philosophical argument would, however, remain without consequence if I did not also address the historical question of to what extent Canadian struggles for equality have been influenced by liberal ideological hegemony. In the light of these two considerations I shall try to outline a notion of equality which might help clarify historic struggles and contribute to, rather than foreclose, structural change in the direction of real equality.

LIBERAL TREATMENTS OF EQUALITY:
SOME PRELIMINARY CLARIFICATIONS

The attitude of liberals to equality has been, to put it mildly, ambiguous. Macpherson notes that bourgeois society has 'demanded formal equality but required substantive inequality of rights.'[2] We are assured on the one hand that 'the principle of Equality is an essential ingredient of Liberalism';[3] yet liberalism has 'come to serve as a rationalization of unjustified social inequalities.'[4] One of the great achievements of liberalism, in Canada and elsewhere, has been its ability to legitimate sharp and increasing inequalities by proclaiming as one of its highest ideals the equality of all men.

To examine how this has been accomplished, I wish first to review schematically how the word 'equality' is used; secondly, I will review the historic process of ideological concealment of basic interests by the liberal use of the word.

Equality, we are told, is a slogan admitting of many meanings, and for this reason of not much help either as a social goal or as a criterion for decisions. To clarify what equality means, we must, Isaiah Berlin assures us, 'isolate the pure ore of egalitarianism proper from those alloys which the admixture of other attitudes and ideals has at various times generated.'[5] Berlin is insisting that equality be taken as a 'unit-idea', to see 'whether it possesses any inherent plausibility of its own.'[6] A unit-idea is a phrase coined by Lovejoy in developing what he meant by the history of ideas; it is an idea which can sustain a detachment from any and all systems of thought in which it is at various times embedded, without losing its essential characteristics.[7] Equality is not such a unit-idea. To treat it as such is either to fall into a moralistic idealism or to drive the notion either to absurdity or to a vacuous formality.

Equality is pushed to absurdity fairly easily when, as an idea, it is contrasted with the 'reality' of empirical inequalities. People do not have the same IQ, the same ambitions, dreams, goals, drives; nor the same capacities for work, saving, and planning; they have different needs, tastes, etc.

Aristotle distinguished the notion of equality into two types: quantitative equality and proportional equality. Many of those who push equality to absurdity are taking the quantitative sense as the only true meaning of equality, without bothering with the distinction. They can then insist that if you want to take the meaning of the word seriously, that is, if you do not water it down to mean simply fairness, then it must be related to sameness. 'Persons have (received) an equal distribution, equal treatment or equal rights, etc., if and only if they have (received) the same distribution, treatment, rights, etc.'[8]

Once one has set up this straw man, there are, so to speak, two ways to blow it down. One way is to point out that the goal of equality as sameness is a dull, constraining uniformity. Bedau says that 'egalitarians have had a certain understandable wariness of the uniformity and conformity connoted by "equality."'[9] More than academic philosophers take this tack. People have generalized from Stalinism to socialism and equate any real push towards equality with police-controlled totalitarianism; but short of that, since they equate freedom with freedom to spend, they identify equality with drabness.

Another way to push quantitative equality to absurdity is to argue that such equality would be inequitable. A person earning $35,000 is fined $300 for speeding; a person earning $8,000 is fined $300 for speeding. Is this equal treatment equitable? It certainly tends to explain why our provincial jails are still, to a great extent, debtors' prisons where people serve sentences for non-payment of fines. In 1976, 44 per cent of those admitted to provincial correctional centres in Nova Scotia were admitted for non-payment of fines. In 1970-71, 57 per cent of native people admitted to Saskatchewan correctional centres were admitted for non-payment of fines. These natives comprised one-third of all admissions and 70.9 per cent of all admissions for non-payment of fines.[10] In more general terms, the criminal trial has as a basic rule to treat people 'equally'; and this equality in a class society constitutes the basic injustice of the criminal justice system.[11]

Economic and political equality can also be fruitfully distinguished. Economic equality refers to an equal distribution of economic goods. The stance of the liberal tradition with respect to economic equality has been quite clear. While admitting that there is some rudimentary equality regarding basic needs, and that there must be some provision for an equitable distribution of goods covering at least these basic needs, the liberal economist insists that the distinction between basic needs and mere wants is fuzzy at best; that it is beyond the legitimate competency of the public authority to act on the basis of this distinction since it would offend against both Pareto-efficiency and liberty. The liberal tradition is, as Moscovitch has elaborated, against public moves towards equality of economic outcome.

Further, apologists for equality admit that absolute political equality – that is, an absolute sharing of power – would mean anarchy.[12] If all share power equally at all times, then each decision (no matter how trivial) would require not only consensus but continual consensus. If, once a decision were made, I began to notice unwanted consequences, I would be able to withdraw my consensus, and the decision would need to be reviewed by all. Because of the need for a basic stability in the community, political equality cannot be antithetical to legitimate political authority and political obligation.

It can, therefore, be argued that not everyone can be equal or be treated equally in every respect; we must choose which equality we want; 'we must choose one of several ways of treating men as counting for only one.'[13] Clearly the basis for this choice is not equality itself but some other value, such as liberty or fairness or community. In fact, equality understood quantitatively and as a unit-idea is so obviously unsatisfactory as a criterion for choice or as a social goal that I am tempted to suspect that those who insist that equality must be so construed have an underlying hostility to any equality.

What then of proportional equality? Its trouble is that of itself it is easily shown to be an empty formality. It has been called the 'weak' principle of equality because, in John Rees' words, when it tells us to treat others equally unless we have a good reason, 'it contains no instructions as to what count as "reasons."' [14] For example, Aristotle, the father of the notion of proportionate equality, adduced reasons which he felt established that some men are by nature (i.e., appropriately) slaves. These reasons seem so threadbare today that it is understandable that some might consider his notion of proportionate equality to be empty.

Obviously there are many empirical, natural inequalities. Some of these natural inequalities are the basis for justifiably unequal treatment. But one cannot stop here. The division between natural and socially produced inequalities is extremely problematic. Further, it is not clear what constitutes a sufficient reason for differential treatment: ought people be treated according to their need, their worth, their contribution, their effort, or, indeed, according to agreements struck?

EQUALITY AND PLURALISM

Throughout the preceding section, I have argued by implication that the liberal treatment of equality has been somewhat less than serious and has often been hostile. It could be pointed out that all I have really done is to show that equality as a value, as a social goal, as a criterion for policy decisions, cannot sustain analytic scrutiny. To this I would reply that as a unit-idea equality can indeed by shown to be either too abstract to be a criterion for political choice or else too vague to be anything except an empty rhetorical device. Equality must be understood in relation – often in tension – with other key notions which make up a vision of humans as developing, free individuals who must work out their destiny in community, politically. If a political tradition considers other values to be more important than equality, then when it discovers tension between equality and those more important values, it will find ways to discount equality, even while proclaiming equality as a central value.

I will now show why I think the liberal tradition has done just that and try to point out the applicability of these ideas to Canadian struggles and dilemmas.

In order to clarify matters, I suggest using equality and pluralism as a pair of opposites. In general, pluralism refers to differences among people. I suggest that we use 'pluralism' instead of 'inequality' since pluralism has, within the liberal tradition, a very high evaluation. However, pluralism can be understood somewhat differently from the perspectives of a conservative, a liberal, and a socialist political vision. I hope by way of these contrasts, as well as by an examination of the liberal understanding of pluralism, to establish my main contention; namely, that the liberal construction of equality itself constitutes through ideological obfuscation a barrier to equality.

The conservative vision

The conservative vision of pluralism is that there are natural differences between people, based on blood, virtue, or other personal qualities; and that these differences constitute a valid reason for differential treatment. One variant of this vision was held by most English-speaking Canadians throughout the nineteenth century. But this vision has a long history, with Plato and Aristotle being important early spokesmen.

The classical vision of a society which is naturally hierarchic was inherited by medieval Europe. Since the liberal tradition understands 'modernity [to] consist in a transition from feudal domination to the gradual liberation of the individual,'[15] that is, from a traditional allocation of goods according to status to a market allocation according to contractual agreements, it becomes helpful to contrast the conservative vision of pluralism-equality with the liberal vision.

The medieval conservative vision insisted that it was the moral duty of the public authority to treat people differently. The 'goodness' of various groups and of their interests had to be grasped and judged by the public authority, and on the basis of such moral judgments, decisions were to be made. This was so because the medieval vision could locate people and events only within a value-laden hierarchic universe; their place depended upon their 'goodness.' Goodness was understood to be, at its limit, the 'fullness of being.' God was good; God was the fullness of being; and other things had both their being and goodness by sharing God's fullness.

There was, according to the medieval vision, a natural order in society which mirrored the ordered sharing in the fullness of being and goodness. The primary responsibility of the ruler was the respect of maintenance of this natural moral order. Hence the ruler's *duty* to discern moral differences in his subjects and in their interests, and to treat them differentially. To demand of a ruler this moral discernment required that the culture provide him with a clear set of guidelines about the 'fullness of being' or 'goodness.' Further, there needed to be a clear consensus around these guidelines, though it is questionable, given peasant uprisings, how complete the consensus ever was. Even when this consensus was at its height, the treatment of Jews in medieval Europe, for example, shows us the profound weakness in this conservative vision.

Whatever the merits or demerits of the medieval vision at the time when it represented a consensus, the consensus itself was in tatters by the seventeenth century. There was, to begin with, religious dissent, and the medieval response – persecution in the name of order – finally escalated into catastrophes such as the Thirty Years' War. Besides, the newly emerging merchant class could not rest content with a notion of natural order based on the superiority of landed gentry, according to which values were allocated.

While the medieval vision in its integrity could not withstand the onslaught of new historical factors, a modified version of Toryism did survive. It hung on to the vision of a natural order, worked out over time and manifesting the wisdom of past generations, upon which human progress depended. As the competing liberal vision was able to forge more adaptable political institutions, these became part of the community's heritage and were often incorporated into the Tory framework. As the British Empire grew in size through the eighteenth and nineteenth centuries, its moral legitimacy remained couched in Tory terms. By Victorian times it claimed that the Anglo-Saxon race was destined to govern, and it cited as evidence the lead Britons had taken in both democratic and technical affairs.

English-speaking Canadians shared this Tory vision. They derived a sense of power and destiny for the new Canadian nation, as Carl Berger has argued, from the British connection.[16] They spoke of the Anglo-Saxon race, but they were more broadly elitist since they quietly assumed the superiority of British traditions, attitudes, and qualities. In addition, they applied to Canada the Tory vision of the natural order in which class inequality and ruling class obligation to the lower order were taken as given. Thus it was quite unselfconsciously assumed that both those who spoke French and – later – European immigrants (especially from the South and East) were inferior.[17]

This rather generally accepted Toryism converged neatly with the interests of the Tory merchants who pushed through Confederation in order to have a larger stable hinterland to exploit. This was the meaning of Macdonald's National Policy as interpreted by W.L. Morton: 'Confederation was brought about to increase the wealth of central Canada and until that original purpose is altered and the concentration of wealth and population ceases, Confederation must remain an instrument of injustice.'[18]

The liberal vision

Despite the strength of the British connection among most Canadians, the economic and political implications of Toryism could not be swallowed by enough of them for the party of Macdonald to remain in power. With the hanging of Riel in 1885, any pretence on the part of the national elites to protect minority rights collapsed. When the Manitoba Schools question became an election issue in 1896, it was Laurier's doctrine of provincial autonomy in educational and cultural matters which carried the day. Since then, the Liberal party has been the party of French Canadians and, for the most part, of English-speaking Catholics as well. Since it had been seen from the beginning as the farmers' party and was able to capture the western farmers' vote until 1921 and again from 1926 to 1958, the Liberal party has usually been the governing party in Canada since 1896.

Just as the Tory party is a manifestation of a long Tory tradition, so the Liberal party in Canada shares important apsects of the liberal tradition. Canadian Liberals, as other liberals, have always had equality as a war-cry. The nineteenth-century Grits were against colonial privilege; Laurier's party was the party of language minorities and of farmers; Mackenzie King became leader because he promised to give the country labour peace based on humanity and co-operation. On the other hand, despite many decades of Liberal rhetoric about equalization, the Canadian community has not experienced any real equalization of outcomes. My quest is to clarify the reasons – at an ideological level – for this 'failure.'

It is important to understand that historically the liberal tradition has stood in reaction to the Tory vision. The Tory vision saw differentials between people as traditionally given and as legitimate. The implication of these natural differences is, I have argued, that people's interests are legitimate only if they fit within this natural scheme. Nobody could have legitimate interests if they would take him beyond his appointed 'station.' Liberals, by contrast, attacked the legitimacy of the traditional differentials and advocated a legitimate plurality of interests. These interests, even though they will inevitably be in competition with one another, will not destroy civil peace, the liberals argued, because they can all be accommodated by two institutions: the market and the political arena.

This understanding of pluralism is at the root of the liberal notion of liberty: because each person's interests are legitimate, each is at liberty to pursue those interests without interference by the public authority. There is, however, also a deep connection between the liberal vision of pluralism and the liberal vision of equality.

Many thinkers and politicians have over the past 350 years contributed to the liberal vision of pluralism, liberty, and equality. I wish, however, to confine my analysis here to the way Hobbes' equality postulate laid the philosophical foundation for subsequent liberal thought. Macpherson has singled out this postulate as a 'leap in political theory as radical as Galileo's formulation of the law of uniform motion was in natural science, and not unrelated to it.'[19]

Galileo's law of uniform motion had heralded the end of the medieval cultural system. If all beings and events were located in a value-laden universe according to their 'goodness,' then 'motion' within the medieval vision was never neutral, but always connoted either better or worse. In order to articulate theoretical mechanics, Galileo had to abandon that medieval cultural assumption; and his law of uniform motion serves notice that he did just that.

Thus Macpherson correctly points to the similarity between Hobbes' equality postulate and Galileo's law of uniform motion: 'It was Hobbes' *refusal to impose moral differences on men's wants*, his acceptance of the equal need for continued motion as the suffficient source of rights that constituted his revolution in moral and political theory.'[20]

Thus, while the conservative notion of pluralism was clearly at odds with equality, the liberal notion implies a certain formal, abstract equality. Macpherson has argued definitively that this vision of equality constitutes an ideological concealment of forces which result in our present inequality of outcomes.

Macpherson has insisted that Hobbes' notion of equality is empirical, so that Hobbes' argument to derive political obligation is from facts, not metaphysical fancy. Thomas Lewis has argued that the crucial point in Hobbes' equality postulate is that it is not empirical, not a declarative statement but a recommendation statement.[21] Hobbes is not saying that all men are equal; he is saying that *if* you want civil peace, then you would be well advised to treat all men's interests as though they were equal. Hobbes says in *Leviathan*: 'If nature therefore have made men equal, that equality is to be acknowledged: or if nature have made men unequal; yet because men that think themselves equal, will not enter into conditions of peace, but upon equal terms, such equality must be admitted.'[22]

While Lewis seems to be making a significant qualification to Macpherson's thesis, still Lewis' point can be squared with Macpherson's historical work. Hobbes' contemporaries (and Hobbes himself) assumed that when he analysed what he called 'the state of nature' he was speaking of all men at all times. But, says Macpherson, Hobbes 'got at the "natural" proclivities of men by looking just below the surface of contemporary society.'[23] From there, Macpherson's definitive contribution was to argue that only one set of social conditions would validate Hobbes' argument for a self-perpetuating sovereign: a possessive market society.[24] Some men will have to sell their labour power to others who already own the means of production. Given this condition, plus the assumption that some men will want more possessions and power than others, Hobbes can conclude there is a war of all against all.

Hobbes' method, as Macpherson has demonstrated, met exactly the requirements of the newly emergent interests of the new merchant class. His method met their requirements so well that it was as though a door to reality had been opened. Unfortunately, it was only the 'door opening' which was experienced by Hobbes' readers and followers; what they overlooked, because misled by the very structure of his argument, were the concrete historical interests which had evoked the invention of the method.

Hobbes chronicled the revolution of interests and projects occurring around him; but because of the masking, ideological apsect of his theory, he chronicles in order to justify that revolution. However, his chronicling is so accurate and effective that it is easy to overlook his justificatory interest.

Macpherson is willing to grant that Hobbes, even while elaborating a vision which had the political effect of justifying bourgeois interests, was at the same time trying to develop an impartial, scientific analysis of his situation. However, he insists that since 1820, when liberals felt they could advocate democracy and at the same time equal class differentials, the liberal analysis could no longer be construed as simply mirroring the very nature of things. From that time the task of liberal political theory became 'deceptive'; that is, it concealed from itself its own fundamental assumptions about humanity and community.[25]

I suggested that equality cannot stand by itself since criteria are needed to establish what are sufficient reasons for unequal treatment and what are sufficient reasons for insisting on equality. Since pluralism, as I have tried to define it, is a basic liberal value (even liberty derives from this notion of pluralism), the liberal has enormous difficulty with the very notion of 'sufficient reason.' Since all men's interests are to be counted as equal, without inquiry, how can we now establish criteria for differential treatment? John Wilson sums up the contemporary liberal's difficulty: 'Intrinsic equality suggests that the wills, choices and values of each man are as valid as those of any other man ... But more than this: for his belief is not properly represented by saying that the will of one man, as it were, *weighs as much as* the will of another, as if we were entitled to judge the weight of both by some external criterion ... His belief is rather than *we are not entitled to weigh the wills of other men by our own criteria at all.*'[26]

The liberal notion of equality is thus fundamentally at odds with any real, concrete equality of outcomes. The liberal tradition is predicated on the assumption that nobody can know what the fullness of humanity might be;

and even if that were possible, that there could be no peaceful, fruitful communication between those who might differ concerning the ideal end-state of human beings. The great breakthrough of liberal political thought was, given these assumptions, to advocate political and legal structures which would protect people seeking their own goals in their own ways, provided Mill's 'harm rule' was obeyed.

It was pluralism in this sense which Laurier invoked in the election of 1896, when he advocated stronger provincial autonomy rather than promising to afford minority rights federal protection. Mackenzie King invoked the same principle when he refused to intervene in 1922, when BESCO cut the Cape Breton miners' wages by one-third. With their families going hungry, the men struck 'on the job,' doing two-thirds of a day's work for two-thirds pay. Even Arthur Meighen saw their logic and supported their plea for a royal commission. But King held firm, even accusing the men of 'loafing on the job.'[27] He was convinced of the 'folly of our invading Provincial jurisdiction in matters of this kind.'[28]

King has been berated for his decision, especially since federal troops were sent to Cape Breton three times between 1923 and 1925. King was able to say that, under the Militia Act, he had no discretion to refuse military aid to the civil powers.[29] However, during 1923 and 1924, despite considerable pressure to amend the Militia Act, the changes finally brought down by his government were, as he put it, 'not very significant.'[30] He had been in a position to allow himself discretion and had not acted. I would contend that his actions were entirely consistent with his liberalism.

There are two considerations to be made to bolster this contention. The first is that the liberal, wishing to avoid authoritarianism and – worse – totalitarianism, has adopted an understanding of pluralism which cannot but aid those who already are in positions of dominance. Since in the liberal view of pluralism it is neither effective nor even meaningful to differentiate the proprietary interests of the owners of BESCO from the interests of a corner store owner or, indeed, from those of a homeowner, each of these 'owners' is entitled to pursue his property rights as he sees fit within the scope offered him by the market. To suggest that one exercises more power than another is to introduce language foreign to the liberal framework. Little wonder, then, that 'a socialist egalitarianism is not readily compatible with a pluralist political order of the classic western type.'[31]

The second consideration takes us to a crucial element of modern liberalism. From Adam Smith on, and certainly more explicitly since the Keynesian formulation of governmental responsibility in economic matters, liberals have been sure that if they concentrated on the enhancement of production (a technical question), this would take the edge off the more thorny political question of distribution. There can, they would admit, be economic growth without justice, but there can be no justice without economic growth. Seen from this angle, Mackenzie King's labour strategies throughout his career are thoroughly liberal. Whitaker characterizes King's 'supreme central tenet in his conception of the role of the state in labour relations' to be 'industrial "peace" at all costs.'[32] For, without peace, production would be disrupted and economic growth would suffer. Distressed though he might have been at BESCO's intransigence, King was consistent when he acquiesced to the presence of federal troops in Cape Breton. While workers should be brought into the decision-making process, they should remain subordinate and above all, be prevented from becoming violent.

TOWARDS A CRITIQUE OF THE LIBERAL VISION

The ideological triumph of the liberal vision puts an opponent in an extremely difficult position, for two reasons. First, it is difficult to argue against any dominant ideology simply because it has become embodied in every major institution so that any other way of seeing things is hard to imagine, let alone to believe. The second difficulty stems from the content of liberalism. Because the liberal notion of pluralism construes every group's interests simply to be data not to be scrutinized in the light of the demands of values such as equality, it becomes meaningless within the terms of public political debate to make discriminating judgments on the basis of a vision other than that of liberal pluralism. The ideological hegemony of the liberal vision means that the liberal has not only won the political argument but he has been able to pre-empt any further discussion. Any criticism of unequal outcomes can be written off as mere empty moralizing and self-righteous posturing based on mere personal idiosyncrasy.

Within the dominant liberal tradition it is meaningless to distinguish consumer preferences into essential and frivolous or downright harmful; hence it is meaningless to scrutinize the interests of those who both play to, and manipulate, those consumer preferences. Indeed, such criticism often is called worse than meaningless: it is often construed to be the first step towards totalitarianism since it presumes to tell others what their best interests are.

Ideological hegemony has, then, the effect of keeping any public debate within the bounds which it sets. The task of emancipation thus entails, it seems to me, trying to find a recognizable basis in people's experience for language which can break beyond the limits set by liberal ideology. Can we, in other words, recast our notions of both equality and pluralism so that they become mutually reinforcing instead of antagonistic?

I take my lead in this quest from those British thinkers who are serious egalitarians, who consider themselves in the tradition of R.H. Tawney, and who have insisted that the ultimate objective of social policy should be 'the development of the capacities of all men in their richest diversity' and that this is not only compatible with the demands of equality but essential to genuine equality. [33] By contrast, the received liberal wisdom insists that it is precisely in those aspects of our common humanity wherein we are the same that we are to be treated equally, and that to the extent to which our individual creativity and self-development render us different, we should be treated differently. [34]

This view is distortive since it is based on the logical relationship between abstract ideas. The concrete reality of humanity is quite different: our common humanity gives rise to both our similarities and our differences. When a modern examines primitives, for instance, he easily ascribes the similarities between them to their common humanity. I would also insist that the differences – arising as they do from human ingenuity, human creativity, and human symbol-making ability – are equally ascribable to our common humanity.

If serious egalitarians turn to the Kantian notion of 'respect' to explain what they mean by equality, it is, in large measure, in order to break past the pale abstractions of the liberal tradition. What Kant means by respect is the response appropriate to the concrete living person, the moral agent, the actor in history, capable of deciding which values to identify with and entitled to free and secure space to pursue those values. [35] Respect is not the response appropriate to a doctrine about individuals; it is what ought to be accorded to the individuals themselves.

Each person, as a person, is entitled to equal respect. This differs from a liberal view in that the autonomy and creativity of the person is precisely that which gives rise to the empirical differences among people. The liberal tradition, on the other hand, insists that only empirical similarities can be the basis of equal treatment. This difference, while it might seem merely academic, has had very real consequences. I have remarked that latterly the liberal understanding of equality has amounted to equality of opportunity. It is perhaps fruitful at this point to examine that notion.

Wollheim, who declares that the principle of equality is the fundamental principle of liberalism, has more baldly than most revealed the ideological obfuscatory function of equality of opportunity. He notes that equality of rights can mean either that 'everyone has a right to equal x' or 'everyone has

an equal right to x.' Since his examples of 'x' are all quantifiable, he is sure
that his first formulation is the same as quantitative equality. Without explicitly rejecting this formulation, he notes that the second, an articulation of
proportional equality, belongs to the tradition of liberalism.[36]

Is it, I would interject, accidental that all of Wollheim's examples are
quantifiable? I would argue that it is not accidental. The liberal tradition
assumes a vision of man as rational, as a maximizer of individual satisfaction
through strategies shaped by suspicion in a market situation.[37] It has, in other
words, reduced values in use (which are quantitatively diverse for different
individuals and groups) to values in exchange, to factors of production or to
indifference maps. If, from a liberal view, man is no more than a consumer
of utilities, then 'a right to equal x' can only mean quantitative equality and
as such can be contradicted by experience.

Wollheim is, however, constrained to ask whether 'an equal right to x'
means anything more than 'everyone has such rights as he has.'[38] If this is
so, then 'equal' means nothing. Equal opportunity is simply a special case of
proportional equality: each has an equal right to wrest from the market what
he can; each is entitled to equal treatment, provided each relates equally to
the demands of the market. Schaar, in his attack on equality of opportunity,
would seem to have been justified in remarking that people really only get an
opportunity 'to develop those talents which are highly valued by a given
people at a given time.'[39]

The ideological function of this is clear. It has become culturally unlikely
for people to catch a glimpse of a larger vision of humanity than 'consumer.'
But the vision of consumer isolates people and pits them against each other
in inevitable competition. This becomes the implicit argument for construing
equality of opportunity as the untrammelled opportunity to foster bourgeois
values and to pursue entrepreneurial interests.

The liberal vision of pluralism and of equality is self-contradictory and
bankrupt. One of the great historic breakthroughs of our civilization – since
the days of Jeremiah and Socrates – has been its ability to appreciate the
value of the individual human and, despite backslidings and aberrations, to
embody that value institutionally. But the liberal doctrine of individualism is
not necessarily the best cultural form with which to defend and foster the
value of the individual. Liberal individualism pictures individuals abstractly,
as given, with given interests, wants, and purposes; it pictures society and
the state as modifiable arrangements designed to meet those needs and interests; it is sure only of its knowledge of the individual as a set bundle of
needs; and can understand society and its institutions only derivatively. I
have been arguing (with Lukes) that this doctrine, because it is incompatible

with equality of respect, is also incompatible with a genuine valuing of the individual.[40]

The liberals have been warning us, I noted in the last section, that to abandon the liberal vision of pluralism will be too costly and that equality is not worth it. However, given the distortive abstraction upon which liberal pluralism is based, can we count its abandonment as such a cost?

LIBERAL IDEOLOGY AND CANADIAN STRUGGLES

Before I attempt to counterpose a critical notion of equality, I think it wise to turn to history for help. I have already suggested that liberalism has been hegemonic in Canada during most of the twentieth century. It therefore seems helpful at this point to inquire as to how the liberal notion of equality has constituted an ideological barrier to equality in Canada.

Because liberalism has exercised hegemony, those whose vision of equality has been to the left of the liberal have not simply been in the role of opposition. They have usually been ostracized as illegitimate; that is, as either unrealistic or irresponsible or both. Labouring under this marginal stigma, they were under considerable pressure to modify their position in order to be 'effective.' Where the line lies between effectiveness and accommodation is, of course, the endless debate.

Asking how they responded to this marginalization-accommodation dilemma, I propose to examine briefly three egalitarian movements: the women's suffragists, the agrarian protest, and the labour movement. Once the CCF was on the scene, it became the focal point of these debates; and its history has been written from many points of view. I propose to concentrate more on the years just after 1916, when it must have seemed to many that a breakthrough towards real equality was imminent.

Women's suffrage
While the ideas concerning political equality for women were imported from the United States and Britain, the tone of hostility was lacking in the Canadian debate, where 'rational persuasion' won the day.[41] However, tone and content are often interrelated, and Gorham argues that it was possible for traditional attitudes concerning maternal feminism to survive in Canada, whereas the harshness of the struggle in other countries disabused women of illusions.

If women's suffrage was won with rational persuasion, what were the arguments? How did the movement, as its leaders articulated it, understand its goal of equality? It seems safe to turn to the writings of Nellie McClung since she, by all accounts, emerged as the most important spokesperson for the movement. She was already a well-known novelist and short story writer when she took up the suffragist cause; and she brought to the cause both a vision and a remarkable gift as a humourist.

She was perhaps at her best when reducing to shreds with her cutting wit the essentially Tory argument that women are too good, too refined for the dirty business of politics. In a 1912 short story, 'The Elusive Vote,' she detailed the antics of both parties to bring out the vote of the village idiot. Perhaps the high point of her campaign was the mock parliament she staged in Winnipeg in 1914, when she satirized what she had earlier heard the Tory premier say about women being too good to vote. For three nights to packed houses she played the premier of a women's parliament when men came to petition for the vote.[42]

If her wit was devastating, what vision powered it? She believed in the assimilative powers of Anglo-Saxon culture, but it was an Anglo-Saxon culture purified of its Ontario narrowness.[43] In Nellie's West, a demonstration started by an angry Orangeman turns into a picnic with the local Catholics.[44]

Her admiration of the pioneer women of the West, of whom she wrote so glowingly, led her to reject 'chivalry' with its implications that women need protection and that pretty women get more than plain ones.[45] She is sharply aware of the class bias in this chivalrous protection: 'They cannot bear, they say, to see women leaving the sacred precincts of home – and yet their offices are scrubbed by women who do their work while other people sleep – poor women who leave the sacred precincts of home to earn enough to keep the breath of life in them, who carry their scrub-pails home, through the deserted streets, long after the cars have stopped running. They are exposed to cold, to hunger, to insult – poor souls – is there any pity felt for them? Not that we have heard of.'[46] She was, she told Premier Roblin, decidedly 'not nice' in the Victorian sense of nice ladies since she did care about 'those factory women, working in ill-smelling holes, and we intend to do something about it.'[47]

Unfortunately, while Mrs McClung personally worked for welfare programs as an MLA, the movement at that time did little about factory women. The movement's rational argument, repeated often by Mrs McClung, rested on the assumption that the majority of society would give everyone a 'fair deal,' 'where every race, colour and creed will be given exactly the same chance; where no person can "exert influence" to bring about his personal ends; where no man or woman's past can ever rise up to defeat them; where no crime goes unpunished; where every debt is paid; where no prejudice is allowed to masquerade as a reason; where honest toil will insure an honest living; where the man who works receives the reward of his labour.'[48] It would be difficult to give a better description of what I have been calling the liberal notion of equality, with its reliance upon the market and parliamentary democracy.

There are also evident traces of the Tory vision, which Nellie would have learned as a child, throughout her writings. Her argument that women are morally superior to men, for instance, is essentially Tory. These 'visions' which I am trying to delineate in this paper are, after all, ideal types, and few people would hold one to the absolute exclusion of the others.

It makes more sense, however, to assess a movement in terms of the vision which characterizes and bounds it. The women's suffrage movement in Canada, apart from Nellie McClung as one of its important spokespersons, accomplished what it set out to achieve: formal political equality. The vision of the movement, courageous at the time in its quarrel with Tory privilege, was bounded by the liberal tradition. Its analysis of the obstacles to genuine equality did not impel the women in the movement – mostly economically independent – to press for structural change.

Agrarian protest

The position of farmers in a capitalist economy is ambiguous. They own the means of production; there is a legitimate reason for considering them as independent commodity producers; yet they experience exploitation. The instrument is not the wage relationship but the structure of the markets in which they buy their factors of production and sell their products. The hegemonic liberal vision insists that the market is the most important social structure whereby equality is available to people.

Since the 1880s, and in most provinces at one time or another, there have been significant farmers' organizations. Depsite the variations in these different groups, it seems possible to draw some useful generalizations from the major organizations, their leaders' articulation of their goals, and how they dealt with liberal hegemony.

With the exception of the Patrons of Industry,[49] farmers' organizations avoided direct involvement in politics, preferring, for the most part, to rely on the Liberal party. However, during the First World War, when farmers regrouped into the United Farmers movement, electoral success was almost instantaneous.[50] However, with the exception of Alberta, where the UFA held power until 1935, the success hardly lasted past the next election. This bursting bubble has been discussed from many viewpoints. It would seem reasonable to ascribe the brevity of the farmers' political success to the instability of their populist vision.

There were, of course, differences within the movement. The basic tension was between those who, following Crerar and Forke, were never far from the Liberals and those who subscribed to the non-partisan populist vision of Henry Wise Wood and William Irvine of Alberta and W.C. Good of Ontario.

From the beginning the farmers' goal was to restrict the monopoly power of the 'Big Interests.' They sought more perfect competition and held 'no enmity to capital.'[51] This led them to react hostilely to the tariffs of the National Policy.[52] In this fight they relied on the Liberal party of Laurier. However, when Laurier listened to the farmers and fought the election of 1911 on reciprocity, he was deserted not only by major Toronto business and financial powers – who issued a manifesto which could be dismissed as simply representing the Big Interests – but even by people within his own caucus such as Clifford Sifton, owner of the Winnipeg *Free Press*. The reaction of the farmers to this set-back and to the handling of the conscription issue by the Union government during the war – where, again, Liberals such as Crerar did not adequately represent their interests – was to reorganize and enter politics directly.

During the period of farmers in politics, some of their leaders – notably Drury, UFO premier of Ontario, and Crerar, first leader of the federal Progressives – always thought of the farm bloc as constituting a party and, in order to 'broaden out,' sought to form alliances with the Liberals.

But the bulk of the farmers and their representatives firmly believed that non-partisan, open, honest, business-like government would salvage both democracy and the free market. H.W. Wood was the foremost spokesman for this vision and during the heyday of direct political action was pivotal in keeping the farmers' involvement non-partisan. Wood's vision was of a co-operative society: 'Human perfection could be achieved only through group organization – never through political parties, because the latter were controlled by plutocratic interests. The people, organized on a democratic class basis, must strive to destroy competition or be destroyed by it ... True progress can come only as a result of thoughtful, continuous co-operative effort. This progress will be slow, but it must be continuous.'[53] Wood in fact believed that, since co-operative democracy was in harmony with the laws of nature and of God, it could not help but succeed. W.C. Good, a confirmed Ontario populist, pondering this question in 1925, just as the Progressive party was foundering, remained optimistic since he had the 'deep-seated conviction that in the long run "the common sense of most" is more trustworthy than the wisdom of any person or small group ... that, with all its faults, democracy is the only system *that contains within itself the seeds of progress* because it emphasizes as no other system can do, the vital need of general and efficient popular education.'[54]

Populists saw that between the good sense of the electorate and government policy there was a blockage. Their analysis isolated party discipline as this blockage. Thus they could content themselves with a strategy which encompassed only parliamentary reform. Their lack of party discipline, on the other hand, enabled Mackenzie King to confuse and divide them in the Commons. More basic, their vision of 'group government' assumed co-operation between groups. This assumption was based on the experience of the independent commodity producer who, in Macpherson's terms, could have the impression of living in a 'simple market economy.'[55] What a populist failed to notice was the parallel between his position in the market and the position of the urban worker, and that the disability of each stemmed not from monopolistic distortions in the market but from the structure of the market itself.

The populist vision was, then, unrealistic, and could not succeed. As the populist political movement faltered everywhere but in Alberta, a forthrightly socialist agrarian movement sprang up in Saskatchewan. In 1922 the Farmers' Union of Canada (FUC) was formed. In the preamble of its constitution it stated: 'Modern industrial society is divided into two classes – those who possess and do not produce and those who produce ... In the struggle over the purchase and sale of farm produce the buyers are always masters – the sellers always workers.'[56] In line with this analysis, the FUC strove for the 100 per cent pool; that is, they planned to organize a majority of farmers, then insist that the government hold a referendum and give monopoly control of grain marketing to the winner. By 1923 each of the Prairie provinces had organized a voluntary wheat pool and these came together in a Central Selling Agency. By 1927 there were 140,000 farmers involved, which was between 50 and 60 per cent of the wheat market.[57] The Saskatchewan group, facing the difficulties of the world slump after 1929, pushed again for a compulsory pool (opposed by Wood who still saw co-operation as the only way). They had the Grain Marketing Act passed, only to see it struck down by the Supreme Court of Saskatchewan.

In summary, the farmers' populism was unable to deal squarely with the farmers' original ambiguous relationship to capital and hence contained internal contradiction. Thus when populists gained power, they could not deal with the problems. The majority then adopted a liberal approach to equality (and to the market) while a significant minority took and still take a socialist position. I shall return to the question of why the majority took a liberal position, after examining the labour movement's handling of its marginalization-accommodation dilemma.

The labour movement
Wage earners do not have an ambiguous relationship to capital. The inequality of this relationship is difficult to avoid. Nonetheless, while there have been radical segments of the labour movement since the 1880s, and while the labour movement has been the home of sustained radicalism, it is fair to say that Gomperism has characterized the mainstream of the labour movement. During the 1880s, when the 'labour question' emerged violently in the United States, both the radical Knights of Labor and Gomper's American Federation of Labour (AFL) came to Canada. But by the end of the decade, the Knights had all but disappeared and the AFL was solidly established, having formed the Trades and Labour Congress in 1886.

At its worst, Gomperism is a cynical disregard for equality. More usually, Gomperism has connoted a liberal reliance on the balancing forces of the market and of liberal democracy to bring about equality. It has always, of course, been characterized by its proponents as practical, pragmatic.[58] Gomperism was a doctrine of opposition to direct labour involvement in formal politics, advocating that labour 'reward its friends and punish its enemies.' In a large federal polity such as Canada, this has often meant a splintering of labour's vote and, more generally, a dissipation of labour's power.

The triumph of Gomperism certainly did not stem from a lack of powerful radical spokesmen.[59] One who stands out among the early leaders, both for the vigour of his language and the numbers who read him, was Phillips Thompson. Writing from 1883 to 1887 in the daily Toronto *News*, in the weekly *Palladium of Labour*, as well as in his book, *Politics of Labour*, he gave Canadian working people a radically egalitarian vision and strategy.

He saw the structure of the labour market itself to be the source of inequality. The employers, he saw, were moving towards monopoly power 'combined with absolute and unrestricted competition among the wage earners'; hence his metaphor of monopoly above and competition below being the 'upper and nether millstones between which the toiler is crushed.'[60]

Thompson also had little faith in liberal democracy. Capitalism was 'entrenched behind the ramparts of party.'[61] Labour's votes were captured through promises nobody intended to keep. 'Energy and intelligence which ought rightly to be devoted to the solution of the labour problem are worse than wasted over the petty, misleading, idle issues which partyism keeps in view; and the attention of the people is distracted by campaigns which, whatever the result, settle no question of real significance.'[62] Meanwhile, he queried, who discusses or votes for the decisions to lay men off or to cut their wages 'as a cure for industrial ills?'

Thompson called for a party to fight for the interests of working people, though he knew that real equality would involve a long struggle and a different education for workers.[63] His rejection of equality of opportunity is unequivocal. The opportunity to better oneself is as much a solution to the disabilities of the working man's lot, he says, as the possibility of escaping Sing Sing would lessen the sufferings of prisoners there.[64] Despite Thompson's forceful words, party discipline and patronage co-opted labour leaders.[65] The Knights disappeared shortly after their sudden emergence. It has been argued, however, that Thompson had lasting influence.[66]

Whatever Thompson's influence, Gomperism was not without challenge. Over the next thirty years (until the end of the First World War) there were several labourite and socialist parties which emerged from the ranks of labour. They had some success, especially in British Columbia, where six labour representatives held the balance of power from 1898 to 1904. But from our present vantage point they remained marginal; and I would argue that their marginality was the issue around which they fought and splintered. Some opted to try for success at the polls; others, notably the Socialist Party of Canada, were against electoral politics as class collaboration, opting instead for educational work of a relatively doctrinaire kind.[67]

Marginality and doctrinaire ideas seemed to reinforce each other. The movement was not able to use socialist ideas to analyse specifically Canadian problems and propose specifically Canadian solutions. It was thus left with Hobson's choice of either learning about the socialist ideas of Europeans or entering electoral politics on essentially liberal terms. One wonders if the Canadian left has yet broken out of this dilemma.

Two major events, perhaps more than others, shaped how Canadian working people dealt with the marginality of radical egalitarianism. These two events were the Russian Revolution and the Winnipeg General Strike.

The success of the Bolshevik revolution, in the first instance, was that it gave enormous encouragement to the small embattled groups of Canadian radicals. Socialist speakers such as J.S. Woodsworth, J.W. Curry, and W.A. Pritchard now found packed houses when they toured. People even spoke of a 'speedy termination [of the] ... system which deprives [the working class] of the fruits of their labour, [so] that poverty may give place to comfort, privilege to equality and slavery to freedom.'[68]

The Bolshevik revolution also led to a realignment of egalitarian forces in Canada. Because success seemed imminent, socialists were motivated to break more clearly from labourites and social democrats to unite under the banner of international communism, which meant 'the bold translation of revolutionary propaganda and theory into practice.'[69] As Penner says: 'By the end of 1921, the Canadian socialist movement had been decisively transformed. The Social Democratic Party and the Socialist Party of North America had ceased to exist. The Socialist Party of Canada was reduced in numbers and in influence. The Communist Party had emerged with a new brand of Marxism based on the Russian experience and the teachings of Lenin.'[70]

Organizationally, the CPC's 'industrial concentration' was successful. It 'pioneered two of the most important themes in Canadian trade-union history: industrial unionism and the organization of the unorganized'[71] and earned the loyalty of many within the labour movement despite the savage attacks over the years.

Ideologically, however, it remained weak. While it did much to bring socialist ideas to bear on Canadian problems, its reliance on the Third International, hence on a Stalinist line, led to disastrous mistakes and turnabouts. Despite its heroic and sustained efforts within the labour movement, it was destined to remain marginal because it was 'foreign.'

The other important event was the general sympathetic strike which took place in Winnipeg during May and June, 1919. It came at a time of great unrest, and probably was partially the result of that unrest. Organized labour, especially in the West, had become more and more impatient during the latter years of the war. Since the Ontario-based majority in the TLC would not deal with their issues satisfactorily, western labour leaders met in Calgary in March 1919 to discuss secession. At that meeting the idea of the One Big Union (OBU) was born. It was not really to be an industrial union. Its aim was syndicalist, predicated on the idea that direct union action (without political involvement) would bring about structural change.

It seems clear that the idea of the OBU was not necessarily acceptable to a large majority of union members, even in the West.[72] Certainly many progressive union leaders actively opposed the OBU.[73] However, a referendum being held in all western locals to decide on membership in the OBU was interrupted by the Winnipeg General Strike.

The strike, begun when metal workers walked out in order to force their employers to bargain in good faith, was intended to be an orthodox strike with orthodox aims. It was brutally broken and its immediate objectives were not attained. What is perhaps the most significant thing about the strike is the violence perpetrated by the federal government on the strikers and their leaders. Arthur Meighen and Gideon Robertson, sent by Borden's Union government to mediate, acted out of fear of revolutionary syndicalism and, in Peter Heenan's words, 'were more interested in breaking the strike than in settling the strike.'[74] There had been in the preceding forty years at least thirty-three interventions by the military in strikes.[75] Perhaps it was that the Winnipeg strike had so much popular backing, that it came at a time when change seemed so imminent that the violence unleashed by the government had such a profound impact on Canadian political life. The set-back in Winnipeg, McNaught argues, led to 'an intensified class feeling, a deepened suspicion of elite-controlled state violence, a fresh drive for independent labour politics.'[76]

At the sedition trial of the strike leaders, W.A. Pritchard, arguing in his own defence, outlined clearly the reasons why working people, in order to achieve real equality, had to work for an indigenous democratic socialism.[77] The Winnipeg strike and the fury it unleashed scattered any illusions about how easy this task would be.

At this point the stories of the agrarian and the labour involvement in politics come closer together. The election of 1921 sent sixty-five Progressives and a 'Labour Group' of two to the House of Commons. While Mackenzie King was able to manipulate and confuse many of the Progressives, Woodsworth stood firm and eventually was able to form an alliance with the 'Ginger Group' of Progressives. This was the group which demonstrated both a full understanding of equality and a realistic appreciation of the obstacles. It became the parliamentary base for the Canadian experiment in democratic socialism, the CCF.

It has, of course, been argued that the CCF fought only one election – in Saskatchewan in 1934 – as an explicitly socialist party, and that after its resounding defeat it began to change into a social democratic party.[78] That this shift occurred points once again to the exigencies of the marginalization-accommodation dilemma facing any egalitarian who would be effective in Canada.

Conclusions: the market and equality
In general, the history of Canadian movements shows the difficulty of clarifying one's position in opposition to any hegemonic ideology. More specifically, the difficulties and ambiguities which have beset the agrarian and labour movements point to elements needed for a clarifying, critical understanding of equality.

Both the agrarian and labour movements suffered because they lacked clarity (both ideologically and strategically) about their relationship to private property. As I have argued, the liberal tradition has successfully rendered meaningless any criteria whereby the interests of property could be evaluated. Indeed, since it has been generally, or at least officially, accepted that corporate property interests, rationally pursued, bring economic growth, these property interests tend to be themselves the criteria against which other interests are evaluated.

The populist vision of the agrarian movement has not served farmers well. Since the majority of farmers have prized their 'independence' – that is, their status as property owners – they have remained overcapitalized, overburdened with debt, caught in a cost-price squeeze, and thus vulnerable to a process of 'rationalization' which has drastically cut the number of farms and stripped the family farm of its socially normative status.[79]

Despite what seems a far less ambiguous relationship between wage earners and corporate private property. Gomperism nonetheless seems to have been more successful than agrarian populism in its reliance on the market to serve working people's interest. Certainly, as I think the history of Canadian labour shows, a notion of equality which is critical of property and profit has remained historically marginal. This is perhaps because, in the context of an international exploitative order, many Canadian workers are net beneficiaries since they have been treated as part of the metropole.

The question is, of course, how much longer this will last. The large international unions, whose wagons are hitched to the multinationals' stars, seem bent on a continued policy of Gomperism. However, many of the workers in the public sector are beginning to suffer from the long-term fiscal crisis; many Canadian workers, active within the peripheral economy, have no stake in the continuance of the exploitative arrangements which benefit the stronger unions; and even the international unions might begin to have second thoughts if, as the American empire suffers further reverses, the multinationals cease to treat Canada as a kind of privileged extension of the metropole.

I would venture to suggest that the exploitative market relationships have become starkly clear to many primary producers. Despite the ambiguities created by real class differences among farmers and fishermen, organizations such as the National Farmers Union and the Maritime Fishermen's Union – small though they be – reflect a clarity of analysis born of struggle, which puts them in the vanguard in Canada. Perhaps there is still hope in Canada for an alliance of primary producers and labour.

TOWARDS A CRITICAL NOTION OF EQUALITY

The most important lesson to be learned from Canadian struggles is that equality of opportunity masks exploitative property relationships. A critical notion of equality must make clear its incompatibility with the institution of private property as it now exists in capitalist society.

What characterizes property in the liberal tradition is exclusivity.[80] To own property, especially land or capital, is to be in a position to dominate non-owners, even to the point of keeping them from using something which is necessary for their human development or, indeed, even for their survival. This ability to dominate others is radically incompatible with equality of respect as I have developed the notion.

It does not follow that to achieve equality, a society need abolish property. Such 'vulgar communism' stems from envy rather than an emancipatory strategy. The notion of property need not entail exclusivity. The classical argument for property was based on human development: to achieve human responsibility, a man must be in a position to appropriate that which he needs to meet the future. It is only, as Macpherson demonstrates, when the liberal tradition adduces the further assumption that each individual must face a hostile market that this argument entails the acquisition of property in an exclusivist sense. If taking possession were to mean appropriation and the consequent human development rather than exclusion; if it were to 'presuppose a similar activity by other men' and have as its goal to increase the social surplus rather than to increase a surplus socially generated but privately appropriated then the institution of property would enhance equality.[81]

However, because this relationship to property is not clarified, Canadians continue to show reluctance to accept that private property and equality are incompatible. They tend, then, to confuse the freedom that a fully developed person enjoys with the freedom held out to them by the liberal tradition, namely, the freedom to spend their money as they wish in the consumer market. Thus they see equality as tending towards a grey uniformity.

There is a second source of reluctance to accept the incompatibility between proprietary interest as we now know it and equality. Proprietary interests give structure to the market, and this is the basis of our present social order. It can seem blindly anarchic to abandon social order, no matter how imperfect; thus any questioning of the basic structure of the market is suspect.

The incompatibility between a critical notion of equality and private property leads to a materialist formulation of equality. People, through productive work, are fundamentally contributors to society; equality, then, demands 'from each according to his ability.' A critical notion of equality must, as I suggested earlier, include the development of the capacities of all people in their richest diversity: 'to each according to his needs.' Linked as this notion is to Kantian respect, it is, I would suggest, a more idealist formulation of the critical notion of equality. There is both strength and weakness in this idealist formulation. The weakness is its idealism; it does not necessarily lead to a class analysis of the real obstacles to real equality. Historically, thinkers such as T.H. Greene could enunciate this goal and remain liberals because their idealism kept them from admitting the obstacles to this goal. The materialist formulation, of course, leads immediately to a criticism of equality of opportunity and of exploitative market relationships. On the other hand, the strength of the idealist formulation is that it highlights the need to respect each individual; hence it will not make the mistake of giving up the historic gains which liberalism has won. Thus neither of the phrases in the classic formulation of equality can properly be understood except in dialectic interdependence with the other.

However, it is also true that that stream of liberal thought which has relied upon market relations and equality of opportunity has not accorded much validity to people's full development. To the extent that the liberal tradition has relied upon the market and a 'trickle down' effect to deal with equality, it has also relied upon increasing organizational technology as a social form. Over against this technical-rational form of organizing human beings, there has grown a tradition, essentially romantic, which has affirmed human individuality and potentiality.

It is a mistake to confuse this romantic affirmation of human individuality with the critical notion of equality and respect. The romantic tradition, though it has often sentimentalized the 'common people,' is nonetheless essentially individualistic and elitist. Its most prized virtues – authenticity and sincerity – are considered to set individuals apart from the anonymous, unthinking herd.

This view is born of alienation; and its artistic expression, no matter how attractive, is unable to overcome that alienation. Technical rationality has never had to take it seriously. It is not a critical vision because, having begun as a partial and distortive vision, it has never been able to develop an appropriate strategy which leads towards emancipation.

A more fruitful beginning than this elitist romanticism is Marx's notion of the 'social individual': 'Man is a zoon politikon in the most literal sense: he is not only a social animal, but an animal that can be individualised only within society. Production by a solitary individual outside society ... is just as preposterous as the development of speech without individuals who live together and talk to one another.'[82] This account takes nothing for granted. It starts at the beginning, when we all must learn everything from others. The need to learn is the general rule for communities as well as individuals. If the fullness of human development and autonomy requires at least some liberation from the basic economic necessity of repetitious, soul-grinding reproductive labour – if, in other words, there must be a growing social surplus for there to be human development – then humanizing activity must happen within community, where individuals can build upon the lessons of others.

If, however, the development of each individual becomes the basis for policy, then the thrust of policy will always be towards an increasing diversity of incommensurable needs and interests. Thus equality as a social goal can never simply mean a redistribution of income, any more than an abolition of property. These measures imply a levelling off of needs or, indeed, a simplification of needs. No one act, no one program, not even a revolution can establish equality in society, not if it has adopted as a goal the real development of its members and, therefore, a real increasing diversity of needs.[83]

There is another far more important implication of the critical vision of increasingly diverse and incommensurable needs to be met. The notion of political discourse must be enlarged in order to deal with the decisions. The understanding of politics contained within the conservative and liberal traditions is too simplistic to handle this problem. Each of these traditions is sure that it has measuring devices for comparing needs: the conservative looks to an overarching natural scheme or to the tradition of the community to judge (hence to compare and priorize) differing interests and needs; the liberal looks to the market in order to make the same evaluative judgment. However, a critical understanding of equality will imply that a far more open political discourse should be devised.

True political debate about end-values has been foreclosed, in accordance with the liberal understanding of pluralism, for about two hundred years. In its place there has been developed an administrative rationality which, as ideology, has claimed to effect compromises between conflicting interests but has in fact suppressed (by rendering them meaningless in public discourse) the legitimate interests of the powerless. What is required is discourse which can test the validity of the claims of all interests. Habermas has suggested that the model for this discourse is intersubjectivity, which implies complete symmetry and mutuality.[84] This approach is clearly meant to bring out the ideological aspect of class domination: communication is systematically distorted by the suppression of the legitimacy of one set of interests; political debate has become restricted to technical questions about redistribution; the political imagination becomes fettered.

I have argued that the liberal idea of equality is formal, abstract, and obfuscatory. It lacks critical clarity because it is subordinate to the liberal idea of pluralism, which precludes public examination of how the institution of private property serves the interests of those who own the means of production.

I have also suggested that groups who have struggled for equality in Canada have suffered from a lack of clarity about their goal or about the true nature of the obstacles they have faced. I have suggested that at the ideological level what is required is a critical understanding of equality, which will imply a notion of political debate where the criteria of symmetry and mutuality will be satisfied.

Because the goal is an increasing qualitative diversity of needs, equality (understood as a static position) cannot be the aim of any society, but rather a constant equalization, a constant examination and restructuring of institutions and processes to redress concrete inequalities which have been discovered through genuine political debate about end-values.[85]

NOTES

1 See Allan Moscovitch's 'The Canadian Economy and Inequality,' in this volume.
2 C.B. Macpherson, *The Political Theory of Possessive Individualism* (Oxford 1962), 247
3 Richard Wollheim, 'Equality,' *Proceedings of the Aristotelian Society*, New Series, LVI (1956), 281
4 Sanford Lakoff, *Equality in Political Philosophy* (Cambridge 1964), 126
5 Isaiah Berlin, 'Equality,' *Proceedings of the Aristotelian Society*, New Series, LVI (1956), 326
6 Ibid., 302
7 Lakoff, *Equality*, 7. Lakoff's theme is that equality is not a unit-idea, but has a different meaning within the framework of a conservative, a liberal, and a socialist political vision.
8 Hugo Adam Bedau, 'Egalitarianism and the Idea of Equality,' *Nomos IX Equality* (New York 1967), 7
9 Ibid., 12
10 Of 5,266 admitted to provincial correctional centres in Nova Scotia, 2,322 were for non-payment of fines. Statistics from the Attorney-General's Department of Nova Scotia. Douglas A. Schmeiser, *The Native Offender and the Law*, prepared for the Law Reform Commission of Canada (Ottawa 1974), 45-6, 81
11 See Patrick Kerans, 'Distributive and Retributive Justice in Canada,' *Dalhousie Law Journal*, 4, 1 (1977), 76-95.
12 Cf. John Rees, *Equality* (London 1971), 37-79.
13 Berlin, 'Equality,' 316; see also John Plamenatz, 'Diversity of Rights and Kinds of Equality,' *Nomos IX.*, 94; and Charles Frankel, 'The New Egalitarianism and the Old,' *Commentary*, LVI, 3 (Sept. 1973), 57.
14 Rees, *Equality*, 108; see also Bernard Williams, 'The Idea of Equality,' in Peter Laslett, ed., *Philosophy, Politics and Society* (Oxford 1967), 111.
15 Lakoff, *Equality*, 138
16 Carl Berger, *The Sense of Power: Studies in the ideas of Canadian Imperialism, 1867-1914* (Toronto 1970)

17 This attitude died hard. As late as 1942, after Arthur Meighen was beaten by the CCF in a by-election in York South, he wrote: 'Truly it is discouraging that the foul and despicable methods ... without the slightest regard for truth, could be successful in a constituency almost wholly of Anglo-Saxons.' Cited by J.L. Granatstein, 'The York South By-Election of Feb. 9, 1942: A Turning Point in Canadian Politics,' *Canadian Historical Review*, XLVIII, 2 (June 1967), 157

18 W.L. Morton, 'Clio in Canada: The Interpretation of Canadian History,' *University of Toronto Quarterly*, XV, 3 (April 1946), 232

19 Macpherson, *Possessive Individualism*, 77

20 Ibid., 78 (emphasis added). Brian Barry makes the same point when he distinguishes between 'want regarding' and 'ideal regarding' principles: 'if you discriminate among wants of different kinds for purposes of evaluation then you are an adherent of the ideal-regarding view.' Brian Barry, *The Liberal Theory of Justice* (Oxford 1973), 21

21 Thomas J. Lewis, 'An Environmental Case Against Equality of Right,' *Canadian Journal of Political Science*, VIII, 2 (June 1975), 256-8

22 Thomas Hobbes, *Leviathan*, ed. M. Oakshott, (Oxford 1947), 100-1

23 Macpherson, *Possessive Individualism*, 26

24 Ibid., 53-61

25 C.B. Macpherson, *Democratic Theory* (Oxford 1973), 196-8

26 John Wilson, *Equality* (London 1966), 128-9 (emphasis in original). Within the framework of a far more important argument, Habermas makes much the same point when speaking of 'civil privatism' and its role in forestalling a legitimation crisis, in *Legitimation Crisis* (Boston 1975), 36-7 and 74.

27 Kenneth McNaught, *A Prophet in Politics* (Toronto 1959), 173-6

28 King Diary, 24 Feb. 1925

29 Don Macgillivray, 'Military Aid to the Civil Power: The Cape Breton Experience in the 1920s,' *Acadiensis*, III, 2 (Spring 1974), 63

30 Ibid., 61

31 Frank Parkin, *Class, Inequality and Political Order* (London 1971), 183

32 Reginald Whitaker, 'The Liberal Corporatist Ideas of MacKenzie King,' *Labour/Le Travailleur*, II (1977), 151; see also 165.

33 Rees, *Equality*, 105; see also Stephen Lukes, 'Socialism and Equality,' *Dissent*, XXII, 2 (Spring 1973), 157; and R.H. Tawney, *Equality* (London 1931, 1964), 141.

34 This seems a fair summary of the meritorian notion of justice implied in the received liberal understanding of equality of opportunity. Cf. John Stanley, 'Equality of Opportunity as Philosophy and Ideology,' *Political Theory*, V (1977), 61-74. It is an attack on John Schaar, 'Equality of Opportunity and Beyond,' *Nomos IX.*, 228-49. Stanley cites Robert Simon, 'Equality, Merit and the Determination of Our Gifts,' *Social Research*, XLI (1974), 507.

35 Cf. Lukes, 'Socialism and Equality,' 157; see also Williams, 'Idea of Inequality,' 117; and Stephen Lukes, *Individualism* (Oxford 1973), passim.

36 Wollheim, 'Equality,' 282-4

37 Cf. Macpherson, *Democratic Theory*, 4, 20, 30, 34-5, 56; see also Lukes, *Individualism*, 139.

38 Wollheim, 'Equality,' 287

39 Schaar, 'Equality of Opportunity,' 230

40 This is the argument of Lukes' excellent *Individualism*.

41 Deborah Gorham, 'The Canadian Suffragists,' in Gwen Matheson, ed., *Women in the Canadian Mosaic* (Toronto 1976), 44

42 See Gwen Matheson and V.E. Lang, '"Not a Nice Woman,"' in Matheson, ibid., 13

43 Virginia Strong-Boag, 'Introduction,' in Nellie McClung, *In Times Like These* (Toronto 1915, 1972), xvi

44 Nellie McClung, 'The Way of the West,' *Black Creek Stopping-House* (Toronto 1912), 209

45 McClung, *In Times Like These*, 38-42

46 Ibid., 52

47 Matheson and Long, '"Not a Nice Woman,"' 12

49 In 1894, 17 Patrons were elected in Ontario. Cf. Louis Aubrey Wood, *Farmers' Movements in Canada* (Toronto 1924, 1975), 139.

50 Farmers took power in Ontario in 1919, in Alberta in 1921, and in Manitoba in 1922 and sent 65 Progressives to Ottawa in 1921, where they constituted the second largest bloc in the Commons.

51 Wood, *Farmers' Movements*, 60

52 Ibid., 94, citing the Master's Address of 1890

53 William Kirby Rolph, *Henry Wise Wood of Alberta* (Toronto 1950), 65-6

54 W.C. Good, *Farmer Citizen* (Toronto 1958), 180 (emphasis in original)

55 C.B. Macpherson, *Democracy in Alberta* (Toronto 1953, 1962), 34-5

56 Lorne Brown, 'Peace and Harmony: Breaking Down Myths of Canadian Labour History,' *Canadian Dimension*, 9, 5 (May 1973), 37 (emphasis in original)

57 Rolph, *Henry Wise Wood*, 159

58 The relative significance of a radical segment within a generally liberal labour movement, and the reasons for its minority status are questions which historians puzzle over. Cf. Martin Robin, 'Determinants of Radical Labour and Socialist Politics in English-Speaking Canada between 1880 and 1930,' *Journal of Canadian Studies*, II, 2 (1967), 27-39; Martin Robin, *Radical Politics and Canadian Labour, 1880-1930* (Kingston 1968), especially 268-94; Gad Horowitz, *Canadian Labour in Politics* (Toronto 1968), esp. 1-59; Norman Penner, *The Canadian Left* (Scarborough 1971), 6-39; David Jay Bercuson, 'Labour

Radicalism and the Western Industrial Frontier,' *Canadian Historical Review*, II, 2 (May 1967), 154-75.

59 Penner, *Canadian Left*, names a number of labour leaders who considered themselves Marxist.

60 Thomas Phillips Thompson, *The Politics of Labour* (1887, Toronto 1975), 22

61 Ibid., 104

62 Ibid., 103

63 Ibid., 81, 104

64 Ibid., 152

65 Robin, *Radical Politics*, 3, 4, 12

66 Russell Hann, 'Brainworkers and the Knights of Labour: E.E. Shepherd, Phillips Thompson and the Toronto News, 1883-1887,' in G.S. Kealey, ed., *Essays in Canadian Working Class History* (Toronto 1976), 56

67 Ivan Avakumovic, *Socialism in Canada* (Toronto 1978), 23; see also Penner, *Canadian Left*, 43; Robin, *Radical Politics*, 102.

68 Penner, *Canadian Left*, 63

69 Robin, *Radical Politics*, 145

70 Penner, *Canadian Left*, 68

71 Ibid., 143

72 Robin, *Radical Politics*, 179

73 D.J. Bercuson, 'Western Labour Radicalism and the One Big Union: Myths and Realities,' S.M. Trofimenkoff, ed., *The Twenties in Western Canada*, National Museum of Man History Series (Ottawa 1972), 44

74 Cited in the 'Introduction' to Norman Penner, *Winnipeg 1919: The Strikers' own history of the Winnipeg General Strike* (Toronto 1975), xvii; see also 'The Heenan Disclosures,' ibid., 229 ff.

75 Kenneth McNaught, 'Violence in Canadian History,' John S. Moir, ed., *Character and Circumstance* (Toronto 1970), 80

76 Ibid., 82; see also Penner, *Winnipeg 1919*, xxi.

77 Penner, *Winnipeg 1919*, 256-7

78 Peter R. Sinclair, 'The Saskatchewan CCF: Ascent to Power and the Decline of Socialism,' *Canadian Historical Review*, LIV, 1 (March 1973), 423

79 The National Farmers' Union has chronicled this process. See also *The Land of Milk and Money: The National Report of the People's Food Commission* (Toronto 1980), 18-25, 39-54 For a brief statistical overview, see Leo Johnson, 'The Development of Class in Canada in the Twentieth Century,' Gary Teeple, ed., *Capitalism and the National Question in Canada* (Toronto 1972), 148-51.

80 Macpherson, *Democratic Theory*, 127-31, where he argues that private property, understood as exclusivity, is essential to the liberal tradition.

81 Ferenc Feher and Agnes Heller, 'Forms of Equality,' *Telos*, 32 (Summer 1977), 14-17

82 Karl Marx, *A Contribution to the Critique of Political Economy* (Moscow 1970), 189

83 Feher and Heller, 'Forms of Equality,' 9-12. They develop the distinction between qualitatively different needs and those needs reducible to quantitative measure. See also ibid., 26; and Istvan Meszaros, *Marx's Theory of Alienation* (London 1970), 267-72. Both warn against a non-dialectic understanding of policies which can simply substitute a 'despotic' notion of egalitarianism for the vacuous liberal notion of equality of opportunity. See also Parkin, *Class, Inequality and Political Order*, 168-80.

84 Cf. Habermas, *Legitimation Crisis*, 86-9, 100-2, 111-18; see also Habermas, 'Toward a Theory of Communicative Competence,' in Hans Peter Dreizel, ed., *Recent Sociology No. 2* (New York 1970), especially 140-6. Habermas' call for a communication ethic is perhaps the *point d'accrochage* between this essay and Rawls' monumental work.

Given the comprehensiveness of Rawls' book, it seemed that either I should deal with him as a primary concern or only mention him once. (1) While Rawls' elaboration of the 'initial position' is a device for delineating the role of reason in social ordering, his role of reason is 'want-regarding.' (2) While, according to Rawls, justice would demand not only that unequal distribution be justified (as the best arrangement for the least advantaged) but justified in an open process; nevertheless that process would examine distribution and not production relationships. (3) Rawls' contractarian position precludes a careful accounting for the dialectic between community and personal development; hence, he presupposes an individual facing a competitive market. Rawls remains within the liberal tradition.

85 Feher and Heller, 'Forms of Equality,' 26

3
The Canadian economy and inequality

ALLAN MOSCOVITCH

What is the meaning of economic equality and inequality in a capitalist society such as Canada? There are, it is asserted here, four general approaches to economic equality: equality of opportunity, of outcome, of wealth, and equality at work. In setting out to consider these four different concepts in the context of the Canadian economy, the central argument posed is that the dominant ideological conception is equality of opportunity, predicated on the historic legitimacy of, and the necessity of, inequality of outcome, of work, and of wealth. It is further argued that the competitive market system, through which equality of opportunity is in theory to be satisfied, is the foundation of economic inequality in a capitalist society. Expressed in the negative, equality of opportunity constitutes the specific negation of equality of outcome, work, and of wealth in Canadian society. However, before proceeding to consider equality of opportunity, let us first examine economic inequality in the dominant ideology.

THE IDEOLOGY OF ECONOMIC INEQUALITY

In the context of a Canadian society, dominated by the ideology of equality of opportunity (and of private enterprise), how can we seriously raise for public debate the issue of moving towards economic equality? The most common response to a demand for equality of outcome (wages, salaries, incomes) is pragmatic, the 'motivation' argument: 'If everyone gets paid the same amount of money then who will run the corporations, and who will do the skilled jobs? Without economic incentives the right people will not get the necessary training, and without the possibility of earning more money, people will put in minimum hours at a leisurely and unproductive pace.' The pragmatic response often continues like this: 'I'm in favour of helping the poor when they want to help themselves, but what you are proposing will destroy the economy. I want everyone to have a choice at a larger piece of a bigger pie.'

A further response is the 'sameness' argument, which poses a view of what economic equality might mean in practice: 'Do you mean to say that everyone has to have exactly the same things, the same housing, the same clothes, and the same food? Determined by some government bureaucrat?' While the first response is more serious, the second serves to trivialize discussion, leading possibly to a conclusion of the following type: 'That's tyranny you are talking about; you're opposed to individual initiative, to creativity, to people doing what they want, how they want to do it. I say that if people want to get ahead, and if the government doesn't stop them, they will.'

These are popular expressions of the dominant ideology in capitalist society – an ideology in which equality is taken to mean equality of opportunity, and in which opportunity means the opportunity to compete for incomes, commodities, and jobs. This competition is assumed to take place in a society which is competitive in the sense that no individual or group can exert any significant measure of control over the buying or selling of commodities or over jobs. The implication drawn from the latter is that a competitive society is a good society.

But why does competition result in the formation of a good society? First, it is asserted that competition is good because it is a natural process; human beings are naturally acquisitive and competitive. Second, it is asserted that what makes competition desirable is that it requires little conscious organization; the competition of the many individuals in society requires only acquisitiveness to spur people on and some regulation to ensure that no one in society breaks the rules thereby allowing either unfair or self-destructive competition to take place. Therefore, with a modicum of regulation and administration, this competition (in the economic sphere) automatically results in the good society, in the sense of the greatest (material) good for the greatest number.

The dominant ideology in capitalist societies can be illustrated by use of the metaphor of the machine. Society is, in this view, a machine over which no individual can have any particular control, a machine which takes differentiated inputs of human beings and turns out, in an inexorable manner, the outcome that they merit as a result of its operation. If equality of opportunity exists, then everyone in society has an equal chance to enter the machine as a low or high quality input, and, therefore, each individual's outcome is just in the sense of being directly commensurate with input quality and quantity.

We would not expect outcomes to be equal unless the quality and quantity of human inputs were equal. If there is observed inequality of outcome, then either it is the result of a low quality and quantity of input or a malfunction in the machine, or both. In the case of a malfunction either the machine is self-correcting or it can be corrected by a mechanic. In the case of the quality and quantity of inputs, it is argued, some correction may be made by the individual, by the machine, or by the mechanic; but there is a limit – the fundamental difference in human capacity, and the individual choice of quality and quantity of work.

If such is society, then how do individuals act, being simply input in the machine? In essence all individuals conform to the same rule of behaviour: they act to maximize their own individual or family benefit. They do this whether they act as suppliers of labour input to the machine or as consumers spending their wages or salary on commodities. In each case, each individual acts to maximize his benefits (utility) through his choice of job, with its accompanying pay and conditions of work, and through the choice of commodities to purchase. Choice is constrained in the former case by the number of working hours in the day, in the latter by disposable income. In this sense, and this sense alone, each individual is rational.

It is this conception of rational economic man, developed primarily by the European economists of the late nineteenth century and summed up so succinctly in Veblen's critical phrase as 'a homogenous globule of desire of happiness,'[1] which remains the dominant conception in late twentieth-century capitalist societies. The presumed advantages of competition, the free market-place, free trade, the state as neutral referee of economic affairs, the free movement of labour and capital; and the presumed limitations of state intervention to support social programs, minimum wages, trade unions, and a redistributory tax system – these remain the common themes of the day. The arguments as theory and as ideology are little more than the case for economic inequality. The doctrine of equality of opportunity is the means by which in capitalist societies economic inequality is justified.

This is not to suggest a lack of ideological diversity; it is a diversity of degree, not of kind. The material and intellectual developments of the past two hundred years have confirmed two major streams of thought within the dominant ideology in Canada as in other capitalist societies: liberal and conservative. While the virtues of the idealized competitive free market society are generally accepted (even by most social democrats as the basis of social analysis), differences still remain as to the extent to which each society conforms to this capitalist ideal. The particular combination of economic variables, which are currently the key to the explanation of the economy, and the nature and extent of state intervention are all the subject of continuing controversy, even among the faithful. [2]

For example, the current fashion among economic conservatives is for explanations of economic malaise based on the expansion of government expenditures and the supply of money. Consequently, their solution is to cut government programs, particularly social programs such as unemployment insurance and welfare, which act as 'disincentives to work,' and to cut the growth of the money supply.[3] Economic liberals continue to stress the importance of the level of consumption, savings, and investment in explaining current economic problems. Consequently, they turn to a mix of selective monetary and fiscal policies, including a variety of job creation programs, in order to control inflation and unemployment. They have turned and continue to turn more readily to state regulation, including wage and price controls. Economic liberals have also been more prepared to turn to the implementation of social programs when occasion warrants.[4] However, despite this seeming diversity, whether expressed by individuals, organizations, political parties, or by the state, there is a core of ideas which is common to all: the doctrine of equality of opportunity and the operation of the perfectly functioning economic machine, which constitute the dominant (economic) ideology.[5]

The existence of a dominant economic ideology is neither conspiratorial nor accidental. It is not that there is somewhere a room in which meet the captains of industry, the owners of the media, and the leading members of the government of the day, who between them decide what people in society should believe, and that like drones, we accept it. Neither does it simply happen that there exists a set of views often held by people in all classes in society, even though those views are largely to the benefit of the dominant class. A particular set of views comes to predominate neither through conspiracy nor accident, but through the conscious efforts of the dominant class to give expression to their economic, social, and political dominance. Equality of opportunity – fundamentally an expression of economic dominance – is, from the conventional point of view, a key weapon in an ideological arsenal used by the dominant class to express the legitimacy of its dominance and the justice of the subordination of other classes. In *The German Ideology* Marx and Engels provided the most elegant yet succinct of explanations:

The ideas of the ruling class are in every epoch the ruling ideas, i.e. the class which is the ruling *material* force of society, is at the same time its ruling *intellectual* force. The class which has the means of material production at its disposal, has control at the same time over the means of mental production, so that thereby, generally speaking, the ideas of those who lack the means of mental production are subject to it. The ruling ideas are nothing more than the ideal expression of the dominant material relationships, the dominant material relationships grasped as ideas; hence of the relationships which make the one class the ruling one, therefore the ideas of its dominance. The individuals composing the ruling class possess among other things consciousness, and therefore think. Insofar, therefore, as they rule as a class and determine the extent and compass of an epoch, it is self-evident that they do this in its whole range; hence among other things rule also as thinkers, as producers of ideas, and regulate the production and distribution of the ideas of their age: thus their ideas are the ruling ideas of the epoch.[6]

In each capitalist society the ideas of dominance take precedence, but they must find expression, they must be interpreted to fit the occasion, and they must be available when occasion warrants. Given the range of sometimes competing interests within the dominant class, and the range of middle-class and working-class organizations with allied and competing interests, we would expect to see a public diversity of views, expressed by a diversity of individuals and organizations, but with a common core of ideas linking them.[7]

This diversity is best illustrated in Canada by a range of lobby groups expressing the views of particular sectors, industries, professions, trades, regions and localities, and by a group of sophisticated, specialized organizations. These latter organizations may be public, semi-public, or private, but their role is similar: to interpret the economic interests of the dominant class, to articulate them as the national interest where national interest is to be understood as the interest of the dominant class, and to disseminate these ideas as widely as possible.[8] They serve as the popularizers of theoretical and empirical formations and investigations of questions which are defined by the academic version of the dominant ideology, itself referred to as a paradigm.[9] They also serve as the bridge between the university-based high priests, the industry, and state-based technicians, although all are no less servants of power.[10]

The most prominent and most important of those organizations are the C.D. Howe Research Institute, the Fraser Institute, and the Conference Board in Canada – three private and primarily business-funded research groups. The Fraser is the most recent (1974) and the most conservative of the three. As a stepchild of the (British) Institute of Economic Affairs, its board of directors is dominated by well-known right-wing American and British economists. It is a purveyor of a brand of conservative economics gaining prominence in both countries, which has as its most distinguishing feature a simple and single-minded attack on state expenditures in general, on social programs in particular, and on taxation, together with a defence of economic individualism and so-called free markets.[11] In its own words the Fraser has as its objective 'the direction of public attention to the role of competitive markets in providing for the well-being of Canadians. Where markets work, the Institute's interest lies in finding the reason. Where competitive markets have been replaced by government control, the interest of the Institute lies in documenting objectively the nature of the improvement or deterioration resulting from government intervention.'[12]

Other organizations are less overtly conservative and business oriented. The Conference Board in Canada is the Canadian subsidiary of an American parent whose 'sole purpose [is] to promote prosperity and security by assisting in the effective operation and sound development of voluntary productive enterprise.'[13] Its orientation has been to problems internal to the organization of large-scale private enterprise and only secondarily to current economics.[14] The more liberally oriented of the three has been the C.D. Howe Institute (founded in 1973, though beginning life in 1957 as the Canadian-American Committee). It has posed as a more objective and research-oriented organization. Its mandate is 'to undertake research into Canadian economic policy issues, especially in the areas of international policy and major government programs.'[15] In practice it has promoted private enterprise and free trade, leaning more to the liberal side of the dominant (economic) ideology.

Also prominant are a range of public organizations such as the Economic Council of Canada, which was founded in 1963 as a high-level planning agency under the federal government. A prominent liberal economist has said that the Economic Council is a blocking institution, 'an institution that would give the appearance of being a planning body, but would be so structured that it would not be capable of any planning whatsoever.'[16]

There are also several more socially oriented institutions which are the purveyors of the same ideology in the welfare field. Equally infused with equality of opportunity, they have evinced a concern for the victim, for those who clearly have been excluded from, or have been damaged by, the operation of the economic machine. One such organization is the National Council of Welfare, a government-appointed and funded organization which is advisory to the Minister of Health and Welfare. It has commissioned a number of innovative studies of the extent of poverty, of reform proposals (particularly the Guaranteed Annual Income), and of the differential effects of the tax system. Commenting on the report, *The Hidden Welfare System*, Howard Buchbinder said:

It assumes that the solution to poverty lies within the tax system and/or redistribution of income. It further assumes that the focus on how the rich 'rip-off' the poor will generate the response necessary for reforms ... All of these proposals, including this one, ignore the issue of wealth and concentrate the struggle in the area of income. All of them including this one, ignore the causes of poverty and devise adaptive measures to provide a cushion to those among the most exploited and victimized while preserving the process of their exploitation.[17]

These and other such organizations are the institutional ideologists of the bourgeois order. They and the individuals who represent them publicly, expend considerable amounts of energy and money in justifying the benefits of competition, private enterprise, individual initiative, and the ultimate wisdom of the inequality manifest in Canadian society. All share a fundamental belief in the virtues of equality of opportunity, more or less tempered by various kinds of social programs.

EQUALITY OF OPPORTUNITY

What is equality of opportunity? Popularly, it suggests that everyone has an equal chance to strike it rich or to get a well-paying job, or both. The assumptions which underlie it are that life is a competition, a race which everyone starts at the same place, and that the competition is a fair one. Now if everyone has equal talents and abilities, equal education and training; is prepared to put out the same effort for the same period of time, under the same conditions, with the same information about these conditions; then everyone should arrive at the same point at the same time. The key to this race for life requires the competition to be fair, that it be privately run, that it be held under a clear set of rules, and that there by a clearly acknowledged referee who will enforce the rules and arbitrate disputes in a fair manner. According to the doctrine this is what we can expect from life, but since the whole process is not only natural but the most efficient, the most rational, and the most democratic of forms of social organization, it is also *all* we should expect.[18]

If, according to thise view, equality of opportunity does not prevail, if people do not have an equal chance to compete, there must be a breakdown or a blockage associated with the individual, the competition, the rules, or the referee. The challenge is to determine why society departs from this idealized picture of a capitalist economy and to take what steps are considered reasonable to ensure that a fair competition is established.[19] After all, fair competition under the conditions described should produce equal incomes for all individuals in the race. However, equal incomes have not been the result in capitalist societies. The unequal distribution of incomes is widely recognized and is persistent. In Canada since 1951 the proportion of income received by quintile has changed little. If anything, income distribution is more unequal since the proportion of incomes received by the bottom 20 per cent of individuals and families actually fell from 4.4 per cent in 1951 to 3.8 per cent in 1977, while the proportion received by the top 20 per cent remained relatively constant.[20]

Such inequalities have been rationalized, but these explanations fail to account for more than small variations in income because they ignore the most fundamental of divisions in society – the division between those who own capital and the means of production, and those who do not. Equality of opportunity, fair competition – these are the ideological means used to obscure the real social relations in society, to mask the exploitation of those who work by those who own. Competition, or more specifically, the labour market, is a convenient fiction, a way of masking a system of social organization which forces the propertyless to compete with each other for the owners' jobs, to work to earn enough to carry on, while the owner accumulates profits and capital by virtue of ownership alone.

Whether in the public sector or private, in small- or large-scale operations, in mines, factories, or offices, jobs are hierarchically organized with few high-paying jobs and many low-paying jobs. In addition, jobs tend to be stratified. One segment corresponds to those areas of the economy which tend to have high profits with high capital concentration, high capital/labour ratios, a considerable degree of control over the price and conditions of sale of the product, and a well-established structure of jobs, with hours, wages, fringe benefits and advancement paths determined in a union contract. The other segment contains jobs which are located in relatively small labour-intensive, low technology, highly dispersed, and competitive companies with small profit margins. These jobs are associated with low pay, ill-defined hours, and few benefits. They also tend to offer employment to workers who are not unionized. These jobs require fewer skills, lower credentials, and less training from workers who are employed in them.[21] Consequently, not everyone in society can have high-paying jobs because there are few of them, and once they are filled there is no more space at any one time. If equality of opportunity means that everyone has a chance for a 'good job,' then the actual probability of getting one, for many people, is very low – low enough to be very close to zero. The fact that there are individuals occupying high-paying positions, such as corporate directors, managers, and supervisors, is no proof that those who manage do so because they are best suited for the job. There is now ample evidence of the systematic intergeneration transfer of types of jobs, as well as evidence that many, if not most, directors of

Canadian corporations acquired their positions through prior economic power and influence. Their abilities, training, and intelligence have little to do with their position. In any case, their acquisition of skills, experience, and training is closely related to that of their parents, family, and social circle. Further, the connection between social class and job is systematic and general, rather than accidental and particular. Such competition as exists is primarily among unskilled workers for unskilled, low-paying jobs. The higher up the job hierarchy we travel, the more structured and less competitive jobs are until we reach the upper echelons, in which we find the largely self-selecting corporate elite.[22]

The result is that the capitalist labour market provides the illusion of social justice through an ideology of undifferentiated and fair exchange (of labour power for wages and salaries) while hiding the reality of the exploitation of labour, which is the basis of profit and growth in a capitalist economy. The usual conclusion, on the other hand, is that the market provides the result which no other form of social organization can provide, so that is justice for workers and efficiency for society. This conclusion could not be achieved without the complete separation of the idea of markets from actual economic conditions and their consequent reification.

The ideology of the capitalist job market is, then, the key to understanding the continuing importance of equality of opportunity in the dominant ideology. If the market provides justice, who are mere human beings to tamper with this just, natural, and technical arrangement, in which the unseen hand operates for the good of all, capitalists and workers alike? What we must do (say bourgeois apologists) is make it possible for everyone to compete. The fallacy, of course, is that capital and labour, owner and worker are not alike, and that to the extent that exchange value of labour rises, then, other things being equal, surplus must fall. Equality of opportunity is simply the right to compete with other workers for jobs which are offered by those who own and direct the corporate wealth in society. The free job market is only free in the sense that the worker is divorced from wealth and is, as a consequence, compelled to sell labour power in order to subsist from day to day. Since the job market has become simply a way of filling hierarchically organized job slots with wages and salaries attached, equality of opportunity presupposes inequality of outcomes.

INEQUALITY OF OUTCOMES

In order to explain the persistence of major inequalities of outcome, theorists and popularizers have developed a series of defences (some might say apologies). Here we review five of them: differences in intelligence, individual choice, human capital, marginal productivity, and labour-market imperfections. These arguments should be properly understood as relating to differentials in earnings, although each has a counterpart which is used a posteriori to justify profits. The avowed purpose of these defences is to provide a series of explanations for the rationality and efficaciousness of equality of opportunity, for competitive labour-markets, and, consequently, for considerable inequality of outcome. We also review the consequence of this inequality on the amount and quality of goods and services obtainable.

DIFFERENCES IN INTELLIGENCE

The oldest and longest standing defence of equality of opportunity is the linking of individual characteristics with outcome. If outcomes are different, given all other assumptions of the idealized competitive world, then such differences are due to variations in innate ability. The supposed observed fact of such a positive link has led to suggestions that those at the top are there primarily on the basis of their intelligence, and secondly, that educational programs directed at increasing the opportunities of people with low incomes are likely to fail, for the reason that low intelligence is associated with low income. The argument is based on two propositions: first, that intelligence as measured in IQ tests is largely inherited, and second, that IQ is a major determinant of income.[23]

The latter proposition is more important for our purposes here. Much, of course, depends on the measurement of intelligence in any testing. It would be possible for example to find a set of IQ test questions which would, when applied, generate a distribution of results similar to the distribution of income. This would not, however, indicate a correspondence of intelligence with income. Consequently, the results of statistical studies of intelligence and income must be treated with caution, if not scepticism. In a series of published articles Bowles and Gintis have explored the statistical relationships between genotypic IQ, socio-economic (family) background, childhood IQ, years of schooling, and income using American data collected in the early 1960s.[24] Where the main correlates were socio-economic background and income, Bowles found, in a decomposition of the statistical relation between these two variables, that the 'genetic inheritance of IQ (even assuming a relatively high degree of heritability) accounts for only a miniscule portion of intergenerational immobility.'[25] In other words, earnings differentials are more dependent on inequality of education and on the direct effect of socio-economic status itself.

Bowles further emphasizes the importance of family, school, and work-place in generating and reinforcing character traits of workers: 'personality traits relevant to the work task, modes of self-presentation ascriptive traits, and credentials appear to be integral to the process of intergenerational immobility.'[26] On the other hand, achievement and skills appeared to be of limited importance in determining economic success, independent of schooling and socio-economic background. The socialization of children of workers in particular occupational categories serves to prepare them for similar work as their (like gender) parents.

An alternative way to look at the same problem was that taken by Veblen. The supposed link between intelligence (ability, capacity) and income was a key assertion of the Social Darwinism of the latter years of the nineteenth century. The present-day argument is a twentieth-century inheritance. Veblen argued that this most venerable of bourgeois self-justifications could as easily be turned on its head. Hofstadter explains Veblen's critique this way: 'The process of selection under the conditions of modern society, has caused the aristocratic and bourgeois virtues – "that is to say the destructive and pecuniary traits" – to be found among the upper classes, and the industrial virtues, the peaceable traits, largely among the "classes given to mechanical industry." '[27]

INDIVIDUAL CHOICE

Economic ideology is based on the existence of a defined perfectly rational representative individual. It is not surprising that a most important defence of equality of opportunity, and of observed inequalities is that the latter may be the result of differences in individual choice. The argument runs as follows: each person chooses to spend each day's working hours at work or in leisure. Such choices are made subject to a range of assumptions which go to make up the archetypic rational economic man. One additional assumption is added about the nature of work – an assumption drawn directly from nine-teenth-century utilitarian philosophy – that work is always undesirable and leisure always desirable. The only reason for working then is to acquire money. Given all these assumptions and the wage rate or salary, people with varying tastes choose different combinations of work and leisure, resulting in some measure of observed inequality.[28]

In other words, people are poor because they like the leisure that comes with poverty. Others work long hours for their relative affluence. Since there is no doubt an element of truth in this argument, the question is whether the argument is a general one, or simply a special case. As high theory this utilitarian approach and more sophisticated versions of it have been completely discredited as unscientific. Versions of the theory have been severely criticized on the grounds of the underlying assumptions; these criticisms create of the theory not a general case (from which exceptions can be noted) but a special case.[29] For example, most workers do not have the range of information or choices of jobs with the flexibility implicit in the assumptions. The range of occupational choices of any given worker is limited by the interrelation of family background, schooling, training, and locations; those jobs which are realistic choices at any time, depending on market conditions, are limited. For the most part these jobs have a determinate wage and minimum hours attached to them. The jobs may entail enforced lay-offs on the one hand, or overtime, determinate sick-pay, holidays, and other fringe benefits on the other hand. Choices of jobs and flexibility in the job tend to increase, up to a point, with greater access to capital, with higher credentials, and with greater skills. Typically the hierarchy of jobs is such that better pay is matched by greater flexibility and the possibility of working fewer hours, particularly since professionals and managers may be able to set their own hours.

Revenue Canada data based on 1976 tax returns show that the highest average occupational income is that for self-employed doctors and surgeons, at $49,310, while the average income of employees is $13,125. Self-employed professionals account for 76,155 taxpayers, while there are an additional 773,551 others who could be similarly classified, making 849,705 out of a total of 8,806,731, or 18.4 per cent.[30] On this rough measure possibly 18.4 per cent of taxpayers have the potential flexibility implied. If we account for those who are self-employed but in marginal businesses, and those who obtain their flexibility through UIC or welfare, and for managers listed as employees, we still do not arrive at a very large percentage of people with the requisite flexibility implied by the theory. When further account is taken of the fact that individual choice is only one of several rationalizations offered, it does not loom as a serious argument.

Another hole in the argument is that people in low-paying jobs simply cannot afford the luxury of leisure if they are to survive. They are trapped in jobs from which they cannot advance and which may require them to work long hours when they work, or may require them to take enforced leisure in the form of a lay-off. This is as much the case for women as for men, the former entering the labour force in larger and larger numbers principally because of the impossibility of leading a decent family life without two wages or salary cheques.[31]

Lastly, we should recall that many of the statistically identified poor (possibly about 40 per cent) are outside of the labour force, and not by choice. Their 'leisure,' either as a result of their being natives, female heads of families, handicapped, retired, or injured, is enforced since neither the employment flexibility nor the institutional support necessary for them to work is apparent. Of those they called the welfare poor, the Special Senate Committee on Poverty had this to say:

Not all the poor are able to join the ranks of the working poor. Eighty-four percent of the adults who depend on the welfare system have no alternative means of support. They require assistance simply because they are not capable of earning a living. They are the ones left behind by our economic system – the elderly, the sick, the disabled, and women in charge of families which require their presence in the home.

The remainder, slightly more than one in ten, are prospective members of the labour force who are not currently working. To categorize all of these persons as shiftless, irresponsible, or inherently lazy is to ignore the realities of the current employment picture.[32]

No matter how well these points are documented, nor how many times, individual choice continues to be presented as a major reason for observed inequalities.

HUMAN CAPITAL

A further choice is the decision to seek training or education. To do this the individual must in most cases forego an income in order to acquire educa- tion, skills, or training; this is assumed to provide the 'human' capital which will lead to a higher future income. Accordingly, the individual calculates and compares the present value of a future higher income. He need only program his home computer to obtain the results in several minutes.

The argument draws on a parallel to the economic explanation for interest and profit, the latter being the return for the capitalist's prescience and defer- ral of gratification. Specifically it is argued that owners of capital agree to forego present consumption, using their capital to augment production and receiving a return in future as a result. However, the latter theory presup- poses the existence of capital and cannot explain where it (and, therefore, profit) comes from.

Human capital theorists explain differential earnings in a similar way, in that, if individuals are to undergo training, they must forego earnings, which they could be receiving during the period of training. They must also pay for the cost of training itself. Assuming (1) that everyone has the same opportunity to undergo training and (2) that the economic system primarily works according to qualifications, skills, and training, then the observed differential earnings should be explained by this theory.[33] The problem with this approach is that it assumes, but cannot show to be the case, that there exist equal opportunities and a perfectly competitive labour-market in the textbook sense. In addition, the approach assumes that the individual decision to acquire skills and take training is independent of the structured inequality of a class society and of the socialization of class. In other words, the theory cannot explain the reasons why the individual acquired training or why there is a necessary relation between qualifications, skills, training, and jobs. For example, is it clear that the son of the owner of the family firm who goes to business school is doing so on the basis of some estimate of the rate of return to acquiring that training? Is there any evidence that training is then a necessary prerequisite to acquiring the job of vice-president of the corporation?[34]

The results of empirical work based on human capital theory, if not in accord with predictions, have been explained on the basis of the existence of so-called imperfections in the capital market for the financing of training.[35] Such imperfections are the deviations of reality from the theory that finance is available on a perfectly competitive basis. This rationalization has provided a means by which, for example, arguments have been put for the improvement of student loan programs rather than for the provision of free tuition, the former reinforcing market inequalities and simply ignoring the existence of class inequality, loading those with low incomes who do actually borrow with large future debts.

MARGINAL PRODUCTIVITY

While the previous rationalizations of inequality of outcome are based on the individual workers' decisions, a further rationalization is to be found in explanations of the behaviour of capitalists in the labour-market. The marginal productivity theory suggests that workers be paid according to the marginal contribution to output of the last worker hired. Theoretically this leads to a fair return to labour since workers are collectively paid according to their contribution to national output. It is in this sense that the claim is made that capitalism has eliminated exploitation.[36] Several questions may be raised about this assertion. It is clear that if workers are collectively paid according to their marginal contribution to output, they cannot necessarily be paid according to their total contribution. Why this should be considered fair or just is not explained. On an individual basis how logically, in a complex process of production and distribution, can the marginal contributions of each worker be established separately so that each may be paid according to his/her productivity at the margin? Further, argues Nell, marginal productivity does not provide a guide to remuneration in cases where the connection between labour and output is indirect and where status and power, and social conventions are important. If this is so, with the number of white-collar and service workers, farmers, managers, foremen, supervisors, and with companies having less than full knowledge of production possibilities or market circumstances, then 'as a theory of wages we can say that marginal productivity applies part of the time and not always well to a tiny minority of the labour force, perhaps no more than 3 per cent or 4 per cent. Clearly such a theory should be thought of as a special case.'[37]

Why then should payment according to marginal product be the subject of economic sermons since its formulation by Clark at the turn of the century? The answer can only be that the doctrine of wages according to marginal product, is an apology and a mystification of the process of determination of unequal wages in a capitalist labour-market. For example, that part of the output not paid to labour is paid to capital, on the presumption that capital is productive in exactly the same fashion as labour power: capital is to be paid according to its marginal product. But capital presupposes an owner, and as a consequence the marginal productivity theory simply provides a convenient justification for the returns to ownership. In other forms of the theory some portion of output may be attributed to so-called entrepreneurship, but this portion cannot be measured except in relation to what the entrepreneur or capitalist can appropriate for himself – profits. In other words, there must be entrepreneurship. Otherwise where do profits come from?

LABOUR-MARKET IMPERFECTIONS

The capitalist labour-market is a shorthand term for the matching of buyer and seller, of worker and job slot, of labour and capital.

Jobs, it is argued, call for particular skills, experience, ability, intelligence, etc. Equal opportunity means that each worker with the appropriate mix of requisite characteristics has an equal chance at each such job. The labour-market is, in other words, the perfect mechanism for generating a meritocracy. Competition for jobs throws up those with the attributes and temperament to be managers, supervisors, and industrial leaders in the search for human progress. Just as individual attributes are matched by appropriate rewards, so also they are matched by appropriate jobs to which a reward is attached. Further, as we have seen, it is argued that some mis-matching occurs by choice since some workers are unprepared to move or prefer to work in jobs which do not provide a challenge commensurate with their abilities and capacities. Some may resist acquiring the skills and training which would provide entry to more responsible (and higher-paying) jobs in favour of immediate remuneration in less responsible jobs.

There are, of course, abuses which may occur. Discrimination by employers or by a combination of employers may prevent a particular worker from appropriate employment, but, it is argued, the market is bound to prove employer discrimination unprofitable.[38] Persistent discrimination may call for state regulation to encourage the employer to restore fair competition. In the most extreme form of the argument employee combinations (trade unions), representing an impediment to the free entry of labour into the market, should be closely regulated by the state in order to eliminate such a market imperfection. In another version trade unions should be encouraged where appropriate – where the employer has monopoly powers, or where manual workers are involved. Shortages and surpluses of labour which arise due to fluctuations in the economy may provoke temporarily high wages or lay-offs and unemployment. For all these reasons the capitalist labour-market may fail to be the perfect instrument for the translation of equal opportunity into action.

While discrimination may be put down to happenstance or to the result of the actions of individuals, such explanations are not sufficient. What is dismissed as discrimination, as an aberration, or a departure from the norm is in fact endemic. Discrimination against women, as a growing number of studies show, is profitable.[39] Women have been relegated to particular occupations, doing the same tasks as male workers in particular sectors, but for less pay. They make up the preponderant numbers of part-time workers, serving as a cheap flexible surplus of labour as demands on production change. At home they labour to ensure that the household's workers are prepared for work and that the next generation's labour force is prepared for what lies ahead. Labour-market discrimination against French-speaking people[40] and native peoples[41] has proved by its longevity that it too will not disappear of its own accord. Discrimination, it must be recognized, has served to enhance the profitability of capital. Yet profitability is the purpose for which labour is in general hired. Discrimination in this sense must be understood not as aberrant, but as endemic.

Trade unions have also been the subject of the rationalization of inequality. In one version of the story unions prevent the smooth operation of the capitalist labour-market. Consequently, unions cause some workers to be unemployed or to be kept out of unionized employment. Undoubtedly, union activity has an effect on the availability of work and on the general living standards of workers. On the one hand some workers may be kept from employment; on the other, union activity has led to the capitalization of industry, the search for new technology and new markets, and in general has been an important historical factor in economic expansion. In addition, while union wage demands have been an ingredient in inflation, they have also forced up wages and standards for all workers. Lastly, union militancy has been a key ingredient in effecting state regulations which have benefited all workers.

An alternative and now more common argument is that although unions create 'distortions' in the distribution of income, they should nonetheless be encouraged where there is already considerable corporate power, in order to provide a countervailing force, both in the workplace and in the political arena. As Albert Rees explains it, 'if the union is viewed solely in terms of its effect on the economy, it must in my opinion be considered an obstacle to the optimum performance of our economic system. It benefits those workers who would in any case be relatively well off, and while some of this gain may be at the expense of the owners of capital, most of it must be at the expense of consumers and the lower paid workers.'[42] In other words, the union still introduces inequality, but on the positive side it provides 'protection against the abuse of managerial authority.'[43] The union also functions to inculcate and disseminate bourgeois values and faith in free enterprise: 'By giving workers protection against arbitrary treatment by employers, by acting as their representative in politics and by reinforcing their hope of continuous future gains, unions have helped to assure that the basic values of our society are widely diffused and that our disagreements on political and economic issues take place within a broad framework of agreement.'[44]

The last of labour-market arguments is that observed inequalities are due to temporary fluctuations in the economy. Such an argument cannot of course explain the persistence of inequality of outcome over time or the persistence of inequalities which leave workers in specific regions, occupations, and ethnic, religious, and sex groupings at the bottom. Neither can it explain the persistence of unemployment at levels greater than those which could themselves be explained by frictional unemployment, unemployment due to some workers simply being between jobs. Rather, if fluctuations and imbalances are long-term structural features of capitalism, at least some inequality must be a permanent feature, not amenable to removal by state policy.

In reviewing each of the five arguments – differences in intelligence, individual choice, human capital, marginal production, market imperfections – we have tried to show that each has a kernel of truth but is limited in what it can explain of inequality. Like equality of opportunity itself, these arguments play an important ideological role. By suggesting that workers primarily get what they deserve, what they ask for, or are the subject of anonymous market forces, they assist in rationalizing the existence of widespread inequality in income and wealth. The rationalizations allow equality of opportunity to remain a part of the dominant ideology despite the persistence of inequality.

INEQUALITY OF CONSUMPTION

Equality of opportunity presupposes, as we have seen, considerable inequality of outcome. It is with widely varying incomes that workers, professionals, farmers, managers, and capitalists alike approach the consumer market. The result is widely varying standards of living. Data from the *Urban Family Expenditure, 1976* survey,[45] reveal that the average family (and individual) in the first decile of income distribution pays $1,189.30 per annum on food for an average family size of 1.44, or $825.90 per person. In the tenth decile, average food expenditures are $4,798.50 for 4.06 persons, or $1,181.90 per person. While differences in family composition might temper the data, the figures indicate that the average tenth decile family spends 300 per cent more, or 40 per cent more per person, than a first decile family, the tenth decile family also spends 20 per cent more per person on shelter, 310 per cent more on clothing, and 560 per cent more on travel and transportation. Nonetheless, the average tenth decile family still has enough income, after spending considerably larger sums in all other areas as well, to be able to save $5,031.80, or $1,239.40 per person. The first decile family is on the average *using up* $122.30 of savings, or $84.90 per person per year.

It is very clear from these data that inequality of incomes directly translates into major inequalities in the quality of life. Yet these data do not account for the considerable implicit income derived from ownership of housing and durable goods, furniture, clothing, books, etc., which have been purchased in the past and which would tend to further reinforce inequalities. Differences in income also have other important dimensions affecting consumption, as several studies have shown. Credit, bargains, discounts, special treatment, and wider choice all come with higher income.[46]

Yet the dominant ideology tells a different story, in which market exchange constitutes the centre-piece of the analysis of a capitalist economy. It is this analysis which has prompted the charge that reality is presented as nothing so much as a corner store, with each person in society represented as a rational economic calculator of pleasure and pain, come to make purchases. Nowhere can we see more closely the relation between ideas and the social class that gives rise to them. The fundamental unit of analysis, it is posited, is the individual, the fundamental task consumption, and the fundamental method, the rational utilitarian calculus of less and more. There are no social classes or forms of socialization to interpose on the nature of the task: what the undifferentiated consumer consumes is up to him or her, and it is the undying task of the undifferentiated productive unit (the corporation) to supply. Consumer and producer meet as equals in a technical relation which determines the best for all.

The observed differences in consumption are, as a consequence, often explained as simply the result of the different choices made by 'utility' maximizing individuals. If, for example, people are observed to live in poor housing, this is explained at least in part by their choice to do so.[47] There is no understanding of the social relations which engulf the individual, which lead to and delimit choice. Inequality of consumption is simply assumed to be the result of low income and/or individual choice since, as with the job market, the consumer market is a perfectly functioning, well-oiled machine. No doubt this view offers insight into the operation of the bourgeois mind, but it can only be, as an understanding of the economic reality of the mass of people, a thinly veiled attempt to attribute all the attitudes and habits of the bourgeois to all in society.[48] It should be clear than in a very real way, the consumer, the worker as buyer in exchange, is not sovereign as is claimed, for choices are made not according to some abstract set of notions – a little of this or that – but on the basis of what the owners decide to have produced and to make available. If indeed workers attempt to get the most for the wages accorded to them, it provides no evidence of their unchecked self-interest, but rather a reasonable reaction to circumstance – a given amount of earnings from which to purchase necessities to accomplish a reasonable social standard.[49]

INEQUALITY AT WORK

Equality of opportunity presupposes only that under particular conditions all workers have an equal chance for similar employment. Since employment is primarily offered by privately owned enterprise, it also presupposes a division between workers and owners of enterprise. However, equality of opportunity says little about the structure of work in the enterprise. What it does say is that the relations between labour and capital and between various kinds of labour (the division of labour) are determined according to the most cost-efficient technology of production. Inequality at work; the undemocratic organization of the capitalistic work process; the subjugation of the worker to the machine; the destruction of traditional skills; the uprooting of the worker from the land which created the 'free' labourer, free to sell labour to owners of capital – all these characteristics are considered to be the necessary results of the division of labour. André Gorz explains the point this way:

The tyranny of the factory is as old as industrial capitalism itself. The aim of production techniques and the work organization they dictate has always been a double one: Labour must be made as productive as possible for the capitalist, and thus maximum output must be forced from the worker through the organization and the objective requirements of the means of production. The production process must be organized so that the worker experiences the coercion to maximum output as an unalterable requirement of the machine or an imperative inherent in matter itself. Inexorable and incontestable, this imperative seems to be a result of the apparently neutral laws of a complex machine, beyond volition and dispute. The worker must submit to the quantity and the nature of his daily work as the only possible way to serve a machine. And he must see the machine as the only possible one: the only possible solution to the technical problems of production.[50]

Existing production technologies do not fall from the sky or necessarily constitute the most efficient means of producing a particular output. Rather, they are *chosen* by particular owners for the reason that these production methods constitute a means of ensuring that production takes place at a particular speed, intensity, and duration, utilizing a particular combination of labour and capital to produce output of a particular type and quality. They are secondarily chosen because they constitute the cheapest means by which a particular level and quality of output can be achieved with given costs of materials and labour power.

The division of labour is not specific to capitalism; nor can it be taken to be the same as the specific division of labour under capitalist production. It was an integral part of production in pre-capitalist periods: the peasant did not attempt to perform all aspects of farming simultaneously; that is, from plowing to seeding to tending to reaping. But what distinguishes the division of labour under capitalism is the separation of tasks into discrete units to be performed simultaneously by different workers. In a characteristic passage Marx explains that

by decomposition of handicrafts, by specialization of the instruments of labour, by the formation of detail labourers, and by grouping and combining the latter into a single mechanism, division of labour in manufacture creates a qualitative gradation, and a quantitative proportion in the social process of production; it consequently creates a definite organization of the labour of society, and thereby develops at the same time new productive forces in the society. In its specific capitalist form – and under the given conditions, it could take no other form than a capitalistic one – manufacture is but a particular method of begetting relative surplus-value, or of augmenting at the expense of the labourer the self-expansion of capital – usually called social wealth ...

It increases the social productive power of labour, not only for the benefit of the capitalist instead of for that of the labourer, but it does this by crippling the individual labourers. It creates new conditions for the lordship of capital over labour. If, therefore, on the one hand, it presents itself historically as a progress and as a necessary phase in the economic development of society, on the other hand, it is a refined and civilized method of exploitation.[51]

The division of labour, while integral to the productive achievements of the factory system and the industrial system and the assembly line, performs three very specific and important functions under capitalist production: the provision of a role for the owners, directors, and senior managers in the co-ordination of production, through the separation of planning from execution; the individuation of workers by limiting training and introducing task work through a monopoly of knowledge of the work process and through the subjugation of the worker to the machine; and the creation of a job hierarchy accompanying the introduction of the detail division of labour, as a means of encouraging workers to compete by creating differentiated levels of work and rewards, and as a means of control over the alienated work of mass production. Of these, conventional theories attempt to explain only the role of the capitalist by reference to the capital he supplies to production, presupposing the legitimacy of private property and its use in the appropriation of the surplus in production. On deskilling and the dominance of the machine, conventional theories have little to say except that if they persist it is because they represent the most efficient form of production. About job hierarchy they say the same.

The early system of manufacture depended upon both the specialization and separation of tasks. While the specialization of the tasks required to manufacture a particular commodity formed the basis of the rapid expansion of output, it was also accompanied by the separation of tasks in space. The early capitalist sought advantages by standing between the producer and the market, controlling the output. The stability of his position and the size of profit was ensured by separating the tasks to be performed not simply in time but in space, between different workers in different locales. This was the basis of the putting-out, or contract, system. In the early eighteenth century, factories began to appear in England, grouping detail workers in one place. Technological change, the introduction of new machinery (it has often been argued) prompted the development of the factory. Equally plausible, Marglin notes, is the argument that factories developed as a means of ensuring control over the work process – the speed and pace of work by the workers. The factory was also a means of controlling the quality and type of materials used in production and of protecting the profitability of new innovations in machinery. The factory system was an efficient system of production not simply because of the saving in time and energy in production, but because it afforded an easier means of control not only over output but over aspects of the work process itself.[52] In Marx's analysis of the division of labour he concluded that the 'division of labour within the workshop implies the undisputed authority of the capitalist over men, that are but parts of a mechanism that belongs to him.'[53]

The introduction of more complex machinery confirmed the role of the capitalist since it was clear that no individual worker or household could afford to buy it. But the full triumph of the capitalist awaited the introduction of the principles of scientific management, beginning in the latter years of the nineteenth century. The preservation of the putting-out, or contract, system of labour in the factory meant that control over the work process still largely rested with the workers. The aim of scientific management was 'the dictation to the worker of the precise manner in which work is to be performed.'[54] This was accomplished not by accident but as the result of conscious effort to expand productivity by breaking the hold of the worker over the process of work. The principles by which owners operated were a part of what was called scientific management, the systematic study of work and application of the results to the organization of the work process. The terminology is important because as Braverman notes, it was not called scientific workmanship. F.W. Taylor, who is often credited with initiating scientific management, argued that there 'are many workmen who are intellectually just as capable of developing a science, who have plenty of brains and are just as capable of development a science as those on the managing side. But the science of doing work of any kind cannot be developed by the workman. Why? Because he has neither the time nor money to do it.'[55]

It is an interesting argument in that it ran counter to the still prevalent ideas of survival of the fittest. Yet it is an argument for the appropriation of the fruits of science by management 'for the very same reason that machines, factory buildings etc. belong to them, that is, because it costs labor time to conduct such a study, and only the possessors of capital can afford labor time.'[56] The result is that 'not only do the workers lose control over their instruments of production, but they must now lose control over their own labor and the manner of its performance.'[57] While the capitalistic division of labour, the factory system, the revolution in the instruments of labour, and the separation of planning and execution have all contributed towards making capitalism an enormously productive form of social organization, they do not represent inexorable forces. They have been the result of a conscious endeavour on the part of an ascending class of owners of capital and have in fact presupposed the existence of capital and the existence of propertyless free labour. They have been introduced to make labour power more productive for capital and to expand the appropriation of surplus labour by capital, an appropriation based solely on the capitalists' own enforced claims of legitimacy.

The capitalist division of labour, the factory, the introduction of complex machinery, and the introduction of scientific management also had their effects on the workers. They have, over centuries, served to reduce the artisan to a detail worker repeating the same task as a part of the collective labour of the workshop or factory, and being subject to the discipline of the capitalist and of the work process and the machine. The worker is degenerated from a creative, independent artisan with a profound knowledge of production to an automaton of repetition, only vaguely aware of the total production process. Individually and collectively the worker becomes an extension of capital. Again we turn to Marx for an analysis of the effects of the capitalist division of labour on the worker:

In manufacture, as well as in simple co-operation, the collective working organism is a form of existence of capital. The mechanism that is made up of numerous individual detail labourers belongs to the capitalist. Hence, the productive power resulting from a combination of labours appears to be the productive power of capital. Manufacture proper not only subjects the previously independent workman to the discipline and command of capital, but, in addition, creates a hierarchic gradation of the workmen themselves. While simple co-operation leaves the mode of working by the individual for the most part unchanged, manufacture thoroughly revolutionises it, and seizes labour-power by its very roots. It converts the labourer into a crippled monstrosity, by forcing his detail dexterity at the expense of a world of productive capabilities and instincts ...[58]

The capitalist division of labour also brought with it the introduction of a wage hierarchy. This served as a means of achieving cost reductions through a system of differential pay according to levels of skill. This was accomplished in the process of introducing a detail division of labour in which a much more restricted level of skill was demanded of workers: to repeatedly perform a limited range of tasks. Often such 'deskilling' was accompanied by the introduction of a higher level of capitalization, which reduced the size of the labour force at the same time as it substantially increased individual worker productivity. Consequently, wage and salary differentials can be seen to be the result of this process of the breaking down of the traditional crafts' methods of production, which continued to dominate the factory system until the turn of the twentieth century. In the process of separating planning from execution, planning was given a higher level of importance over execution. Similarly, a hierarchy of jobs (and wages) according to (reduced) levels of skill introduced further differentials among workers and served as an incentive to workers to expend more effort. The wage hierarchy represented the full triumph of capital over labour, in that it broke from the piece-work system, which had tied workers' wages to the market price of the commodity. With control of the speed and pace of production, workers retained a close connection to output, the market, and their own returns. The elimination of piece-work, as Braverman clearly points out, marked the end of that connection and control.[59] But the expected growth in class conflict, in absenteeism, labour turnover, and in trade unionism was mediated in part by pitting worker against worker through the development of wage incentive schemes involving wage hierarchy and internal promotion. In addition, sophisticated systems of industrial welfare were put in place to tie the worker to the company and to instill company loyalty.[60] In a study of the destruction of the contract system in the American steel industry, Katherine Stone argues that the

advantage of the job ladder arrangement was that it gave the employers more leverage with which to maintain discipline. The system pitted each worker against all the others in rivalry for advancement and undercut any feeling of unity which might develop among them. Instead of acting in concert with other workers, workers had to learn to curry favor with their foremen and supervisors, to play by their rules, in order to get ahead. As one steel worker described the effect this had on workers during the 1919 organizing campaign, 'Naw, they won't joint no union; they're all after every other feller's job.' This competition also meant that workers on different ladder rungs had different vested interests, and that those higher up had something to lose by offending their bosses or disrupting production.[61]

The conclusion is that the fundamental division between owners and workers gives rise to a particular form of the relations of production in which the direction and control of production is handled by owners and those who work for them on behalf of them directly. The relations of production give rise to an authoritarian relationship in the work process and a hierarchical structure of wage and salary differentials, such that there are internal inequalities within the work-force. Inequality at work is a consequence of, and a means of, reinforcing the competition for jobs which is equality of opportunity.

INEQUALITY OF WEALTH

A fundamental proposition in this paper is that the ideas which justify and/or commend existing economic relations and consequently economic inequality are the dominant ideas in society because they are provided by, or on behalf of, the dominant class in society. These ideas which are presented as having their own rationality, as being divorced from the interests of any particular individual or class in society, appear so as the result of this dominance. Accordingly, inequality of outcome and inequality at work appear as the result of an inexorable technical process run by creative entrepreneurs and set in motion by the aggregated choices of rational economic individuals. To this point, we have presented the ideas used to justify inequality; we have examined them theoretically and empirically: and we have rejected them. We have argued that equality of opportunity, in turn, leads to and presupposes inequality of outcome and inequality at work. Each of these aspects of inequality is based on a fundamental difference between those who own wealth or do the work of owners, and those who do not. By wealth we mean here not simply ownership of material goods (in consumption) or of labour power (human capital), for this would trivialize the distinction (and it is the means, of course, by which the distinction between owners and workers is trivialized), but also the means of production. These we define as those physical commodities which are used in the production of other commodities, or that pool of calls against present and future commodities which is aggregated in the form of finance. This difference is not simply an idea, an abstraction; it is also a concrete recognition of the nature of social relations, which are both cause and effect of this fundamental distinction.

There are several points here. First, inequality of wealth is not simply one of several forms of economic inequality; it is the fundamental inequality since the existence and maintenance of the 'free market' is predicated on a division between owners of wealth and non-owners of wealth who must depend on their wages and salaries received from their daily work. Equality of opportunity, the dominant ideological guise for inequality, presupposes inequality of wealth; without it, there would be no compulsion on workers to compete in the job market.

Second, a distinction must be made between corporate wealth, the means of production, and personal wealth. If we treat inequality of wealth as simply inequality in a societal continuum of asset holdings, we abstract from the nature of economic power in society, which is the direction of, and control over, wealth as productive capacity. A concentration of wealth appears in each sphere: the concentration of corporate wealth refers to the number and extent of pools of capital held in corporations, while the concentration of individual wealth refers to the extent to which ownership over those pools is diffused or concentrated. The distinction is important since the concentration of corporate capital does not necessarily imply the existence of a group of significant owners of capital.

The conventional response to the accumulation of corporate wealth has been variously to deny its significance, to redefine the notion of competition, or to argue that corporate concentration leads to increased efficiency in production. This is to be contrasted with the predominant attitude towards accumulation of individual wealth, which is considered both a natural right and evidence of the thrift and entrepreneurial initiative of the owner. Individual wealth holding has also been defended on the grounds that property ownership is the best defence of democracy and the inevitable result of differential outcomes and differential tastes for savings. One consequence of inequality of outcome is that there will be some people with a high enough wage or salary such that they will be able to save. It follows, then, that such inequality, if it is indeed to create the incentive to draw out entrepreneurship, must be supported by the right to transfer capital from one generation to another. Otherwise, it is argued, the incentive to accumulate is significantly reduced. The chain of reasoning is, then, that inequality of outcomes is a likely result of equality of opportunity. Further, some inequality of wealth is a necessary adjunct to inequality of outcomes. Consequently, equality of opportunity requires inequality of wealth.

An alternative defence against the charge that the free market system promotes the concentration of economic power is the argument that economic power is actually highly diffuse. Canada, it is argued, is a country of people's capitalism. The first question the diffusion thesis poses to critics of capitalism is, what is the definition and extent of concentration of individual wealth holdings? A second and related question is, what is the nature and extent of control over corporate wealth? Finally, a third question is, does equality of opportunity still mean that it is potentially possible for anyone to become a millionaire?[62]

In order to assess the first question, of the extent of diffusion, we must have a definition of individual wealth. Should wealth include all assets, including deposits in finance companies, bonds, shares, partnership interests, other capital, housing, and consumer goods, or should it be confined to a more restricted list? In addition, should a definition of wealth also include so-called human capital? For our purposes here in identifying ownership of capital in the sense of means of production, wealth is defined as ownership of the voting stock of corporations. It is voting stock which carries the potential to influence corporation policy, including the present and future use of corporate assets.

The only surveys of wealth holdings in Canada have been provided by Statistics Canada, and recent results are available for the years 1970 and 1977.[63] These data link together income and wealth so that wealth holdings by themselves are difficult to discern. Nonetheless, the data do give us some indication. The data show that in 1970, 87.7 per cent of families and unattached individuals covered in the survey *did not* hold publicly traded stock holdings; share ownership by Canadians was confined to 12.3 per cent of individuals and families. By 1977 the incidence of ownership had fallen to 8.5 per cent of those surveyed. There is indication here not only of limited diffusion of share ownership but of a fall in the extent of diffusion in recent years.

Looking first at the results of the 1970 survey, we find that of the 12.3 per cent of families and individuals that did hold publicly traded stocks, only 0.6 per cent held blocks priced at $25,000 or more. The average holding among shareholders was $6,211, but among individuals and families with $25,000-plus income, the average holding was $23,357. More than 50 per cent of those in the $25,000-plus category held some shares; this was far in advance of any other income category. Unfortunately, the question we cannot answer is, what portion of all shares do 0.6 per cent of families and individuals hold? Further, we find that the average stock holding of those surveyed that held $10,000 of stocks or more was $32,562, while the average stock holding in the next category below, that is, between $5,000 and $9,999, was considerably lower at $6,791. Those holding $10,000 or more of publicly traded stock constituted 1.7 per cent of the sample.[64]

Additional data (previously unpublished) on the inequality of wealth holdings in general can be found in an article by J.R. Podoluk. She suggests that 'within nearly all income groups the top 5% of wealth holders held approximately ⅕th to ⅓rd of the assets of that income group.'[65] Consequently, within the category of those asset holders with $25,000 or more annual income who own 61.9 per cent of total assets, we might expect an even greater concentration of ownership of assets.[66]

Changes in questions asked, sample size and reliability, and report format mean that the results of the 1977 survey are not easily comparable to those of the 1970 survey. However, in 1977 the average holding of stocks was $10,946, but among families and individuals with $25,000 to $34,999

income it was $7,766, and among those with $35,000-plus income it was
$32,373. In these same two income categories the incidence of share owner-
ship was 16.4 per cent and 29.6 per cent respectively, the latter being more
than three times the average incidence.[67]

The distribution of wealth by income categories in the 1977 survey also
suggests considerable concentration of ownership of shares. The incidence of
share ownership in the highest income category, $300,000-plus, was 31.4 per
cent, almost four times the average incidence, and 26.5 per cent in the next
category of $150,000 to $299,999. Average share holdings in each category
were $76,553 and $25,538, as compared to the average holding of $10,946.
Lastly, looking at the distribution of share assets, 45.3 per cent were owned
by families and individuals in the $300,000-plus category, and 21.5 per cent
in the $150,000 to $299,999 category for a total of 66.8 per cent of share
assets held in the two top wealth categories.[68]

What we cannot obtain from the data is an estimate of the concentration of
share holdings by wealth categories. None the less, we may safely conclude
from these data that there is an indication of considerable concentration of
holdings of publicly traded shares among Canadians on the basis of the
sample data. We could also expect that the data understate the extent of
concentration for the reason that reporting among the wealthy is notoriously
bad.[69]

A second aspect of the diffusion thesis is that corporate control is not
concentrated among shareholders of individual corporations. Power is diffused because most corporations no longer have dominant or even minority
shareholders; boards of directors are largely made up of corporate managers
who owe their position not to ownership of shares but to a rise in the corporate hierarchy. The implication is that there are no longer a significant number of capitalists; an occupational elite has replaced an economic elite.

A recent study examined the nature of the control exercised in 136 of the
largest Canadian corporations as of 1975. The results indicated that 12 corporations were subject to absolute control, 28 majority control, 52 minority
control, and 44 (32 per cent) to internal or managerial control. On a sectorial
basis, only in transportation and utilities were there a majority of corporations under internal control (93 per cent). In addition, the largest companies
in each sector in the study (except real estate) were under managerial
control.[70]

Reviewing this evidence, we find that diffusion, while sizeable, is still
limited to a minority of major Canadian companies. In addition, some doubt
must be cast on the reliability of the 'internal control' category as is noted in
the study. The use of trustees and dummy shareholders, and the absence of

requirements to report a less than 10 per cent holding of shares, make it difficult to properly identify shareholders and the extent of diffusion. Further, and related to the unreliability of reporting, is the fact that particular companies ostensibly under internal control have a long history of directors from the same family. Davis family members on the board of Alcan, the Richardson family and Inco, the McLean family and Canada Packers – these are all examples of continuing family connections, despite ostensible diffusion. The persistence of these relationships may be further evidence of hidden shareholding.

In sum the data do not suggest significant diffusion among major Canadian corporations. Internal control is the result of either state regulatory policy (primarily American) leading to the breakup of even larger corporations, or the progressive diffusion of shares in a succession of mergers. Such companies that are internally controlled are also more open to a takeover which will restore a stronger form of control. Lastly, from the Canadian point of view foreign-controlled subsidiaries are not subject to diffusion of control, regardless of the position of the parent. Effective decision making is in the hands of the directors of the parent corporation.

The third aspect of the diffusion thesis is that control over the major corporations is not concentrated; therefore, the road to riches is still open to those who work hard. This question has been most recently investigated by Wallace Clement in an extensive study of the directorships of the 113 dominant Canadian corporations and the people who hold them. He concludes that

Canada has been and remains a society controlled by elites. Moreover, its present class system, as the culmination of a long historical development, reflects not a random but a structured inequality. The overseers of this carefully maintained domination, in its economic aspects at least, are the economic elite. They preside over the corporate world, using as their means of power, the central institutions of the Canadian economy – 113 dominant corporations, their subsidiaries, affiliates, investments, interlocking directorships with smaller corporations, family ties and shared class origins. Their power is reinforced by control over the major sources of capital, especially the key banks and insurance companies, and over the paramount positions within most of the central economic sectors. With increasing economic concentration over the past twenty years, the structure has become increasingly closed, thus making it more difficult for those outside the inner circles of power to break through.[71]

Looking first at directorships, Clement established a list of 113 dominant corporations according to whether they had $250 million or more in assets, and an income of $50 million or more. These 113 corporations had 454 directorship positions held by residents and another 301 held outside Canada. However, only 60 per cent of directorships were held by Canadians resident in Canada, and only 54 per cent were held by Canadians born in and resident in Canada. Foreign directors (primarily American) are concentrated in resources, manufacturing, and trade, in that order of importance.[72] In an analysis of the interlocking of directorships (the placing of directors from one board on the board of another dominant corporation), Clement found a considerable degree of density of interrelation between dominant corporations. The highest density was found in the interrelation of finance and utilities sectors of 0.71, where density is 'the potential number of interlocks divided by the actual number.'[73] Similarly, finance and manufacturing stood at 0.62, finance and resources at 0.59, finance and trade at 0.37, and manufacturing and resources at 0.30. He also found a considerable number of corporate interlocks between dominant and middle-range and smaller corporations. Lastly, Clement also found that 54 per cent of directorships were held by 274 or 29 per cent of directors.[74]

Who holds this interlocking group of key positions of power? Based on analysis of the class origins, career avenues, family connections, ethnicity, religion, schooling, and community activities, Clement concluded that access to power has become even more limited than it was according to Porter's study of 1951 data: 'the Canadian economic elite over the past twenty years has become a more exclusively upper class preserve.'[75] Of the Canadian-born and Canadian resident directors for which data could be found (673), 28.5 per cent had fathers or uncles in the corporate elite at some time, 2.4 per cent had fathers in the political or bureaucratic elite, 5.8 per cent married into elite families, and 10.1 per cent had fathers who were 'in substantial businesses which were not dominant but of sufficient size to provide an initial upper class avenue into the elite. This means that 46.8 per cent of the present elite began at or near the top of the class structure.'[76] An additional 47.4 per cent entered the elite from middle-class backgrounds. Only 5.8 per cent of the elite were from lower than middle-class origins. Lastly, Clement notes that the reduction in the numbers of the elite who made it into the elite on their 'own account' has fallen from 7.6 per cent in 1951 to only 2.2 per cent. This reflects in part the much greater difficulty of establishing a major corporation in one generation.

An investigation of the three aspects of the diffusion thesis, with the limited empirical evidence, suggests that ownership of key forms of wealth is not diffuse but concentrated; it appears that there is considerable inequality of wealth in Canadian society. Since inequality of wealth is the basis of the liberal ideal of equality of opportunity/inequality of outcome, it remains for us to examine its origins.

THE FOUNDATION OF ECONOMIC INEQUALITY

If the fundamental barrier to equality is inequality of wealth, the question still remains as to how this inequality is generated. The answer is that the system of economic relations in capitalist societies came into being as a result of, and depends upon, the continuous drive to accumulate. What distinguished this newly emerging system of economic relations from the old, which was based in trade and the consequent accumulation of profits on the part of merchants through trade, was the development of a pool of labourers not tied to the land, either as independent farmers or as peasants, and the emergence of owners of land and of means of production who were eager to employ them.[78]

In Canada as the fur trade slowed and property rights were established and concentrated particularly in central Canada, a group of workers unattached to the land began to develop. At the same time, small-scale local manufacturing began to develop, at first in response to the local demands of trade and the exploitation of the forests, and the growing population of farmers. The quest to continuously develop and extend property rights and to concentrate them was described by Gustavus Myers in his book the *History of Canadian Wealth*.[79] The development of the system of capitalist relations in Canada in Myers' work leans rather too heavily towards the analysis of the acquisition of property essentially through theft and corruption. Nonetheless, in Myers' defence one would be moved to paraphrase Proudhon that 'not all property is theft, but a good deal of theft turns up as property.'

The development of capitalist relations was based on the historic process of the divorce of farmers, free farm workers, peasants, and artisans from the means of production. There consequently emerged a class of owners who enjoyed a monopoly over the means of production, which afforded them the economic power to employ this emerging class of workers who were divorced from those means. The class of owners employed these workers, purchasing their services through the establishment of a money wage paid to the worker in return for the employ of his or her labour power for a given period of time, in the production of commodities. In the process of the hiring and employ of labour in production, there occurred a divorce of the exchange value of labour power (in the form of the wage) from labour's use value, i.e., its value to the owner when combined with means of production to produce commodities. It was this process which Marx studied so very carefully in the first volume of *Capital*.[80] In addition, it is the owner's right by virtue of ownership alone to appropriate a part of the output derived from production. The owner does this as a result of a difference between the total value of commodities produced and the amount which he has had to lay out in the form of wages, rents, and in the form of materials and means of production which have been used up in the production process. This is the process which Marx identified as the *appropriation of surplus value*, the process of exploitation of labour, which is fundamental to capitalist accumulation. However, the drive of the owner is not simply for the accumulation of the direct products of production, but rather for what they can be exchanged for. As a consequence, the owner must sell the output in order to realize in his hands the surplus value, which he then takes in the form of profits – profits which can be used for the further expansion of production through the purchase of additional means of production, and labour power; profits which could be saved and, as a consequence, used for expansion elsewhere or could be used for the consumption of commodities by the owner himself.

Marx's identification of this law of value is crucial to our understanding of the nature of the economic relations of capitalist society. It is through the law of value that we can comprehend the process by which inequality is generated. Inequality pervades economic relations; it is inherent in the unequal and exploitative relation between owner/employer and employee. This is in contradiction of course to the analysis provided by conventional economics and popular ideology which suggests that the relationship between employer and employee is a technical one rather than a social one, and a fair one rather than an exploitative one. For what they both identify as key is the efficiency of the combination of inputs, including labour to produce output. The nature of the relation between employer and employee is portrayed as an exchange between equals, a view which hides and mystifies the structured inequality at the heart of capitalistic economic relations. This is not to suggest that means of production contribute nothing to the production process and, consequently, to the output, but rather that *ownership of them* contributes nothing. Neither should the law of value be interpreted to suggest that to each worker should be accorded all the results of his work. For what is characteristic of the nature of capitalist production is that it is fundamentally social: the division of the tasks of production has been made to correspond with the division of workers such that each must depend on the others to see the task through. This is the case in any particular enterprise and across enterprises as well.

Inequality of wealth, which is both cause and effect of the structured inequality of Canadian society, results from two interrelated processes.

There is first the process by which historically an owning class is established using the legitimating and coercive forces of the state to establish their individual rights to land and other capital. This process of theft is concurrently and/or subsequently legalized. Further, the rights of ownership are extended from generation to generation. Second, and at the same time, the law of value operates to assure owners that the use of their capital by others will expand their capital in providing a return to ownership which can be reinvested.

The conclusion I believe is two-fold. First, we must cast our understanding of equality from a critical perspective which refuses to accept the ideas of the dominant class as determinant and seeks rather to root understanding in the economic relations of Canadian capitalist society. Second, we must be clear in the search for an equalitarian society that inequality is rooted in the structure and existence of capitalist society. To overcome the structure of economic inequality we must overcome exploitative relations themselves. The reduction of inequality of opportunity through whatever means is the path to inequality of outcome, inequality at work, and inequality of wealth. It changes nothing fundamental. The reduction of inequality of outcome leads to some amelioration of the social conditions of some people. In that, it is laudable, but it does not change the system which continues to generate further inequality. It is only by substantially reducing inequality of wealth that the possibility of a more fundamental change is open. It is only by collectively appropriating wealth that we place within our grasp the means for establishing an egalitarian society.

NOTES

The author wishes to thank Leo Panitch, George Warskett, and Bela Egged, who provided valuable commentary on earlier drafts of this paper.

1 Quoted in the 'Introduction' to E.K. Hunt and Jesse G. Schwartz, eds., *A Critique of Economic Theory* (Harmondsworth 1973), 11
2 This point is emphasized by many authors writing of capitalist societies. See, for example, Ralph Miliband, *The State in Capitalist Society* (London 1970), chap. 7.
3 The virtually classic statement of this viewpoint is by Milton Friedman, *Capitalism and Freedom* (Chicago 1963). Friedman has been special adviser to U.S. presidential candidate B. Goldwater and former President Richard Nixon. He has also been special adviser to the Israeli government of Menachim Begin, and the Chilean junta of Augusto Pinochet.

4 Since the 1930s, the bible of liberalism in economics has been J.M. Keynes, *The General Theory of Employment Interest and Money* (London 1964). Keynes has prompted many interpretations and popularizations. Of the former, the most influential were those by J.R. Hicks. (On Hicks, see Alan Coddington, 'Hicks' Contribution to Keynsian Economics,' *Journal of Economic Literature*, XVII, 3 (Sept. 1979), 970-88, for an appreciation of his role in interpreting Keynes to other economists.) As with any Bible there is bound to be a debate on exegesis of the texts. The last ten years has seen a debate over what Keynes 'really said,' a debate not unassociated with growing economic crisis and the rise of economic conservatism. In the debate Keynsianism is separated by some writers from Keynes' own economics: they argue that Keynsians have misinterpreted Keynes. A second stream not directly associated with this debate attempts to extend Keynes and is sometimes identified as Neo-Keynsianism, or in some versions, Neo-Ricardianism. In North America, mainstream Keynsianism has been strongly influenced by the writings of Cambridge, Mass., economists such as Alvin Hansen, Paul Samuelson, Robert Solow, E. Domar, R. Arrow, and J.K. Galbraith. The most important popularization has been Samuelson's textbook on *Economics*. An early Canadian interpretation by Mabel Timlin published in 1942 is entitled *Keynsian Economics*. While there has been a range of debate between conservatives, liberals, and institutionalists over the nature of the economy as a whole, the theory of individual and firm behaviour has evolved with many fewer controversies as a generally accepted core of ideas. Criticisms have not constituted a significant challenge to the continued predominance of individualism as to the philosophic and methodological base.

5 It is arguable that economics is the extreme example of the congruence of science and ideology. However, the position taken here is not that there are no scientific elements in conventional social science, but that there is a core of views common to science and ideology. The language of expression does, of course, significantly differ between the two. Yet the basic role of both scientific economic theory and economic ideology as they exist now in late twentieth-century capitalism is to obfuscate, to substitute explanations of surface phenomena for explanations of underlying structures and relations. Each, as a consequence, contains an element of truth, which assists their continued domination in the realm of ideas. See, for example, Martin Shaw, *Marxism and Social Science: The Roots of Social Knowledge* (London 1975), chap. 4; N. Geras, 'Marx and the Critique of Political Economy,' in Robin Blackburn, ed., *Ideology in Social Science* (London 1972), 284-305; E. Nell, 'Economics: The Revival of Political Economy,' in Blackburn, ibid., 76-95; E.K. Hunt, 'Economic Scholasticism and Capitalist Ideology,' in Hunt and Schwartz, *Critique of Economic Theory*, 186-93.

6 K. Marx and F. Engels, *The German Ideology* (New York 1974), 64 (emphasis in original)

7 Miliband, *The State*, chaps. 4 and 7

8 Ibid., 75

9 The concept of the paradigm was developed by T.S. Kuhn, *The Structure of Scientific Revolutions*, (Chicago 1970). It was a concept used to refer to the core of thought in the physical sciences. It has been stretched to apply to the social sciences. Several such efforts have been made in economics. See, for example, A.W. Coats, 'Is There a Structure of Scientific Revolutions in Economics?' *Kyklos*, XXII (1969), 289-94

10 This idea has been explicated in a paper by Herb Gintis, 'Economists as Servants of Power,' *American Economic Review*, LXIV, 2 (May 1974), 129-32.

11 For an analysis of the history of the Fraser Institute, and in particular, of their publications in the housing field, see Donald Gutstein, 'Corporate Advocacy: The Fraser Institute,' *City Magazine*, III, 7 (Sept. 1978), 32-9.

12 From the inside cover page of the Fraser's first publication, *Rent Control: A Popular Paradox* (Vancouver 1975). This volume is largely made up of reprints of classics of anti-rent control right-wing diatribes by such well-known purveyors as Pennance, Friedman, de Jouvenal, and Hayek.

13 From the inside cover page of the American publications

14 Reports of the Conference Board in Canada state that its main office is in New York and its Canadian office is in Ottawa. Previous chairmen have included Arthur Smith, formerly of the Economic Council, and Robert René de Cotret, former Conservative minister of economic development.

15 From the inside cover page of *A Time for Realism*, ed. Judith Maxwell, (Montreal 1978)

16 Albert Breton, 'A Theory of the Economic Council of Canada,' in L.H. Officer and L.B. Smith, eds., *Canadian Economic Problems and Policies* (Toronto 1970), 100. A further liberal analysis is provided by Gilles Paquet, 'The Economic Council as Phoenix,' in T. Lloyd and I. McLeod, eds., *Agenda 1970: Proposals for a Creative Politics* (Toronto 1968), 135-58. The liberal orientation of the Economic Council has been both in personnel (with former chairmen such as J.J. Deutsch, Arthur Smith, Sylvia Ostry) and in topics and content as brought out by R.W. Phidd, 'The Role of Central Advisory Councils: The Economic Council of Canada,' in G. Bruce Doern and Peter Aucoin, eds., *The Structure of Policy-Making in Canada* (Toronto 1971), 204-45.

17 Howard Buchbinder in *This Magazine*, XI, 1 (Jan.-Feb. 1977), 20

18 Few authors in recent times have clearly explicated the concept of equality of opportunity. Instead, the assumptions and the doctrine appear sometimes stated, sometimes hidden in books on aspects of economics, politics, and soci-

ety. There are exceptions, however, among the more conservative-oriented writers who have been more directly concerned to state positions on the connections between economics and politics. Milton Friedman's *Capitalism and Freedom* (Chicago 1961) is such an exception. The work of Von Hayek, Von Mises, Robbins, and Knight and others has been the key influence among more conservative-oriented economists. Completely unreconstructed laissez-faire as a policy doctrine is a thing of the past; Keynes was himself critical of relatively unfettered laissez-faire as an ideal. (See, for example, J.M. Keynes, *The End of Laissez-Faire* (London 1927). Keynesians born of the depression have tended, like conservatives, to accept the basic 'core' of ideas as presented here but have supported a much broader array of state measures. In addition, much of the discussion of what the state should do has been artificially hived off into so-called normative welfare theory and separated from the 'positive' analytics. This has turned the discussion of welfare (what to do about the lack of opportunity) into complete apologetics, a point made by many authors. See the critiques of welfare theory by James O'Connor, 'Scientific and Ideological Elements in the Economic Theory of Government Policy,' in E.K. Hunt and Jesse G. Schwartz, eds., *A Critique of Economic Theory* (Harmondsworth, Middx. 1972), chap. 15; M. Dobb, *Welfare Economics and the Economics of Socialism* (Cambridge 1969); J.P. Roos, *Welfare Theory and Social Policy: A Study in Policy Science* (Helsinki 1973).

19 Like all generalizations this one too has its exceptions. There are a range of positions around the competitive ideal, within bourgeois economic ideas. Yet the 'challenge' as presented here is undoubtedly the key question in welfare economics – the study of departures from the welfare optimum, and the policies necessary to achieve it. There is no doubt, as well, that economists, utilizing welfare theory as justification for policy tools, analysis, and recommendations, now have considerable weight in the corridors of power in industry and the state. See Peter Self, *Econocrats and the Policy Process* (London 1975).

20 For 1951 data, see Statistics Canada, *Income Distribution* (Ottawa 1969, cat. no. 13-529), table 12; for 1977 data, see *Income Distribution by Size in Canada, 1977* (Ottawa 1979, cat. no. 13-207), table 72.

21 The approach taken here has been identified as labour market segmentation theory or the theory of dual labour markets. See David Gordon, *Theories of Poverty and Unemployment* (New York 1971); David Gordon, Richard Edwards, and Michael Reich, eds., *Labour Market Segmentation* (New York 1974). M. Piore and P.B. Doeringer, *Internal Labour Markets and Manpower Analysis* (New York 1971); a summary from a liberal perspective has been prepared by Glen C. Cain, 'The Challenge of Dual and Radical Theories of the Labour

Market to Orthodox Theories,' *American Economic Review, Papers and Proceedings*, LXV, 2 (May 1975), 16-22. A use of the approach appears in The National Council of Welfare, *Jobs and Poverty Ottawa* (1977); and in I. Adams et al., *The Real Poverty Report* (Edmonton 1971).

22 W. Clement, 'Inequality of Access: Characteristics of the Canadian Corporate Elite,' *Canadian Review of Sociology and Anthropology*, XII, 1 (1975), 38-42

23 On the first point, see S. Rose, J. Mambley, and J. Haywood, 'Science, Racism and Ideology,' in A. Blowers and G. Thompson, eds., *Inequalities, Conflict and Change* (Milton Keynes 1976), 89-103. Their conclusion on the relation between IQ and 'genetics' is that 'the two major premises in which the Jensen-Eysenek position is based, one that behavioral differences between groups can be attributed to a genetic component, and the other that I.Q. tests measure a fundamental biological attribute, are not merely fallacies but meaningless. No type of scientific experiment could ever be designed to answer the question "how much does genetics and how much does environment contribute to the differences in intelligence between two racial or class groups?"' (p. 99)

24 Samuel Bowles, 'Understanding Unequal Opportunity,' *American Economic Review, Papers and Proceedings*, LXIII, 2 (May 1973), 346-56. See also Samuel Bowles, and Herbert Gintis, *Schooling in Capitalist America* (New York 1976), chap. 4.

25 Bowles, 'Unequal Opportunity,' 349

26 Ibid., 351

27 T. Veblen, *The Theory of the Leisure Class*, quoted in Richard Hofstadter, *Social Darwinism in American Thought* (Boston 1955), 153-4

28 This is a very brief synopsis of the work-leisure trade-off model in conventional economics. This model is itself simply a variant of the general model of individual choice which, since Jevons, has been the centre-piece of bourgeois economic theory. It appears in virtually every introductory textbook in economic theory (that by Joan Robinson and John Eatwell, *Introduction to Modern Economics* (New York 1974), is an exception). It is the centre of microeconomic theory whether as the theory of individual maximization of utility choice, revealed preference (Samuelson), or characteristics (Lancaster). It is an elegant but scientifically meaningless approach, thoroughly discredited by such critiques as presented by M. Hollis and E. Nell, *Rational Economic Man* (London 1975); Julius Sensat and George Constantine, 'A Critique of the Foundations of Utility Theory,' *Science and Society*, XXXIX, 2 (Summer 1975), 157-79; M. Shukik, 'A Curmudgeon's Guide to Micro Economics,' *Journal of Economic Literature*,' VIII, 2 (June 1970), 405-35; V.C. Walsh, 'Aspects of a Radical Economics,' Department of Economics, Waterloo Economic Series, no. 44, July 1971.

29 See note 28.

30 Revenue Canada, *Taxation Statistics, 1978* (Ottawa 1978), table 3
31 National Council of Welfare, *Jobs and Poverty* (Ottawa 1977) and *The Working Poor: A Statistical Profile* (Ottawa 1977); Health and Welfare Canada, Social Security Research Reports, *Characteristics of Low Wage Earners in Canada, 1971 and 1973*, Report no. 2 (Ottawa 1976); Hugh Armstrong and Pat Armstrong, *The Double Ghetto* (Toronto 1978).
32 Senate of Canada, Special Senate Committee on Poverty, *Poverty in Canada* (Ottawa 1971), 31
33 A useful review of literature can be found in A.B. Atkinson, *Economics of Inequality* (Oxford 1975), 77-86.
34 W. Clement, in *The Canadian Corporate Elite* (Toronto 1975), chap. 5, presents data on the class origins of the economic elite – the directors of the 113 dominant corporations in Canada in 1972, holding the 1,848 interlocked positions on the boards of these corporations.
35 Atkinson, *Economics of Inequality*, 86-8
36 See, for example, R.L. Heilbroner, *The Economic Problem* (Englewood Cliffs, NJ 1970), 488-9. Heilbroner is careful, however, to distinguish the 'Elimination of Exploitation,' from moral equity. Lipsey and Steiner, another popular textbook, is more restrained in keeping with strict adherence to a narrowly conceived positivist methodology: 'We cannot here enter into normative questions of what constitutes a just distribution of income,' *Economics* (New York 1969), 437. Whether claims for justice are made in the 'positive' economics or reserved for the normative, the marginal productivity theory remains the centre-piece of the conventional theory of micro- and macro-distribution.
37 C.E. Ferguson and E. Nell, 'Two Books on the Theory of Income Distribution: A Review Article,' *Journal of Economic Literature*, X, 2 (June 1972), 444
38 This is a view derived from a study by Gary Becker, *The Economics of Discrimination* (Chicago 1971)
39 See, for example, Armstrong and Armstrong, *The Double Ghetto*, chap. 25; Patricia Connolley, 'The Economic Context of Women's Labour Force Participation,' in P. Marchak, ed., *The Working Sexes* (Vancouver 1976), 10-27; Marylee Stephenson, ed., *Women in Canada* (Toronto 1973), especially M. Meisner, 'Sexual Division of Labour and Inequality: Labour and Leisure,' 160-80; and L. McDonald, 'Wages of Sin: A Widening Gap Between Women and Men,' 181-91.
40 See, for example, La Société des Acadiens du Nouveau Brunswick, *Les héritiers de lord Durham: le plan d'action, mai 1977* (Moncton 1977); André Bernard, *What does Quebec Want?* (Toronto 1978), chap. 2; Jac-André Boulet and André Raynauld, *L'analyse des disparités de revenue suivant l'origine ethnique et la langue sur le marché Montréalais en 1961* (Ottawa 1977); Jac-André Boulet, 'The Origin of Linguistic Disparities in Earnings Between

Francophone and Anglophone Male Workers in the Montréal Metropolitan Zone in 1971,' paper presented to Economic Council Conference on Canadian Incomes, Winnipeg, 1979; Henry Milner and Sheilagh Hodgins Milner, *The Decolonization of Quebec* (Toronto 1973), chap. 3.

41 See, for example, Heather Robertson, *Reservations are for Indians* (Toronto 1973); Hugh and Karmel McCallum, *This Land is Not For Sale* (Toronto 1975); Harold Cardinal, *The Unjust Society* (Edmonton 1969). Harold Cardinal, *The Rebirth of Canada's Indians* (Edmonton 1977); James Burke, *Paper Tomahawks* (Winnipeg 1976); P. Deprez and G. Sigurdson, 'The Economic Status of The Canadian Indian: A Re-examination,' University of Manitoba, Centre for Settlement Studies, Winnipeg, 1969; Jane Norris, 'A Socioeconomic, Statistical and Demographic Profile of Native Indian and Non-Indian Canadians: A Study of Inequality and Poverty,' BA thesis, Carleton University, Ottawa, 1976.

42 Albert Rees, *The Economics of Trade Unions* (Chicago 1971), 194

43 Ibid., 195

44 Ibid.

45 Statistics Canada, *Urban Family Expenditure, 1976* (Ottawa 1978, cat. no. 62-547), table 2 (calculations are my own).

Urban family expenditures by family income decile group, 1976 (selected items)

	1st decile	10th decile	10th decile / 1st decile
Food			
Average expenditure	$1,189.30	$ 4,798.50	4.0
Average expenditure per person	825.90	1,181.90	1.4
Shelter			
Average expenditure	1,354.60	4,592.60	3.4
Average expenditure per person	940.70	1,131.18	1.2
Clothing			
Average expenditure	246.10	2,861.40	11.6
Average expenditure per person	170.90	704.80	4.1
Travel and transportation			
Average expenditure	253.70	4,737.50	18.7
Average expenditure per person	176.20	1,166.90	6.6
Average size of family	1.44	4.60	
Average income before tax	$3,764.00	$43,113.50	11.5
Average income before tax – per person	2,613.90	10,624.00	4.1
Net change in assets	−122.30	5,031.80	41.1
Net change in assets per person	$ 84.90	$ 1,239.40	−14.6

46 See, for example, The National Council of Welfare, *Prices and the Poor* (Ottawa 1974).

47 There is a growing body of literature on housing and the poor. See, for example, I. Silver, *Housing and the Poor* (Ottawa 1971).

48 The piece of bourgeois theory reviewed here is also referred to as the doctrine of consumer sovereignty. It has been the subject of considerable criticism and debate over many years. See, for example, P. Baran, *The Political Economy of Growth* (New York 1957), xi-xviii; H. Gintis, 'Consumer Behavior and the Concept of Sovereignty: Explanations of Social Decay,' *American Economic Review, Papers and Proceedings*, LXII, 2 (May 1972), 267-78; David Mermelstein, ed., *Economics: Mainstream Readings and Radical Critiques* (New York 1970), 'American Capitalism at the Crossroads,' 493-552, and articles by Robert Solow, J.K. Galbraith, Robin Morris, Ralph Miliband, E.J. Mishan, Paul Baran.

49 Gintis, 'Consumer Behavior and the Concept of Sovereignty.'

50 André Gorz, 'The Tyranny of the Factory: Today and Tomorrow,' in André Gorz, ed., *The Division of Labour* (Brighton 1978), 55

51 Karl Marx, *Capital* (London 1970), I, 364

52 Steven Marglin, 'What Do Bosses Do?' in Gorz, *Division of Labour*, 13-54

53 Marx, *Capital*, 355

54 Harry Braverman, *Labour and Monopoly Capital* (New York 1974), 90

55 Cited in ibid., 115-16

56 Ibid., 116

57 Ibid.

58 Marx, *Capital*, 360

59 The discussion here has been heavily influenced by Braverman's *Labour and Monopoly Capital*, especially chap. 4.

60 See Katherine Stone, 'The Origins of Job Structures in the Steel Industry,' *The Review of Radical Political Economics*, VI, 2 (Summer 1974), 127-41.

61 Ibid., 134

62 For a discussion of diffusion, see Clement, *Canadian Corporate Elite*, 18-33; Jorge Niosi, *The Economy of Canada: Who Controls It?* (Montreal 1978), especially chap. 2.

63 Statistics Canada, *Incomes, Assets and Indebtedness, 1970* (Ottawa 1973, cat. no. 13-547), and *Distribution of Income and Wealth in Canada, 1977* (Ottawa 1980, cat. no. 13-570). The data on 'stocks' in the 1970 and 1977 surveys include publicly traded shares, with holdings of mutual fund shares, rights and warrants, and holdings of shares in private investment clubs. No distinction in the data is possible between holdings of voting and non-voting shares. The data do not include holdings of shares in private corporations which are non-

trading. Aggregation of holdings of voting and non-voting shares together suggests that the data may understate the extent of concentration of ownership of voting shares. It is not clear what effect on the data is produced by excluding ownership of shares in private corporations. Ownership of voting shares does not necessarily imply exercise of voting rights in Canada. Surveys were conducted in 1970 and 1977. Each survey asked respondents to provide answers to questions on the basis of their position in the previous year, i.e., 1969 or 1976. I have adopted the practice of referring to data by the year of the survey.

64 Data from Statistics Canada, *Incomes, Assets and Indebtedness*, tables 32 and 33

65 J.R. Podoluk, 'The Size Distribution of Personal Wealth in Canada,' *Review of Income and Wealth*, Series 20, no. 2 (June 1974), 214

66 Statistics Canada, *Incomes, Assets and Indebtedness*, table 8

67 Statistics Canada, *Distribution of Income and Wealth in Canada*, tables 13, 14, and 15

68 Ibid., tables 11, 12, and 16

69 See Gail Oja, 'Inequality of Wealth Distribution in Canada, 1970 and 1977,' in Economic Council of Canada, *Reflections on Canadian Incomes* (Ottawa 1980), 342, 362.

70 Niosi, *The Economy of Canada*, 79

71 Clement, *Canadian Corporate Elite*, 125

72 Ibid., 150-5

73 Ibid., 160

74 Ibid., 159-69

75 Ibid., 172

76 Ibid., 190

77 Ibid., 191

78 Marx, *Capital*. In his section on 'The So-Called Primative Accumulation,' chaps. 26-33, Marx examines the progressive divorce of the peasant from the land, the state assistance given to owners to prevent peasants from remaining on the land, and the colonization schemes which removed excess population from England to the colonies.

79 G. Myers, *The History of Canadian Wealth* (Toronto 1971)

80 Marx, *Capital*, chaps. 7-11

4
The formation of dominion capitalism: economic truncation and class structure

PHILIP EHRENSAFT, WARWICK ARMSTRONG

The term 'inequality' which appears in the title of this book is, sociologically, a polite way of saying 'class.' Class is an ideologically charged word and justly so, for it points to the central organizing force of the kind of society in which we live. Over time, a small fraction of the population has acquired control over the means of production and exercise of force. In order to subsist, the majority of people must offer their most precious possession as a commodity in the market-place: labour time, which becomes the temporary property of the ruling minority.

There are many gradations of control over the means of production and various intermediate classes, but the central organizing relationship is the one just expressed. Class, as a central force in industrial capitalist societies, does not eliminate or subsume other forms of inequality. But these other dimensions of inequality in capitalist societies are bounded and deeply conditioned by the dominating fact of social class. Consequently, our discussion of inequality within the specific form of capitalist organization commonly prevailing in dominion capitalist countries, which include Canada, Australia, New Zealand, Argentina, and Uruguay, focuses upon class control of the means of production and thus of social domination over the process and products of human labour.

The dominion capitalist countries exhibit a specific configuration of economic structures which identify the five national societies as constituting a distinctive category within the world economy. Given the formal historic status of Canada, Australia, and New Zealand as self-governing white dominions within the British Empire, plus the informal economic integration of Argentina and Uruguay as 'honorary dominions' within Great Britain's imperial system up until the Great Depression, we label this specific category as 'dominion capitalism.' Prior to the 1930s, there existed a widespread perception of the fundamentally similar nature of these five prosperous, temperate region colonies or neo-colonies of European settlement. In speaking of dominion capitalism, we are resuscitating and systematizing an older, instinctive, and comparative perspective within the framework of more recent notions of political economy.

The features which define dominion capitalism are the following:

1 Each society was established by colonizing temperate or semitemperate regions which were sparsely populated by indigenous populations when European overseas expansion commenced during the late fifteenth century.
2 Given this geographic and social context, the ruling groups of the colonizing nations found it most advantageous to exploit the regions via a labour force composed of large masses of European emigrants. The sparse indigenous population was eliminated, assimilated, or pushed into distant corners of the hinterland.
3 Most social labour is appropriated by the sale of labour power. Through its class struggles the proletariat attains real salary levels which, by 1930, approximate or exceed those of western Europe. As corollaries to this third characteristic, two other features follow.
4 The population exhibits levels of urbanization, birth rates, and life expectancies comparable to those of modern western Europe.
5 The proportions of gross domestic product (GDP) generated by the primary, secondary, and tertiary sectors also approximate those of modern western Europe.
6 In common with the regions of the world economy generally known as the 'periphery,' most exports from the dominions consist of primary products. In contrast with most of the periphery, however, the entire range of the dominions' exports are produced by technologies and wage levels typical of advanced industrial capitalism.
7 The sixth characteristic is complemented by an industrialization based principally upon the first processing stages of primary production or upon import substitution. The industrial base is sheltered behind tariffs or other forms of protection and is largely confined within national boundaries, i.e., few companies attain world thresholds of cost efficiency and quality which permit sales abroad in a fiercely competitive international market. Unlike the periphery, the high wage levels of the dominions preclude development of labor-intensive manufactured exports.
8 An exceptional minority of companies within some dominions are able to innovate technologically and organizationally such that their products or services penetrate the markets of advanced industrial economies or effectively

compete with the latter in other regions of the world economies. Some dominion capitalist companies establish themselves as bona fide multinational corporations.

9 Nevertheless, branches of multinational corporations whose home base is in the North Atlantic region or Japan occupy a strong or commanding position in manufacturing and mineral production within the dominion.

10 In the half-century after the First World War each society passes from British domination to a primary economic and political domination by the United States, accompanied by secondary domination via the trade and investment interests of the Common Market countries and Japan.

Each of these defining elements of dominion capitalism will receive fuller treatment in the following section. For the moment, let us situate this form of capitalism within a more general historical and theoretical context. First, we see the key formative period for each of the five societies as proceeding during what may be termed the age of classical monopoly capitalism. This age begins from the 1860s onward, when a second wave of industrial revolutions in western Europe, the United States, and Japan increasingly manifested themselves and challenged Great Britain's hegemony over the world economy. It terminates during the First World War – the imperialist war which shattered Europe's century of (relative) peace and heralded the Great Depression. Among the key developments of this period which are most relevant to the study of dominion capitalism, the new world transportation network created by railways, steel-hulled steamships, and refrigeration is of prime importance. This new network, with its drastic lowering of the costs and risks of long-distance trade, rendered the hinterlands of Africa, Asia, and the Americas economically available for large-scale production of low-value-per-weight staples for the western European, American, and Japanese markets.

The temperate regions of the outlying continents helped avoid a Malthusian crisis in western Europe and Japan by supplying grain, meat, cheese, butter, and forest products on a scale not realizable in an age of canals and sailing ships. Minerals entered the list of exports somewhat later. The configurations of cheap transoceanic transport, temperate climate, and sparse indigenous population encouraged ruling groups to resort to European immigration as a source of labour. Conversely, it also enabled European ruling groups to use emigration as one means of solving the Malthusian problem. Production of temperate region commodities further encouraged methods of appropriating labour fundamentally similar to those prevailing in Europe. By the conclusion of the age of classical monopoly capitalism, the favourable resource endowment of the dominion capitalist societies permitted a degree of industrialization through export processing and import substitution such that their social structures were as proletarianized and urbanized as those of western Europe.[1]

Aggregate measures of class, such as relative distribution of wealth and revenue, or rates of social mobility within the dominion capitalist societies, could thus be expected to fall within the same general range as those prevailing in the dominant capitalist economies. This is not to say that the class structures of and the range of inequality in the five dominions are identical to those of western Europe and the United States. There are important differences, both between the five dominions and the dominant capitalist societies, and among the dominions themselves. When one compares the class structures of the dominion capitalist societies to other regions of the so-called periphery, however, their fundamental character as an extension of European social space stands out quite clearly. At the same time, the class structures of the dominion capitalist societies form the basis of a macro-economic structure with relatively shallow backward and forward linkages from the primary production sector.

Given the advanced technology and capital-intensive nature of agricultural, forest, and mineral production in the dominions, capital-labour ratios are in the same range as those of the dominant capitalist societies.[2] But such an aggregate measure masks the structural difference between dominion capitalist economies and those of advanced industrial capitalism. In effect, there is a preponderant element of rent on natural resources, which supports the industrialization and prosperity of dominion capitalism. The economy as a whole is thus subject to the same long-term risks as any rented resource: non-renewable resources may be exhausted; renewable resources may be converted into non-renewable ones through capitalist overexploitation (e.g., the serious decline in the organic content of prairie soils since 1900); competition from newer, lower cost regions; new technologies which provide substitute materials (e.g. innovations which permitted the use of southern pinewood and now Brazilian tropical woods in pulp and paper); or political decisions to seek alternative sources of supply (e.g., the Common Market's restrictions on New Zealand's dairy exports). Dominion capitalist societies are thus both structurally shallow and subject to high risks over the long run; in this sense we may speak of a truncated economic base. Accordingly, the dominions have often been referred to, via one expression or the other, as constituting the 'richest underdeveloped countries.'

'Richest,' as a qualifying adjective, emphasizes a secondary or surface measure of the nature of dominion capitalist societies. What must be brought to the forefront is the conjunction of a full or non-truncated class structure (i.e., class formations similar to those of the dominant capitalist societies) with a truncated economic base. The primary source of this truncation does not, in our view, lie in a reliance upon staple exports as such. The history of industrialization in western Europe and the United States provides ample examples of the manner in which primary product exports may play a powerful role in sparking a full process of industrialization. (Indeed, a certain technocratic version of staples theory – lacking the richness of Harold Innis' thinking – is one of the dominant approaches employed by orthodox U.S. economic historians.[3]) Neither the general context of the world economy – in Gunnar Myrdal's sense that the later a country attempts to industrialize, the more difficult it becomes to break into a competitive world market dominated by more advanced industrial economies – nor such elements as a presumed lack of internal capital – which forces a resort to borrowings from international finance capital, associated with strings that lock the borrower into a 'staples trap' – or distance from markets and tariff barriers blocked the dominions from following the smaller western European powers into a process of relatively full industrialization. This failure is to be found in the economic strategies, explicit and implicit, which the ruling groups in the dominions forced upon their societies. Such strategies and calculations of self-interest emerged within the context of the rulers' struggle for power against other social classes. Thus it becomes crucial to specify the nuanced differences between the class structures and struggles of dominion capitalist societies, as opposed to those of the dominant capitalist systems. Although such differences may appear relatively minor with respect to those prevailing between other dominated economies such as Brazil or India vis-à-vis advanced industrial capitalism, these nuances appear to us to be the most important element blocking a deeper industrialization process in the dominions.

THE SPECIFICITY OF DOMINION CAPITALISM

The ruling groups within each of the five dominion capitalist societies during the age of classical monopoly capitalism envisioned that the pursuit of their own defined and socially imposed self-interest would propel their economies into the ranks of the leading industrial powers. They presented the dominions as new societies offering magnificent opportunities for European investment and emigration, as five new U.S. frontiers. The age of monopoly capitalism was an era of optimism for the ruling elements of the dominions, particularly after the general upturn in the world economy from the mid-

1890s onwards. A rhetoric of optimism was created which amounted to more than vapid words trotted out for national holidays. Canadians spoke nobly of 'Canada's century.' The Australians saw themselves as inhabiting the 'lucky country.' If Uruguayans perceived themselves as the New Switzerland, the British colonizers of New Zealand judged their territory as 'God's Own Country' (but not that of the Maoris, whom they displaced by military conquest). But the Argentinians won this rhetorical competition by declaring that 'Dios es argentino.' This general optimism with respect to the economic future of the dominion capitalist societies, when toned down to the demands of worldly life, was shared by advanced industrial capital.

Before the Great Depression, there was a widespread perception in western Europe of the comparable social and economic organization of Canada, Australia, New Zealand, Argentina, and Uruguay, and of the excellent opportunities this provided for European commerce and settlement. This perception was shared by businessmen, economists, politicians, and government officials, not to speak of the masses who crossed the ocean in third-class holds to the five dominion capitalist societies. Colin Clark, in the first edition (1940) of his *Conditions of Economic Progress*, classified the five societies as 'rich debtor nations' which had already surpassed most of Western Europe in terms of national product per capita. Clark's classification, and the rosy industrial future he envisaged for the dominions, reflected a general international consensus of the times.

Within the dominion capitalist societies themselves there existed a perception of the comparable character of the socio-economic organization of the five nations, but also of a certain hierarchical order among them. Canada was viewed as the 'senior' dominion. In mainstream Australian economic literature one still finds frequent comparisons between the experience of development 'down under' and in Canada. In Canada comparisons with the other dominion capitalist societies are less frequent among orthodox economists: comparisons are rather drawn 'upwards' towards the dominant capitalist economies. By contrast, the work of Innis and other Canadians operating from the staples perspective is of inherent relevance to an understanding of dominion capitalism. To cite one example, the staples theory provoked a major debate during the 1950s and 1960s over the interpretation of Australian economic history.[4] Systematic comparison of the five dominions, however, is not present in the staples literature.

In Argentina the consciousness of the analogous character of the five economies has been much more explicit. Comparisons between Argentina and the two more senior dominions, Canada and Australia, are frequent both in academic and public discourse. For example, during commercial negotiations in London during 1932-33, Julio A. Roca, the vice-president of Argentina, requested that Great Britain formally incorporate his country as a dominion within the Empire. He argued that Argentina had the same social base and degree of economic integration into the British imperial economy as Canada, Australia, and New Zealand and should thus have equivalent political rights to imperial commercial preferences.[5] Finally, with approximately the same total population as New Zealand and a similar geoclimatic setting, plus an economy based upon pastoral exports, Uruguayans compared themselves to New Zealanders practically as an automatic reflex. We should also add that Argentinians and Uruguayans traditionally considered their societies as quite distinct from those of the rest of Latin America, with its generalized poverty and social heritage of Indian, mestizo, and slave plantation structures.

Since the Second World War there has been a sharp decline in the general perception of the similar socio-economic organization of Canada, Australia, New Zealand, Argentina, and Uruguay. Profound crises shook the Argentinian and Uruguayan economies from the late 1940s onwards. In the eyes of international businessmen and economists there was a declassification or 'Latin Americanization' of these two economies. First of all, national product per capita grew quite slowly relative to the post-war rates achieved by the advanced capitalist nations and the senior dominions. (In Uruguay, GNP per capita actually declined during the 1950-60 period.) Secondly relatively rapid growth in Mexico and petroleum exports in Venezuela resulted in per capita national products in the same range as those of the two Latin American dominions. Furthermore, even if one acknowledges the crushing poverty of its masses, Brazil has created an industrial base which is larger in absolute terms and more technologically profound than that of Argentina. Thus it is not surprising that the notion of Argentina's and Uruguay's distinctiveness from the rest of Latin America suffered a decline.

This declassification is based on orthodox measures such as the rate of growth of GNP per capita. While Argentina and Uruguay did not maintain the same growth rates as the dominant economies or more dynamic regions of the 'periphery,' their urban proletarian class structures persisted. The tendency to develop a large lumpenproletariat was checked by the possibilities of re-immigration during times of crisis in each of the dominions, as we shall see below. In spite of the intense crisis experienced by Argentina and Uruguay, the defining structures of dominion capitalism have persisted. In a similar sense we could speak of the declassification of Great Britain as a dominant economy. In neither instance have major economic difficulties implied a fundamental reordering of class structures. The analysis of a given economy as dominant or dominion capitalist respectively, depends precisely upon consideration of class structure rather than orthodox measures such as GNP.

In Argentina and Uruguay economists sought the reasons for the incapacity of their societies to follow the same post-war expansion as experienced by Canada, Australia, and New Zealand. In the light of more recent experience a quite different question might be posed: why have profound structural crises been delayed in the three formal dominions? In our eyes the crises currently traversing Canada, Australia, and New Zealand represent more profound instabilities than those conjuncturally generated by world stagflation. These instabilities are tied to the inherent weaknesses and limitations of dominion capitalism itself. As an economic structure, dominion capitalism was well adapted to the world economy during the age of classical monopoly capitalism. In the pages which follow, we argue that the fundamental structures of dominion capitalism are ill adapted to the pressures created by multinational capital's reorganization of the world economy subsequent to 1945. This is not to say that Canada, Australia, and New Zealand will automatically and necessarily follow the declassification experiences of Argentina and Uruguay. In fact, one cannot maintain with utter assurance that the stagnation of the latter two economies will persist over the long run. The structural weaknesses and instabilities inherent in dominion capitalism exercise profound and persistent pressures towards declassification. Whether these societies succumb to such pressures or not depends upon a series of contingent factors. Continuing discoveries in the mineral rich shield formations of Canada and Australia, for example, may delay the day of reckoning. Most importantly, class struggles, strategies, and alliances may reorganize the foundations of any economy in the face of profound structural crises. Let us now proceed to the task of evaluating whether the class systems of dominion capitalism are capable of, and likely to generate, such a creative reorganization. The first step will be a perception of dominion capitalism as one specific form of what may be termed 'semi-industrial capitalism.'

Industrialization through import substitution and the first stages of export processing have proceeded via diverse routes in those regions of the world economy known as the periphery. These diverse routes are distinguished by different systems of appropriating labour in each society; i.e., by class structure. We see these different class structures as located along a spectrum, with dominion capitalism at one pole and a structure which may be labelled 'classic semi-industrial capitalism' at the other. By way of contrast, we can better seize the specificities of dominion capitalism by briefly comparing them with those of classic semi-industrial capitalism. The following set of elements distinguished classic semi-industrial capitalism:

1 A large part of the labour force is engaged in agriculture and exhibits much underemployment.
2 The proportion of the labour force engaged in industrial factory production remains small relative to the proportion so employed in the centre.
3 A large proportion of the labour force has lumpenproletariat status.
4 Real wages of the industrial working class are far lower than those prevailing in the centre but yield a per capita income markedly higher than those of the rural underemployed and the lumpenproletariat.
5 Relative distribution of income is more unequal than in the centre: income is skewed towards a small middle class and an upper class, which attempt to achieve class levels of consumption prevailing in the centre.
6 A larger fraction of the middle class is employed by the state or performs various services in the private sector, as opposed to being engaged in direct production, than is the case in the centre.
7 Rates of population growth are higher than in the centre.
8 The state, in order to maintain this highly inegalitarian social structure, relies more upon threatened or actual violence than is the case in the centre, where the state relies more upon economic incentives and ideological persuasion to maintain its hegemony.

One consequence of the characteristics just enumerated is that the purchasing power of the masses is quite low, and thus the internal market for industrial products is sharply limited. Consumption of durable goods, which tend to exhibit more backward linkages generating capital goods production than is the case for non-durables such as textiles or food, is largely limited to the small middle and upper classes. Given a rate of population growth lower than that of the masses, and given the slow opening up of middle-class positions in the economy, the expansion of the middle classes as a proportion of the population proceeds slowly, if at all. The resultant sharply limited domestic market, especially for consumer durables such as refrigerators or cars, plus the limits on manufactured exports which prevail in semi-industrial capitalist economies, may result in a levelling-off or eventual stagnation in the industrialization process.

On the other hand, the class structures of classic semi-industrial capitalism may permit a deeper industrial expansion during the coming decades than is likely to be the case for dominion capitalism. First of all, low wages permit the export of light industrial goods such as textiles or shoes. Such exports are fragile, however, over the long term. Both the dominant and dominated economies frequently erect protectionist barriers against light industrial imports; dominant societies protect older industries and jobs while the dominated societies often choose light industry as the easiest first step towards industrialization through import substitution. Furthermore, such export activity is highly mobile; no matter how much existing sweat-shop systems squeeze their workers, there always seems to be a yet more oppressive society over the horizon which can move into world markets. In fact, Quebec's footwear exports during the period of classic monopoly capitalism offer one of the first examples of the importation of a mature light industrial technique into a dominated, low wage region and the eventual decline of its exports in favour of yet lower wage regions. More important than such exports as textiles is the new wave of technologically sophisticated exports which is beginning to flow from countries like India or Brazil. The absolute size of India's middle-class market considerably exceeds that of any of the dominions. Combined with a network of universities and research centres, this permits a growing capacity to master advanced industrial techniques. Fractions of the working class have acquired skills comparable to those of their class equivalents in the dominant countries, while wages remain considerably lower and the political regime more brutally repressive of labour organization. All of the above factors favour the implantation of heavy industries requiring a large input of skilled, disciplined labour, such as the manufacture of machine tools or locomotives. In such fields India is increasingly able to offer exports at world standards of quality but at a relatively low cost.[6] The class structure of dominion capitalism, with its historically high wage rates, precludes this kind of industrial expansion. As absorbers rather than generators of new production techniques, the dominions are ill equipped to place their high wage manufactures on the world market.

In order to begin to understand why dominion capitalism functions as an absorber of innovations in spite of its 'advanced' class structure, we must delve more closely into the set of its defining characteristics previously presented. Let us treat the first two characteristics together: the national society was established by colonizing temperate or semitemperate regions which were sparsely inhabited by indigenous populations when European overseas expansion commenced during the late fifteenth century; the region received large waves of European emigrants; the sparse indigenous population was either eliminated, assimilated, or pushed into distant corners of the hinterland; the large majority of its present-day population is of European descent. To begin with, we must emphasize the distinction between sparsely inhabited temperate regions and sparsely inhabited tropical regions. The latter involved the creation of plantation economies based on transplanted African slave labour (e.g., northeastern Brazil, the Caribbean) and later on, in some instances, indentured labour from India (Trinidad, Guyana). Plantation-based social structures differed quite evidently from those established in the dominion capitalist societies. Furthermore, even though the coffee-growing regions of Brazil received large waves of Italian and Spanish emigrants as did Argentina and Uruguay during the nineteenth and early twentieth centuries, they were integrated into a social system which bore the heavy imprints of a slave-based economy and was thus quite different from the systems of its southern neighbours.[7]

Another word to be emphasized in the above characteristics is the existence of a sparse indigenous population. For example, where Europeans colonized the densely inhabited semitemperate region which became South Africa, the resultant social hierarchy was, to say the least, notably distinctive from those which are the target of our analysis. Though officially a dominion within the pre–Second World War British Empire, South Africa thus falls outside our definition of dominion capitalism. Mexico, Guatemala, Peru, and Algeria are other salient examples of the distinctive social structures created by European colonization in regions of dense indigenous populations.

The *third* characteristic of our definition concerns the appropriation of labour whereby proletarian social relations represent the central force of overall social organization. Outside of Latin America it is not usually recognized that Argentina and Uruguay are proletarianized societies, as are the official dominions, and that this has been the case for several decades. In table 1 we present some selected League of Nations statistics concerning the relative proportions of the economically active population employed in different sectors during the last decades of classic monopoly capitalism. Four of the dominion capitalist societies (figures were not available for Uruguay) are compared with five western European nations plus the United States. The figures speak for themselves, particularly when they are put alongside those in table 2, which concerns levels of productivity per person employed in agriculture. Together, the two tables give us the first indices of the dominions' urban-proletarian social structures joined to agricultural sectors whose labour productivity was quite ahead of most of the 'centre.'

Before proceeding further, let us point out that our discussion in this section frequently cites macro-economic and demographic data in order to get at the more abstract relations of capital to labour. These statistics do not present the 'economy' conceived as the 'base' for social class. 'Economy' itself is a

Table 1
Percentages of economically active population by sector

	Year	Agriculture, fishing, forestry	Mining	Industry
Western Europe, United States of America				
Great Britain	1911	7.7	6.9	38.7
	1921	6.8	7.5	39.7
Germany	1908	35.2	4.3	35.8
	1925	30.5	3.2	38.1
France	1911	41.0	1.2	31.9
	1921	41.5	1.5	28.4
Italy	1911	55.4	0.7	25.9
	1921	56.1	0.6	24.0
Spain	1910	56.3	(13.8)	
USA	1910		2.5	27.9
	1920	26.3	2.6	30.8
Dominions				
Canada	1911	37.1	2.3	27.1
	1921	35.0	1.6	26.9
Australia	1911	24.2	5.3	28.4
	1921	22.9	2.9	31.2
New Zealand	1911	26.1	3.3	30.1
	1921	27.1	1.6	27.5
Argentina	1914	16.8	–	26.6

Source: League of Nations, *Statistical Yearbook, 1926*, 42-4

complex of class relations which generates a flow of commodities. Official statistics, defined and collected according to the narrow and ideologically skewed perspective of orthodox economics, usually measure the surface relationships of things – commodities – rather than the social actions which generate these commodities. Nevertheless, we are forced to use official statistics as best we can in order to grasp the class relations which constitute the economy. Each figure presented above is chosen to present an aspect of class and power.

As a corollary to the third characteristic, we added that the urban-proletarian class structure of the dominions was capable of generating national products per capita which were equivalent or superior to those prevailing in industrialized Europe towards the conclusion of the era of classic monopoly capitalism.

Table 2
Productivity per person employed in agriculture, 1925-34 (international units)

	Persons employed in agriculture per 1,000 hectares of arable land and pasture	Productivity per person employed
Australia	7	1,524
Argentina	7	1,233
New Zealand	20	2,444
Uruguay	23	1,000
USA	25	661
Canada	35	618
Great Britain	70	475
France	134	415
Denmark	146	642
Germany	162	490
Switzerland	166	433
Holland	235	579
Belgium	388	394

Source: Colin Clark, *Conditions of Economic Progress* (London 1940), 246

In table 3 we present some relevant figures which are drawn from Colin Clark's pioneering work on comparative national accounting, *The Conditions of Economic Progress*. These figures on income per capita, which support our corollary, are reinforced by other measures presented by Clark, such as international comparisons of the quantity of different foods consumed per capita.[8] It is to be emphasized, however, that *structural* relations – here the appropriation of labour by capital – are fundamental to the definition of dominion capitalism, rather than income or welfare measures. One measure of this structural relation is the ratio of capital to labour in various economic sectors: Clark's comparative figures for this ratio as of 1913 are presented in table 4. Again, one observes Argentina's equivalent ranking with the formal dominions in terms of the labour-capital ratio, which is one of the key indicators of the development of class forces in a capitalist society.

Another perspective on the capital-labour relation is given in figure 1, where the aggregate level of capital per economically active person is plotted against real hourly wages. The positive correlation which one observes between these two variables is not merely a numerical measure of the technological structure of greater or lesser degrees of development but repre-

Table 3
Revenue per capita, 1925-34 (international units*)

Revenue	Country
1,300–1,400	USA
1,300–1,400	Canada
1,200–1,300	New Zealand
1,000–1,100	Great Britain
1,000–1,100	Switzerland
1,000–1,100	Argentina
900–1,000	Australia
800–900	Holland
700–800	Ireland
600–700	Uruguay
600–700	France
600–700	Denmark
600–700	Sweden
600–700	Germany
600–700	Belgium

* Quantity of goods and services purchasable for
$1.00 USA
Source: Colin Clark, *Conditions of Economic
Progress* (London 1940), 54

Table 4
Capital per person employed, 1913 (international units*)

Total quantity of capital	Country	Sector			
		Agriculture	Railways	Construction	Industry/ commerce
1,000–2,000	Italy Spain	100–300	200–300	200–600	300–800
Approximately 3,000	Great Britain Germany France Sweden	300–400	200–500	900–1,300	1,600
4,000–5,000	USA Canada Australia Argentina	300–500	400–700	1,400–2,400	1,600–2,000

* Quantity of goods and services purchasable for $1.00 USA
Source: Colin Clark, *Conditions of Economic Progress* (London 1940), 417

Figure 1
Capital-labour ratios and real salaries (in international units,
expressed as quantity of goods and services purchasable for
$1.00 USA).
Source: Colin Clark, *The Conditions of Economic Progress* (2nd ed.,
London 1951), 501

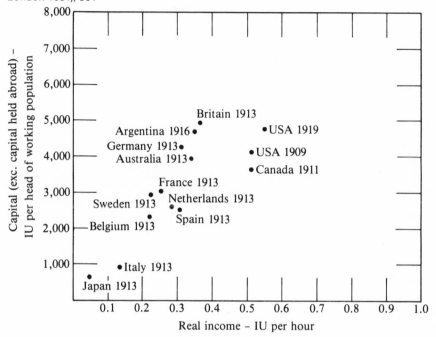

sents one index of the historical struggle between the bourgeoisie and the
proletariat, the latter attempting to increase the socially defined level of subsistence as growth proceeds, and the former moving to substitute capital for
labour precisely because such attempts constitute one of the main motors of
capital accumulation. While the overall accumulation of capital in Argentina,
Australia, and Canada ranks high relative to various industrial capitalist societies of the 'centre,' however, aggregate measures mask the structural weaknesses of capitalism in the dominions. If one breaks down total capital by
such categories as relative distribution between different branches of production, patterns of backward and forward linkages in each branch, average
size of units of production, and patterns of ownership and oligopolization,
then the dominions' high level of capital accumulation – itself an index of

advanced class forces – is less impressive than at first glance, as we shall see below.

In the meantime let us underline the importance of Argentina and Uruguay towards understanding the general category of dominion capitalism. In a report published in 1969, the Economic Commission for Latin America emphasizes that Argentina's two decades of crises must not be viewed as typical of an underdeveloped country, but within the context of a society which was one of the most relatively prosperous units within the world economy during the first half of the twentieth century and had then failed to follow the pace of growth maintained by western Europe during the second half of the century.[9] The experience of this 'honorary Dominion' – with its urban-proletarian, white immigrant, high productivity economy – inclines us towards a rather somber analysis of the long-term prospects for Australia, Canada, and New Zealand unless major changes in policies and practices are introduced.

The *fourth* characteristic of dominion capitalism follows from the structural relation between capital and labour which was just indicated: the population exhibits demographic characteristics, such as urbanization, birth rates and life expectancies, comparable to those of modern western Europe. These demographic characteristics are part and parcel of the process of class formation. At the beginning of this decade 76 per cent of Canada's population resided in settlements of 1,000 persons or more, compared with 86 per cent for Australia, 80 per cent for New Zealand, 81 per cent for Argentina, and approximately 75 per cent for Uruguay.[10] Birth rates, death rates, life expectancies, and rates of natural increase of population for Argentina and Uruguay are similarly within the ranges prevailing within metropolitan countries and the formal dominions.[11]

The *fifth* element of dominion capitalism also follows from the urban-proletarian class structure: the proportions of national product generated in what are usually termed the primary, secondary, and tertiary sectors respectively are within the same range as is the case in the dominant industrial economies. Looking at table 5, we observe the overall correspondence between the two sets of economies. Two exceptions stand out. First, the proportional industrial contribution to national product in Uruguay is a fraction lower than the range of figures exhibited by the other economies. This reflects an industrialization process which built up steam later than that of the other dominions (i.e., during the 1930s) and was thus cut off at an earlier stage of development when the post-1954 crisis arrived. Second, the contribution of agriculture is relatively higher for Argentina and Uruguay than for the other economies listed in the table. In part this may reflect the lack of significant mineral discoveries to supplement agricultural staple exports.

Table 5
Relative weight of different sectors in gross national product, 1971 (percentages)

	Agriculture	Industry*	Construction	Commerce	Transport and communi- cations	Other†
Dominant economies						
USA	3	29	5	18	6	38
Germany	3	45	8	14	6	25
Great Britain	2	31	6	9	7	30
France	6	36	10	16	5	27
Dominions						
Canada	4	26	6	10	8	33
Australia	6	28	8	13	7	27
Argentina	13	37	5	15	9	22
Uruguay	11	21	4	14	8	30

* Manufacturing; mines and quarries; electricity; gas and water
† Finance, insurance, business services, and real-estate sales; social and community services; public administration and defence
Source: United Nations, *Yearbook of National Accounts, 1975*, III, 78-115

New Zealand, with one of the most technologically sophisticated agricultural systems in the world, exhibits a figure for this sector's contribution to national products which is similar to that of the two Latin American dominions.[12]

The higher figures for agriculture are partly due to another factor. Before the Second World War, agricultural productivity depended largely upon favourable geoclimactic endowments, efficient labour organization, and a certain level of mechanization. Subsequent to the war a petrochemical agricultural revolution swept through the industrialized economies. The economic crises in Argentina and Uruguay retarded the application of the new technology, and thus their relative rank in world agricultural productivity suffered a major decline. This rank, however, is still far closer to that of the countries of the 'centre,' than to those of the 'periphery.' Even after two decades of intense crises we are still dealing with a structure of dominion capitalism. Furthermore, recent efforts to apply agribusiness techniques in these two countries may raise their rankings once again.

Now let us look at the industrial sector alone – but for two different periods – in order to provide a provisional idea of the trends in the relative weights of industrial activities (see table 6). This is important because of a

Table 6
Proportion of gross national product generated by
the industrial sector* (percentages)

	1960	1973
Dominant economies		
USA	33	29
Great Britain	37	30
France	40	36
Germany	47	44
Dominions		
Canada	29	26
Australia	30	27
Argentina	35	38 (1972)
Uruguay	21	22

* Manufacturing, mines and quarries, electricity, gas
and water
Source: United Nations, *Yearbook of National Accounts,
1975*, III, 78-115

tendency in popular nationalist discussions within the dominions to see the
relative decline of industry as a proportion of national product as an indicator
of de-industrialization. In fact, this relative decline is also evident among the
dominant industrial economies.[13] In part, this is the result of the increased
capitalization of direct production; in part, too, it is the result of capitalist
accounting systems which count any monetary payment for services as part
of national product. The proliferation of tertiary sector activities, itself permitted by what Marx would term the increasing organic composition of capital, thus receives increasing weight in national accounts. Far from measuring
an industrial decline, the decrease of industrial activity as a percentage of
national product in the dominions indicates a social capacity to absorb
(though not necessarily to generate) advanced technologies. Furthermore,
the dominions share a certain type of actual de-industrialization with the
dominant industrial economies; here it is a question of the decline of light
industries, such as textiles, shoes, or the assembly of electronic and photo-
graphic equipment, in the face of imports from low-cost labour regions. The
question is whether the economy has the capacity to adapt and generate
other compensating activities, which the dominions are less able to do than
the dominant economies for reasons to be treated below.

There is, it must be recognized, one kind of real de-industrialization in the
dominions due to the policies of multinationals. In Canada the major decline

Table 7
Manufacturing as a percentage of
total industrial activity, 1971

USA	86
Great Britain	87
France (1969)	95
Germany	91
Canada	77
Australia	78

Source: Calculated from data in United
Nations, *Yearbook of National Accounts,
1975*, III, 78-115

of automobile parts manufacturing or the software branch of the computer industry due to formal or informal integration into continental corporate strategies is the first example which comes to mind. Furthermore, if one disaggregates the industrial sector into manufacturing, as opposed to mining, quarrying, electricity, gas, and water sectors, one observes a relatively greater weight for the second category as a percentage of total industry, as is seen in table 7, when comparing Australia and Canada to the dominant industrial countries. This is basically an indication of the importance of mining. If we were to disaggregate the manufacturing sector per se, we would see first stages of processing of staple exports stand out as a major fraction of manufacturing.

Much of the capital equipment for mining and manufacturing comes from abroad. If all of this is added to what is already a somewhat lower weight of industry as a whole within the national product of the dominions, as compared to the dominant economies, we feel it is quite justified to speak of a truncated industrial revolution. The problem is not de-industrialization but a whole range of backward and forward linkages which never arose. Given the resources of the five dominions and world market conditions during the times of their industrial revolutions, it seems to us that a deeper industrialization process was quite possible. If this did not occur, it was not the result of reliance upon staple exports as such but rather upon the power of the dominant classes to impose decisions on the use of the surplus generated from these exports which truncated the possibility of a deeper industrialization.

The *sixth* and *seventh* characteristics may be treated together: most exports consist of primary products produced with technologies, capital-

Figure 2
Degree of industrialization in production and exports,
1955 and 1970.
Source: Science Council Committee on Industrial Policies, *Uncertain Prospects*
(Ottawa 1977), 23

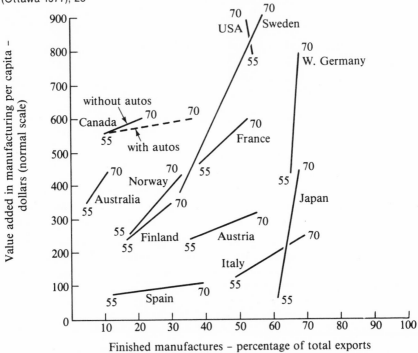

Finished manufactures – percentage of total exports

labour ratios, and salary levels predominant in advanced industrial econo-mies; also, national industry is based upon the first steps of processing raw materials or upon substitution from imports within the context of various protective measures. Figure 2 indicates the relatively high level of value added per capita in manufacturing for Canada and Australia compared to other industrialized countries, but also the very small proportion of the two dominions' exports that is accounted for by finished manufactured products. The figure also indicates the trend in this relationship between 1955 and 1970. Canada seems at first to have tripled the relative weight of manufac-tured exports during this period; but when the continental automobile pact is taken into account, we see that over half of this increase is due to an account-ing process rather than any real increase in industrial exporting capacity.

Neither Canada nor Australia has managed to achieve what is the normal range of manufactures as a percentage of exports that prevails in other economies with similar levels of manufacturing per capita. Furthermore, both the export-processing and import-substituting fractions of the dominions' manufacturing base depend upon advanced but imported technology. One index of this reliance upon technology developed elsewhere is that, while Canada imported 30 per cent of the manufactured goods it consumed in 1970, it imported 52 per cent of the goods which employed an advanced technology. Looking into this more closely, the figures indicate that Canada imports 74 per cent of its machinery and 90 per cent of its computers and office equipment.[14] If we were also to take into account the degree of manufacturing using licensed technology from the dominant capitalist economies, the degree of reliance upon imported technology would stand out to an even greater degree.

The industry of the dominion capitalist countries relies as much upon political protection as upon imported techniques. To cite but one example, one study of Australian industry at the beginning of the 1960s estimated that approximately 60 per cent of the industrial work-force was employed in sectors whose visibility depended upon tariff protection.[15] This protected industry, in turn, as we have just seen, imports most of its capital equipment, as does the export processing sector. This puts perpetual strains upon the balance of payments; a shortage of foreign exchange implies less a decline in discretionary consumer imports than it does a decline in the imports of the means of production. Devaluation may help primary exports in the short run, but the increased expense of imported capital goods may well unleash a general inflation which can cancel out the initial advantage for these exports. The dominion capitalist countries resort to high levels of international borrowing in order to balance their accounts; indebtedness per capita for each of these economies is among the highest in the world. It was quite apt that Colin Clark incorporated the five economies into a category he termed the 'young debtor nations.'

Importation of technology usually raises costs of industrial production relative to those in the dominant economies, but other factors contribute in even more important ways. First, advanced technology is applied within a small market; this limits both economies of scale and specialization of individual factors. The Australian economist, C. Forster, estimates that these two factors together account for at least three-fourths of the gap between the levels of industrial productivity per worker in the dominions as compared to the United States and the Common Market.[16] To this we must add ratios of economic concentration which are higher in the dominions than in the dominant countries.[17] As there is a marked correlation between the degree of concentration and imposition of oligopolistic pricing, here is yet another factor which raises relative production costs in the dominions. In addition, there is a direct relation between concentration ratios and the degree of price increases during inflationary periods.[18] When all of the above factors are taken into account, we realize that the working classes of the dominions purchase manufactured goods whose costs frequently exceed those prevailing in the dominant economies, often by quite a margin. Real wages are not as high as are indicated by international monetary comparisons, and workers are frequently locked into intense struggles in order to maintain what they gauge as metropolitan standards of living. At the level of the economy as a whole, high costs of production render most dominion manufactures uncompetitive on the world market. There is even more reliance upon maintaining staple exports and international borrowing in order to import the advanced means of production necessary to keep the dominion economy functioning than is the case for other primary-product exporters whose industrial sectors and socially defined mass subsistence standards are less advanced.

In spite of the above comments there is an *eighth* element in dominion capitalism which distinguishes it from economies of the 'periphery' which have developed important industrial sectors: a minority of companies which form an exception to the rule in terms of technology and organization are capable of penetrating the world market while paying wages equivalent to those found in the dominant economies. This distinguishes these companies from, for example, Indian machinery exports, which incorporate a relatively advanced technology but depend mainly upon skilled but low-cost labour in order to penetrate world markets. *The Financial Times* of London estimates that there are several hundred specialized manufacturers in Australia who are able to capture world sales on the basis of their technological innovativeness.[19] In Canada the *Financial Post* is now running a more or less regular column on this country's successful industrial exporters. New Zealand organized its first commercial fair in North America during 1978 in order to promote its industrial exports. This limited and exceptional competitive capacity of a minority fraction of dominion capitalists is stronger in activities other than manufacturing. Canadian engineering firms are able to capture large contracts in a highly competitive world market, and the top Canadian construction firms are in the process of a major penetration into the U.S. market. In addition, there are the true multinational companies which have arisen in the dominions such as the Royal Bank or Massey Ferguson in Canada, or Bunge and Borne in Argentina (one of the key members of the international oligopoly in the grain trade). The existence of these exceptional multinationals in the dominions has not, as we shall argue below, been associated with important tendencies to transform the economies of the dominions. In fact, the tendency has been more often to use the dominion economies as a base from which to ship capital towards what are perceived as more lucrative markets.[20]

Finally, the *ninth* and *tenth* elements of the definition of dominion capitalism may be briefly treated as a unit: first, there is the strong presence of multinational corporations in key economic sectors; second, all five dominions passed from an incorporation into Great Britain's imperial network during the nineteenth and early twentieth centuries to contemporary domination by the United States with a secondary penetration by the capitalist interests from the Common Market and Japan. Much ink has been applied to describe and analyse these two elements and, given what we presume to be most readers' familiarity with the issue, we do not intend to enter into details.[21] What we will emphasize is an interpretation which does not envision industrialization by invitation, or mining by invitation, or forestry by invitation as the prime mover in the dynamics and dilemmas of dominion capitalism. The core issue for us is to seek out the balance of class forces and the specific interests (or interpretation of interests) of the dominant classes in the dominions that led them to seek or accept invited (or party-crashing) metropolitan capital. This is not to deny the obviously imposing modern presence of multinational capital in the dominions, or the political difficulties involved if the dominion bourgeoisies were now to reverse their historical decisions to welcome this multinational capital. But the key to multinational domination in dominion capitalist economies is the bourgeoisies in the dominions themselves and their exercise of power vis-à-vis other social classes. Furthermore, the dominion capitalist bourgeoisies would not operate their economies much differently from what is presently the case if they were able to displace the multinationals from the peaks of economic power or establish more home-grown multinationals.

CLASS STRUCTURE

The nature of social class in the dominions may be approached through a critical discussion of the literature on the political economy of staples, despite its general lack of any direct focus on class. For purposes of brevity, let us restrict ourselves to the most productive and theoretically interesting representative of the staples school(s), Harold Innis. Innis was concerned to show how staples production in a 'new country' could exercise differential consequences from those observed in older societies. In the new countries, staples were produced on a large scale via advanced techniques and transportation systems. Certain institutional characteristics of this staples production – e.g., the high, indivisible, overhead costs of transportation systems, plus the subordination of production in the new countries to the needs of more advanced industrial economies – could lock the staple-exporting economy into a relatively shallow degree of economic development despite the use of advanced technologies and the existence of high-income levels.

Let us attempt to recast Innis' approach from a class perspective. First of all, an economy is a system of social relations through which the materials of nature and human labour are appropriated, transformed, and distributed. In Africa, Asia, and most of Latin America, indigenous social structures were incorporated and redirected to fulfil the needs of the new Euro-centred world economy from the sixteenth century onwards. In the 'new societies,' the most dynamic aspects of European social relations were imposed upon 'empty' temperate regions. Only in the case of the North American fur trade was there any systematic incorporation of indigenous social structures into world trade. Otherwise, the constant theme of relations between natives and Europeans has been either elimination or the establishment of reserves and the various other prominent elements of this dismal chapter in the history of the dominions. Given the resource base of the dominions, the advanced social organization of production, the relative labour scarcity, and the intimate communication via immigrants and the printed word of the gains achieved by mass struggles in Europe, the masses of the new countries captured material standards which were among the highest in the world. One consequence of these high standards was the early formation of what Mel Watkins terms 'final demand linkages.' Above and beyond the backward and forward linkages from staple exports, high-income levels provided a prosperous local demand for consumers' goods.[22] Even before the introduction of national policies of protection to foster local industry, consumption linkages were already sufficient to generate a good degree of industrialization through import substitution. When this was added to export processing and equipment manufacturing, one observed an industrial urban working class whose aggregate weight and role looked quite similar to that of the European proletariat. It is in this sense of class structure, rather than ethnic origin and culture per se, that the dominions are to be seen as extensions of European social space.

The role of staple exports can be examined from a class perspective: how is it that the social relations of advanced industrial Europe can shape economies which are truncated and unstable in the long run? One approach to this question is suggested by Albert Hirschman's synthesis of staples theory, of the notion of linkages, and of Marxism into an orientation which he terms 'micro-Marxism.'

Marxist thought has traditionally focused on a very few constellations of productive forces – such as feudal or capitalist modes of production – that are dominant over wide geographical areas and persist over long periods of time; social and political configurations are seen as deriving from these macromodes. The linkage approach also takes characteristic features of technology and production processes as points of departure for understanding social events, but it does so on a much smaller scale, in much more minute detail, and for a much more limited time scale. Hence, 'micro-Marxism' might be a good term for this attempt to show how the shape of economic development, including its social and political components, can be traced to the specific economic activities a country takes up ...

It is characteristic of this micro-Marxist approach to derive important differences in sociopolitical development from comparatively small and initially difficult-to-perceive differences in the structure of the 'productive forces' within which what had generally been considered a uniform historical phase of a homogeneous mode of production ... But micro-Marxism comes particularly into its own when one deals with the development of the countries of the periphery during the so-called period of export-led growth which for most of these countries occupies the second half of the nineteenth century and the first 2 or 3 decades of the twentieth, but goes on even today in some cases.[23]

While we find that Hirschman's understanding of Marx is rather lacking in the 'micro-Marxism' which he forwards,[24] the general notion is quite valuable. What is needed is a wedding of class analysis as the foundation of economic thinking to Hirschman's careful institutional analysis of the differential impact of various staple exports. While a general and abstract theory of political economy is necessary in order to analyse a particular society, the class system in question is the product of a specific national history and cannot be inferred from abstract categories. If the dominant classes use staple exports as one basis of their social power, we must intimately acquaint ourselves with the staples in question in order to grasp a specific system of domination.

Unfortunately, direct use of the staples literature in attempting an analysis of class in the dominions seems to be quite limited. Taking Innis as our example, it is not difficult to see why this is the case: given the profound influence of Veblen's theories on Innis' approach to economic history, one does observe a richness of institutional analysis and a critical edge that is mostly lacking in the more orthodox economics of the times. Although some of Innis' writings make it clear that he had a clear grasp of the history of farmers' and workers' organizations in Canada, broader conceptions of overall struggles and their macroscopic consequences are lacking. Here Innis stands in contrast with such an openly bourgeois theorist as Schumpeter, who had sensed the full range of Marx's intellectual and political challenge to the existing order and attempted to offer alternative explanations across this entire range, including that of class analysis. If he had at least been actively arguing with Marxists, as was Schumpeter, Innis' work could have at least provided the raw material for synthesizing the institutional history of staples production and class analysis. As it stands, there is little to go on. The literature on the political economy of staples is thus a necessary, but far from sufficient step, towards constructing a class analysis of dominion capitalism, even though it does evidence an understanding of the particular consequences of particular kinds of production which is often sadly lacking from more orthodox forms of class analysis. An adequate comprehension of dominion capitalism requires a synthesis of the two streams of thought, albeit with the staples approach as a junior partner: a micro-Marxism, to use Hirschman's phrase. This micro-Marxism is likely to be created via comparative economic history which is theoretically informed, rather than through attempts to construct models of value and development at high levels of abstraction. The latter route looks quite elegant, but we doubt its efficacy in advance of a solid body of comparative history on which to base the necessary abstractions.

Rural class relations and industrialization
Rural class relations prevailing at the beginning of an industrialization process constitute one of the major elements shaping a society's specific path towards proletarianization. These pre-industrial rural relations deeply mark the political nature of class conflicts decades after industrial inputs permit the diminution of the agricultural population to a small fraction of the total labour force. In the five dominion capitalist societies, landholding was sharply concentrated during the first half of the nineteenth century. This concentration, combined with mass agitation to obtain land (with varying results in each dominion), exercised profound effects upon the pace and depth of industrialization and upon the structure and interests of the bourgeois and working classes. The negative consequences of such concentration upon long-run development form a central theme in the critical historiography of each dominion. It is thus rather puzzling that Samir Amin identifies a supposed 'simple commodity mode of production' prevailing in rural Australia, Canada, and New Zealand at the dawn of industrialization, as was also

supposedly the case in the northern United States. This contrasts the British dominions with the bound peasantries of the true 'periphery' and is one of the major characteristics which leads Amin to classify our societies as 'young centers.'[25]

Because of the influence of Amin's writings on critical political economy in the dominions, it will be useful to begin our discussion of rural class relations by confronting his conceptions with the starkly contrasting facts of rural history in Canada, Australia, and New Zealand. By a 'simple commodity mode of production,' Amin refers to family production directly for the market, in contrast to the socially and politically bound peasantries of much of Africa, Asia, and Latin America, or production for market via a rural proletariat. Presumably he also implies a substantial endowment of land and capital inputs (e.g., iron ploughs in eighteenth-century England) to distinguish these European 'petty producers' from the small-scale agricultural producers of regions like west Africa. We thus, more or less, have the yeoman farmer of British rural history or the farmers of Jacksonian America. By inference, we can envisage a double-sided advantage of a yeomanry rural sector compared with the uneven distribution patterns of a bound peasantry or a rural proletariat. First, there is a prosperous market for consumption goods from new industries – consumption linkages, in Watkin's terms. Second, the degree of the yeomanry's control over land and economic surplus encourages capital improvements and thus a market for industrial farm inputs. There is also a third possibility; in the absence of large-scale labour migration from poorer regions or from abroad, industry must offer relatively high wages to attract labour away from the yeomanry rural sector which, in turn, encourages the substitution of capital for labour, thus deepening the industrialization process (conversely, higher wages can discourage indusrial start-ups; the balance depends upon specific historical circumstances). Such would be the basic structural mechanisms through which the yeomanry class structure of the British dominions would encourage their presumed autocentric industrialization as 'young centres.'

An introductory reading of even a few orthodox general histories of Australia indicates a nineteenth-century rural social structure in which rural wealth and power were extremely concentrated in the capitalist sheep-runs of the outback. By the mid-nineteenth century these wool-exporting sheep ranches often exceeded 100,000 acres in area. Wool exports dominated the Australian economy until the First World War period, when extensive industrialization began. Thus Kevin Rowley justly labels the Australian economy previous to this period as one of 'pastoral capitalism.'[26] The alliance of large land-owners and commercial-financial capital in an export-oriented economy, which Amin sees as distinguishing certain regions of the true periphery from the young centres, is precisely the sort of class alliance which prevailed in Australia before the First World War. During the first decades of the nineteenth century, land-owners relied upon transported convict and ex-convict labour for their sheep-runs. Given the military structure of Australia as a penal colony for Great Britain at this time, M. Dunn questions whether these first phases of the pastoral economy were based upon a slave mode of production.[27] Free proletarian labour predominated by the 1840s. Further, the scarcity of white labour in Australia allowed the rural proletariat to capture a level of remuneration superior to that of the industrial proletariat of Great Britain.

From this time onwards, the Australian proletariat fought to keep capitalists from importing Asian labourers. As in the other dominions, racism emerged as a key aspect of the working class's strategy to maintain a high wage level. Rowley presents evidence that the Australian gold boom of the 1850s did not exert the transformatory consequences usually attributed to it in the traditional historiography; neither the rate of economic growth nor the rate of population increase greatly exceeded that of previous decades. It was no more than a temporary defection from the dominance of pastoral capitalism. From the 1860s onwards, there was, permeated by Henry George's single tax ideology, mass agitation to break up the large holdings and distribute the land, but it was only towards the end of the century that such redistribution took effect on a significant scale outside of the colony of South Australia.

In the case of South Australia's yeomanry, the suitability of the land for arable farming in the form of wheat exports was probably more important than the colony's social origins as a private settlement enterprise based upon the ideas of Edward Gibbon Wakefield that yeoman farms are physically more efficient in producing grain than a large-scale unit employing a proletariat. Ranching, on the other hand, exhibits important economies of scale, and large capital still dominates the sheep-runs of Australia, as it does in New Zealand, Argentina, Uruguay, and the American West.[28] The same is true for cattle ranches in the United States, Alberta, Uruguay, and Argentina (aside from the relatively small herds kept by grain farmers to supplement incomes and protect themselves from fluctuations in cereal prices). Thus land was redistributed in parcels suitable for grain farming or dairying, where yeoman farmers were also more efficient than large-scale units until quite recently. This yeomanry was thus quite young when industrialization proceeded in Australia, and it arose within the context of an already urbanized society where high wages predominated. Pastoral capital remained dominant over the rural sector, as it did over the whole society. Wool exports were associated with urban centres that provided support in the form of administration, finance, transport, and diverse services. These urban centres plus the pastoral proletariat provided the mass prosperous base for Australian industrialization.

New Zealand presents a similar story: land was locked up by large-scale pastoral agriculture and speculation during most of the latter half of the nineteenth century. The social structure and class relations were similar to those of Australia and provided the same potential for incipient industrialization, though on a smaller scale. Subsequently, there was a major redistribution of land to dairy farmers, which changed the social and political balance of the colony. Prior to the creation of this dairying yeomanry, there were already the important beginnings of diversified industrial activities in New Zealand. Armstrong has presented evidence as to how the emergence of New Zealand as a specialized dairy exporter was initially associated with a truncation of its industrial sector as commercial and financial capital skewed resources towards the staples sector.[29] Finally, the nineteenth-century history of conflict between the rural proletariat and pastoral capital in both Australia and New Zealand, as well as populist movements for redistribution of land, played an important role in developing a working-class political culture which supported social democratic labour parties committed to intensified industrialization.

Concentration in ownership of agricultural land in pre-Confederation Canada did not have the productive base in terms of the economies of scale of commodity production that operated for the ranches and sheep-runs of Australia, New Zealand, Argentina, and Uruguay. Here, concentration was a function of the power of merchant capital and political pull. In the case of the Maritime colonies and Quebec the major function of agriculture was local production for colonial subsistence in food and as a labour reserve for the export of fur, fish, and lumber. Ontario achieved a certain level of grain exports during the first half of the nineteenth century, later to be succeeded by cheese and butter. In none of these activities was there any advantage in large units of production. Much of the agricultural land held by large individual landlords or chartered companies was locked up for speculative purposes. Gary Teeple argues that such speculative holdings impeded the extent of rural settlement in pre-Confederation Canada and thus limited the extent of the domestic market, as well as forcing emigration from British North America to the United States where land was more easily available.[30]

This reference to the United States poses a problem. Implicit or explicit in the historiography on land settlement for each of the five dominions, one usually finds a contrast between the liberal homesteading policies of the

United States, and the relatively restrictive land policies of the dominion in question, which held back long-run development. But speculative concentration of landholdings in the United States was the object of constant complaints by agrarian movements, and this concentration is a standard theme among economic historians.[31] The United States seems to have industrialized in the face of a pattern of land ownership which was quite concentrated during much of the nineteenth century, and in which land was not nearly as accessible as printed in the historiography of the dominions or Amin's notions of simple commodity production (with respect to the latter, northern U.S. farmers were quite dependent upon paid labour until the 1830s, when industrialized inputs began to displace a scarce and unruly rural proletariat, thus creating the family farm so beloved by American speechwriters). In short, one must systematically compare the degree and pace of speculation and concentration of land ownership in the U.S. 'model' with the levels prevailing in the dominions before identifying such patterns as factors in the economic truncation of these five societies.

Land was unlocked in the Maritimes, Quebec, and Ontario during the latter half of the nineteenth century. In Ontario the yeoman farmer became the norm, with family production associated with relatively large endowments of good agricultural land and mechanization as a substitute for hired labour. The Ontario market for agricultural machinery became an important element in the early phases of Canadian industrialization.

In Quebec things proceeded quite differently.[32] First of all, Quebec has a relatively poor endowment of good agricultural land: 149,000 acres of Class I land as opposed to 5,552,000 acres in Ontario; 2,344,000 acres of Class II land (minor modifications for adaptation to commercial agriculture) as opposed to 5,826,000 acres in Ontario, according to contemporary measurements. By approximately 1820 all the known prime agricultural land was either already occupied, in the case of the seigneuries, or locked up by speculators.

At the same time, the exactions of the seigneurs had been increasing since the conquest of 1760. In La Nouvelle France the seigneuries were usually one of the resources available to a member of the commercial-political elite. With conquest, the seigneurs had to rely upon their land alone since they were displaced from the pinnacles of political and economic power. This led them to press harder upon the habitants. Before 1760 a relative scarcity of population enabled the peasants to bargain advantageously with the seigneurs; overpopulation weakened the habitants' bargaining power. Thus the habitants were doubly squeezed. Given over-population on good land or the occupation of new but inferior soils, poor agricultural practices which exhausted the soil, and the increased exactions of the seigneurs, the Quebec countryside – outside of the Eastern Townships with its Loyalist settlements – underwent a process which André Gunder Frank terms 'passive involution.'

Old practices were repeated on a diminished and impoverished scale. Quebec and the U.S. South became the two regions in North America where one could justly speak of the rural population as a peasantry, in the general sense of producers on small plots of land and little in the way of inputs other than their own labour. This passive involution of the Quebec countryside made a cheap source of labour readily available and served as one of the factors encouraging an emphasis on labour-intensive light industry in the region's industrialization. Subsequent to 1860 the construction of railways, the new steamships, and the opening up of the British market to food imports from the dominions made possible the quite rapid emergence of Quebec as a specialized dairy region (dairying is labour-intensive and can operate with relatively poor endowments of land when other, better endowed regions find a comparative advantage in the production of other commodities). In class terms the Quebec peasantry progressively transformed itself towards the yeoman pattern of other North American dairying regions.

Last but not least, there is prairies agriculture. As of 1971, 35,502,000 hectares of Canada's 43,784,000 hectares of improved farmland were located in the prairies (81 per cent).[33] Wheat and other cereal farming were on the yeoman pattern; in a short while, we shall contrast the structural consequences of this pattern with those implied by the share-cropping of wheat lands in Argentina, which were opened at the same time.

In a forthcoming work Gordon Laxer points to a key difference between land concessions to the CPR and American railways. The CPR was not restricted to alternating sections on either side of its track; it held other areas of choice prairie land either for speculation or to impede competition. This delayed prairie settlement during a favourable conjuncture for wheat exports; i.e., 1896 through to the First World War. Laxer contends that more rapid western settlement would have enlarged the market for central Canadian industry. This, in turn, would have allowed Canadian companies to operate at a large scale and thus be in a better position to avoid inundation by American direct investment. When these prairie lands were finally settled, the Canadian bourgeoisie had pretty much retreated from agricultural lands. Production across Canada was in the hands of yeomen; the bourgeoisie contented itself with indirect seizure of the surplus via such means as transport and storage rates, and the oligopolization of the farm machinery industry.

In terms of land, large capital – both Canadian and American – turned its attention to the forests. Canada has 326.1 million hectares of forest land compared with 68.7 million hectares of total farmland.[34] Large capital controlled forest land either directly, as is predominant in the Maritimes, or indirectly via official ownership by a state easily controlled by the bourgeoisie (concretely, this implies cheap long-term leases). When the forest sector is taken into account, we thus discover a concentration in the control of rural land which is perhaps as skewed as that of Argentina. Furthermore, many of the roots of the proletarianization of Canada's class structure are to be found in the timber and pulpwood hinterland.

Argentina presents a class structure for the appropriation of labour and the economic surplus in its grain-growing regions which is quite different from the yeoman pattern of Australia, Canada, and the United States. Until the early nineteenth century, hides were the major export from Argentina's lush pampas. Herds roamed estates measured in the hundreds of thousands of acres of range land; proprietorship was concentrated in a relative handful of families. After 1810, salt processing of meat for export to Caribbean slave plantations assumed increasing importance, as was also the case in Uruguay. At mid-century, wool replaced meat as the chief export, this production being associated with the arrival of a wave of Italian and Spanish immigrants who served as a rural proletariat on the sheep-runs. Land-owners made the transition to capitalist export agriculture with relative ease, and the pattern of proprietorship and political control remained relatively intact. After 1880 the railway, steamships, refrigeration, barbed wire, windmills, and improved strains of grass made possible two new staple exports from the pampas. First, beef was packed and chilled in large-scale enterprises for shipment to Europe, principally Great Britain. Secondly, grain growing introduced an agricultural revolution into the pampas. But Argentina's great proprietors retained control of the grain lands, resorting to a pattern of tenant share-cropping and temporary occupation of a given plot of land. Once again, the labour for beef ranching and grain farming, and also the labour in the supporting urban and transportation complex, were supplied by mass immigration from Italy and Spain. The means of production stayed in the hands of Argentina's great proprietors while commerce and transportation were largely controlled by British finance capital.[35]

Comparing the Argentine wheat fields with those of Canada and Australia, several inferences may be drawn on the basis of staples theory and the works of J.R. Scobie on Argentina. Farmers in the two British dominions, in spite of the predations of finance capital, appear to have been permitted to retain a greater proportion of their economic surplus than was the case for Argentinian share-croppers. This, plus the occupation of farms in freehold tenure encouraged capital improvements on the land and the purchase of farm machinery. The agricultural implements sector became a key factor in industrialization and helped to raise agricultural productivity.

Argentinian share-croppers were considerably less inclined to make such improvements; their lesser prosperity also diminished their role as consumers. Many more left farming to pursue urban occupations than would have been the case under freehold tenure, and this at a time of favourable conditions for wheat exports. Before the Second World War the great natural productivity of the pampas – grasslands which are among the world's best pieces of agricultural real estate – compensated for the relative lack of capital improvements in grain production. Subsequent to 1940 a petrochemical-based agricultural revolution proceeded in the United States, Canada, and Australia. The pampas' natural productivity no longer compensated for failures in technological innovation, in the context of an extremely competitive conjuncture in the world grain trade from the late 1940s through to the early 1970s. Share-cropping tenancy was one of the major factors behind this failure to innovate.

Finally, Argentina's shifting tenancy system discouraged the development of local social organization and local political initiative. Thus Argentina lacked the vibrant farming communities which provided the basis for the forceful populist movements (sometimes to the left, sometimes to the right) which confronted the merchants and financiers of Canada, Australia, and New Zealand. The urban-based populist movement of Argentina, with its welfare reforms and state encouragement of industrialization through import substitution, never made much of a dent in breaking up the social and economic power of Argentina's great capitalist landlords. The same is true for Uruguay. In both countries, nearly all foreign exchange was earned by exports from the great estates. A certain yeoman sector developed, mainly in dairy and horticultural production for the local market, but it was swamped by the power of large agricultural capital. When world market conditions were no longer able to support a mutually agreeable sharing of an expanding export pie between urban populists and agrarian capitalists, the latter responded via direct military intervention and the establishment of regimes which have become synonymous with torture and state terror.

Formation of the bourgeoisie
The dominion capitalist bourgeoisies must be examined not only in and of themselves but also in relation to their historic conflicts with other classes and social movements. Class conflict not only transforms or fails to transform the working class from a class in itself to a class for itself, but does the same for the bourgeoisie. Without a powerful historic challenge from below, individual elements of the bourgeoisie are able to pursue short-run interests which may undermine the long-term base of their strength as a class. In an essay on South Africa, Ehrensaft makes a first comparison between the rela-

tive organization of the South African bourgeoisie and those of Canada and Australia. In terms of an independent economic base and a cohesive strategy, South Africa's bourgeoisie ranks as the most coherent, Canada as the least, and Australia as in between. Part of these differences relates to the specific nature of different staple exports. South Africa's diamonds and gold, lying in deep vein deposits, required locally-based technological innovations; the extremely high value per mass of these commodities also required local organization of the world oligopoly in diamonds and gold in order to avoid small unplanned supply fluctuations which could bring about drastic price increases. The export of base metals from the Canadian and Australian shield formations employed mostly existing technologies, and oligopolies were administered from the dominant industrial economies.

The other large part of the differences in the relative strengths of the dominion bourgeoisies relates to class conflict. Joint challenges from white working-class militancy and Afrikaner nationalism forced South African capitalists to develop a long-term strategy of relatively independent industrialization. Without the nationalist-labour coalition's electoral victory of 1924, and its policies of forced reinvestment of mining profits in local industrialization, mining capitalists would not likely have made many investments, which turned out later to be in their own best interests. Afrikaner state capitalism and South Africa's international pariah status also reinforced these tendencies (on the other hand, for purposes of political backing in dominant countries, the South Africans sometimes seem to have invited multinational investment where local capital could have accomplished the task alone).[36] In contrast, the Canadian bourgeoisie's success in breaking up worker and farmer movements and in containing the sharper conflicts within regional boundaries permitted the upper class to pursue its short-term interests willynilly. As we shall see below, the Australian bourgeoisie faced a nationally-based social democratic movement from the early twentieth century onwards. In contemporary Australia, multinational investment has deeply penetrated industry and mining, but not yet to the extent it has in Canada. In part, this may be a question of timing; industrialization proceeded later in Australia than Canada, and so did the take-over movement. But one observes many industrial and mining sectors where Australian capital stands on an equal footing with the multinationals, and that this position will likely continue.[37] It seems to us that conflict with a socialist political party was an important factor in forging a relatively greater strategic cohesion among the Australian bourgeoisie as compared with its class equivalent in Canada, and that this cohesion permitted the Australian upper class to create a stronger independent economic base.

A second axis of comparison among the dominion capitalist bourgeoisies concerns the role of merchant and finance capital in the long-term development – or lack of development – of the five economies. In contemporary Canada, discussion of this issue is most closely associated with the work of R.T. Naylor. The central thrust of his complex arguments seems to us to be the following: the men of affairs who controlled Canada's economy at Confederation (1867) and during subsequent decades concentrated their energy in commerce and finance. Capital specializing in circulation of commodities is inclined towards secure short-term investments which, in the context of British North America, meant the movement of staples out of Canada and the importation of manufactured products. As industrialization through import substitution proceeded, merchants and financiers preferred to place their money in branch-plant operations of metropolitan firms and also to direct incentives of the state which they controlled towards the benefit of such branch plants, rather than supporting riskier long-term placement of capital with nascent, indigenous industrialists.[38]

This basic theme of structural contrast and conflict between merchant and financial capital on the one hand, and local diversifying industry on the other, is also present in critical discussions of the bourgeoisies of the other dominion capitalist societies. For Australia, Kevin Rowley contends that 'in the nineteenth and the early twentieth centuries, the urban upper class was based primarily on mercantile, financial, and speculative wealth, and closely interlocked with the pastoral elite.'[39] Similarly, R.W. Connell finds that 'the predominance of mercantile and financial capital in the colonial economy left its work ... All of the major financiers, both banks and insurance companies, of the early 1970's were established in the nineteenth century ... The current set of leading companies, then, was created by the growth of an industrial economy over a mercantile and pastoral base within an imperialist context.'[40]

Neither Rowley nor Connell advance quite the same proposition as Naylor with respect to the consequences of commercial and financial predominance in the late nineteenth-century bourgeoisie, but W.B. Sutch does so for the New Zealand economy: 'both the political parties which called themselves Reform and Liberal were in fact farmers' parties but with a strong element of the merchant, importing, and generally trading classes and, of course, financial groups. All these were interested in promoting what they were doing: importing, merchandizing, warehousing, distribution and lending money. And none of what they were doing gave jobs to the unemployed or promoted policies which would enable manufacturing to develop.'[41] Armstrong's article on New Zealand documents how this cluster of interests, organized around staple exports, enforced policies at the end of the nineteenth century which effectively dismantled the local diversified manufacturing sector which had arisen between the 1860s and 1880s. E. Daniels has also argued that commercial and financial capital in Argentina distorted and truncated the economy of the pampas by subordinating its operation to the needs of staple exports to Great Britain.[42]

Theoretically, this distinction between the differing inclinations of capital specializing in circulation as opposed to production originates in the third volume of *Capital*.[43] This distinction played a key role in the debate over the transition from feudalism to capitalism which took place in the pages of *Science and Society* during the 1950s.[44] There were two ways to industrialization: the first – the revolutionary way – resided in the predominance of production capital over circulation capital and resulted in the thoroughgoing transformation of society; the second involved the predominance of circulation capital over production, which frequently involved accommodation with older social forms rather than their transformation. It is immediately attractive to see this distinction operating in dominion capitalism; merchant and financial capital subordinates social structure to the imperatives of staple exports rather than transforming the local economy into a diversified autonomous entity. However, it seems to us that Marx's theoretical notions here are meant to be applied to the first phase of any industrial revolution. Paul Bairoch's research on the first phase of the world's first industrial revolution in Great Britain supports the utility of Marx's distinction between production and circulation capital: there was little in the way of financial flow between large mercantile capital based in London and the pioneering entrepreneurs of the hinterland, who created the industrial production of textiles.[45]

Contact between large mercantile capital and the new industrial capitalism only assumed intimacy with the advent of railroadization from the 1820s onwards.[46] But here it would be off the mark to speak of a subordination of finance capital to a revolutionizing production capital. In creating the base of modern share-capital and company financing, British finance capital both transformed itself and helped unleash vast new productive forces through, in Schumpeterian terms, facilitating the second great epoch-making innovation of the industrial era, the railways. From the 1820s onwards, one may speak of production and circulation capital as both revolutionary and transforming forces, at least in the centre of the world system. Furthermore, a distinction which may be crucial for understanding the first phases of the first industrialization may no longer hold force for the first phases of subsequent waves of industrialization in various regions of the world economy. U.S. economic history is replete with examples of merchants who moved into industrial production in a quite revolutionary way. To cite another example, merchant capital in Brazil played a key role in initiating the industrialization of the Sao Paulo region.[47]

In the dominion capitalist societies the dominant circulation capital of the latter half of the nineteenth century seems to us to have been quite inclined to support local manufactures characteristic of the first phase of the Industrial Revolution (with textiles as the epoch-making innovation) or the second phase (with railways and steel as the epoch-making innovations). In fact, one of the central themes in left Australian historiography is the manner in which nationally owned banks backed industrialization while British-owned banks skewed capital almost exclusively to the pastoral export sector. Thus the progressive indigenization of Australia's banks after the First World War was seen as facilitating the ensuing industrial revolution. However, the Canadian experience should caution the Australians from placing too great an emphasis on indigenous ownership per se. One cannot reach conclusions about the role of circulation capital in industrialization by considering it as an abstract theoretical category; its role in a given context depends upon specific circumstances of time and place, and calculations of advantage. Circulation capital acted for or against industrialization according to specific historical conditions.

Where the bourgeoisies of the dominions did falter was in their common hesitancy to remain in, or even to attempt to undertake, or encourage, local entry into industries characterizing the third and subsequent phases of industrialization: chemicals, automobiles, in fact, the gamut of dynamic sectors in twentieth-century industrial economies. Such sectors became, with few exceptions, the preserve of branch plants. By the time that the dominion capitalist economies were poised to move into third phase industries, these industries had already passed into a monopoly capital stage in the central capitalist economies. The dominion bourgeoisies found it more prudent to restrict their markets rather than take on central monopoly capital in these new sectors: Henceforth, a long-term truncation of the dominion capitalist industrial base began to unfold. This prudent truncating choice on the part of the bourgeoisies cannot be comprehended apart from their conflicts with workers in the dominions.

The working class

Why is Australia a world of absolute silence? You will ask, by the way, how is it possible to be an Australian? Yes, it is possible, there are Australians; one can even be comfortable, it seems, being an Australian, even have a slightly better chance (statistically) of being a tennis champion. One can even *become* an Australian; functionalism is a thing you can get hooked on. So let all the technocrats in the world be automatically sent to Australia, they will like it there.[48]

The last sentence of the above quotation, from Samir Amin's 'In Praise of Socialism,' is quite off the mark: it was not technocrats but hundreds of thousands of proletarians from England, Ireland, Scotland, Wales, Italy, and Greece who went to Australia. There is a long history of intense class conflict in Australia and a thriving socialist intellectual milieu. It is thus difficult for us to conceive how Amin has created such an inaccurate image of Australia. The uranium miners of the Australian or Canadian shields, or the asbestos miners of Quebec, whose health is steadily ruined in the workplace, would be quite surprised to discover that they dwell in a land of technocratic functionalism. Class exploitation is the central social fact of dominion capitalism, and this exploitation has not been, and is not, imposed without an active opposition by the workers of the five societies.

In the pages which follow, we present a brief comparative delineation of the role of workers in the formation of dominion capitalism. This is probably the most difficult aspect of our analysis, for comparative class histories require one to enter into great detail concerning the economic, political, and social formation of the masses in each dominion. It will require several years for us to accomplish this task, so the following paragraphs should be viewed as a preliminary orientation of work in progress. Furthermore, history is all too rarely written from the vantage point of the masses: even when concerned with the workers, one usually finds histories of the leadership of working-class organizations rather than a direct focus on the workers themselves. Nevertheless, we do, at present, see several broad trends in the formation of the working classes of Canada and the other dominions.

First of all, the staples and protected import-substituting sectors seem to have created working classes whose short-run interests depend upon supporting a continual truncation of the economy by the dominion bourgeoisies. Radical working-class movements have often functioned in support of policies which reinforce this truncation. This reinforcing role must be viewed against the backdrop of the particular natures of their industrial revolutions. In contrast to Europe, each society was well along the path towards proletarianization in advance of industrialization. Wage-labour relationships prevailed both in the cities and in the mines, forests, and pastoral agricultural regions of the dominions. As we have seen, the yeoman farmers of the cereal and dairying regions of Canada, Australia, and New Zealand employed rural wage-labour during the first part of the nineteenth century, after which industrial inputs began to replace field hands. Transportation networks from staples-producing hinterlands to port cities involved a relatively greater overhead expense for the dominions than was the case in Europe, and these networks were built and manned by proletarian labour. In short, both class relations and average income were equal to or in advance of those prevailing in much of western Europe.

Consequently, even such a small society as Uruguay could institute welfare measures, state intervention in the economy, and formal worker participation legislation quite on a par with those of the dominant economies even before its industrial revolution. On the basis of its pastoral exports Uruguay's population expanded from 200,000 in 1860 to 1,000,000 by the turn of the century; most of this increase coming from Spanish and Italian immigration. Until 1935 there was very little industry outside of the big meat-processing plants in Montevideo. Nevertheless, beginning in 1904 with the victory of the *Colorado* president, José Batlle y Ordoñez, Uruguay began to institute a series of welfare and parliamentary measures which, along with the nation's prosperity, earned this society its reputation as the Switzerland of Latin America.[49] When Uruguay changed its policy towards an active state encouragement of industrialization through import substitution subsequent to 1935, rapid progress was achieved due to the relatively advanced class nature of its internal market. As we shall see later, however, this industrialization strategy did not change either the composition of Uruguay's exports or the class power of the big pastoral capitalists; the ultimate result was economic decline and one of the world's nastier dictatorships.

At times, the working class, along with capitalists whose interests were attached to staple exports, opposed even industrialization through import substitution. This was the case for Argentine workers and their associated socialist party at the beginning of the twentieth century: industrial protection was opposed on the grounds that free trade and an open staples economy provided workers with lower and more stable prices for consumer goods.[50] On the basis of pastoral and cereal exports, population had jumped from 1.8 million in 1869 to 8 million as of 1914, with some 53 per cent classified as urban.[51] The transportation and transformation of staples, plus urban service occupations, provided the masses with a real standard of living which was quite high by world standards. Consumption linkages in this relatively prosperous market entailed the creation of a certain degree of import substitution, beginning with the First World War, in advance of systematic protection. As with Uruguay, however, active state fostering of industry came after the onset of the Great Depression. Even when workers constituted a key element in Juan D. Peron's first urban populist coalition (1946-55), the kind of industry which was fostered involved protected import substitution. In effect, importation of producers' goods replaced importation of consumers' goods. This created jobs and thus had the support of Argentine workers from 1930 onwards but did not change either the composition of exports or challenge the class power of the large agricultural capitalists.

Australia's industrial 'take-off' may also be said to have proceeded from the First World War onwards, but the workers' stance towards industrialization was more complex. In 1851 Australia's gold rush began; not until 1870 did wool once again displace gold as the most important export.[52] As the major diggings in the colony of Victoria were exhausted, pressure arose both on the part of workers seeking alternative employment, and fledgling manufacturers seeking protective tariffs. After tentative legislative moves, the colony embarked upon strict protectionism with its tariff bill of 1879. In contrast, Australia's other major colony, neighbouring New South Wales, remained committed to free trade (for a variety of reasons: the relatively greater weight of pastoralists in the total economy, more free land both to absorb surplus population and to generate revenue through sales of Crown land to investors, and coal mines to absorb some workers from exhausted gold fields).[53] After the creation of a federation of the Australian colonies (1901), protectionism versus free trade remained one of the country's most heated political issues until protectionist forces won out with the tariff bill of 1908. By this time most workers allied themselves on the protectionist side; when the Australian Labour party, for the first time in its existence, gained an absolute majority in both Houses of the Commonwealth Parliament in 1910, protectionism was continued, as well as the level of state intervention to encourage industrialization. However, at no time in its various terms in office was there any systematic attempt to move Australia's industrial base beyond its largely import substitution role.

In New Zealand, as in the other dominions, industrialization presented dual and conflicting tendencies: one towards truncation, and the other towards a deeper structural transformation, with the ultimate victory of the former tendency. New Zealand was officially annexed by Great Britain in 1840; intensive settlement and capital investment commenced after the military conquest and seizure of Maori lands between 1861 and 1869. During the following two decades, there were hopes that New Zealand would emerge as the 'Great Britain of the Pacific.' Structurally, there was a certain reality to these hopes: W.B. Sutch has described an emerging industrial sector, alongside the staple exports of wool and gold, which was capable of producing and exporting a wide range of goods – from textiles to farm machinery and dredges – and of supplying the New Zealand network with locally made locomotives and ships.[54] Subsequent to 1890, capital was directed towards a more specialized role in the exportation of agricultural products. Land redistribution both created a yeomanry for the production of dairy exports and helped win the masses over to the new specialization. Fledgling manufacturers sweated labour to an extent that this practice greatly weakened the possibilities of an alliance between workers and capitalists in the industries concerned. Buoyant agricultural exports, with their associated transportation and processing activities, seemed to offer more jobs in the short run. Subsequent to a government commission of enquiry into sweated labour, and then a major class confrontation in 1890, the state began to institute a series of measures involving arbitration of industrial disputes and welfare for workers. This also helped to win over the working class to the skewing of New Zealand's resources towards a highly specialized role as a high technology overseas farm for Great Britain. Several decades later, when the Great Depression jolted New Zealand's export-based economy, the Labour party won the 1935 elections and ruled through 1949. The party opted for a policy of industrialization through import substitution as one major line of response to the Great Depression. It did not, however, seek to revive the tendencies towards a deeper and more autonomous industrialization, which had existed during the 1870s and 1880s.

The relation between these observations and the earlier part of the paper can be appreciated if we refer back to table 7. We saw that, in spite of the urban and proletarianized nature of their labour forces, the dominions had a slightly lower proportion of the working population employed in industrial occupations than was the case for the dominant economies; within the industrial category, a lower proportion of workers were employed in manufacturing in the dominions than was the case for dominant capitalist countries. This reflects both the emphasis on staple exports and the failure to develop backward linkages with such exports; it also reflects the shallowness of import-substituting industrialization. When the working class in the dominions has achieved state power, either through social democratic or urban populist parties, it has basically continued this pattern of truncated industrialization. The contemporary truncated structure of the dominions is thus, in part, the product of the strategies – or non-strategies – of working-class movements during the dominions' respective industrial revolutions.

A second strand of our observations on the working classes of the dominions concerns the role of immigration. In nineteenth and early twentieth-century Europe, industrialization and the transformation of rural economies were accompanied by a steady stream of inter-continental emigration. Between 1846 and 1932, approximately 51.7 million Europeans went over

Table 8
Inter-continental migration to 'new societies'

Country	Period	Thousands of immigrants
United States	1821-1932	34,244
Argentina	1856-1932	6,405
Brazil	1821-1932	4,431
Canada	1821-1932	5,206
Australia	1861-1932	2,913
Uruguay	1836-1932	713
New Zealand	1851-1932	594

Source: W.W. Rostow, *The World Economy* (Austin 1978), 19

seas.[55] In table 8, we present figures for the 'new societies' which were the main recipients of these European migrants: the United States, the dominions, and Brazil. Europeans sought the land rather than the labour of the indigenous peoples. Military conquest and land seizure were associated with a profound racism towards native peoples. There was also a steady resistance by European workers against the immigration of Asians, who came from regions where the socially defined standard of subsistence was far below what Europeans would accept, and could thus be used by capitalists to lower wage rates. In Australia, white workers successfully battled against the use of indentured labourers from the South Pacific islands – the 'Kanakas' – in the cane fields of Queensland. In general, workers steadfastly opposed the importation of 'coolie labour' and staunchly supported the white Australia policy. In Canada, racism against Chinese and Japanese immigrants in the West was one of the uglier chapters of our history. Given the key role of immigration in the dominions and workers' fears that the bourgeoisie would use non-white labour to break wage rates, a profound racism permeated the masses and hindered class mobilization.

Each of the dominions exhibited a high rate of emigration as well as immigration. Thus Corradi estimates that, of the four million Europeans who arrived in Argentina between 1890 and 1914, only 2.4 million stayed permanently.[56] The same general range of net immigration prevailed for Australia, Uruguay, and New Zealand. Many immigrants arrived as target workers; that is, they intended to accumulate money and return home after a limited stay. Others were discontent with their new surroundings and returned home. In either case, one would hypothesize that this re-emigration diluted the capacity of the working class to mobilize itself. This is especially

Table 9
Net migration, Canada, 1861-1941 (thousands of persons)

Years	Immigration	Emigration	Net migration
1861-71	183	375	−192
1871-81	353	440	−87
1881-91	903	1,109	−206
1891-1901	326	506	−180
1901-11	1,759	1,043	716
1911-21	1,612	1,381	231
1921-31	1,203	974	229
1931-41	150	242	−92

Source: Donald Avery, *'Dangerous Foreigners'* (Toronto 1979), 193

the case during times of economic crisis, when new emigration has served as a safety valve in each of the dominions. Canada constitutes the extreme case of re-emigration in the dominions: between this factor plus the emigration of persons born in this dominion, more persons left than entered Canada for five of the eight decades between 1860 and 1940, as is seen in table 9. This is most important in explaining the relative lack of mobilization of the working class in Canada as compared to the other dominions.

The high proportion of the dominion populations which were born abroad implied that much of the working class was engaged in the first stages of socialization in a new setting and thus might sense itself unready to enter the fray of workplace and political organization. Some sense of the newness of the population in the dominions may be grasped from the following examples: Germani estimates that one-third of Argentina's population as of 1914 was composed of immigrants; for the year 1916, only 13 per cent of the European population over 55 years of age had been born in New Zealand.[57] But other factors acted counter to this implied tendency towards non-participation. First of all, for Australia and New Zealand most immigrants came from Great Britain during the 1870-1930 period and readily felt themselves to be citizens within the Empire and immediately entitled to the citizenship rights prevailing in the home country. In Canada, British migrants constituted a large majority among the newly arrived through the early years of the twentieth century. By 1913, however, 48 per cent of new immigrants were from southern and eastern Europe.[58] Ethnic differences were compounded by the shunting off of southern and eastern Europeans into sweated industries in the cities, or into hard labour in newly opened staples-producing regions. This segmentation, which fueled the fears of established workers that a new labour reserve army would break existing wage levels, as well as cultural prejudices, hindered the mobilization of the working class as a whole. But these non-British workers also confronted the leading edges of Canadian capitalism: both the large agglomerations of capital in staples regions, and mass unskilled work in import substitution industries. The polarized class conditions, both of the immediate workplace and the localities in which they lived, often produced more violent and class-conscious responses by the ethnic workers than was prevalent among established workers. Ethnic sub-community organization could also facilitate class mobilization in specific industries. Despite the bourgeoisie's attempts to culturally isolate these ethnic workers as 'dangerous foreigners,' effects were spread from their radicalism to the working class as a whole. Furthermore, as Clare Pentland has shown in his essay on the labour radicalism of the Canadian West, workers of good British stock were just as subject to the infectious ideas of Marxism and anarcho-syndicalism as their southern and eastern European or Yankee counterparts when class conditions were appropriately polarized.[59]

The third strand in our comments on the working classes of the dominions concerns Canada's exceptionality as the only dominion in which no working-class party has ever held national political power. Let us begin by comparing the Canadian working class with that of Australia. Both societies are of continental proportions but are sparsely settled relative to the land mass within their national frontiers. Like the concentration of most of Canada's population along an east-west axis just north of the frontier with the United States, over 80 per cent of Australia's population of 13.9 million (1976) lives within a 200-mile band along the 'Boomerang Coast,' which stretches from Port Pirie to Brisbane.[60] The majority of Australia's resources, like Canada's are located in the sparsely populated hinterland. However, southern Queensland, New South Wales, Victoria, south Australia, and western Australia each presented comparable regional economies based upon pastoral agriculture, grain growing, minerals, and manufacturing (northern Queensland, with its semitropical climate, presented a different economic and social structure). The structure of the working class was broadly similar in each region. Cheap coastal transportation facilitated population mobility between the different Australian colonies even before the construction of railways. This contrasts with the difficulties and expense of transportation across the Canadian Shield, even after the transcontinental railways. Secondly, there is the relatively greater ethnic homogeneity of Australia through the Second World War: tensions between Irish Catholic workers and those of English and Scottish Protestant origins never approached the intensity of French-English conflicts in Canada. These two factors facilitated the formation of radical working-class culture, a strong national union movement, and the political expression of this movement in the form of a labour party, which shook the political confidence of the Australian bourgeoisie: 'The expansion of the union movement in the later nineteenth century, its rise to electoral success in the Labour Parties of the early twentieth century, and the deepening militancy of industrial workers around the time of the First World War, posed a threat to the entire position of the ruling class. However mild the Labour Parties may appear in historical retrospect, they were certainly seen as a wild and dangerous force by property owners.'[61]

Connell proceeds to describe the reaction of the bourgeoisie: 'One response, as is well known in the history books, was a closing of ranks, a "fusion" of free traders and protectionists against labour in parliament. Another response, less well recognized because it developed over a longer time, was the emergence of a new leadership in the ruling class. A specialized political leadership of the ruling class as distinct from its business leadership. In the nineteenth century, business leadership and political leadership had been so closely intertwined they were often impossible to separate. Now they were prised apart.'[62]

While the same process of specialization and separation of bourgeois political leadership ensued in Canada, the degree of fusion and cohesion of different fractions of capital did not approach that prevailing in Australia. Without the challenge of even a mild social democratic movement on a national level, the Canadian bourgeoisie was relatively free to pursue its short-term interests willy-nilly, as was noted above. The degree of bourgeoisie's self-organization is, in large part, related to the challenges it faces from working-class mobilization. In Canada the working class was less able to pose such challenges than in other dominions.

Certainly the Canadian working class was not lacking in militancy, as is readily observed in Stuart Jamieson's account of labour unrest in Canada between 1900 and 1966.[63] Indeed, the high proportion of the proletariat engaged in staples extraction encourages militancy. Single industry resource towns evidence strong developments of informal independent proletarian culture and social organization which facilitate class mobilization. Wage conflicts can spiral into more inclusive protests against an entire context of life which is formed and controlled by large-scale resource capital.[64] Relative quiescence of labour alternates with fierce escalation of conflicts. While the distance between resource towns tends to isolate struggles, the Australian experience indicates that this difficulty is not insuperable.

One major barrier to the political mobilization of workers in Canada was the victory of Gomperism – craft organization of unions which were branches of U.S. unions and shunned formal affiliations with political parties. Gomperism's victory was rooted in the regional diversity of Canada's class structures and ethnic composition, but once victorious, Gomperism accentuated this diversity to an extent that rendered the possibilities of a cross-dominion working-class mobilization considerably more difficult. The most important event in Gomperism's dominance of the Canadian union movement was the Trades and Labour Congress (TLC) of 1902 in Berlin, Ontario.[65] The TLC's constitution was amended to exclude from membership those unions that conflicted with existing units of the American Federation of Labor; representation was refused to any central city labour organization which did not have a charter from the TLC. These measures resulted in the expulsion of dual unions – skilled and unskilled workers in a given industry joined within one union – and of a number of independent Canadian unions. District trade assemblies of the Knights of Labor, which were present in a number of cities, most importantly Montreal, were also expelled. The 1902 decisions disrupted the union movements of the West, the Maritimes, and francophone Quebec and alienated many workers there from the TLC. In addition, the TLC also adopted the AFL's practice of seating only bona fide card-carrying union members, thus excluding many representatives of worker-based political parties.

Let us examine this victory of Gomperism within the context of a comparative analysis of class. First, there were very strong motivations on the part of the AFL to intervene in Canada's union movement. Among these motivations was the political battle which Gompers and his followers fought against populism, syndicalism, and socialism in the U.S. labour movement. If the United States and the dominions constituted an extension of European social space, these new societies constituted, between themselves, a common ideological space. The Knights of Labor, founded in 1869 in the United States, exercised a wide appeal in Canada, Australia, and New Zealand. While U.S. membership peaked in 1886 and thereafter suffered a precipitous decline, the Knights were strong and growing in Quebec and the Maritimes in the years after 1890.[66] Gompers wished to defeat the Canadian Knights in order to ensure that the last nail had been pounded into the coffin of the Knights in the United States. Syndicalism was present mainly in the form of such unions as the Western Federation of Miners and, later, the Industrial Workers of the World (IWW). Syndicalism exerted an even greater influence in the western Canadian labour movement than in the western United States;[67] Gompers viewed the prairies and British Columbia as a key battlefield in his struggle against the western American radicalism which he thought had spilled over into Canada. Secondly, James Weinstein has demonstrated that the U.S. Socialist party was a thriving institution through the end of the First World War; its influence spread not only among immigrants but also among the native born – American socialism was an indigenous plot.[68] Thus Gompers was also anxious to do battle against social democratic notions which might be transmitted to the United States via Canadian workers.

From the Canadian side of the equation, a good portion of the disputes at the Berlin conference may be understood as consequences of the different balance of industrial and class forces within Canada's regions. For example, Pentland contends that western labour tended toward radicalism because workers there usually confronted large agglomerations of capital engaged in the extraction or transportation of staples, resulting in highly polarized class situations, both in the immediate workplace and in company towns. In this polarized context, dual unionism made more sense to western workers than craft unionism. Workers in central Canada, by contrast, faced capital which was more plural in structure. The large agglomerations of capital were complemented by small and medium blocks of capital which prevailed in the import-substituting industries of the Toronto-Montreal manufacturing axis. The structure of industry thus provided a social base more receptive to Gompers' craft unionism. In addition, the border at this time was quite permeable in both directions, which increased the appeal of Gomperism to a mobile work-force. The AFL had little real power over Canadian locals and organizers during the early twentieth century. Fundamentally, Gomperism prevailed over the union movement because the majority of workers in Canada's industrial heartland judged that affiliation with U.S. craft unions would best serve their interests in a very nasty struggle with the dominion's bourgeoisie. Whether, in the absence of Gomperism, a certain modus vivendi would have been possible between the diverse strands of Canada's union movement, must remain one of history's 'might have beens.'

Let us speculate a bit further about this 'might have been.' One hypothesis would be that the development of a working-class political party across Canada would have made little difference in the overall structure of the economy, given what we said at the beginning of this subsection concerning the shaping of the working class and its political movements in the other four dominions. Another hypothesis would be that Canada, as the senior dominion, possessed an industrial structure which was sufficiently profound to provide a far more autonomous development than we have experienced. A sharp challenge from the working class might have forced the Canadian bourgeoisie to act more as a class-for-itself. The 'staples trap' was neither automatic nor inevitably permanent. Given a challenge from below, it is not implausible that the Canadian bourgeoisie might have organized itself to use staple exports as the basis for autonomous economic development. This historical speculation becomes all the more interesting in the context of resource shortages in the world economy of the latter twentieth century. Staple exports might well serve as a solid basis for fuelling a fundamental reordering of the dominion economies if a new balance of social forces can be created.

CONCLUSION

Dominion capitalist societies flourished during the period we have labelled classic monopoly capitalism. In the first part of this paper we examined the defining characteristics of dominion capitalism, and the truncated overall economic structure which resulted from the conjuncture of this distinctive set of features. Following this, we presented some aspects of the class origins of the truncation of dominion capitalist economies. We conclude by a brief examination of the fragility of the truncated dominion economic structures within the context of the world system subsequent to the Korean War. Throughout this paper we have implied that Canada, Australia, and New Zealand share the same *tendency* toward structural crises as became evident in Argentina and Uruguay during the mid-1950s. Whether the tendency actualizes itself in the other dominions to the extent it did in Argentina and Uruguay depends upon a complex web of factors related to the differences in class structure and resource endowment among the five societies. The persistent and troubling presence of this tendency is best seen in the case of New Zealand.

New Zealand is the first of the three formal dominions to experience an economic set-back to the degree that we may question whether a process of declassification or 'Latin Americanization' is proceeding. From 1973 to 1976, real personal income fell by 15 per cent. Since the 1960s, GNP per capita slipped from the fourth highest in the world to the twentieth. Between June of 1976 and the same month of 1978 there were 120,000 emigrants from New Zealand (one out of every thirty persons).[69] Despite these grim figures, it is probably too early to assert that New Zealand is definitively moving along the path followed by Uruguay and Argentina towards declassification. First of all, let us contrast New Zealand with Uruguay, which has a similar population base and array of exports. Both societies were hit hard by post–Korean War price declines. In New Zealand, economic tensions led to the entry of the Labour party into national political power between 1957 and 1960. Its strategy was the traditional one of social democracy in the dominions: state-fostered intensification of industrialization through import substitution. When the Conservative party regained power (1960-72), it basically continued Labour's policies.

In contrast, post-1954 economic tensions in Uruguay eventuated in the 1958 electoral victory of the Partido Nacional, 'los Blancos,' which was controlled by large pastoral capital. During the Great Depression there had been a confluence of interests between urban populists and pastoral capital in promoting the first stages of import substitution industrialization as a solution to the country's economic ills. By the mid-1950s, consumer goods imports had been progressively displaced by imports of producers' goods; the demand for the latter was inelastic, as the urban industrial economy could not function without imported equipment and components. This was even more the case for Argentina, which had a far larger and deeper industrial structure. In the context of contracting export revenues, the industrial base could be maintained only by making major inroads into the surplus captured by pastoral capitalists. In neither Uruguay nor Argentina had urban populists touched the social base of the pastoral capitalists, who earned most of these dominions' export revenues. In order to preserve their class power and existing surpluses, pastoral capitalists in Uruguay began to institute International Monetary Fund open economy policies which threatened most of the gains won by the masses through urban populism since 1904. Mass resistance to pastoral capital's policies eventuated in the latter class instituting a reign of systematic state terror and torture. Rogelio Garcia Lupo has documented how Argentinian pastoral capital was careful to maintain direct control of the officer corps of key branches of the military.[70] This control was utilized in the military coups of 1966 and 1976. As in Uruguay, state terror and torture were systematically employed to enforce policies in the interest of pastoral exports. It was precisely because the dominion class structures of Argentina and Uruguay permitted the creation of a highly organized state which was very much part of European social space that torture could be systematized as a form of government.

In contrast, the class basis of New Zealand's pastoral exports differs from that of Argentina and Uruguay. Dairy production is organized by yeoman farmers and is more important in total exports than wool produced on large estates. Furthermore, New Zealand's agriculture employs high technology, and it has an independent base in agricultural science which is quite respectable by world standards. The major immediate cause of New Zealand's economic plight is Great Britain's abandonment of this dominion as a major source of its dairy consumption, this being done in order to enter the Common Market. Given the class forces and high technology of New Zealand's farm exports, plus a growing world population pressing on food resources, it is not out of the question that efforts to diversify both export markets and the range of agricultural products may pay off in the intermediate run. Such a strategy would be more difficult for Uruguayan and Argentinian agricultural capital. The class power of Argentinian and Uruguayan pastoral capital enabled them to continue to extract large surpluses from exports while lagging behind in adoption of new agricultural techniques. The relative productivity of their agriculture has declined in a competitive international market; whether this class can construct a desired modern agribusiness sector is problematic.

If Canada and Australia have avoided the post-1954 declines suffered by the other dominions, this is due mainly to the mineral deposits of their shield formations. In spite of these minerals, Canada has the distinction of exhibiting the highest rate of unemployment among industrialized societies since 1967. Australia has experienced its most severe recession since the 1930s, and both the financial press and critical political economists see this as a longer-term structural crisis rather than just a reflection of the general world economy.[71] For both countries, modern mining is too capital-intensive to absorb a large fraction of the work-force. The same may be said of the energy-intensive agricultural system of New Zealand as well as Canada and Australia, and Argentina and Uruguay if their agribusiness modernization succeeds. As we have seen above, the dominion economies lack many of the backward linkages one might expect from high technology export sectors; much if not most production equipment is imported. In order to resolve the structural malaise of the dominion economies, a fundamental reordering of the economy must be put on the agenda. Given the class forces within the dominions and the dominant economies, this will not be an easy task.

The traditional policy of protected import substitution, combined with political demands for further processing of staple exports, worked fairly well for the dominions between 1870 and the Second World War. This is no longer the case. Another proposed strategy was to encourage the consolidation of dominion companies in order that they may attain the scale to compete on the world market. We have seen above that there is an exceptional minority of such companies which already exist in the dominions. The historical experience with such companies has been that they maintain monopoly prices at home while often using their dominion base as a source of capital for investment either in the dominant economies or in the 'periphery.' Such world-scale dominion companies prosper without initiating structural transformation of their home economies. Then there is also the thorny question of the industrial role of smaller societies in the age of multinational capitalism. Countries such as Belgium or Holland, with more balanced industrial structures than those of the dominions, are experiencing the same multinational domination of advanced technology industries as the staple-exporting dominions. In fact, it is natural gas exports which are presently permitting Holland to delay the consequence of a profound structural malaise in its economy. Sweden, which is often cited in Canada as an example of how a small society may use staple export earnings to build an independent industrial and technological base, is itself undergoing what may be a process of declassification. Sweden's traditional product lines are losing their competitive edge while the country's much vaunted multinationals seem to be pumping capital out of Sweden towards more profitable regions. In short, the answers will not be easy.

On the other hand, it is potentially quite advantageous to be a staple exporter to a resource-short world during the latter part of the twentieth century. If the surplus from such exports could be socially mobilized in a creative fashion, it is not impossible to envisage a structural adaptation of the dominion economies to a changing world context. Given the composition and behaviour of the dominion bourgeoisies, we doubt much creativity can be expected on their part. Any solution is likely to rise in spite of them, and in the face of their political opposition. The traditional industrial policies of social democracy and urban populism are equally unlikely to resolve present quandaries. A resolution of the structural truncation and fragility of dominion capitalism will require a mobilization of the working class around new priorities. It is only in this way that there will be potential for a transformation of the peculiar structures of inequality of dominion capitalist societies.

NOTES

1 The partial exception is Uruguay, which was in the very first phases of its industrialization at the outset of the Great Depression. The tendency then, however, was quite clearly towards the same level of urbanization and proletarianization as in the other four dominions.

2 The capital-labour ratio measures the priced relation between labour and capital rather than value relations – the direct measure of class exploitation. Capitalist states, however, do not have the habit of collecting data according to labour value categories, nor are value relationships easily inferred from official statistics.

3 See, in particular, Douglas C. North, *The Economic Growth of the United States, 1790-1860* (Englewood Cliffs, NJ 1971).

4 J.W. McCarty, 'The Staple Approach in Australian Economic History,' *Business Archives and History*, IV, 1 (Feb. 1964), 1-22; J.P. Fogarty, 'The Staple Approach and the Role of Government in Australian Economic Development: The Wheat Industry,' *Business Archives and History*, VI, 1 (Feb. 1966), 34-52

5 Personal communication, Professor Jorge Niosi, Département de sociologie, Université du Québec à Montréal

6 Parpsh Chattopadhay, 'Reflections of India's Industrialization,' in Hamza Alaui and Catherine Gough, ed., *The Sociology of South Asia* (London 1980). For Brazil, see J. Serra, 'The Brazilian Economic Miracle,' in J. Petras, ed., *Latin America: From Dependence to Revolution* (New York 1973).

7 C. Furtado, *The Economic Development of Brazil* (Berkeley 1965)

8 Colin Clark, *The Conditions of Economic Progress* (2nd ed., London 1951), 370-1. Hector Dieguz maintains that there was still an important gap in terms of GNP per capita between Australia and Argentina as of 1930. See 'Argentina y Australia: algunos aspectos de su desarollo economica comparado,' *Desarollo Economico*, VIII, 32 (1969), 543-64. We are more in accord with Clark's figures, which attempt to estimate real income via a purchasing power index for each country. Furthermore, it is the structure of appropriating labour and the forces of production which define capitalism, not income per capita. For example, even at a quite advanced stage of its development, Japan's GNP per capita was considerably below the prevailing levels in other dominant capitalist economies.

9 Economic Commission for Latin America, *Economic Development and Income Distribution in Argentina* (New York 1969), 19-20

10 *Quarterly Economic Report, Argentina*, Annual Survey (1977), 5; J.D. Crysdale and C. Beattie, *Sociology Canada* (Toronto 1973), 143; D.V. Cloher, 'A Perspective on Australian Urbanization,' in J.M. Powell and M. Williams, ed., *Australian Space, Australian Time* (Melbourne 1975), 104; T.E. Weil et al., *Area Handbook for Uruguay* (Washington 1971), 104

11 C. Furtado, *Economic Development of Latin America* (London 1970), 47; ibid., (2nd ed., 1976), 11; *Quarterly Economic Report, Argentina*, 5

12 Unfortunately, the UN does not homogenize New Zealand's accounts into its comparative data, so this dominion is not listed in the table.

13 Steve Moore and Debby Wells, 'The Myth of Canadian De-Industrialization,' in John Saul and Craig Heron, ed., *Imperialism, Nationalism and Canada* (Toronto 1977), 34-47, use a similar set of figures to reach conclusions quite different from our own.

14 John M. Britton and James M. Gilmour, *The Nearest Link* (Ottawa 1978), 45-9

15 K. Rowley, 'The Political Economy of Australia Since the War,' in J. Playford and D. Kissner, ed., *Australian Capitalism* (Victoria 1972), 280

16 'Economics of Scale and Australian Manufacturing,' in C. Forster, ed., *Australian Economic Development in the Twentieth Century* (London 1970), 166-7

17 P. Brown and H. Hughes, 'The Market Structure of Australian Manufacturing Industry, 1914 to 1963,' ibid., 184-5

18 J.M. Blair, 'Inflation in the United States,' in J.M. Blair, ed., *The Roots of Inflation* (New York 1975), 33-68

19 K. Randall, 'Australia's Industrial Exports,' *Financial Times*, 1 June 1976

20 For the roots of this tendency in Canada, see Tom Naylor, *The History of Canadian Business, 1867-1914* (Toronto 1975), II, 218-75.

21 For surveys of the role of multinationals in the dominions, see E.L. Wheelright, *Radical Political Economy* (Sydney 1971); W.B. Sutch, *Takeover New Zealand* (Wellington 1972); North American Congress on Latin America, *Argentina in the Hour of the Furnace* (New York 1975), 29-41; W. Clement, *Canadian Corporate Elite* (Toronto 1975), and *Continental Corporate Power* (Toronto 1977).

22 Mel Watkins, 'A Staple Theory of Economic Growth,' in W.T. Easterbrook and M.H. Watkins, ed., *Approaches to Canadian Economic History* (Toronto 1967), 55

23 Albert O. Hirschman, 'A Generalized Linkage Approach to Development, with Special Reference to Staples,' *Economic Development and Cultural Change*, XXV, Supplement (1977), 92-3

24 Hirschman, ibid., 92-3, maintains that 'Marx and the more perceptive Marxists moved themselves in the micro direction when they were dealing with specific events and country experiences ... Marx predicts a very different path for Germany and continental Europe in relation to England because of the absence of factory laws and in general because of a variety of social and political residues from feudalism that did not exist in England. In this manner, Marx presents elements for a comparative analysis that considerably qualifies and in effect contradicts the generalization with which he starts out.

It is remarkable ... and characteristically un-Marxist ... that Marx differentiated between England and Germany on the basis of certain elements in Germany's judicial institutions and historical heritage.'

Hirschman is quite condescending in seeing Marx's ability to differentiate various national experiences as 'un-Marxist.' This implies that Marx was too intelligent to apply his theory very strictly. While we do not wish to rush to a defence of Marx's theoretical apparatus (assuming that one could choose from among the plethora of competing views on what this apparatus really is), it is at least important to meet a man on his own grounds. There are different levels of abstraction in Marx's theory as in any other useful theory. Volume I of *Capital*, for example, begins with a highly abstract discussion of the nature of a commodity. At this level of abstraction, one can simplify and assume that the organic composition of capital is equal in different branches of production, and thus value-prices and exchange or money prices will be equal. But in volume III, Marx moves down a level of abstraction and makes a more realistic assumption where, as in the world we observe, different branches of production evidence different organic compositions of capital. But now value and prices are not equal, and thus we have the famous transformation of value into the prices problem.

We chose the transformation problem as our example of moving between levels of abstraction for two purposes. First, by pointing to such an example, we see how Marx consciously and purposively moves from one level of abstraction to another. The inference is that for some purposes, one must ignore the difference between Germany and England; for others, one must take them into account; it all depends upon the problem at hand. Therefore, Marx's differentiation between the two countries is, in fact, quite Marxist. Secondly, we share Meghnad Desai's view that the transformation problem does not represent an arcane domain for faithful Marxist economists but is rather central to Marx's entire theoretical project. The theory of value represents an attempt to demonstrate how class exploitation and class struggles underlie and shape the surface phenomena of observed prices in capitalist societies. As such, Marx's attempt, erroneous or not, to show how value and observed price relationships may be mutually translated is not marginal but rather central to his system of thought. And here we see how Hirschman once again misses the boat on what Marx was about, when the former remarks that 'the linkage approach also takes characteristic features of technology and production processes as points of departure for understanding social events.' On the contrary, the 'social events,' i.e., class exploitation in capitalist economies, constitute the point of departure for Marx; particular technologies are viewed as particular social arrangements for appropriating labour.

25 Samir Amin, *Unequal Development* (New York 1976), 15, 57, 202, 365
26 *Intervention*, no. 1 (April 1972), 9-26
27 'Wage Labour or Slave Society,' in E.L. Wheelright and K. Buckley, eds., *Essays in the Political Economy of Australian Capitalism* (Sydney 1975), I, 12-32
28 See A.G. Ball and E.O. Heady, eds., *Size, Structure and the Future of Farms* (Ames, Iowa 1972).
29 'New Zealand: Imperialism, Class, and Uneven Development,' *Australia and New Zealand Journal of Sociology*, XIV, 3, Part II (Oct. 1978), 297-303
30 'Land, Labour, and Capital in Pre-Confederation Canada,' in G. Teeple, ed., *Capitalism and the National Question in Canada* (Toronto 1972), 44-66
31 Frederick Merk, *History of the Westward Movement* (New York 1978); John T. Schlebecher, *Whereby We Thrive* (Ames, Iowa 1975), 57-70, 139-50; Michael Perelman, *Farming for Profit in a Hungry World* (Montclair, NJ 1977), 38-41. From the above sources, we may make the following tentative statement: it is

not clear how readily land was really available before the Homesteading Act of 1862. The northern U.S. exhibited marked concentration of land in various regions and periods, including the much-vaunted New England village democracies, where ownership was highly skewed and often in the hands of absentees. Speculators were ingenious at finding loopholes in legislation when it was not a case of outright fraud and bribery in order to amass land. It is quite possible that, in relative terms, land was not less monopolized in the pre-1862 U.S. than in pre-Confederation Canada; it may have been the sheer absolute size alone of the farm population which created such an advantageous internal market. Now was it completely smooth sailing to keep speculators out of the homesteading regions after 1862. Furthermore, when one adds the lands of the plantation South to western ranches and the large-scale proletarianized fruit and vegetable farms of the sun belt, this adds up to a big chunk of U.S. agricultural land which was never too available to the yeoman farmer. The yeomen operated largely in dairying regions, the corn-hog belt, and the wheat fields of the Great Plains; these three regions do provide an agricultural hinterland staggering by European standards. On the other hand, it took a fair amount of capital to set up as a pioneer, and this was often beyond the means of much of the population. Finally, we have been speaking of agricultural land. Forest reserves largely fell into the hands of corporate capital or the state it controlled after the Civil War. Taken with the above, this means that the U.S. may have industrialized in the face of a pattern of land ownership which was quite concentrated.

32 This paragraph is a summary of material to be found in P. Ehrensaft and B. Marien, 'De l'agriculture à l'agro-business,' in P. Fournier, ed., *Le capitalisme au Québec* (Montreal 1978), 191-7.

33 Canada, Department of Agriculture, *Orientation of Canadian Agriculture*, I, part A (Ottawa 1977), 29

34 C.R. Stanton, *Canadian Forestry* (Toronto 1976), 16-17

35 J.R. Scobie, *Argentina* (London 1971), 64-87, 112-35; J.E. Corradi, 'Argentina,' in Ronald H. Chilcote and Joel C. Edelstein, eds., *Latin America: The Struggle with Dependency and Beyond* (New York 1974), 316-31

36 See P. Ehrensaft, 'Polarized Accumulation and the Theory of Economic Dependence: The Implications of South African Semi-Industrial Capitalism,' in P. Gutkind and I. Wallerstein, eds., *The Political Economy of Contemporary Africa* (Beverly Hills, Cal. 1976), 58-89.

37 Bob Connell and Terry Irving, 'The Making of the Australian Industrial Bourgoise: 1930-1975,' *Intervention*, 10 and 11 (Aug. 1978), 5-38

38 'The Rise and Fall of the Third Commercial Empire of the St. Lawrence,' in Teeple, *Capitalism*, 1-42; *The History of Canadian Business* (Toronto 1975), I

and II; 'Trends in the Business History of Canada, 1867-1914,' in The Canadian Historical Association, *Historical Papers* (1976), 255-67

39 Rowley, 'The Political Economy of Australia, 282; see also Peter Cochrane, 'Australian Finance Capital in Transition,' *Intervention*, 6 (1976), 21-39.

40 R.W. Connell, *Ruling Class, Ruling Culture* (London 1977), 68-9

41 Sutch, *Takeover New Zealand*, 28

42 'From Mercantilism to Imperialism: The Argentine Case,' parts I and II, in *NACLA Newsletter*, IV, 4 and 6 (July-Aug. 1970 and Oct. 1970)

43 Chaps. 20, 36, and 47

44 The debate is reprinted in R. Hilton, ed., *The Transition from Feudalism to Capitalism* (London 1976).

45 *Révolution industrielle et sous-développement* (4th ed., Paris 1974), 45-69

46 E.J. Hobsbawn, *Industry and Empire* (London 1969), 109-19

47 Warren Dean, *The Industrialization of Sao Paulo, 1889-1945* (Austin 1969)

48 *Monthly Review*, XXVI, 4 (Sept. 1974), 14 (emphasis in original)

49 Martin Weinstein, *Uruguay: The Politics of Failure* (Westport, Conn. 1972), 20-79

50 Corradi, 'Argentina,' 339

51 Scobie, *Argentina*, 304

52 Geoffrey Blainey, *The Tyranny of Distance* (Melbourne 1966), 144

53 See R.M. Crawford, *Australia* (London 1970), 119.

54 Sutch, *Takeover*, 49-50

55 W.W. Rostow, *The World Economy* (Austin 1978), 18

56 'Argentina,' 333

57 G. Germani, 'Mass Immigration and Modernization in Argentina,' in I.L. Horowitz, J. De Castro, and J. Gerassi, eds., *Latin American Radicalism* (New York 1969), 333

58 Donald Avery, *'Dangerous Foreigners': European Immigrant Workers and Labour Radicalism in Canada, 1896-1932* (Toronto 1979), 37

59 H.C. Pentland, 'The Western Canadian Labour Movement, 1897-1919,' *Canadian Journal of Political and Social Theory*, III, 2 (Spring-Summer 1979), 53-78

60 Blainey, *Distance*, 146

61 Connell, *Ruling Class*, 52-3

62 Ibid., 53

63 *Times of Trouble*, Privy Council Task Force on Labour Relations, Study no. 22, (Ottawa 1968)

64 See R.A. Lucas, *Minetown, Milltown, Railtown* (Toronto 1971).

65 The Description of events at Berlin is drawn from Robert H. Babcock, *Gompers in Canada* (Toronto 1974), especially 85-97.

66 Ferrand Harvey, 'Les Chevaliers du Travail, Les Etats-Unis et La Société Québecoise, 1882-1902,' in Fernand Harvey, ed., *Aspects historiques du mouvement ouvrier au Québec* (Chapleau 1973), 33-118
67 Pentland, 'Labour Movement,' 67-71
68 *The Decline of Socialism in America, 1912-1925* (New York 1967)
69 Barry Newman, 'New Zealand Staggers from Two Hard Blows to its Economic Base,' *Wall Street Journal*, 22 Jan. 1979
70 *Mercenarios y Monopolios en La Argentina* (Buenos Aires 1973)
71 'Financial Times Survey: Australia,' *Financial Times*, 18 September, 1978: M. Brezniak and J. Collins, 'The Australian Crisis from Boom to Bust,' *Journal of Australian Political Economy*, 2 (1977), 4-32

5
Women's inequality and the family

DOROTHY E. SMITH

A central theoretical and political issue in the women's movement is that of the relation between the struggle for women's equality and the struggle for socialism. The theoretical debate focuses upon alternative accounts of the basis of women's inequality. One view grounds women's inequality in the relation of domination of men over women. This relation may be seen as arising from women's child-bearing functions,[1] from some prehistoric drama in which women were subjugated to men,[2] or some similar account focusing upon the specificity of relations between the sexes. Such reasoning gives no grounds for supposing that socialism will change anything. Women's liberation must be fought between women and men and on the basis of exclusive organization among women.

The alternative views identify women's inequality as arising from private property and class,[3] and look to socialism to liberate women from the family into the work-force, hence liberating them from the drudgery and dependence on which their unequal position is based.[4] This position returns us to class rather than sex as the basis of organized struggle against capitalism.

More recently socialist thinkers among women have begun to put forward analyses articulating the two inequities of class and sex through examining and formulating in various ways the relation between capitalism and 'patriarchy,' thus establishing a conceptual basis uniting the two struggles.[5] This paper shares that concern. It is an inquiry into family relations, linking them to class and the changing historical development of capitalism.

Though it is a serious over-simplification to treat the family as the sole basis of women's inequality, it is the social organization of women's labour in the home and outside, and the relations between the two which *are* women's inequality, and it will be argued here that the character of inequality and of its history differs in different class settings.

The strategy adopted here is that of a consciously open-ended inquiry into the actual processes which are now and have been at work in our society. Such an inquiry is grounded less in the theoretical and political debate – however important that has been in formulating the central issues addressed – than in the experience from which the theoretical debate arises and which it originally expressed directly. The concept of patriarchy as it has been developed in the women's movement locates and conceptualizes women's direct personal experience of inequality in their personal, and indeed sometimes intimate, relations with men.[6] By contrast, as intellectuals we begin ordinarily *outside* experienced actuality and *within* the discourse – the conversation-in-texts going forward among an intelligentsia. In this inquiry I have sought to return to the actuality in which such experience arises and to explore the larger social and historical process which is the matrix of that experience. Rather than detaching patriarchy as a phenomenon to be examined in relation to capitalism, this inquiry turns, however partially and imperfectly, to that world in which we have needed such terms to speak politically of our experience.

Engels' *The Origin of the Family, Private Property, and the State* suggests the method of analysis which will be used here. This method takes an actual work process and locates it in a determinate social relation. When we do this we can see how the articulation of an individual's work to the social relations of a given mode of production determines how *she* is related and the ways in which she becomes subordinate. There is, on the one hand, a work process, an actual activity, and on the other, social relations (and activities) which articulate and organize that work as part of a division of labour in society. This method is illustrated in the following passage from Engels' work: '[With the shift from communal to private property] the administration of the household lost its public character. It was no longer the concern of society. It became a *private service*; the wife became the first domestic servant, pushed out of participation in social production.'[7]

Engels over-simplified, but the method he used is important. He did not see the division of labour simply as a distribution of work in work roles. Rather, he saw the work process as articulated to social relations, which defined its relation to other processes and hence defined how the doer of that work was related in society. Here we don't draw a boundary between the mode of production and the door of the home. Instead, we see that home and family are integral parts of and moments in a mode of production. Our method of work is one which raises as an empirical question the work which is done and the relations which organize and articulate that work to the social, economic, and political processes beyond and outside the home. Thus we don't cut across class or other divisions such as rural/urban differences in a society to discover the lineaments of the family and then return to the abstracted family to discover how it 'varies' in differing class and historical contexts. We begin with a method which locates the family and women's work in the home and in the actual social relations in which they are embedded. Thus we shall be trying to understand the inner life and work of the family and the personal relations of power between husband and wife as products of how family relations are organized by and in economic and political relations of capitalism. The relation between internal and external, between the personal dimensions of relations – those relations wherein particular individuals confront, co-operate, and work together as individuals – and those relations which are organized as economic and political ones are all key to women's experience of the personal as political and as a relation of inequality.

Behind the personal relations of women and men in the familial context are economic and political processes which provide the conditions, exigencies, opportunities, powers, and weaknesses of the interactional process. The economic and political processes are there as a continual presence giving shape, limits, and conditions to what goes forward, and – as in every other aspect of a capitalist mode of production – supplying change and necessitating adaptation, rendering the examples of lifetime experience of previous generations irrelevant as models for each succeeding generation. Our strategy seeks for the determination and shaping of the interpersonal forms of domination and oppression of women in the economic and political relations in which the family is imbedded.

In the analysis which follows, class and family – or class and patriarchy – will not be viewed as opposing and incompatible terms placing us in an either/or situation at every point. Rather, our strategy will be one relating the specific form of the family to the class organization of a changing capitalist society. The conception of class we will use is a Marxist one, which identifies classes on the basis of differing relations to the means of production. For instance, the ruling class appropriates and controls the means of production. In turn, it is supported by a class which labours to produce the subsistence of the ruling class as well as its own. In a capitalist society this relation takes the form of the mutual constitution of capital and wage-labour. Surplus value is the form in which surplus labour appears and is then appropriated by the ruling class. This dichotomous class structure, however, does not become visible in a simple way for reasons which will be discussed, in part, throughout this paper. We shall see that an analysis of family relations, rather than leading us away from an examination of class, brings them into focus as a feature of an everyday world. By beginning with class as a dynamic relation central to capitalism; by recognizing families as organized by and organizing social relations (among them, class relations); and by avoiding the use of the abstracted concept of the family to make differences between classes unobservable, we can begin to see the social organization of class in a new way. We discover that the forms of family work and living are integral to the active process of constructing and reconstructing class relations, particularly as the ruling class responds to changes in the forms of property relations and in the organization of the capitalist enterprise and capitalist social relations.

It is important to preserve a sense of capitalism as an essentially dynamic process which continually transforms the 'ground' on which we stand, so that we are always looking at a continually changing historical process. It is one of the problems of the 'head world' strategy that our categories and concepts fix an actuality into seemingly unchanging forms, and then we do our work in trying to find out how to represent society in that way. We must avoid this. We must try to see our society as part of a continually moving 'surface' and avoid introducing an artificial fixity into our perceptions. The society as we find it at any one moment is the product of an historical process. It is a process which is not 'completed,' in that the various 'impulses' generated by the *essentially* dynamic process of capitalism do not come to rest in their own completion or in the working-out to the point of equilibrium of systemic interactions. The process of change is itself unceasing, and at any moment we catch only an atemporal slice of a moving process. Hence, to understand the properties, movement, and 'structure' of the present, we must be able to separate the strands of development which determine their present character and relations.

Our discussion here of the present bases of women's inequality and its relation to class and family will sketch the differing histories of women and the form of the family in the historical development of classes within capitalism. Behind the course of change and the experience of women in different classes is the same overall historical course which capitalism has taken in North America, particularly in Canada. That common course of development has shaped the histories of classes and the widely different experiences of family living for middle-class and working-class women.[8]

THE PETIT-BOURGEOIS FAMILY

Our analysis of the forms and bases of inequality among women of different classes follows an historical course, tracing changes in key relations over a period of some two hundred years. For some writers the change in women's status from pre-capitalist to capitalist forms of the family coincides with the shift of production from the family to the factory. Women's work in the home was no longer part of a productive enterprise; hence its value as an essential contribution to the productive process declined.[9]

A rather different picture will be presented here. Here, we will focus on a process of development in the social relations of capitalism, taking property as that key relation which has organized the relation of the bourgeois and petit-bourgeois family. This is not a fixed relation. Rather, it is a reciprocal process; on the one hand, of changes in the forms of property relations *fundamental* to capitalism, and on the other hand, of processes of advance and elaboration of capitalist social relations and of a deepening penetration by capital of all aspects of society. Capital reorganizes the *forms* of property relations and the specific character of the relation of property-owning 'units' to capitalist social relations. At the outset the characteristic form of property holding, the characteristic property basis of capitalist enterprises, is that of the individual – a man – whose civil person subsumes that of his wife, so that in marriage they constitute a single person equatable to him. Over the last hundred years in particular, that form of property basis for the capitalist enterprise has been displaced, though not eliminated, by the corporate form, whereby the unit becomes the corporate entity (of whatever kind) and not the individual. The implications for the family and for women's status in the family are major, for the emergence of the second form of property relation as a predominant form means that capital has been disconnected from its grounding in the bourgeois family. It means that family relations, which were formerly penetrated and organized by this relation to the individualized property form and the individualized organization of the enterprise, are now severed from that direct relation. The family is no longer constitutive of property relations under monopoly capitalism.[10]

Nevertheless, the enterprise identified with an individual owner who participates directly in the labour process has persisted, most notably in agriculture, but also as a generally recurrent form.[11] This is the typically petit-bourgeois type of enterprise. Here, perhaps most distinctly, we can see two aspects of the process described above. On the one hand, forms of property ownership permit the husband to appropriate the wife's labour in the enterprise. On the other hand, the reorganization of the relation of household to enterprise – of women's domestic work and her work directly for her husband's enterprise as being that enterprise – is articulated to changing capitalist social relations including changing financial institutions and fiscal practices, and, in general, to the increased domination of monopoly capitalist forms and thereby of finance capital.

The general emphasis here is on the significance of the economic relations to which the family is articulated as these organize the inner structure of the family, particularly with respect to the subordination of women and their domestic labour to the economic unit identified with the individual man. The Canadian record is distinctive in this respect because the character of the Canadian economy does not allow us to make use of a linear model. As new lands were opened up by the advent of the railroad in the West, the home-steading patterns which developed the eastern farmlands were replicated (though with a somewhat different technological base). In the 1930s, home-steading patterns in Dawson Creek (British Columbia)[12] showed a division of labour little different from that described by Susannah Moodie[13] and Cather-ine Parr Traill[14] in the early nineteenth century in Ontario. But behind the scene in Dawson Creek were the commercial, property-holding institutions and market processes developed to a very different level. Once the home-stead of the 1930s developed beyond the subsistence stage, it was articulated to an economic organization very different from that characteristic of early nineteenth-century Canada. Developments in Canada are characteristically truncated as indigenous processes. The development of economic institu-tions and systems elsewhere – in Britain or the United States – have entered the Canadian economic scene as fully fledged forms subordinating and arti-culating the indigenously developed economic formations. Similarly, the economic institutions which matured in eastern Canada organized and arti-culated the localized forms of enterprise developing the western provinces.

In the context of this history we can contrast earlier forms, in which the commodity-producing enterprise and the household producing the direct subsistence of both domestic and productive 'workers' formed comple-mentary sides of a single economic unit, with the more advanced forms of capitalist social relations. Where accounts were kept of this economic unit, domestic and personal expenses were included in the overall accounting for the enterprise.[15]

The reciprocal dependence of household and enterprise is visible in nine-teenth-century Canada in more than one form. At least one of the house-holds Katz describes in his study of late nineteenth-century Hamilton suggests just such a relation between household and enterprise:

John Mottashed, a 52-year-old Protestant shoemaker, born in Ireland, lived on Hughson Street in a two-storey stone house which he rented from T. Stinson. With him in 1851 lived his 40-year-old second wife Mary Ann; his married, 24-year-old son Jonathan, a miller, and his 20-year-old daughter-in-law, Mary Anne; his other sons, John, twenty-two, George, seventeen, Roger, fourteen, Joseph, six, and Charles, one; his daughters, Mary, twelve, and Anne, eight; and his stepchildren, John Calvert, an 18-year-old shoemaker, and Sarah Calvert, fifteen years old.[16]

This was the household in 1851. It is not clear whether the adult sons were working as shoemakers, but in 1861 the relation of household to enterprise is more clearly established. Mottashed's three older sons have taken up his trade, and his son, the miller, and his daughter-in-law are no longer part of the household.

For a farm of a slightly later period, Nellie McClung's autobiography gives us a picture of this type of organization of household and enterprise:

An Ontario farm, in the early '80's was a busy place, and everyone on our farm moved briskly. My father often said of my mother that she could keep forty people busy. She certainly could think of things for people to do. Maybe that was one reason for my enjoying the farmyard so much. I loved to sit on the top rail of the fence, and luxuriantly do nothing, when I was well out of the range of her vision. Mother herself worked harder than anyone. She was the first up in the morning and the last one to go to bed at night. Our teams were on the land, and the Monday morning washing on the line well ahead of the neighbours'.[17]

It is clear from McClung's account that the woman in charge of the household with this relation to the enterprise has a role going beyond that merely of labouring to produce subsistence. It is an organizational and managerial role. The daily scheduling of work, the mobilizing of available labour resources to get the work done – these were part of the housewife's work role. Characteristically, men produced the means of production and produced for the largely local market while women produced the means of direct subsistence. Dependence upon money was minimal in the farming context. As far as possible, the subsistence of family members, servants, and hired hands employed for harvesting would be produced by the women – wives, daughters, and servants. A substantial farm, such as that described by Nellie McClung, would have employed servants of both sexes. Women in such households established rights in their own products so that when there was a surplus they could market it themselves.

At an earlier time the successful homestead would develop towards the type of household-enterprise organization described by Nellie McClung. At later stages homesteading enters a very different set of economic relations: it constitutes a subsistence economy. The division of labour between husband and wife and children as they become of age to participate produces their own survival. The contribution each makes is indeed essential, and it is hard to see how issues of relative power and status arise in such a context. However that may be, when the homestead develops to the point of producing a marketable surplus and enters economic relations already formed to constitute an economic unit of a determinate type, in which men are the economic agents, the force of these relations becomes apparent. In the mid-west, this experience was part of the impetus to women's suffrage and to the changes in matrimonial property laws (minimal though they were) which followed on the success of the campaign for suffrage.

There is an experience which is superficially similar to the work organization and division of labour of the Ontario farm described by McClung, but very different in its actualities both as an experience and in its underlying structure. In a Canadian novel based on her own experience as a schoolteacher boarding with a farm family, Martha Ostenso tells a story of tyranny of a farmer over his wife and daughters, and of the special drudgery of his wife's existence.[18]

To understand this radical difference in the internal organization of the farm family we must examine how the later farm family is articulated to the later agricultural economy. The change is a departure from the form in which the production for the subsistence of those labouring on the farm was integral to its economy. In this farm, as we've seen, women played a key role. What has happened in between the childhood scene described by Nellie McClung and that described by Ostenso in her novel are changes in the political economy of Canadian farming. Political and economic policies in Canada during the late nineteenth and early twentieth centuries combined railroad expansion with land settlement through promoting extensive immigration.[19] The latter was a political imperative in defence of the threat of incorporation of western Canada into the United States and also served to develop a commodity (wheat) on which the railroad could depend for freight. As a bonus, the railroad created, and to a large extent dominated, a highly speculative real-estate market. The immigrants who built up the wheat economy of the Canadian prairies were, in many instances, financed by mortgages on their land and bank loans for tools, seed, and other necessities for which their crop stood as collateral. They did not begin, as homesteaders characteristically did, by producing their own subsistence and remaining to a large extent outside the market economy.

Ostenso's novel attests to the fact that survival for the immigrant farmer in this squeeze depended on the production of a single cash crop. Everything must be subordinated to that. In this context, then, women's labour is substituted for hired labour both in working the land and in the production of subsistence for the family. Furthermore, her labour is substituted as far as possible for labour in the form of manufactured commodities for which money must be found. Increased inputs of her labour eke out the lack of money at every possible point in the enterprise. Her time and energy, indeed her life, are treated as inexhaustible. She must, in addition, bear children because their labour is also essential. Women were virtually *imported* into Canada at this period to serve these functions.

Further, in this relation she is totally subordinate to her husband. She has no independent economic status or independent source of money. There are no local sources of employment for women. And, while such laws as property, debt, and credit endow him with full economic status, they do not do the same for her. He is responsible for the debts on the land; he owns it insofar as he can be said to own it; the monetary income from the crops is his. Her labour contributes to his capacity to act in the economic sphere but does not further her own. These forms of matrimonial property law establish title to land in such a way as to provide for its standing as collateral to loans, or for being mortgaged. They are integral to the constitution of that type of economic organization in which the family functions as a small business in a fully developed capitalist economy. Moreover, the functioning of a highly speculative real-estate market was facilitated by single and unencumbered titles to real property. The patterns of drudgery and tyranny described as the farm woman's experience by Ostenso and others are generated by a political economy of this kind.

The extraction of surplus labour through mortgages and loans to farmers and homesteaders at this period took a distinctive form in relation to this rural petite bourgeoisie. The interest on loans and mortgages concealed, as did the wage, a relation of exploitation in which the farming household produced surplus value for the capitalist. The property form identified the farm with the individual male farmer. His success in accumulating over and above what he had to pay out in interest depended generally upon exploiting the labour of women, both domestically and as supplementary labour on the land. This is the situation Nellie McClung presents to typify the injustices and suffering of farm women:

I remember once attending the funeral of a woman who had been doing the work for a family of six children and three hired men, and she had not even a baby carriage to make her work lighter. When the last baby was three days old, just in threshing time, she died. Suddenly, and without warning, the power went off, and she quit without notice. The bereaved husband was the most astonished man in the world. He had never known Jane to do a thing like that before, and he could not get over it. In threshing time, too![20]

Farm women of that period were vividly conscious of this relation and of the injustice of laws which deprived them of the fruits of their own labour and permitted its appropriation by men as a basis for economic activity. For example, in 1910 a Saskatchewan farmeress (self-styled) stated the issue as follows:

It may not be so in every part of the province, but here it is not the bachelor who is making the most rapid progress, buying land and in every way improving the country, but it is the married men – and why? One wonders if the women have nothing to do with this. Who does the economizing if not the women? And pray tell me what incentive a woman has to work longer hours everyday than her husband, if she is to have no say in the selling or mortgaging of land her hard work has helped to pay for? Is it not the women who deny themselves most when the bills come due? It is not for myself that I so much want our rights as for our unfortunate sisters who, no matter how hard they toil, can never get what they merit. Several women in this neighbourhood have land, and I do not know of one who is not anxious for the dower law and homesteads for women, and most of them for equal suffrage.[21]

In the political economy of prairie development, women at this period were doing much the same kind of work as they did in the farm of the nineteenth century. Yet the social relations organizing their work and their relation to their husbands were very different. Rather than playing a leading managerial role in the household/enterprise as a whole, they became subordinated to a market and financial structure through their husband, who, as property owner, acted as economic agent. The husband extracted surplus labour from his wife, the results of which were allocated through the mortgage and loan system between him and those to whom he paid interest. Writings of this period expressing the perspective of women – whether in novel or journalistic form, such as those of the Saskatchewan farmeress[22] or Nellie McClung[23] or the U.S. writer, Freeman – show an implicit or explicit hostility of women to men and a sharp recognition of women's interests as opposed to those of men. Women sought various means of limiting and controlling how they were exploited. Securing some rights in the property they helped to accumulate was only one way. Suffrage also was a means to this.

There were other ways. One major form was the withdrawal of women's participation in the labour on the farm, which accompanied the increased affluence of Canadian farming. A friend in British Columbia described how her mother prevented her from acquiring the manual skills and strength which would make her useful in 'his' enterprise and thus make it less likely that she would be called upon to help. Kohl indicates that this may be a more general practice.[25] Property rights constituting the man as economic agent have only very recently begun to be modified. The celebrated Murdoch case drew the attention of rural women to the fact, of which many were unaware, that their labour did not entitle them to a share in the property. Mrs Murdoch had worked for twenty-five years on her husband's ranch, doing more than the domestic work. A large part of the work of cattle ranching she did herself since, in addition to what she did when her husband was there, she took over the whole enterprise for the five months of the year he took paid employment. Yet her labour did not, in the view of the courts, entitle her to a share in the property she had helped to create. Even the dissenting opinion of Bora Laskin did not recognize the wife's contribution of labour to the overall enterprise as constituting a claim on the property. He dissented only on the grounds that her contribution had been exceptional. Women's labour as such – as the labour of a wife – had no claim.

Though petit-bourgeois forms of production are no longer the predominant form in Canada, the farm as an economic unit, as well as other independent businesses, still organize and incorporate women's labour in much the same way. The husband is constituted as economic agent appropriating his wife's labour as part of the enterprise. He cannot pay her a wage and deduct it from his income tax, according to Marchesault-Lussier: 'La loi de l'impôt dit: lorsqu'une personne a reçu une rémunération à titre d'employé de son conjoint, le montant de cette rémunération ne doit pas être déduit lors du calcul du revenu du conjoint ni inclus dans le calcul du revenu de l'employé.'[26] (The tax law states: when a person has received remuneration as the employee of his or her spouse, the amount of the remuneration cannot be deducted in the calculation of the income of the spouse nor added in the calculation of the income of the employee.) A wife working in her husband's business cannot pay into the pension plan and is not insured for injuries on the job. Other than in Ontario and in Quebec (where the marriage contract may make provision), a wife has no assurance of a share in the assets of the business to which she has contributed directly – let alone the indirect contributions she has made in the form of domestic labour.

In the farm setting there is no physical separation of household and enterprise. Women's work in and around the household – both as direct producer of primary resources (gardening, keeping hens, etc.) and in processing and storing farm produce in general – sharply reduces the monetary costs of maintaining the family labour force. Nevertheless, the earlier complementary relation has disappeared, and with it the managerial role played, for example, by Nellie McClung's mother.[27] The organization of the farm as an economic unit is vested in the person of the husband. Wives, according to Carey, are not viewed as part of the enterprise: 'Men view women as "helpers," and women themselves often underestimate their own indispensable contribution to the farm.'[28] The man as economic agent and property owner articulates the farm as a productive process to the structure of large-scale agribusiness. In this relation, women's domestic labour, the economies she can achieve, combined with work on the farm and sometimes part-time employment outside, contribute to the profits of agribusiness. Carey points out that 'Agribusiness corporations have indirectly admitted that they cannot pay anyone to work for them as cheaply as a farmer, his wife and children would work for a family farm.'[29] Individual ownership by the man and his legal capacity to appropriate the unpaid labour of his wife enter into very different relations at different points in the development of capitalism. It is in this relation that 'value' arises, and it is this relation which organizes the internal relations of the family.

THE RISE OF MONOPOLY CAPITAL AND THE
CHANGING MIDDLE-CLASS FAMILY

The development of the corporate forms of ownership and economic agency increasingly separate the spheres of economic relations and of the family and household unit. The social construction of the individual man as agent or actor arises at the juncture of these two spheres. The forms of property and the social relations of the economy organize domestic labour in relation to the individual man in determinate ways. Under capitalism these relations are in a continual process of change, producing an ever-increasing concentration of capital. Quantitative changes have been accompanied by major modifications in the forms of property ownership, in the organization of the market and of financial and commercial processes, as well as of management and technology. These changes have also radically modified the organization of the middle-class family.

In the *Grundrisse*, Marx writes of commodity production and the market process as externalizing relations of dependency among individuals that were previously embedded in the particularized feudal relations of lord and serf to land.[30] This process continues with the rise of monopoly capital and begins to develop as an externalization of property relations and an objectification of managerial and organizational processes. The continuity and accumulation of capital so precariously provided for by individual forms of property were externalized as corporations, trusts, cartels, joint-stock companies, etc. Markets organized earlier as a series of independent transactions are progressively integrated as a single sequence of ordered transactions from original seller to final destination. This required co-ordination at a different level than could be met by economic units tied into the household and family. Economic organization became increasingly separated from the local organization of the household. Men moved to and from the two 'levels' of organization, participating in each. With the rise of corporate forms, they became the agents of capital by virtue of their positions in an organization, whatever their capacity. Director, manager, so-called owner – the relations, powers, and activities of each are features of large-scale organization.[31] Their relations, roles, and performances are mediated by the corporation as a property-holding form. The new forms of property are a differentiated structure externalizing property relations as a system of specialized roles.

The concentration of capital in the corporate form developed rapidly in Canada in the period just before the First World War, when the number of companies actually declined.[32] These developments coincided with similar ones in the United States. They were marked there in the Progressive Era by an explicit linkage of government to corporate interests; the development through government support of essential administrative structures, regulative processes, legal forms, and economic knowledge; and an attempt to incorporate trade union organization into an integrated corporatist conception of society.[33] The development of corporations and the concomitant administrative and professional structures in Canada was slower; agriculture did not lose its leading position until the 1930s, and Canada's development of a secondary industrial structure has never been strong. But the process has been essentially the same, and insofar as American companies have penetrated the Canadian economy, it has, of course, been the same process.

Over a period of time the corporate form becomes the legal constitution for all sizes of business, although for small business it is elective. Organizationally, it completes the separation of family and household from economy – or rather from the economy as differentiated and specialized processes. Economic relations are increasingly differentiated and specialized at national and international levels. Earlier forms of externalized economic relations still depended upon networks of kinsfolk in varying degrees. The middle-class family was a broader conception than the household, representing an organization of common interests vested in more than one privately owned enterprise or professional occupation. The separation of family and business world was blurred. Economic organization was supported and organized by kin and familial relations. The primarily domestic work of women was not isolated from the relational politics of business, quite apart from other ways in which women's skills could be involved in business enterprise. The advancement and security of the family involved the active participation of women in more than one way. Allegiances, decisions about character, the back-door informational processes known as gossip – these were all part of the ordinary world in which business was done and were integral to it. But the corporate form supplants these processes with its own. Those employed must owe allegiance to the organization and not to the family. Specific competencies and qualifications become of greater importance than family ties. Alliances established within the business structures and networks themselves become more central than alliances in the local area or within a kin network. As the economic process is sealed off, women in the household are isolated, and the domestic world becomes truly privatized. The locus of advancement for the individual ceases to be identified with his family connections and with the advancement of the kin constellation. It becomes identified with his individualized relation to the corporate enterprise. It is this which later becomes institutionalized as a career. The domestic labour of the middle-class household is increasingly organized as a personal service to the individual man. Its relation to the business enterprise in which he is an actor arises in how the household work and organization are subordinated to its requirements as they become his.

The relation through which men appropriated women's labour is changed. The relation is no longer part of the organization of the enterprise in relation to the economy, in which women are included. Now an individual man appropriates as his the work done by his wife or other women of his family. The individual man becomes the enterprise so far as the family is concerned. The earliest and most typical form of this is that of the individual professional. It becomes general as the *career*, rather than individual ownership, structures the entry and activity of the individual as economic agent. As the corporate form of organizing agency and ownership become primary, the individual's agency and relation to the means of production are organizationally mediated. The relation of appropriation becomes highly personalized. It becomes a general form characterizing the relations of middle-class women and men in work situations in the home and outside.

This is visible in many forms. It is present, for example, in what we do not know about women in the past. It is present in our ignorance, until recently, of the fact that the public figure of British astronomer William Herschel concealed that of a second astronomer, his sister Caroline, who shared his work, perhaps shared his discoveries, made discoveries of her own, kept house for him and acted as his secretary.[34] When a group of eminent sociologists wrote accounts of how one of their major pieces of work was done, some described a very substantial contribution by their wives. No one raised questions about the fact that the husband appropriated that work as his and that the wives' work contributed to the advancement of their husbands' careers and reputations and not to their own.[35]

The middle-class relation of appropriation by men of women's work is incorporated into professional, bureaucratic, and managerial organizations. It appears as a differentiation of men's and women's roles, providing for the structuring of a career for the former in positions which are technically specialized and superordinate, and a truncated structure of advancement for the latter in positions which are skilled, but ancillary and subordinate to those of men and, of course, lower paid. Women were and still are secretaries, graduate nurses, dental hygienists, and elementary class-room teachers. Men were and still are managers, doctors, dentists, and principals and vice-principals of elementary schools. Prentice's study of 'the feminization of teaching' in nineteenth-century Canada indicates that as the school system expanded, the structuring of women's and men's roles was consciously designed to permit men in the teaching profession a career and salary at a professional level. This was possible only by allocating a substantial part of the work to women teachers, whose rates of pay were depressed and whose advancement was limited.[36] Until recently these forms of employment for middle-class women were institutionalized as a transitional status between childhood and marriage. Possibly competition and social contradiction between women's occupational status and marriage and subordination to the husband were avoided by terminating employment on marriage or by ensuring that married women did not occupy professional positions of any authority.[37]

In these developments we find the social and material bases of the form of family which we have taken as typical. We only now become aware of it as a distinct, historical, and cultural form in moving away from it. This is the household and family organization which is a distinct economic unit, primarily a 'consuming' unit; that is, one in which women's domestic labour producing the subsistence for the individual members depends upon a money income. Household and family are increasingly tied to the individual man's career and less to an interlinking of family relations and enterprises. Household and family are enucleated. The interests of the wife are held to be intimately bound up with her husband's career. In various ways she is expected to support him morally and socially, as well as through the ways in which her domestic labour ensures both his ordinary physical well-being and his proper presentation of self. His career should pay off for her in increments of prestige in the relevant social circles and in home furnishings, a larger home – in general, in the material forms in which his advancement in the organization may be expressed in relations between neighbours, friends, and colleagues. As corporations increase in size and the managerial structure is increasingly objectified, a sharp contradiction arises between individual autonomy and subordination to authority. There is a peculiarly difficult combination of the need to exercise initiative, to give leadership, and to take risks as ingredients of a successful career and the requirements of conformity to organizational exigencies, norms, and criteria of achievement in a hierarchical structure. Hence 'tension management' comes to be seen as an important responsibility of middle-class wives.

As the professional, government, and corporate apparatuses become consolidated as a ruling apparatus, forms of action in words and symbols become fully differentiated. Language is constituted as a discrete mode of action. This requires a division of labour which will organize and provide for the necessary material aspects of communication. Processes of action which are merely communicative depend on specific divisions of labour as well as a technology; hence the elaboration of clerical work. But women's domestic labour also comes to be organized specifically to service this conceptually organized world of action. As I have written elsewhere:

It is a condition of a man's being able to enter and become absorbed in the conceptual mode that he does not have to focus his activities and interest upon his bodily existence. If he is to participate fully in the abstract mode of action, then he must be liberated also from having to attend to his needs, etc. in the concrete and particular. The organization of work and expectations in managerial and professional circles both constitutes and depends upon the alienation of men from their bodily and local existence. The structure of work and the structure of career take for granted that these matters are provided for in such a way that they will not interfere with his action and participation in that world. Providing for the liberation from the Aristotelian categories [of time and space] of which Bierstedt speaks, is a woman who keeps house for him, bears and cares for his children, washes his clothes, looks after him when he is sick and generally provides for the logistics of his bodily existence.[38]

The home, then, becomes an essential unit in organizing the abstracted modes of ruling in the context – the necessary and ineluctable context – of the local and particular.

These changes introduce a new subordination of the home to the educational system. The technological, accounting, and communicative practices of the emerging ruling apparatus require appropriate skills as a condition of entry and of action in its modes. Language skills, indeed, perhaps just those styles of speech identified originally by Bernstein as an elaborated code,[39] are essential to participation in this form of action and being. The work of mothering in relation to the work of the school becomes an essential mediating process in the production and reproduction of class relations among the bourgeoisie and against the working class.

The educational system and access to the educational system, mediated and controlled by family, home, and, above all, by the work of women as mothers, come to provide the major transgenerational linkage of class. Children are no longer prospective actors in the moving history of family relations entwined with property and economic enterprise. Sons are no longer prospectively those who will carry on family businesses and hence provide for the continuity of capital built in the work of one generation towards the next. Daughters are no longer those who will consolidate alliances or relations linking social, economic, and political relations into a network of kin. The child progressively becomes the object of parental work, particularly the work of mothers, aimed at creating a definite kind of person, with distinct communicative skills in speech and writing and with capacities to take advantage of an educational process through which he or she can become advantaged.

Much of the literature on the relation between family, class, and education fails to recognize that it is the product of the work of women. The school as an organization of work presupposes prior and concomitant work which is done by women in the home. This work is never named as such. It is seen in ways which render the time, skill, and effort involved as invisible. It is translated into love and responsibility or is merely treated mechanically – home as an 'influence' on school performance; the family as an 'influence' on school achievement; etc. But the relation is not recognized as an actual work process. Here, for example, is a description of a 'home' setting which is favourable to the successful child:

David is the son of professional parents who have themselves been educated in a grammar school. They provide him with facilities for doing homework in a separate room and light a fire when necessary. There is therefore little interruption from other members of the family or from television and radio. If he has trouble with his homework he can turn to either his mother or father for help, and many books of reference are available. His cultural background is constantly a help to him at school and in his homework. Mother or father may even inspect his homework regularly or occasionally.[40]

The authors are properly aware of the significance of economic factors in this picture, and it is indeed contrasted with the situation of a working-class boy of similar age and abilities. What is not visible to them, apparently, is the work of mothering – which provides the facilities, inhibits interruption, cleans, lays the fire, feeds, provides an orderly environment – and, indeed, the work involved in providing the 'cultural background' which becomes his. In general, middle-class mothers are both expected to and do spend a great deal of time and work in organizing the home to facilitate their children's work in school and in developing their children's skills in the non-specific ways summed up in 'cultural background' or 'language abilities.' Somehow it is often described as if the language skills of a child are acquired by some kind of osmosis merely from the atmosphere of the home. There is a lack of recognition of the amount of actual work and thought which middle-class women, having time, opportunity, and skills, expend upon their children. Mothers train their children in the responsibilities of school work, in scheduling, in 'mood control,' and in the organization of physical behaviour adapting them to the class-room. Mothers may correct their children's deficiencies and prevent errors, lapses, and delays from becoming visible at school and, hence, from being consequential in the child's record. This is work. It is an important part of how middle-class women's work in the home serves to organize and sustain the inequalities of class.

The emergence and progressive integration of the new form of ruling apparatus, distinctively a communicative practice, is also an ideologically informed and organized practice. Determinate social organization differentiates and separates the enterprise from particular individuals and particular places. We can find in Weber's analysis of the bureaucratic type of authority, the essential prescription for the formation of a managerial or administrative structure serving the objectives of an enterprise quite independent of the objectives of those who 'perform' it, make its objectives theirs, and thereby bring it into being. The bases of access to positions in the ruling apparatus change. As these no longer clearly differentiate on sex lines but call for technical knowledge, qualifications, and so forth, the barriers to women's entry are weakened. In response, the barriers are artificially and actively reinforced, and ideological forms aimed specifically at the organization of middle-class women's relation to the ruling apparatus are developed.

The rise of monopoly capitalism, rather than instantly precipitating women into the private sphere, initiates a struggle. On the one hand, the barriers to women's participation are reinforced and reorganized; and on the other, women strive to break through barriers already weakened by the advance of capitalism. This struggle has focused particularly on women's education. The conception of a specialized education for women preparing them for domesticity points to a new need to plan and organize women's relation to the home. It also provides that the very ideological channels through which women's potential access to a wider arena opens should be those through which they would learn the practice of their confinement. Ideological organization has been central in organizing the role and social relations of middle-class women.

As education became the key link in the access to economic agency, women's access to education had to be regulated. Steps were taken to exclude women from professional, bureaucratic, and political positions as these were found to be vulnerable.[41] Active forms of ideological and state repression responding to incursions by middle-class women were developed. An educational system systematically differentiating boys from girls was put in place. Girls were streamed so that they would be disqualified for the kinds of advanced training giving access to the professions. The hidden curriculum trained them to be open and conforming to the ideological initiatives and technical practices increasingly originating from experts located in academic settings.

Women's post-secondary training, insofar as it is not in subordinate forms of professional training, such as nursing, pharmacy, and teaching, emphasizes arts and social science. The stress of school and post-secondary education is on women's language abilities, on their knowledge of social science, on psychology, on art and literature.[42] Women are prepared for their ancillary clerical roles in management. They are provided with the language skills needed to give the 'cultural background' on which their future children's success in school will depend. They are also trained to respond to the work of psychological and sociological experts, to psychiatrists, and to physicians as authorities, and to make practical use of their understanding of the new ideologies produced by such specialists. These ideological skills link the private domestic sphere to the professional, bureaucratic, and managerial controls of the ruling apparatus. The ideological organization co-ordinated and still co-ordinates the family and women's roles in relation to the changing and various needs of the ruling apparatus. Education not only ensured that middle-class women would not end with the types of skills which would give them an undeniable claim to entry as active participants to the ruling apparatus, but it also laid down specific ideological controls through which the changing relations of a rapidly shifting capitalist development could be reformulated and reorganized as they were fed through to the family and to women's work in the family. What mothers did in the home affected what children did in school. But what went on in the home was the 'wild' factor uncontrolled by the hierarchical structure of the educational process. Ideological organization, originating in a scientific establishment and mediated by the mass media, came to co-ordinate the private and state sectors of responsibility for children, as indeed it did in other spheres.

These relations among ideological organizations – first, a family form subordinating women in a subcontractual relation[43] to a ruling apparatus of government, management, and professions mediated as personal services to husband and children, and second, an educational system preparing women for these family functions and for the essentially subordinate clerical and professional roles – are the matrix of the experience of patriarchy among middle-class women. The authority of men over women is the authority of a class and expresses class 'interests.' The inner complicity of women in their own oppression is a feature of class organization. The concept of 'patriarchy' explicates as a social relation between women and men the conjunction of institutions locking middle-class women into roles which are ancillary but essential to the ruling apparatus and specifically silencing them by giving them no access to the ideological, professional, and political means in which their experience might be communicated to other women.

THE CHANGING MATERIAL BASES OF DEPENDENCY

Dependence of married women, and particularly women with children, on men and men's salaries or wages is a feature of both middle-class and working-class family relations in contemporary capitalism. This is not simply a matter of a universal family form characteristic of a species rather than a culture or mode of production. Women's dependency must be seen as arising in a definite social form and, as we have suggested, must be organized rather differently in differing class settings and relations. One view identifies the emergence of this type of family organization with the rise of capitalism. As the productive process is increasingly taken over by the industrial organization of production, the family becomes a consuming, rather than a producing, unit, and women's domestic labour ceases to play a socially productive role and becomes instead a personal service to the wage earner. Her domestic labour reproduces the labour power of the individual worker. Here is Seccombe's account:

With the advent of industrial capitalism, the general labour process was split into two discrete units: a domestic and an industrial unit. The character of the work performed in each was fundamentally different. The domestic unit reproduced labour power for the labour market. The industrial unit produced goods and services for the commodity market. This split in the labour process had produced a split in the labour force roughly along sexual lines – women into the domestic unit, men into industry.[44]

But as we acquire more historical knowledge of women we find that the sharpness of this supposed historical moment becomes blurred. The emergence of the dependent family form is slow and seemingly contingent upon elaborations and developments of the original separation of the domestic economy from the industrial process. As we explore the dynamic process at work we can recognize a contradiction in the rise of capitalism so far as women and their relation to the family are concerned. It seems that the same industrial capitalism leading apparently to a restriction and narrowing of the scope of women's work in the home and to her own and her children's dependence on a man's wage is also a process which potentially advances women's independence by creating conditions under which women can earn enough to support themselves, and perhaps even to support their children. Earlier productive labour was tied to sex differences by varying physical and biological situations and also by the intimate ties of skills, which represented a true specialization of persons from childhood or youth onwards. As production is increasingly mediated by machines and increasingly organized as a form of enterprise specifically separated from particular individuals and their local relations, it also becomes increasingly indifferent to social differentiations, such as gender or race.[45] At every new level in the development of productive capacity in capitalism, this contradiction is apparent. Capitalism continually presents the possibility of women's independence and, at the same time, engenders conditions and responses which have constituted a fully dependent form of family unit. The dependence of both middle-class and working-class women on the individual man's salary or wage must be examined in relation to the organization of the labour-market and employment possibilities for women outside the home.

Let us look first at one rather straightforward and simple picture of the relation. It is taken from the 1961 Census of Canada, as the data were available for that year. A husband, wife, and two children can model for us the family which exactly reproduces itself. Podoluk estimates that for 1961 a money income meeting the basic needs of a family of four would be $3,500.[46] Podoluk kept her estimates pretty tight. This figure represents what it would cost just to live – no frills, no discretionary purchases. If we imagine the same woman, the same children, but no man, we have a family of three, and their basic income should be $3,000. Just barely managing, but making it.

Table 1 is striking. It shows us that in 1961 only the earnings of managerial and professional women would have been sufficient to maintain at a basic level a family of two children.[47] These categories represent a rather small proportion of women in the labour force. By far the majority earn less than the income sufficient for a family of three. By contrast, the majority of men's

Table 1
Basic no frills income for four-member and three-member families,
by occupation, average earnings, and sex, 1961

	Four-member family – basic no frills income $3,500	Three-member family – basic no frills income $3,000
	Occupations and average earnings: men	Occupations and average earnings: women
Earnings more than base income	Managerial (6,673) Prof. and tech. (5,448) Sales (3,908)	Managerial (3,207)
Breaking even (or −$100 of base income)	Clerical (3,409) Transp. and comm. (3,419) Crafts and prod. (3,566)	Prof. and tech. (2,996)
Earnings less than base income	Service and recr. (3,161) Farm (1,401) Labourers (2,157)	Clerical (2,340) Sales (1,367) Service and recr. (1,158) Farm (607) Crafts and prod. (1,788) Labourers (1,449)

Source: based on J. Podoluk, *The Incomes of Canadians* (Ottawa 1968)

average earnings are at the break-even level or better, and only workers in service and recreation, farm workers, and labourers earn less than the basic income for a four-member family. Women's earnings are insufficient to provide for the four-member family in every category of women workers. Indeed, the average earnings for women in most categories fall below the basic, no-frills income needed for a two-member family ($2,500). Women's average earnings would not, for the most part, support a woman and her child. It is clear then, that as soon as a woman has a child to support, her options are sharply reduced. Quite apart from the lack of adequate child care and other sources of support, such as school meals, etc., women's earning possibilities incapacitate them from independence. Men can (or could) count on earnings which would provide both for children and a wife. Women cannot count on earnings sufficient for themselves and children.

Over time, working-class and middle-class patterns of family organization have become more alike with respect to the wife's dependence on her husband's wage or salary. But the history of that relation is very different.

Among the middle class the earlier civil status of a man simply obliterated his wife's as she was subsumed in the family economic unit identified with him. She had no place in civil society, no capacity for economic action, at least so long as she was married. What she produced and what she earned, if she did earn, were his. Later, her domestic labour becomes subordinated to the enterprise of his career, and employment outside the home is organized to ensure that the jurisdictions of male authority and appropriation of women's labour inside the home and outside it do not interfere with one another. Dependency is part of a perpetuated pattern of excluding women, and married women in particular, from functioning as independent economic agents and making their domestic and other services available to those who do.

The history of the present family form among the working class is very different. It does not begin with women's exclusion from economic activity and it does not involve the formation of a property-holding unit identified with the man. The legal forms were the same and these gave men the right to women's earnings, but the actual practice and organization of work relations and economic contributions did not conform to the middle-class pattern. The exclusive dependence of women on men's wages is only gradually established and is differently structured. For working-class women, dependence is directly on the man's wage-earning capacity and role, and the man's status and authority in the family are directly linked to his capacity to earn. Moore and Sawhill summarize the sociological studies on the effects of wives' employment outside the home on marital power relations, drawing attention to the greater effect among working-class women: 'A number of studies have found that wives who are employed exercise a greater degree of power in their marriages. Marital power is higher among women employed full-time than those working for pay part-time or not at all, and it is greatest among women with the most prestigious occupations, women who are most committed to their work, and those whose salaries exceed their husbands'. Working women have more say especially in financial decisions. This tendency for employment to enhance women's power is strongest among lower and working-class couples.'[48]

As we learn more of women's history we find that the emergence of the dependent form of the family among the working class was far from an abrupt and immediate consequence of the rise of industrial capitalism. The subsistence work of women in relation to the household as an economic unit has only gradually been supplanted by the industrial process. And only gradually have women been weaned from contributing to the *means* of household subsistence, as contrasted with labour applied to the direct production of the subsistence of its members. On the one hand, women came into competition with men for jobs in industry; on the other hand, their labour was essential in the house, so that home and family were in competition with industry for women's labour. The dependence of the mother-children unit on the male wage earner emerges rather slowly. Anderson describes, for early nineteenth century-Lancashire, a form of family in which all its members, with the exception of the very young and the very old, worked outside the home and pooled their earnings.[49] Scott and Tilly have identified a distinct form of working-class and petit-bourgeois family economy, which they describe as the 'family wage economy.'[50] It is one in which each member earns and contributes to a common fund out of which the family needs are met. They argue that, although a relatively small proportion of married women were employed in industry until relatively late in the nineteenth century, the pattern of women not working outside the home and not contributing actively to the household economy came very late. A wife who did not work and contribute directly to the means of subsistence, and who had to depend upon her husband's wage, was most definitely undesirable. Married women worked outside the home and brought money or goods into the home in all kinds of ways. Many had gardens and produced for their families and could sell the small surplus they might produce. Women were small traders, pedlars, went into domestic service, were laundresses, seamstresses, farm labourers, scavengers, as well as industrial workers.[51]

Cross's study of women's work in Montreal in the latter part of the nineteenth century shows a wide variety of enterprises in which women were employed.[52] In addition to domestic service, women worked in textile, clothing, boot and shoe, and tobacco factories. Also, 'there were many small dressmakers', milliners' and tailors' shops, and seamstresses and dressmakers worked in private houses on a daily basis.'[53] Women also did productive work in the home. Manufacturers put work out to women at piece-rates. Sometimes manufacturers supplied machines to women working at home. The manufacture of men's clothing 'was farmed out to women working in their own homes on machines that were either rented or supplied by the manufacturer. In 1892, the J.W. Mackenzie Company had 900 hands on their outside payroll and the H. Story Company had 1,400 in addition to the 130 employed in the factory.'[54] Other paid work done by women in the Montreal area at that period included running a boarding house and working in small businesses.

Of course many women workers were single, but it is also clear that many were married. It is married women who would have been working in the home. Moreover, the very rapid response to the *salles d'asile* (day-care nurseries) established by women religious orders in the 1850s indicated the extent of the need. The surviving records of two such *salles d'asile* show that many children were from families in which both parents went out to work.[55]

Under the 'family wage' economy, children are essential contributors. Children might be employed in factory work, but they had also a wide variety of opportunities for contribution, ranging from the care of younger children while parents were at work, to housekeeping, gardening, many ordinary chores such as fetching water, and, as well, odd jobs when these were available. As attendance at public school came to be enforced, the school comes into competition with the needs of the family for children's labour.[56]

With the institutionalization of universal education, children cease or have already ceased to be regular wage earners contributing to the family wage. They cease progressively to contribute to the everyday work activities of household tasks and child care. Previously the work of children would have relieved the mother of at least some of her household obligations and made it easier for her to undertake employment outside the home. The withdrawal of child labour from the household, as well as from the labour force, required the presence of mothers in the home. Indeed, the home comes to be organized around the scheduling of school and work so that the mother is tied down to the household in a way which was, in fact, new. Both the husband and children might come home for a midday meal. The school imposed standards of cleanliness, which represented a serious work commitment on the part of women, who had to pump and heat water for washing.[57] In the school context the child appears as the public 'product' of a mother's work. Her standards of housekeeping and child care begin to be subject to the public appraisal of the school system through the appearance and conduct of her child in the school. The working-class home as a work setting began to be organized by a relation to the school, as well as to the place of work. The school itself set standards for women's work and, in various ways, enforced them.

Hence the family wage economic organization is shifted to the new enucleated family form, in which wife and child make no contribution to the family economy in terms of inputs from outside, and in which both depend upon the man as wage earner. The wife, in addition, depends upon the husband for the means to reproduce the domestic order, while she is to provide him with personal service in the form of domestic labour in the home, as well as other more immediate personal services. These changes were part of the developments in capitalism and of the institutionalization of responses and adaptations to such developments. The segregated labour force we find today results from these changes. This process is the other face – that which regards the working class – of the same developments in capitalism, earlier described in relation to the bourgeoisie and middle class.

THE SUBORDINATION OF WOMEN IN THE WORKING-CLASS FAMILY

The dynamic process of capital accumulation is also one of an increasingly extensive use of machines making labour more productive, displacing labour, and making the productive process more generally indifferent to differentials of physical strength. From this process, two consequences flow for working-class women. One is the actual or potential broadening of the range of jobs and industrial settings in which women work. A second is the tendency of capitalism to generate a surplus labour population which cannot be absorbed into developing sectors and hence function as a reserve army of labour. These factors together create a highly competitive situation, which becomes acute at times of recession.

The traditionally lower wages of disadvantaged groups such as women and blacks give them an advantage in competing for jobs. Through the nineteenth and twentieth centuries this problem was a recurrent theme in male working-class views concerning women in the labour force, and in policies of trade and labour unions. The issue of women displacing men in the workforce is complemented by a concern for the implications for the family and men's status therein.[58] Conceivably, women might be paid a wage which would effectively compete with the family for women's labour. Conceivably, women might be economically independent of men. Certainly it happened that some women were earning when husbands, brothers, and sons could not.[59] These complementary themes recur again and again in the attack on women workers made by leading sectors of the trade union movement from the early nineteenth century on. Even in the 1960s, the American Federation of Labor refused its support to any kind of quota system which might rectify the inequalities experienced by blacks and women. Of the early nineteenth century, Malmgreen writes:

There was a psychological as well as an economic basis for the male workers' uneasiness, for the chance to earn a separate wage outside the home might free wives and daughters to some extent from the control of their husbands and parents. The piteous image of the sunken-cheeked factory slave must be balanced against that of the boisterous and cheeky 'fact'ry lass.' Lord Ashley, speaking on behalf of the regulation of child and female labour in factories, warned the House of Commons of the 'ferocity' of the female operatives, of their adoption of male habits – drinking, smoking, forming clubs, and using 'disgusting' language. This, he claimed, was 'a perversion of nature,' likely to produce 'disorder, insubordination, and conflict in families.'[60]

The voice here is that of the ruling class, but on this issue the working-class man and the ruling class have often been united. Malmgreen notes that in the early nineteenth century this view appears particularly prevalent among leading artisans in the working-class movements of Britain. It is the interests of a similar type of worker – crafts and trades workers – which were represented in the American Federation of Labor (AFL). The AFL played a leading role in the organization of a sex-stratified (as well as a racially stratified) labour-market as corporate capitalism began its great rise in North America in the late nineteenth and early twentieth centuries.[61] During this period the AFL contributed to the institutionalization of the sexually stratified labour force we find today. These relations were imported into Canada as the so-called international unions came to dominate Canadian union organizations.[62] Industries in which both women and men worked, such as the tobacco industry, boot and shoe manufacture, textiles and clothing, printing, and the like, established an internal stratification ensuring exclusive male access to the more highly skilled and better-paid positions.[63] Under Gompers's leadership, the trade union movement in North America became for women a systematic organization of weakness relative to men, and a systematic organization of preferential access to skills and benefits for men. In marked contrast to the class orientation of the Industrial Workers of the World (IWW), there was little interest in unionizing women other than as a means of control.[64] There was a fear that bringing numbers of women into a union would result in 'petticoat government.'[65] Women's locals were sometimes given only half the voting power of men on the grounds that they could only contribute half the dues.[66] The Canadian Trades and Labour Congress in the early twentieth century had as an avowed goal the elimination of women, particularly married women, from the work-force.[67] The failure of the 1907 Bell Telephone operators' strike in Toronto is, in part, tied to the absence of serious support or effort by the International Brotherhood of Electrical Workers to organize the women operators, even though the strikers themselves sought unionization.[68]

Struggles to restrict women's participation, and particularly married women's participation in the labour force, went on under various guises. It does not seem likely, however, that union efforts, even when supported by at least some sections of the women's movement at that period, would have been effective in reconstituting the family in a way that maintained women's dependence on men's wages, without the active intervention of the bourgeois state apparatus. The corporatist ideology enunciated by Mackenzie King formulated the principles of, and legitimated, the administrative and regulatory forms through which trade union organization was articulated to state mechanisms aimed at controlling and deploying the labour force in the service of monopoly capital.[69] In these contexts the implicit alliance between state and trade unions with a common interest – stemming from very different bases – becomes effective in subordinating women to domestic labour and in restricting their participation in the labour force.[70]

The emergence of national and international market and financial organizations; of an organization of productive processes implanted into local areas rather than arising indigenously and conforming to standardized technical plans and standardized machines, tools, and other equipment; and of a universalizing of managerial and technical processes called for a new kind of labour force. Similar exigencies arose also in relation to the military requirements of imperialist expansion and the devastating wars resulting from the conflict of rival empires. This new labour force had to be capable of entering the industrial process anywhere in the society. The need was not only for technically skilled workers, but more generally for a *universalized* labour force, stripped of regional and ethnic cultures, fully literate, English-speaking, familiar with factory discipline and the discipline of the machine, and, in relation to the military enterprise in particular, physically healthy. In the production of this labour force, mothering, as a form of domestic labour, was seen as increasingly important.

In the legislation passed during this period, we can see two aspects of state interest: on the one hand, a concern to restrict the ways in which industry competed with the home for women's labour; on the other hand, an interest in laying the legal and administrative basis for a family form in which the costs of supporting the wife and of providing for children would be borne by the wage of the man.[71] The latter motive has obviously special attractions during periods of economic depression. For the United States, an active campaign involving government, the media, and unions to get women, and married women in particular, out of the labour force has been described.[72]

From the early twentieth century through to the mid-twenties there are a series of legislative measures directed towards the family and women.[73] These served to reorganize the legal and administrative basis of the family. Laws which earlier entitled the husband and father to appropriate the earnings of his wife and children disappeared. New legislation was passed requiring men to support their families whether they lived with them or not.[74] Welfare policies were developed incorporating similar principles. These have been built into the welfare practices of today so that, for example, a man sharing the house of a woman welfare recipient may be assumed to be supporting her and her children, hence permitting the suspension of her welfare payments. Unemployment insurance and pension plans, introduced subsequently, also created an administrative organization enforcing women's dependence on men in marriage. The seemingly genial and recent legal recognition of the common-law relation is in fact part of the same theme. Furthermore, the state entry into the socialization of children through the public education system provided an important source of control. Streaming patterns similar to those characterizing the experience of middle-class women prevented working-class women from acquiring the fundamental manual and technical skills on which access to skilled, and even semiskilled, work in industry came increasingly to depend. Thus a significant part of the increased cost of producing the new kind of labour force, including the costs of women's specialization in domestic labour, would be borne directly by the working man's wage.[75]

It would, however, be a serious mistake to view the interests of the trade unions at the earlier period as representing a simple patriarchal impulse. Subsistence of both men and women, and their children depended upon the work of women, in a way which is no longer so. The provision of shelter and heat, the purchase and preparation of food, the making and maintenance of clothing, and the overall management of wages were survival work and survival skills. The physical maintenance of the male bread-winner was essential. When food was short, women and children went without to ensure that the 'master' got enough, or at least the most of what there was.[76] It must be emphasized that this was an interdependent unit which maximized the survival possibilities of all its members. Black describes the dilemmas arising for women when unemployment or low wages made it impossible to support a wife and family, thereby forcing women to wage-labour. She must choose at that time between the care she could give her children by staying home on a wage, which meant that they would starve, and the risks of leaving them to go out to work to earn enough for them to eat.[77]

Characteristic of the working-class family, in which the man is the bread-winner and the women and children are dependent, is a marked subordination of women to men. Control over funds is a distinct male prerogative. A husband's resistance to his wife's going out to work goes beyond the practicalities of the family's economic well-being.[78] Working-class women learn a discipline which subordinates their lives to the needs and wishes of men. The man's wage is his; it is not a family wage. Varying customs have developed around the disposal of this. Sometimes there appears to be a survival of the 'family wage' tradition whereby the wife takes the whole wage and manages its various uses, including a man's pocket-money. But it is also open to men not to tell their wives what they earn and to give them housekeeping money or require them to ask for money for each purchase. It is clearly *his* money, and there is an implicit contract between a husband and wife whereby he provides for her and her children on whatever conditions he thinks best, and she provides for him the personal and household services that he demands. The household is organized in relation to his needs and wishes; mealtimes are when he wants his meals; he eats with the children or alone, as he chooses; sex is when he wants it; the children are to be kept quiet when he does not want to hear them. The wife knows at the back of her mind that he could take his wage-earning capacity and make a similar 'contract' with another woman. As wages have increased, the bread-winner's spending money has enlarged to include leisure activities which are his, rather than hers – a larger car, a motorcycle, a boat. Even a camper often proves more for him than for her, since for her it is simply a transfer from convenient to less convenient conditions of the same domestic labour she performs at home.

For working-class women this relation has a political dimension. The discipline of acceptance of situations over which they have no control and the discipline of acceptance of the authority of a man, who also has in fact no control over the conditions of his wage-earning capacity, are not compatible with the bold and aggressive styles of political or economic action which are characteristic of working-class organization. Women's sphere of work and responsibility is defined as subordinate and dependent to that in which men act. The children's well-being, the production of the home – these require from women a discipline of self-abnegation and service as exacting sometimes as that of a religious order. Masculinity and male status are, in part, expressed in men's successful separation from, and subordination of, the sphere of women's activity, as well as the visibility of his success in 'controlling' his wife (what may go on behind the scenes is another matter).

The fact that the wage relation creates an uncertain title to male status and authority, by virtue of how its conditions are lodged in the market process, makes the visible forms of relations all the more important. Men subordinate themselves in the workplace to the authority of the foreman, supervisor, and managers. A condition of their authority in the home is this daily acceptance of the authority of others. Men assume also the physical risks and hazards of their work. They live with the ways in which capital uses them up physically and discards them mentally and psychologically. They also undertake a lifetime discipline, particularly if they elect to marry and support a wife and children. That responsibility is also a burden, and it can be a trap for working-class men as much as for working-class women. Through that relation a man is locked into his job and into the authority relations it entails. His wife's subordination, her specific personal and visible subservience, her economic dependence are evidence of his achievement. Her 'nagging,' her independent initiatives in political or economic contexts, her public challenges to his authority – these announce his failure as a man. In the political context, we find a subculture prohibiting women's participation in political activity, other than in strictly ancillary roles essentially within the domestic sphere. Thus when women organized militant action in support of the men striking in the Flint, Michigan, strike in 1937, they had to go against norms restraining women from overt forms of political action.

Earlier we cited Malmgreen's description of an instance of ruling-class fear of the 'ferocity' of female operatives. Lord Ashley clearly identified the subordination of women to men in the home with their political suppression. The ideology of weak and passive women, needing protection and support, and subordinated 'naturally' to the authority of men in the home – as it was adopted by working-class men and working-class political and economic organizations – served to secure the political control of one section of the working class by another.[79] The subordination of working-class women to men in the family, which was progressively perfected over the latter half of the nineteenth and the first quarter of the twentieth centuries, was part of the attempt of the ruling class to establish a corporate society subordinating workers through their union organization. The range of organized working-class action was progressively narrowed to economic organization restricted to the workplace. A whole range of concerns and interests arising outside the workplace in relation to health, housing, pollution, and education, remained unexpressed or expressed only indirectly. Inadvertently, working-class men combined to suppress and silence those whose work directly engaged them with such problems. Indirectly, and through the mechanism described above, they came to serve the interests of a ruling class in the political and economic subordination of half the working class.

At the outset we confronted the terms 'patriarchy' and 'class' as key terms in contrasting and opposing accounts of women's inequality in contemporary capitalist society. Resolution of the opposition has been sought in an empirical questioning of family organization as a basis for women's subordination to men. As we have examined the development of a form of the family in which women depend upon men, and the ideological and political institutions which enforce this dependency, we can begin to see patriarchy (in the sense of men's political and personal domination over women) in relation to class as part of the institutions through which a ruling class maintains its domination. At different stages in the transformation of property relations from the individual to the corporate form, middle-class women have been subordinated to the changing requirements of class organization and of the transgenerational maintenance of class. For working-class women we have seen the emergence of a dependent form of family subordinating women to men, locked in by legal and administrative measures instituted by the state, and a stratified labour-market fostered by trade unions, capitalists, and the state. These are the institutional forms which have secured the uses of women's domestic labour in the service of a ruling apparatus, ensuring and organizing the domination of a class over the means of production. They are political institutions in the sense in which the women's movement has come to understand that term, in that, they involve the exercise of power as such, whether it is a feature of specialized political institutions, such as political parties, government, and the like, or not.

Throughout the foregoing analysis we have been aware of capitalism as continually generating changes in material conditions, and of these changes as they are fed through to the 'surface,' necessitating innovations, adaptations and reorganization. Forms of political and ideological organization which are relatively successful in stabilizing the position of the ruling class at one point may, at the next, confront situations in which they are no longer effective or appropriate. This is surely the situation with respect to women today. The institutions of patriarchy organize and control in a material context that which they can no longer handle effectively. The ground has shifted under our feet.

We have pointed to a major contradiction arising for both middle-class and working-class women as capitalism advances. It is the contradiction between a capital which is becoming essentially indifferent to the sex of those who do its work, and the claims of domestic economy as an essential basis for its property relations and the reproduction of class and the labour force. With the rise of corporate capitalism, the balance begins to shift away from the domestic. In relation to middle-class women the extension of corporate capitalism, the professions, the governmental process, the elaboration of the ruling apparatus characteristic of contemporary capitalism – these require skills based on education and specialized advanced training which are not differentiated by sex. Women's exclusion becomes, then, a political institution built into the organization of education, into the uses of power characteristic of the self-governing process of professions and professional organizations, and into the conjunction of the interests of a ruling class and its male members. Earlier the contradiction emerged as a latent, and sometimes actual, competition between the domestic and the political economies for women's labour – a competition resolved for some time by restricting women's access to the labour force after marriage and, in general, by a limited range of occupations with an earning capacity below that enabling them to maintain a family unit without a husband. The political aspects of women's subordination are the institutions of patriarchy. But they could not have been effective without a corresponding material base.

Earlier too, women's domestic labour was essential to subsistence. There were no alternatives. Domestic labour has also been essential to advances in the family standard of living, which would have been originally unobtainable without the interposition of women's work in the home. Women of both the middle and working classes at different income levels could, by their personal skills, hard work, and commitment, take the wage and salary, purchase materials and tools, and combine these with labour and skill – their knowledge of cooking, cleaning, managing, laundering, shopping, etc. – to produce a subsistence level (or better) essential for family health, comfort, and, under minimal income conditions, survival. Over time, the labour women contributed to the domestic production of subsistence was displaced by labour and skill embodied in the product of industry. Progressively, capital has interposed a labour process into the home and has reorganized the work process there. At some point, what women can contribute in the form of labour no longer balances off in a comparison with what she can earn and hence add to the purchasing power of the family. The wife can no longer reduce costs to the wage earner by contributing more of her labour to the household process.

The slow but consistent upward creep of the labour force participation of married women, and, indeed, of women in general, points to the diminishing power of the domestic economy to compete with paid employment for women. The demand for certain types of women's labour increased greatly as corporate capitalism called for clerical, sales, and service workers at low cost, a demand which has more and more been met by women. The 'compact' restricting the employment of married women, and hence the direct competition of paid employment with the domestic economy controlled by the husband, has been weakened and is in decline. The assertion of individual authority by a man in restraining his wife from taking on paid employment outside the home is weakened by the disappearance of complementary restrictions in the work setting. With inflation and increasing levels of unemployment, more and more married women enter the labour force. Money earnings are essential to the family, and if the man's wage or salary does not bring in enough, then a woman's responsibilities to her home and family increasingly demand that she seek employment outside the home.

The same developments within capitalism which elaborate the apparatus of ruling are also those which result in the ever-increasing problem of the surplus labour population. Rates of unemployment have been slowly and steadily increasing, but in the current period of economic crisis they have risen sharply. For the first time, the concentration of capital in a machine technology has begun to create a surplus labour population among the middle class. The state, management, and professional organizations respond to these problems by a resort to the measures which worked earlier and, on the part of professions, by the adoption of protectionist strategies reinforcing discriminatory practices against women. The state attempts to reduce unemployment and reduce state responsibility for unemployment by using the well-worn mechanisms for forcing women into dependence upon men through its welfare policies, unemployment insurance practices, the withdrawal of subsidies for child care, etc. But these measures now function vacuously. The relation of dependency is no longer fully viable. The status quo ante cannot be reinstated. These measures, rather than having practical force in articulation to a material base, merely become the arbitrary exercise of political power.

The earlier political and ideological accommodations, institutionalized in the labour-market and the educational system, function so as to depress arbitrarily women's capacity to earn a living, to survive, and to provide for children. Of course, there are segments of both the middle class and the working class where earlier forms are successful because the underlying relations have not disappeared. Contemporary capitalism is a complex form, and Canadian political economy characteristically develops unevenly and via transitions which are often abrupt, as new levels of capitalist organization invade and overlay earlier forms. At the same time, the dislocations and the arbitrary oppression of the patriarchal forms begin to emerge. Among middle-class women and sections of the organized working class, the women's movement advances an ideology and establishes political and economic organizations through which the latent inequities are given objective expression and become the focus of organized action.

In the course of this inquiry, what the women's movement has made visible as patriarchy has been explicated as an integral part of the institutional process by which the capitalist ruling class has maintained its domination over society. It has taken different forms in relation to women in the middle classes and in the working class. The differences in class are real. They are the bases of differing formations of interest among women struggling against inequality, but the enemy is the same.

NOTES

Parts of this paper will form part of a more extensive treatment of women and class to be published as a book by New Star Books, Vancouver.

Acknowledgments: I am very much indebted to David Smith for criticisms and editorial comments. Thanks also to Vivian Crossman, Beverly Bingham, and Gordon Reichelt who typed the drafts, pieces of drafts, and final version of the paper.

1 For example, Shulamith Firestone, *The Dialectic of Sex* (New York 1970). Firestone's was one of the earliest and most influential statements of this position.
2 See Juliet Mitchell, *Psychoanalysis and Feminism* (New York 1974).
3 Engels' work is the principal theoretical foundation for this line of thought. Engels, *The Origin of the Family, Private Property and the State* (Moscow 1968)
4 V.I. Lenin, *On the Emancipation of Women* (Moscow 1974)
5 For example, Zillah Eisenstein, 'Developing a Theory of Capitalist Patriarchy and Socialist Feminism,' and 'Some Notes on the Relations of Capitalist Patriarchy'; Heidi Hartman, 'Capitalism, Patriarchy, and Job Segregation by Sex,' in *Signs*, I, 3, Part II (Spring 1976); Marlene Dixon, *Women and Class Struggle* (San Francisco 1978); Annelte Kuhn, 'Structures of Patriarchy and Capital in the Family,' in A. Kuhn and A. Wolpe, eds., *Feminism and Materialism, Women and Modes of Production* (London 1978)
6 Kate Millett's *Sexual Politics* (New York 1970) was a key work in establishing this formulation.
7 Engels, *Origin of the Family*, 73 (emphasis in original)
8 The terminology of class used here is descriptive rather than analytic. The current state of the debate on class and stratification is quite inconclusive and does not yield a decisively satisfactory terminology, let alone a theoretical account. I am currently working on the topic of women and class, and in doing so, I have treated the capitalist elite, the middle classes, and the petite bourgeoisie as a single class in relation to contemporary forms of property. It is an internally differentiated class articulated to the regional basis of the capitalist economy, actively organized and reorganized as a class by ideological processes, by the organization of networks of personal relations, and by the maintenance of privileged access to state services, including education, governmental regulation, and so forth. Within this class we can distinguish between a petite bourgeoisie in which the individual owner contributes his/her own labour to the enterprise, a middle bourgeoisie (which I have continued to describe here as the middle class since this is the customary term and I don't want to introduce new terminologies in this paper), and a great bourgeoisie occupying key positions in the ownership and marketing of capital as a com-

modity. The working class can also be seen to be stratified, but its overall internal structure as a class is not actively organized by the working class itself but largely as responses and adaptations to conditions and events originating in the economic process. Trade unions do not organize the working class as a whole.

9 See Naomi Griffith, *Penelope's Web* (Toronto 1976), 141; Eli Zaretsky, 'Capitalism, the Family and Personal Life,' *Socialist Revolution*, 13-14 (Jan.-April 1973), 69-125; ibid., 15 (May-June 1973), 19-71; and Wally Seccombe, 'The Housewife and Her Labours Under Capitalism,' *New Left Review*, 83 (Jan.-Feb. 1974), 3-24.
10 This development will be examined later in the paper in the section 'The rise of monopoly capital and the changing middle-class family.'
11 Seena B. Kohl, *Working Together: Women and Family in Southwestern Saskatchewan* (Toronto 1976). Kohl also describes a perpetuation of father-son inheritance of the family enterprise among farm families in Saskatchewan. This pattern of inheritance consolidates as capital the accumulated surplus of the previous generation's work.
12 Ida Scharf Hopkins, *To the Peace River Country and On* (Vancouver n.d.), privately printed
13 Susannah Moodie, *Life in the Clearings*, ed. Robert L. McDougall (Toronto 1959)
14 Catherine Parr Traill, *The Backwoods of Canada, Being Letters From the Wife of an Emigrant Officer, Illustrative of the Domestic Economy of British America* (facsimile ed., Toronto 1971)
15 See Alfred D. Chandler, Jr, *The Visible Hand: The Managerial Revolution in American Business* (Cambridge 1977), 66; and Leonore Davidoff, 'The Rationalization of Housework,' in L. Barker and S. Allen, eds., *Dependence and Exploitation in Work and Marriage* (London and New York 1976).
16 Michael Katz, *The People of Hamilton, Canada West: Family and Class in a Mid-Nineteenth Century City* (Cambridge, Mass. 1975)
17 Nellie McClung, *Clearing in the West: My Own Story* (Toronto 1964), 27
18 Martha Ostenso, *Wild Geese* (Toronto 1967)
19 V.C. Fowke, *The National Policy and the Wheat Economy* (Toronto 1973)
20 Nellie McClung, *In Times Like These* (Toronto 1972), 114
21 Ramsay Cook and Wendy Mitchinson, eds., *The Proper Sphere: Women's Place in Canadian Society* (Toronto 1976), 111
22 Ibid., 111
23 McClung, *Clearing in the West*, and *In Times Like These*
24 Mary E. Wilkins Freeman, *The Revolt of the Mother and Other Stories* (Old Westbury, NY 1974). The title story is a moving and humorous drama on this theme.

25 Kohl, *Working Together*, 70-1
26 Lucie Marchesault-Lussier, 'Une femme comme les autres, ou la femme collaboratrice – une travailleuse non-reconue,' *Canadian Women's Studies*, I, 2 (1978), 7-10; see also Patricia Carey, 'Farm Wives: The Forgotten Women,' in the same issue of *Canadian Women's Studies*, 4-5.
27 McClung, *Clearing in the West*, 27
28 Carey, 'Farm Wives,' 4-5
29 Ibid.
30 Karl Marx, *Grundrisse: Foundations of the Critique of Political Economy* (New York 1973), 163-4
31 Chandler, *Visible Hand*, 145-87
32 Wallace Clement, *Continental Corporate Power: Economic Linkages Between Canada and the United States* (Toronto 1977), 55
33 See James Weinstein, *The Corporate Ideal in the Liberal State, 1900-1918* (Boston 1968).
34 See H.J. Mozans, *Women in Science* (Cambridge 1974), 182-90.
35 Philip E. Hammond, *Sociologists at Work: Essays on the Craft of Social Research* (New York 1964)
36 Alison Prentice, 'The Feminization of Teaching,' in S. Trofimenkoff and A. Prentice, eds., *The Neglected Majority: Essays in Canadian Women's History* (Toronto 1977)
37 See Kathleen Archibald's account of the establishment of this structure in the federal civil service, in her *Sex and the Public Service: A Report to the Public Service Commission of Canada* (Ottawa 1973), 14-17.
38 Dorothy E. Smith, 'Women's Perspective as a Radical Critique of Sociology,' *Sociological Inquiry* XLIV, 4 (1974), 10
39 Basil Bernstein, *Class, Codes and Control: Theoretical Studies Towards a Sociology of Language* (St Albans, UK 1973)
40 R.R. Dale and S. Griffith, 'The Influence of the Home,' in Maurice Craft, ed., *Family, Class and Education: A Reader* (London 1970), 86
41 See, for example, Mary Roth Walsh, *Doctors Wanted, No Women Need Apply: Sexual Barriers in the Medical Profession, 1835-1975* (New Haven 1977); and Albie Sachs and Joan Hoff Wilson, *Sexism and the Law: A Study of Male Beliefs and Judicial Bias in Britain and the United States* (Oxford 1978).
42 See A. Leslie Robb and Byron G. Spencer, 'Education: Enrolment and Attainment,' in Gail C.A. Cook, ed., *Opportunity for Choice: A Goal for Women in Canada* (Ottawa and Montreal 1976); and J. Vickers and J. Adam, *But Can You Type?* (London 1977).
43 Dorothy E. Smith, 'Women, the Family and Corporate Capitalism,' in Marylee Stephenson, ed., *Women in Canada* (Toronto 1973)

44 Seccombe, 'The Housewife,' 6
45 See Patricia Connelly, *Last Hired, First Fired: Women and the Canadian Work Force* (Toronto 1978).
46 J. Podoluk, *The Incomes of Canadians* (Ottawa 1968)
47 These are average earnings including full-time and part-time. It can be argued that this distorts the picture because if women did not depend on their husbands, they would have to seek full-time work. But we have to take the organization of the labour force as it is. A good part of the work available to women is just part-time work. To examine only the earnings of women in full-time positions would be to select not only an unrepresentative segment of the labour force, but also an array of types of jobs unrepresentative of much that was and is available to women with children. We are not concerned here with the possibilities for *individual* women who choose to attempt independence. We are concerned with the *general* situation for women.
48 Kristin A. Moore and Isabel U. Sawhill, 'Implications of Women's Employment for Home and Family Life,' in Ann H. Stromberg and Shirley Harkess, eds., *Women Working: Theories and Facts in Perspective* (Palo Alto, Calif. 1978), 206
49 Michael Anderson, 'Family, Household and the Industrial Revolution,' in Michael Anderson, ed., *Sociology of the Family* (Harmondsworth 1971), 78-96
50 Louise A. Tilly and Joan W. Scott, *Women, Work and Family* (New York 1978)
51 Ibid., 123-9
52 Suzanne D. Cross, 'The Neglected Majority: The Changing Role of Women in 19th Century Montreal,' in Trofimenkoff and Prentice, *Neglected Majority*
53 Ibid., 73-4
54 Ibid., 73
55 Ibid., 74-5
56 See, for example, the records of truant officers excerpted by Alison Prentice in Alison L. Prentice and Susan E. Houston, eds., *Family, School and Society in 19th Century Canada* (Toronto 1975).
57 Mrs Pember Reeves, *Round About a Pound a Week* (London 1913)
58 See, for example, Edward O'Donnell, 'Women as Bread Winners: The Error of the Age,' in R. Baxandall, L. Gordon, and S. Reverby, eds., *America's Working Women: A Documentary History – 1600 to the Present* (New York 1976). R. Geoffroy and P. Sainte-Marie provide a number of instances of such views; see, for example, their *Attitude of Union Workers to Women in Industry*, Studies of the Royal Commission on the Status of Women, no. 9 (Ottawa 1971), 57, 58, and 101-2; see also Philip S. Foner, *History of the Labor Movement in the United States*, vol. III, *The Policies and Practices of the American Federation of Labor, 1900-1909* (New York 1964), 244.

59 O'Donnell, 'Women as Bread Winners,' 168, writes: 'The rapid displacement of men by women in the factory and workshop has to be met sooner or later, and the question is forcing itself upon the leaders and thinkers among the labour organizations of the land. Is it a pleasing indication of progress to see the father, the brother and the son displaced as the bread winner by the mother, sister, and daughter?'

60 Gail Malmgreen, *Neither Bread Nor Roses: Utopian Feminists and the English Working Class, 1800-1850*, a 'Studies in Labour History' pamphlet (Brighton, UK 1978), 23

61 Foner, *Policies and Practices*, 219-55

62 Jack Scott, *Trade Unions and Imperialism in America*, vol. II, *Canadian Workers, American Unions, How the American Federation of Labour Took Over Canada's Unions* (Vancouver 1978)

63 James J. Keneally, *Women and American Trade Unions* (Montreal 1978) 18

64 Joan Sangster, 'The 1907 Bell Telephone Strike: Organizing Women Workers,' *Labour: Le Travailleur*, III (1978), 109-30

65 Ibid., 126. Other unions simply refused to admit women or to recognize locals organized by women. See Foner, *Policies and Practices*, 224-25, and Keneally, *Women and Unions*, 24.

66 Sangster, 'Bell Telephone Strike,' 127

67 Ibid.

68 Ibid., 125-7

69 See Reginald Whitaker, 'The Liberal Corporatist Ideas of Mackenzie King,' *Labour: Le Travailleur*, II (1977), 137-69.

70 The state, of course, also represented the specific interests of segments of the capitalist class in the low-cost labour provided by women. For an account of the state process co-ordinating the various interests and the exclusion of working-class women, see Marie Campbell, 'Early 20th century Trade Unionism and Women in British Columbia: Discovering Oppression,' forthcoming in *Our Generation*.

71 See National Council of Women in Canada, *Legal Status of Women in Canada* (Ottawa 1924).

72 See Jane Humphries, 'Women: Scapegoats and Safety Valves in the Great Depression,' *Review of Radical Political Economics*, VIII (Spring 1976), 98-117; and Ruth Milkman, 'Women's Work and Economic Crisis: Some Lessons of the Great Depression,' ibid., 73-97.

73 Sachs and Wilson, *Sexism and the Law*

74 National Council of Women, *Legal Status*

75 Mary Inman, 'In Women's Defense,' (Los Angeles: Committee to Organize the Advancement of Women, 1940) in Gerda Lerner, ed., *The Female Experience: An American Documentary* (Indianapolis 1977)

76 Richard Hoggart, *The Uses of Literacy* (London 1958)
77 Clementina Black, *Married Women's Work* (London 1915), for examples, see pp. 91 and 138.
78 Lillian Breslow Rubin, 'Worlds of Pain: Life in the Working Class,' (New York 1976), 177-84
79 Malmgreen, *Neither Bread Nor Roses*, 35; see also Jill Liddington and Jill Norris, *With One Hand Tied Behind Us: The Rise of the Women's Suffrage Movement* (London 1978), 216-17.

PART II
SOCIAL WELFARE AND INEQUALITY

6
Income redistribution

GLENN DROVER

Lack of opportunity has been viewed as a major cause of low income in recent years. People are poor, according to this perspective, not because they wish to be poor, but because they lack the qualifications to participate in a modern economy. Given greater opportunity through job retraining, wider accessibility to social services, elimination of tax loopholes, diminished regional disparities, and expanded transfer payments, the poor, it is assumed, will overcome their own disadvantages. An earlier version of poverty that held individuals responsible for their own penury has thus been replaced by a kindlier version which accepts that people cannot really be blamed for having the wrong attributes or being in the wrong location.

Buttressed by these beliefs, the Canadian liberal state set about in the sixties and seventies to correct unequal opportunities and to promote greater equality of income. The idea of redistributing income on a more egalitarian basis was a key plank in the federal government's 'just society' program. Speaking on income security in 1970, Prime Minister Trudeau stated that he believed the government of Canada was obliged to redistribute income between persons and provinces in order to equalize opportunity.[1] A consequence of these concerns was the creation of a comprehensive review of Canada's social security system, which resulted in the orange paper of 1975. One of the goals of the review was to establish a basis for a guaranteed income. Another was to determine how income could be redistributed in a more efficient and equitable manner. The same Liberal government under Pearson had earlier launched DREE, medicare, manpower development, social housing programs, CAP, LIP, LEAP, CYC, a new unemployment insurance scheme, and tax reforms. Collectively they added up to a formidable array of measures, all of which were directly or indirectly presented as methods of modifying the existing distribution of income and specifically aiding the poor.

But what they also had in common was a basic assumption that individuals simply needed the means by which to pull themselves up by their own boot-straps. None of the measures was directed to the underlying structures of society, which served to reinforce poverty. To suppose, however, that the problem of income distribution is resolved by finding the best method of transfer or the right mix of programs ignores a basic fact articulated by Marx: 'The prevailing distribution of the means of consumption is only a conse-quence of the distribution of the conditions of production themselves ... The capitalist mode of production, for example, rests on the fact that the material conditions of production are in the hands of non-workers in the form of property in capital and land ... If the elements of production are so distri-buted, then the present-day distribution of the mass of consumption results automatically.'[2] In a free market, private enterprise economy, this essentially means that the bulk of unearned income remains in the hands of the few while the mass of workers compete on the market to divide up the rest.

Programs based on the concept of equal opportunity are not only restricted because of the nature of capitalist production; they are also inhibited by the role of the state. As Panitch has shown in a recent Canadian study, the state does not simply act as a neutral arbiter between capital and labour or between various pressure groups in society. Instead, it functions primarily to promote capital accumulation and to maintain social control.[3] It is the state's dominant role as a promoter of capital accumulation that generally prevails when there is a conflict of interest. When measures to redistribute income are proposed, the state's capacity to undertake major reform is likely to be limited by capitalists' need to accumulate. Reforms are tolerable only to the extent that they do not interfere with private appropriation of profit.

Essentially, therefore, the purpose of this paper is to explain why present Canadian methods of promoting a more egalitarian distribution of income are unlikely to succeed, and to explore alternative measures. To meet this double objective, the paper is divided into five sections. Section I briefly examines size distribution of income in Canada in order to show that govern-ment measures have not appreciably changed the pattern of distribution in the post-war period. Section II explains and critically evaluates the orthodox rationale for income distribution in capitalist countries based on principles of efficiency, equity, and incentives. Section III looks at the rationale of income distribution in socialist countries, followed by section IV, which compares income distributions of both the East and West. Finally, in section V, implications of the analysis are suggested for Canada. The case is put for a socialist strategy based on public savings, income disclosures, and social expenditures.

Table 1
Percentage distribution of total pre-tax income of families and
unattached individuals by quintiles, 1951-79

	Q1	Q2	Q3	Q4	Q5	Total
1951	4.4	11.2	18.3	23.3	42.8	100
1954	4.4	12.0	17.8	24.0	41.8	100
1957	4.2	11.9	18.0	24.5	41.4	100
1959	4.4	11.9	18.0	24.1	41.6	100
1961	4.2	11.9	18.3	24.5	41.1	100
1965	4.4	11.8	18.0	24.5	41.4	100
1967	4.2	11.4	17.8	24.6	42.0	100
1969	4.3	11.0	17.6	24.5	42.6	100
1971	3.6	10.6	17.6	24.9	43.3	100
1972	3.8	10.6	17.8	25.0	42.9	100
1973	3.9	10.7	17.6	25.1	42.7	100
1974	4.0	10.4	17.7	24.9	42.5	100
1975	4.0	10.6	17.6	25.1	42.6	100
1976	4.3	10.7	17.4	24.7	42.9	100
1977	3.8	10.7	17.9	25.6	42.0	100
1978	4.1	10.4	17.6	25.2	42.7	100
1979	3.9	10.5	17.7	25.9	42.2	100*

* Estimates only, 1979
Source: Statistics Canada, cat. nos. 13-529 and 13-207. The series includes farm and non-farm
families, beginning 1965.

I. INCOME DISTRIBUTION IN CANADA

The fact that the distribution of income in Canada, both before and after
taxes, is highly skewed in favour of the rich is well known. There is, however,
a well-entrenched myth that Canadian society, through transfer payments and
government expenditures, has become increasingly more redistributive in the
post-war period.[4] Recent evidence tells us there is no apparent trend toward a
reduction in inequalities and possibly even a deterioration.

Speaking about pre-tax income to the Empire Club of Canada in 1974,
Marc Lalonde, at that time minister of health and welfare, noted that the
shares of low-income families and individuals have remained relatively constant over the post-war period.[5] This can be seen from table 1. The lowest
quintile of families and individuals received about 4 per cent of income from
1951 to 1979 while the highest quintile received about 42 per cent. With the
exception of the early 1970s, when the lowest quintile actually declined rela-

tive to other groups, there has been virtually no variation in income distribution. A more dramatic shift in distribution was noted by Johnson. By disaggregating earned income into deciles and by focusing on individual tax returns, he observed that (1) the proportion of income received by the five lowest deciles actually declined from 1946 to 1971 while the top five increased, and (2) the loss of income by the poorer income earners was accompanied by a decline in purchasing power.[6]

It can be argued, of course, that the skewness in the original distribution of income is unimportant, providing disparities are levelled by a progressive tax system. But, again, evidence runs counter to this point of view. A 1972 study by Maslove examined the effective tax rate in fourteen income groups.[7] He found that taxes were extremely regressive at the lower end of the income scale, with little progressivity over the remainder. Indeed, for the lowest-income groups (below $2,000), the tax rate was actually in excess of 100 per cent; so that without transfer payments this group would have paid all of its income to the tax-collectors. The high burden of taxation for low-income groups was also confirmed more recently by Gillespie.[8] He found that taxes were regressive up to a level of $6,000 family income, mainly due to the influence of local and provincial taxes. Only federal income taxes were found to be consistently progressive, but even in this case, not sharply so.

A more important belief, which dies hard, is that inequality of income distribution has been ameliorated by transfer payments and the minimum wage. In the face of pre-tax inequality the Canadian government has introduced new transfer programs and expanded old ones. The effect has been that transfer payments accounted for $4.4 billion of government expenditures in 1970 and $9.0 billion in 1974.[9] Yet, in spite of this increase, they have not led to a reduction in the inequality of income. At best, they have only offset the trend toward greater inequality noted in the pre-tax distribution and at worst they have followed the same trend. One reason why this happened is that the rich have benefited from some transfer payments at the expense of the poor. Green noted this in the period from 1967 to 1971. He developed measures of elasticity for the public income transfer system and observed that those in the income group under $5,000 and those between $5,000 and $10,000 received reductions in the share of transfers. On the other hand, those above $10,000 received proportionately more than the increase of families warranted. Similar trends have also been described by the National Council of Welfare.[10]

Another reason why there is little change in income is that minimum wage rates are frequently below the poverty line constructed by the Special Senate Committee on Poverty. This is demonstrated in table 2. Thus the net effect

Table 2
Difference between the minimum wage and the revised poverty line
for families of various sizes in five cities, 1979 (in dollars)

	One adult	Two adults	Two adults, one child	Two adults, two children
Halifax	772	−1,454	−3,196	−4,687
Montreal	1,932	−443	−2,342	−3,882
Toronto	954	−1,421	−3,295	−4,901
Winnipeg	1,396	−830	−2,572	−4,063
Vancouver	954	−1,421	−3,295	−4,901

Source: Statistics Canada, unpublished data, and Labour Canada, unpublished data. Annual income at minimum wage is calculated on the basis of 40 hours per week at 52 weeks. Family allowances, at applicable provincial rates, have been added to minimum income; children are assumed to be less than 12.

of programs has been to promote horizontal rather than vertical distribution. This pattern of horizontal distribution has been confirmed most recently by Gillespie. In a book entitled *In Search of Robin Hood*, he investigates the effect of federal budgetary policies from 1970 to 1977 and finds that the federal government has not improved the economic position of the poor relative to the rich.[11]

In addition, the inegalitarian distribution of Canadian income is highlighted in two other ways. First, estimates of male/female wage differentials indicate a persistent gap between sexes in the same job. For all occupations, it appears that while the ratio of male to female earnings in Canada improved between 1972 and 1977, the dollar differences between men's and women's average earned income actually increased except for employees working 0 to 9 weeks, where there was a dramatic improvement (table 3). Secondly, it is possible that Canadian income studies overestimate the redistributive benefits to the poor because the effect of foreign ownership is not usually calculated. In 1977, for example, close to $2 billion of national income was paid to non-residents. Since this is in the form of dividend income, it would normally benefit higher-income groups if retained in Canada. The main reason for this is that wealth is more unequally distributed than income, as Moscovitch has noted in his paper on the Canadian economy.[12]

In general, then, it can be seen that neither the original distribution of income in Canada nor taxes and transfers have led to a reduction in income inequalities. If anything, there has been an erosion in the relative position of the poor and low-income earners in spite of an expansion of old-age security,

Table 3
Average earned income of women and men employees by weeks worked,
Canada, 1972 and 1977

Weeks worked	Women ($)	Men ($)	Women/ men (%)	Difference between women's and men's earnings ($)	(%)
(1972)					
50–52	5,166	9,455	54.6	4,289	83.0
40–49	3,784	6,485	58.4	2,701	71.4
30–39	2,648	4,940	53.6	2,292	86.6
20–29	2,003	3,416	58.6	1,413	70.5
10–19	1,221	1,986	61.5	765	62.7
0–9	437	802	54.5	365	83.5
(1977)					
50–52	9,143	15,818	57.8	6,675	73.0
40–49	6,137	10,289	59.6	4,152	67.7
30–39	4,528	7,409	61.1	2,881	63.6
20–29	3,709	5,852	63.4	2,143	57.8
10–19	2,740	4,204	65.2	1,464	53.4
0–9	1,721	1,852	92.9	131	7.6

Increases from 1972 to 1977

	Dollar increase		Percentage increase		Increase in the difference between women's and men's earnings	
	Women	Men	Women	Men	($)	(%)
50–52	3,977	6,363	77.0	67.3	2,386	55.6
40–49	2,353	3,804	62.2	58.7	1,451	53.7
30–39	1,880	2,469	71.0	50.0	589	25.7
20–29	1,706	2,436	85.2	71.3	730	51.7
10–19	1,519	2,218	124.4	111.7	699	91.4
0–9	1,284	1,050	293.4	130.9	−234	−64.1

Source: Labour Canada, Women's Bureau, *Women In the Labour Force* (1977 ed., Ottawa 1979)

guaranteed income supplements, pensions, social assistance, unemployment insurance, workmen's compensation, and family allowance. The problem is that reliance on taxes and transfers ignores the 'production of income which generates the redistributive question that these programs attempt inadequately to deal with.'[13] By examining the factors that affect the original distribution of income we can appreciate the major forces that social policy is trying to influence.

II. EXPLANATIONS OF INCOME IN CAPITALIST COUNTRIES

In attempting to explain income distribution in capitalist countries, it is important to start with the obvious observation that factor shares are divided essentially among rent for land-owners, profits for owners of capital, and wages for labour. The important distinction, though, is between wages and profits because, while wages result from the labour of workers, profits are assumed to arise from the sacrifices and foresight of capitalists. Therefore, the present distribution of income, in which many high incomes are made from profits, is considered fair and equitable.[14] Moreover, differentials in wages are also considered to be just to the extent that they reflect variations in individual contributions to economic development. These individual contributions, in turn, are reflected in prices paid for workers in the labour-market. Thus in a capitalist society, as in any society, income distribution is intricately related to the kind of society desired. Differences arise around the way efficiency, equity, and incentives are viewed and implemented.

Efficiency
Efficiency may be defined as the ratio of result to effort, and in the widest sense given to the term it is the degree to which the aspirations of people as a whole are met.[15] Typically, in a capitalist society efficiency is taken as being reflected in the market because it equilibrates cost-preference relations. Choice and cost, for example, are seen to be closely related because choice implies not only a mere ranking of preferences but also a consideration of foregone alternatives.[16] Hence, emphasis is placed on the private choices of individuals, and the market is considered to be the best way to register and respond. Choice is maximized when no new increase of any good is preferable to what would be foregone to achieve it. In economic jargon, marginal value is considered at this point to be equal to marginal cost. A similar logic follows for the allocation of resources. Since any product can be produced in alternative ways and any resource can be employed in alternative ways, the most efficient process for economizing is achieved when 'no marginal unit of any resource can advantageously be moved to another use.'[17]

The efficiency of capitalism as an allocative device for labour, therefore, presupposes that markets tend to optimize the use of scarce resources. Given production possibilities and income constraints, prices, including the price of labour, are determined by supply and demand: 'If there is pure competition the market mechanism will allocate resources to each industry according to the cash demand for its product.'[18] Supply is based on the firm's cost of production. In theory the most efficient firm will not only maximize profit but be able to pay higher wages than its competitors. The rewards of efficiency will be reflected in income distribution.

Evidently the market, in the sense described, is superior in efficiency to non-market allocative mechanisms such as bureaucracies or queuing. However, the superior efficiency relates only to allocative processes and implies nothing about technological efficiency in the production of goods and services.[19] Also, one can criticize the approach as a narrowly conceived concept partly because efficiency, in this sense, applies under conditions of pure competition, rather than monopoly capitalism, and partly because the relative power that each individual brings to the market-place is ignored. Furthermore, as is clearly evident from unemployment levels in Canada, this concept of efficiency promotes an economic system in which man and machines are frequently underutilized.[20]

Equity

From the concept of efficiency just described, it follows that an equitable income distribution in a market economy is related to the concept of marginal productivity. The concept has been used to explain both factor shares and the size distribution of income.[21] The idea is that the price of labour is equivalent to the marginal contribution to total production of the last worker hired. Wages also depend on supply and demand. Accordingly, changes in the price of labour will also have an output effect in terms of the supply and demand of a product as well as a substitution effect by shifting prices of other factors of production. Marginal productivity is based on diminishing marginal returns, which suggests that each additional input of labour will produce marginally less output. Therefore an employer will only employ as many persons as revenue from sales will permit. By doing this, employers maximize profit, and workers' wages are equal to marginal productivity.

One limitation of marginal productivity theory has to do with a contradiction in its internal logic. The theory holds that marginal physical productivity for each factor of production measures or represents the actual portion of the product created by the marginal unit of that factor. However, according to Gerdes, it is one thing to argue that a factor will be used to the point at which its cost to the user will equal the revenue which its addition to the factor mix produces. It is quite another thing to suggest that its contribution to output is exactly matched by an equivalent reward in money.[22] When labour and capital are mixed, one can only say how much each additional unit of labour produces under certain limiting assumptions. Another limitation of this explanation, accepted even by those who are proponents of this approach to income determination, is that even if it did reasonably well explain the general wage level of labour, it cannot necessarily explain wage structures.[23] The reason is that the marginal productivity concept as stated only establishes the demand schedule for labour; it does not influence the supply side. Hence in this crude form the theory is somewhat of a tautology as wage differentials are used to explain wage differentials. Because of this inherent weakness the marginal productivity approach has placed increasing emphasis on another theory, which we shall examine in relation to incentives. But before doing this, two fundamental criticisms of the orthodox explanation need to be considered. First, it does not take into account institutional factors which reinforce existing patterns of distribution. Secondly, it ignores the class system of a capitalist economy.

The most important institutional characteristic influencing income distribution in a capitalist country is the right to private property and the private appropriation of profit. Both lead to enormous concentration of wealth and the share of total income from wealth. There have been no extensive studies of wealth in Canada, but results from England, where incomes are more equally distributed than in Canada, illustrate the problem. In 1960 fully 83 per cent of total wealth in that country was owned by the top 10 per cent of income earners, and 81 per cent of company stocks and shares were owned by 1 per cent of income earners. The net effect was that 99 per cent of the total share of income from wealth was received by the top 10 per cent while the other remaining 1 per cent was distributed to the other 90 per cent of income recipients. The Provincial Bank of Canada recently reported that 60.8 per cent of total assets were held by the richest 20 per cent in this country.[24]

Second, the theory also suggests that redistribution results from a benevolent state which intervenes in the market only to help low-income workers.[25] Yet as Michelson and others suggest, this ignores a more fundamental reality, namely, that the original distribution of income results in great measure because state activity functions to favour upper-income classes against lower-income classes.[26] For example, by defining and enforcing property rights and biasing factor shares in favour of capital, the state works against the poor rather than remaining neutral as orthodox theory implies. Gillespie finds this criticism unconvincing because he cannot understand why the state would act initially to alter the original distribution in favour of the rich, only to offset this by redistributing to the poor.[27] His reservation seems plausible unless it is accepted that the net effect of initial distribution to capitalists followed by secondary distribution to workers or the unemployed leads to less reduction in inequality than may otherwise be necessary to legitimize the social order.

A third institutional factor which must be taken into account in examining income distribution is the influence of corporations. As Gordon suggests, wage differentials reflect not only relative productivity but also employer power and increasing balkanization of the labour force.[28] In addition, the corporations highlight another weakness – the difficulty of measuring productivity. Corporation executives are among the highest paid individuals in a market economy, but it is impossible to determine empirically whether the price they are paid is equal to their marginal product.

Finally, there is the issue of class structure in advanced capitalism. Several authors in Canada have recently demonstrated how the economy in Canada is controlled by a small elite.[29] Vertical and horizontal integration of companies, interlocking directorates, government regulation of finance capital, support of political parties, and control over the press are only some of the ways in which inequalities in capital holdings and income are preserved. In addition, by means of investment, dismissal of workers, closure of branch plants and movement of capital abroad, it is clear that a relatively small class can sabotage public attempts to implement egalitarian policies.

Incentives

Income differentials under capitalism are also justified on grounds that they provide incentives for employment. The assumption is that individuals basically prefer leisure to work, and therefore material incentives are essential to make them produce. Inequality, therefore, is not only inherently just but also economically necessary. It is just because it promotes individual initiative and reward; it is necessary because it provides societal disincentives to leisure. The first is explained by the human capital approach to income distribution, while disincentives are corrected by welfare measures.

We noted above that marginal productivity theory establishes the demand schedule for labour; human capital theory focuses on supply. According to this version of income distribution, 'earnings differentials depend on the degree of training required in terms of both formal education and of on the job training and are just sufficient to compensate for the costs of this training, taking into account length of working life, uncertainty of earnings, unemployment and non-pecuniary benefits.'[30]

At first sight, the human capital approach seems to salvage the concept of marginal productivity, but evidence from studies is not convincing. Friedman and Kuznets, for example, in an early study noted that expected differences between professionals and non-professionals (allowing for costs of training, longevity, and costs of borrowing) were 55 per cent to 70 per cent while actual differences were 85 per cent to 180 per cent.[31] More recently, Mincer has noted that about one-third of regional differences of income in the United States could be explained by education, while Chiswick has suggested that the rate of return and schooling explain about 65 per cent of provincial differences in Canada.[32] Within regional variations, however, these are not so easily explained. Estimates by Mincer initially implied that less than 10 per cent of variation was attributable to education in the United States; he has since revised this to 25 per cent.[33] But this still means that three-quarters of the variation in regional income distribution is not explained by human capital theory.

In any case, whatever the results of specific studies, a more basic criticism of this approach is that it ignores the determinants of schooling. For example, the rate of return on capital borrowed assumes in the first place that everyone can borrow without regard to position or education involved. It also presupposes that quality of education and socio-economic background are unimportant. Yet as Bowles has indicated, the effect of the length of schooling on earnings is probably of minor significance and independent of social background.[34] Moreover, an individual's IQ – which we might suppose to have some influence on academic achievement – has also been found to be weakly related to economic success.[35] This leads one author to conclude that affective traits are probably more important than cognitive ability in predicting rates of return to schooling.[36]

The welfare approach to incentives is the opposite side of the coin to the human capital perspective. On the one hand, welfare must provide an income platform for unemployed workers in order to maintain political stability; on the other hand, it must also make life sufficiently uncomfortable so that in times of economic upturn, marginal labourers can be nudged back into the work-force.

The incentive function of welfare has been highlighted by Polanyi in *The Great Transformation*.[37] Looking back over four centuries, Polanyi asked himself how capitalism developed initially in England. He provided three answers. First, he associated the rise of free finance capital with mercantilism. Second, he showed how common lands were made private by enclosure. Third, he demonstrated how a new form of welfare was needed to promote labour as a commodity. In effect, the Elizabethan Poor Law (which was part of the labour code) was an encumbrance to the development of capitalism because it assured full employment backed up by yearly wage assessments.

The measure broke down under enclosure, but features of it were strengthened by Speenhamland (1795) because people, though no longer guaranteed work, were guaranteed an income equivalent to work. Thus it was not until the poor law amendments of 1834 that the deterrent principle and the less eligibility principle were introduced to 'free' labour. The deterrent principle simply meant that society no longer had an obligation to support an individual. The less eligibility principle implied that any benefits that were given were to be less than the poorest paid work. True welfare was to be found on the market, and the role of government was to guide the poor to their freedom. Polanyi refers to this as the real beginning of capitalism.[39]

In a contemporary study of welfare, Piven and Cloward show that the same two principles are still enforced, but that the severity with which they are applied varies with political unrest. They put forward the thesis that welfare rolls expand in response to domestic turmoil caused by rising unemployment and contract in times of economic growth in order to reaffirm the work ethic.[40]

In summary, then, an inegalitarian pattern is built into the original income distribution of capitalist countries on grounds of efficiency, equity, and incentives. In addition, it is strengthened by institutional and class structures. Consequently, any effort to shift income by government social policy is likely to have a marginal impact on the original distribution. Market pressures, backed up by ideological biases, will quickly reorder income differentials close to their original ranking. For these reasons, it is understandable why existing measures of redistribution are unsuccessful and why proposed methods are unlikely to work. Therefore, in the next section of this paper, we shall look at alternative structures for income distribution in socialist countries and the rationale behind them. To do so, we shall begin he discussion where we left off, by examining how socialist countries cope with the same problems of equity, incentive, and efficiency. This will be followed by a brief comparison of incomes in the East and West.

III. SOCIALIST ALTERNATIVES

In turning to socialist countries it is important to recognize at the outset that the distribution of income does not reflect the total distribution of resources. Is is widely recognized that the elite of socialist countries, like the elite in capitalist countries, have command over resources that are not measured by income. Nevertheless, since the preceding discussion of capitalist countries dealt with income, the analysis of socialist countries will be similarly focused.

Income distribution under socialism refers essentially to the determination of wages and salaries. Since property is owned by the state, there is no income in the form of rent. Profits, which are distributed through dividends and interest in capitalism, serve a different role under socialism. In general, there is a high degree of centralization and control over the determination of wages. Thus prior to the 1960s, wages in most countries were decided for management on the basis of reaching or exceeding planned targets and on the basis of piece-work for workers.[41] Differentials were presumed to reflect individual effort, though the ratio of wages between skilled and unskilled workers was kept to about 2:1.[42] Since 1962, however, the distribution of the wage fund has been increasingly supplemented by an incentive fund based on enterprise profit. This shift is usually associated with Libermanism in the Soviet Union and self-management in Yugoslavia.[43]

Termed 'market socialism' by some authors, this allocation process duplicates in some respects a capitalist labour-market except that allocation of resources on a macro scale is still determined by the state; basic pay differentials are decided centrally; the percentage of national income distributed for social expenditures (schools, hospitals, housing) is decided in advance of wages; and the means of production are socialized. There is, however, a fundamental distinction between the European socialist bloc and countries such as Cuba and China with respect to the function of the labour-market. Instead of relying upon material incentives and the labour-market as an allocative and distributive mechanism, Cuba and China initially opted to promote greater equality (recent events suggest this is changing) through social consumption and wages; hence, less stress is placed on material incentives for economic growth and rapid industrialization. Basic wages are supplemented by various forms of symbolic reward in order to promote socialist emulation rather than profit-sharing.

Nevertheless, in all socialist countries an egalitarian ethic prevails, and in order to explore wage differentials it will be useful to examine equity, incentive, and efficiency in that order, rather than considering efficiency first as we did in evaluating income distribution in capitalist countries.

Equity
Oskar Lange argues the economist's case for socialism on the grounds that it alone can attain maximum social welfare. 'In any system with private ownership of the means of production,' he states, 'the distribution of income is determined by the distribution of ownership of the ultimate productive forces.'[44] Since labour is the only factor of production credited with the capability of creating value, it alone can be remunerated.[45]

This principle of income distribution is based on Marx's labour theory of value, which implies that the value of a commodity is determined by the labour time necessary for its production. Surplus value, therefore, is created by workers but, unlike a capitalist economy, part of it is not appropriated by owners of capital.[46] Because the means of production are socialized, owners and workers are in theory the same people so that the power to reduce income differentials can be realized.

More equality, however, does not mean total equality from a Marxist perspective, at least in the short run. The principle 'From each according to his ability, to each according to his need' is perceived to belong to a higher stage of society in which material abundance and level of productive organization would promote complementary, not contradictory, social interests.[47] On the other hand, Marx also suggested in the *Critique of the Gotha Programme* that under socialism remuneration would be measured according to labour's contribution.[48] Moreover, it is generally accepted that distribution according to labour is not to be taken to refer only to duration of labour but also to intensity of effort, skill, and possibly economies in the means of production.[49] This new basis of distribution was only intended to be transitional, but as has already been suggested, the distinction made by Marx is the basis for different approaches to income distribution in the Eastern socialist bloc and countries such as China and Cuba.

Incentives

The motivation of labour in a socialist country is different from that in a capitalist country partly because private enrichment and social distinction based on private wealth are minimal and partly because the right to work is guaranteed.[50] Therefore the fear of unemployment, the *sine qua non* of incentives in capitalist countries, is absent and social security is taken for granted. There is, however, another reason why incentives are more complex under socialism than under capitalism. They are intended not only to provide inducements in contemporary society but also to promote a more egalitarian society when distinctions between skilled and unskilled, mental and physical, urban and rural labour are eliminated. Thus a discussion of motivation under socialism must necessarily take into account material and moral incentives.

Attention to material incentives has been a distinguishing feature of Eastern European socialist countries. There are two apparent reasons for the emphasis. First, it is simply stated that non-tangible benefits will have an impact on workers only during times of ideological fervour; they will produce extra effort for short periods of time.[51] Second, following the idea that the earlier phase of socialism will not provide sufficient abundance to satisfy the principle of 'to each according to his need,' income distribution is intended to provide stimuli for growth of social production. 'The right of the producers is proportional to the labour they supply: the equality consists in the fact that measurement is made with equal standard, labour ... The equal right is an unequal right for unequal labour. It recognizes no class differences, but it tacitly recognizes unequal individual endowment and thus productive capacity as natural privileges.'[52]

The exclusive attention given to material incentives in Eastern European socialist countries has been questioned by Sweezy. In commenting on Libermanism, he states: 'Its mentality and attitude have been and are being shaped by an economic system in which the goals and initiative of the individual are indistinguishable from those of capitalism. The types produced by such an environment range from the philistine through the unprincipled opportunist to the greedy corruptionist ... It is necessary not only to abolish private property in the interest of production but also production for profit.'[53]

Until recently the dual objectives of promoting industrialization and socialization of the work-force in China were generally accepted as compatible. But, in general, where the two goals were in conflict, it was assumed that collectivization of man and structures would take precedence. In reshaping motivational mechanisms, therefore, increasing attention was given to non-material incentives.[55] This was intended to transform society by promoting (1) egalitarian payment arrangements with narrower differentials, (2) minimization of material compensation, and (3) replacement of individual motivational schemes by group mechanisms. Thus the focus of moral incentives was on remodelling 'economic motivation, moulding the socialist style of life, stimulating democratic initiative, cultivating the collective reason.'[56]

Nevertheless, the main test for determining whether a society relies primarily on moral incentives is to assess if it succeeds in abolishing the labour-market as the chief motivating device. Bernardo thinks Cuba made more effort in this direction than China.[57] In the early days of the Cuban revolution, every eligible person was assured a job and the provision of basic goods (shelter, food, health services, education, transportation). Payment other than minimum basic wages was non-material.[58] To do this, competition was incorporated in a group process, and workers were encouraged to increase output not only for themselves but for others. Neither wages nor moral incentives were used to allocate labour; that was done through a central agency. The ultimate goal was to transform the role that money plays in the economy. It was intended that it no longer serve as a 'means of accumulation, nor an instrument of exchange, nor a measure of value ... Stripped of its historic characteristics, it will be fundamentally a means of distribution.'[59]

Efficiency

In the folklore of capitalism is the belief that a socialist economy is inefficient. There seem to be two basic reasons for this belief. First, it is assumed that in the absence of market mechanisms there is no automatic adjustment of prices as a means of allocating resources. Second, it is assumed that since the means of production are socialized, bureaucratic bungling will get in the way of efficient production. In fact, however, efficiency is as much a concern in socialist countries as in the West (more so if employment is taken into account), providing the pursuit of efficiency does not interfere with socially desirable goals such as the distribution of national income. As a means of promoting efficiency two methods have been developed: (1) computationally on a centralized basis, and (2) competitively on a decentralized basis. Each has implications for income distribution.

In the centralized approach, prices perform a micro-allocative function in the sense that they influence personal consumption and assist planners in determining consumer preferences. On the other hand, macro-economic goals are established by planners in accordance with political objectives. The actual prices are arrived at by considering a large number of different plan variants. In doing so, prices are assumed to reflect all costs, and in some ways the approach approximates the marginality concept of capitalist countries, at least in terms of competition among plans.[61] However, basic wages are not determined in a labour-market.

The decentralized basis of resource allocation was originally postulated by Oskar Lange. In his model of a socialist economy, property is publicly owned, but individuals are free to choose the goods and jobs they wish. Consumer preferences determine the production of consumption goods, while a planning board determines the rate of capital accumulation. Prices for intermediate goods are determined by the planning board using a trial and error procedure based on past performance and likely trends.[62]

It is this approach to efficiency or adaptations of it[63] that has become associated with the self-management schemes of Yugoslavia. The effect is the development of shadow prices for allocating resources, including labour, and the central motivating force is individual material gain. Under this approach, the functions of the labour-market are essentially identical with a capitalist economy. In China and Cuba, this form of decentralization (as distinct from commune production) was re-evaluated because of the implied reliance on material gain and income differentials. Thus there was a shift in the efficiency debate so that concern was not how to absorb workers' productivity in the economy but how to raise production levels in order to satisfy the needs of people on an egalitarian basis.

IV. INCOME DISTRIBUTION IN SOCIALIST COUNTRIES

Comparison of incomes between East and West is difficult and the information available is scanty. This is particularly true of Cuba and China. However, what evidence there is suggests that incomes are more likely to be equitably distributed in socialist than in capitalist countries, due mainly to collective control of investment capital and government expenditures.[64]

Tables 4 and 5 are taken from a recent study on comparative economic policies of Eastern and Western countries. Table 4 shows that the Eastern European distribution of wage and salary earners is more equal than Western countries. It does not reflect the impact of government expenditures, which weigh more in Eastern countries in promoting equality of consumption. The area of concentration is, on the average, higher in the West. Similarly, the spread of income between highest and lowest quintiles is smaller in the East. Finally, it is also clear that the Eastern countries have a more homogenous spread of income than the West as indicated by the coefficients of variation. Studies by Wiles and Markowski show similar results, though they have reservations about the Soviet Union, where wage differentials, due to Libermanism, created greater disparities than other Eastern countries.[65] Tables 4 and 5 indicate the trend of income change between the mid-1950s and the mid-1960s. In the East it appears that three countries actually improved the original distribution in an egalitarian direction while two remained constant. On the other hand, in four of the capitalist countries, movement was in an opposite direction, the only exception being West Germany.

There are two reasons for these differences. First and foremost, income in socialist countries is derived from labour, and, therefore, rents, interest, and dividends, which constitute a significant percentage of revenue of high-income groups in capitalist economies, would not be present. Thus one would expect the main difference in tables 4 and 5 to be accounted for by differences in income of the lowest-and highest-income groups, not the middle range. This hypothesis is partly supported by table 6, which shows after-tax wages and salaries in East and West Germany. The second, third, and fourth quintiles are not identical in the two countries. But the basic difference lies in the fact that the lowest quintile in East Germany receives 10 per cent of total income and the highest quintile 31 per cent, whereas in West Germany the figures are 6 per cent and 46 per cent respectively.

Second, differences in standard pay rates are established centrally in most socialist countries. Therefore, to the extent that egalitarian policies prevail, differentials are likely to be narrower in the East than the West. On the other hand, to the extent that material incentives and Libermanism prevail, wage

Table 4
Western and Eastern income distribution of wage and salary earners, 1959-64

Countries	Years	Concentra-tion area	Ranking	Coefficient of variation	Ratio of quartiles	Symmetry coefficient
West						
Belgium	1964	0.175	4	0.65	2.10	1.43
France	1962	0.169	3	0.70	1.97	1.44
Germany (FR)	1964	0.136	2	0.51	1.76	1.03
Netherlands	1962	0.195	6	0.74	2.62	0.73
Sweden	1963	0.178	5	0.67	2.62	0.90
United Kingdom	1963-64	0.134	1	0.49	2.04	1.16
Average		0.165		0.63	2.19	1.12
East						
Czechoslovakia	1959	0.092	1	0.33	1.61	1.16
Germany (DR)	1959	0.094	2	0.34	1.62	1.33
Hungary	1959	0.100	3	0.36	1.67	1.36
Poland	1962	0.112	4	0.40	1.82	1.33
Yugoslavia	1963	0.124	5	0.45		
Average		0.105		0.38	1.72	1.32
East-West ratio		0.64		0.60	0.79	1.18

The high figure for Sweden is surprising at first sight, but one should remember that only wage and salary earners are considered here; if all incomes were included, the Swedish figure would be the lowest in the West (0.20) and the French figure the highest (0.26). The 'area of concentration' under the Lorenz curve measures dispersion from equality. Complete equality between income and population is zero, and complete inequality is 0.5. 'Ranking' of the countries is determined by increasing order of concentration area. 'Coefficient of variation' is defined as the ratio between the standard deviation and the mean of the distribution of means. Zero is complete equality. 'Ratio of quartiles' gives an idea of the spread of income in the top and bottom quartiles. 'Symmetry coefficient' is defined as the ratio between quartile and median. Greater than one corresponds to concentration of population in low-income groups; less than one, the opposite.
Source: E.S. Kirschen, ed., *Economic Policies Compared*

structures and differentials may be similar. Studies by Wilczynski seem to warrant this conclusion.[66] It appears that the spread of differentials in Cuba and China are also not very different from those in Eastern Europe, in part, because the scales were adopted from the Soviet Union.[67]

In fact, it is the recognition of inequalities built into standard wage rates that caused China and Cuba to place greater stress on social wages than

Table 5

Comparison of the ratio of quartiles and of the symmetry coefficients for
wage and salary earners for two different years in Western and Eastern countries*

Countries	Years		Ratio of quartiles	Symmetry coefficient*
	Initial	Terminal		
West				
Belgium	1955	1964	106.0	91.7
France	1956	1962	104.2	108.3
Germany (FR)	1955	1964	90.7	104.0
Sweden	1954	1963	104.0	95.6
United Kingdom	1954	1964	104.1	97.5
East				
Bulgaria	1957	1962	100.0	98.6
Czechoslovakia	1959	1964	98.8	99.1
Hungary	1955	1964	94.7	90.6
Poland	1955	1964	95.8	87.8
Soviet Union	1956	1959	100.0	103.9

* The coefficients are expressed as indices, the value in the initial year being taken as 100.
Source: See table 4.

Table 6
Net income by quintiles for East and
West German households, 1970

Quintile	W.G.	E.G.
1	5.9	10.4
2	10.4	15.8
3	15.6	19.8
4	22.5	23.3
5	45.6	30.7
Total	100.0	100.0

Source: Martin Schnitzer, *Income Distribution*

individual wages. In any case, what is apparent from the data is that, even
without consideration of social consumption, which is generally higher in
socialist countries than in capitalist countries,[68] money incomes are more
equally distributed in the East than in the West. And what is also suggested is

that the original distribution of income is determined by basic productive forces influenced by concepts of equity, incentives, and efficiency.

V. IMPLICATIONS FOR CANADA

Since current methods of achieving equality of income in Canada have been unsuccessful, what other ways of promoting equality can be found? From the review of income determination in socialist countries, it is clear that the task is not easy, even when there is an egalitarian ethic. In countries such as Canada, where even the goal does not exist, the task is obviously more complicated. Moreover, since public ownership of the means of production in Canada is not imminent, the more egalitarian distribution of income in socialist countries due to that difference is unlikely to occur in this country in the foreseeable future. Furthermore, given the nature of the state and the power elite in Canada, there can be little optimism that income distribution will be changed substantially in an egalitarian direction. 'The changes that can be made within the context of a capitalist system as regards equality between owners and employers, men and women, and one region and another cannot in the nature of things be of a very far reaching kind.'[69]

This is not to suggest, of course, that capitalist countries are incapable of modifying income distribution, at least on the margin. Sweden has achieved more equality of income distribution than most capitalist countries. On the other hand, there is less evidence that most capitalist countries, including Canada, have substantially altered income distribution in the post-war period. In light of this, two current proposals to promote a more egalitarian distribution of income through negative income tax and education need to be briefly considered before turning to suggestions for structural alternatives.

The model of income guarantees that underlies recent proposals to redistribute income in Canada is the negative income tax.[70] In its broadest terms, the idea behind it is to 'round out the income tax system so that it not only collects money from higher-income families but also provides benefits to lower-income families.'[71] If adopted, it would provide an administratively tidy means of redistributive income, but for several reasons it is doubtful that it will have any appreciable effect in reducing inequalities.

The first reason is that it is unlikely that the federal government and the provinces will adopt basic guarantees or tax rates that will alter the existing distribution. If they do, market mechanisms and higher-income earners are likely to respond quickly to neutralize the effects, particularly if there is any impact on capital accumulation. Second, the tax system is inadequate as a redistributive mechanism simply because 'taxation practices differ markedly from what appear to be taxation policies.'[72] This results not only because of tax loopholes for high-income groups but also because governments rely heavily upon regressive taxes for revenue. Third, and perhaps most important, a negative income tax system with a high guarantee and low deduction rate will not work because it is counter-productive to marginal productivity and capitalist ideology. Such a tax would not only upset incentives but would also imply that 'the supplier of labour does not make the correct choice of his job since the difference in marginal productivity is not brought out by incomes after tax.'[73]

Unlike the negative income tax, those who support education as an equalizer try to directly influence the original distribution of income. Jan Tinbergen, the Dutch economist, is an ardent advocate of this point of view. By taking into account criticisms of human capital theory, Tinbergen and others have shown that the ratio between qualified and less qualified income in capitalist countries has fallen considerably from 1900 to 1960.[74] He further states that the reduction of inequality is not an automatic consequence of rising average income but is made 'possible only if the expansion of education overtakes the expansion required by technological development.'[75] In this way, he assumes that the supply of skilled labour will increase relative to demand, thus reducing wage rates. The converse will happen with unskilled labour whereby demand will exceed supply, thereby forcing up wages.

Evidently this approach is an extension of the principle of meritocracy, that people of higher ability are educated at economic costs 'in order to perform more important jobs and, therefore, should be rewarded for their ability and educational investment. The assumption is that the meritocracy coincides with social and economic contribution, a doubtful belief.'[76] In fact, Tinbergen admits the elitism built into the proposal, not only because the approach implies all the weaknesses of human capital theory, noted earlier in this paper, but also because it implies reward based on capacity to produce. But since this, in turn, depends on personal wealth and personal qualities, both of which are unequally distributed, the capacity for greater productivity is rewarded without regard to effort. To compensate, Tinbergen advocates a tax on capacity in order to equalize wages but accepts that the idea is not realistic until there are adequate psycho-technical tests.[77] In the meantime, we would have to be satisfied with a meritocratic substitute.

It would appear, then, that neither of these proposals is likely to change the distribution of income in Canada. Nor is this surprising since the basic distribution of power and property is in no way changed by these modifications. For this reason, other methods of achieving equality must be found. Two possibilities are proposed. First, the influence of capitalists can be reduced from above through increased public savings. Second, industrial democracy, or worker management, can be extended from below through controls over income disclosure, social consumption, and employee savings.

The idea of using public savings to reduce the effect of unearned income from property has been proposed by Arthur Lewis.[78] In capitalist countries the justification for private property is that it is a major source of private investment capital. Therefore if sufficient funds are going to be developed for investment, either private property must continue or the government must assume greater responsibility for savings. Nationalization of industry is not enough because that simply puts physical assets in the hands of the state; the rich are as rich as before because owners are compensated. What is important to the growth rate of private wealth is not whether enterprise is public or private, but whether saving is private or public. In other words, if public savings are adequate to finance economic expansion, private wealth will not grow as quickly, whether enterprise is nationalized or not. An example of this approach is Petro-Canada.

The case for industrial democracy, or worker management, as a strategy for change in Canada has been well stated by others.[79] It need not be repeated here except to note the need to extend the concept to consideration of income distribution. One possibility, which may seem trivial but has important consequences, is to promote public disclosure of income. In most capitalist countries income is considered a private matter. By making such information publicly available, it will indicate just how wide income differentials are, sensitize people to the discrepancies, and create demands for change. This will be particularly true within industrial sectors as managers are called upon by workers to prove their greater marginal productivity. Second, industrial democracy implies that workers could become involved directly in the allocation of funds for social consumption. In capitalist countries this is usually considered to be the responsibility of government, but if expenditures for such programs as housing, health, transportation, and welfare were more closely related to employment, workers would see more clearly the connection between money wages and social wages. This is particularly important in Canada because public expenditures are somewhat redistributive, even though Gillespie has recently shown that there has been no change in the redistributive effect from 1961 to 1969.[80] Finally, employee savings, particularly forced savings such as pensions or retirement plans, a means by which workers can have an impact on investment and the direction of company funds. At present most pension funds are invested by employers without consultation. In return, the worker only receives a small interest payment or cumulated dividends. By direct involvement in investment of the funds, workers could promote another vehicle for diminishing the influence of private property on income distribution in Canadian society.

This paper has attempted to indicate why income inequalities will continue in Canada in spite of existing and proposed redistributive measures. The basic reason behind the failure of reform proposals is that income inequality is inherent in an economy based on private investment. Furthermore, existing income differentials in capitalist countries are justified as fair and equitable on grounds that they provide incentives and promote efficiency. By contrast, equity and efficiency in socialist countries are related to a labour theory of value. The means of production are also socialized, thereby eliminating differentials arising from private ownership of capital. Income inequalities which persist are due in large measure to divergent views about incentives. Eastern socialist countries tend to rely on material rewards, and countries such as Cuba and China (until recently) upon moral persuasion. In spite of these differences, however, one message which is clear from the socialist experience is that inequalities are unlikely to be substantially reduced in capitalist countries unless the basic distribution of power and property is altered. To do this, a change in strategy has been proposed, based on increased public savings combined with worker control over income disclosure, social consumption, and employee savings.

NOTES

1 P.E. Trudeau, *Income Security and the Social Services* (Ottawa 1970), cited in W.I. Gillespie, 'On the Redistribution of Income in Canada,' *Canadian Tax Journal*, XXIV, 4 (July-Aug. 1976), 419
2 Karl Marx, *Critique of the Gotha Programme* (Peking 1972), 18
3 L. Panitch, 'The Role and Nature of the Canadian State,' in L. Panitch, ed., *The Canadian State: Political Economy and Political Power* (Toronto 1977), 3-27
4 Douglas Fullerton, 'A Society Transformed: Robin Hood Runs Out of Funds,' *Saturday Night* (May 1976)
5 Marc Lalonde's address, 'Income Distribution: A Question of Community Ethics,' is referred to in Gillespie, 'Redistribution of Income,' 420. For government documents on income distribution, see the report of the Special Committee on Poverty, *Poverty in Canada* (Ottawa 1971); Ian Adams et al., *The Real Poverty Report* (Edmonton 1971); Economic Council of Canada, *The Challenge of Growth and Change* (Ottawa 1968); Jenny Podaluk, *Incomes of Canadians* (Ottawa 1968).

6 Leo Johnson, *Poverty in Wealth* (Toronto 1974), 5. Johnson's findings have been heavily criticized by sociologists Hamilton and Pinard on the grounds that distribution of family income more reasonably reflects actual distribution than individual tax returns. Johnson argues, however, that family income hides the real spread of income distribution by treating all members of the family other than the head as secondary earners. See Richard Hamilton and Maurice Pinard, 'Poverty in Canada: Illusion and Reality,' *Canadian Review of Sociology and Anthropology*, XIV, 2 (May 1977), 247-52; L. Johnson, 'Illusions or Realities: Hamilton and Pinard's Approach to Poverty,' ibid., XIV, 3 (Aug. 1977), 341-6.

7 Allan Maslove, *The Pattern of Taxation in Canada* (Ottawa 1972)

8 Gillespie, 'Redistribution of Income'; also W. Irwin Gillespie, 'The Redistribution of Income in Canada, 1969,' Carleton University, Ottawa, 1975. Gillespie's study on income distribution, like Johnson's, has been criticized on methodological grounds, including the following: (1) orthodox studies of fiscal incidence view government as a neutral arbiter of income distribution rather than a protagonist of dominant classes; (2) the studies also assume that dollar outlay accurately reflects benefits (i.e., each dollar spent on police protection for the rich is equivalent to each dollar spent on welfare for the poor); (3) income from personal wealth holdings other than housing is not included; (4) it is taken as given that the state doesn't bias the pre-tax distribution of income in favour of capital; and (5) information on the very highest-income groups is not disaggregated. See, for example, Larry Sawers and Howard Wachtel, 'Theory of the State, Government Tax and Purchasing Power and Income Distribution,' *The Review of Income and Wealth*, Series 21, no. 1 (March 1975), 111-23.

9 Christopher Green, 'The Distribution of Transfers: The Income Transfer System and the Implementation of Income Supplements,' Dalhousie University, Halifax, Seminar on Income Distribution, mimeo., 1974, p. 1

10 Ibid., 5-7; see also National Council of Welfare, *Bearing the Burden, Sharing the Benefits* (Ottawa 1978).

11 W. Irwin Gillespie, *In Search of Robin Hood* (Montreal 1978). Similar findings are reported in a more recent study by David Ross, *The Canadian Fact Book on Income Distribution* (Ottawa 1980).

12 For recent studies of women's wages, see Morley Gunderson, 'Work Pattern,' in Gail Cook, ed., *Opportunity for Choice* (Ottawa 1976); also Hugh Armstrong and Pat Armstrong, 'The Segregated Participation of Women in the Canadian Labour Force, 1941-71,' *Canadian Review of Sociology and Anthropology*, XII, 4 (Nov. 1975). Regarding the impact of foreign ownership on income distribution, there are no studies to my knowledge. However, the dis-

tribution of wealth is reported through Statistics Canada. As reported in the Provincial Bank of Canada, *Economic Review*, V, 5 (Sept.-Oct. 1975), the richest 20 per cent of Canadians owned 60.8 per cent of total assets. If dividends paid to non-residents went to Canadians, it can be assumed that the major beneficiaries would be the rich. Dividends paid to non-residents and net national income from 1970 to 1977 are the following:

Year	Dividends to non-residents ($ millions)	Net national income ($ millions)
1970	952	64,235
1971	1,079	70,327
1972	1,032	78,746
1973	1,246	90,755
1974	1,646	113,850
1975	1,835	130,031
1976	1,729	147,838
1977	1,823	161,758

13 S.M. Miller and Martin Rein, 'The Possibilities of Income Transformation,' paper prepared for the Nuffield Canadian Seminar on Guaranteed Annual Income, Canadian Council on Social Development, Ottawa, 1972, p. 28

14 This is seldom stated directly in an economic analysis of income, but it is implied in standard texts. See Paul Samuelson and A. Scott, *Economics* (3rd ed., Toronto 1971).

15 J. Tinbergen, 'Does Self-Management Approach the Optimum Order?' in J. Broekmeyer, ed., *Yugoslav Workers' Self-management* (Dordrecht, Holland 1970), 119

16 These ideas are usually discussed in terms of competition, prices, utility, and production in standard economic books. Again, see Samuelson and Scott, *Economics*.

17 Robert Dahl and C. Lindblom, *Politics, Economics and Welfare* (New York 1953), 167

18 E.K. Hunt and H.J. Sherman, *Economics: An Introduction to Traditional and Radical Views* (New York 1968), 208

19 Ibid., 206

20 Ibid., 208

21 David Gordon, *Theories of Poverty and Underemployment* (Lexington, Mass. 1972), 25

22 Carl Gerdes, 'The Fundamental Contradiction in the Neoclassical Theory of Income Distribution,' *The Review of Radical Political Economics*, IX, (Summer 1977), 39-64

23 John Dunlop, *The Theory of Wage Determination* (London 1964), chap. 1

24 A.B. Atkinson, *Unequal Shares: The Distribution of Wealth in Britain* (London 1972), 20-36; The Provincial Bank of Canada, *Economic Review*, 2

25 S. Michelson, 'The Economics of Real Income Distribution,' *Review of Radical Political Economics*, II, 1 (Spring 1970), 86. See also David Gordon, 'Taxation of the Poor and the Normative Theory of Tax Incidence,' *American Economic Review, Papers and Proceedings*, LXI, 2 (May 1971), 319-28.

26 Gordon, ibid. See also R.C. Edwards et al., *The Capitalist System* (Englewood Cliffs, NJ 1972), 235-43.

27 Gillespie, 'Redistribution of Income,' 25 f.

28 Gordon, *Theories of Poverty*, 70 f.

29 John Porter, *The Vertical Mosaic* (Toronto 1965); Robert Chodos, *The CPR: A Century of Corporate Welfare* (Toronto 1973); Don Mitchell, *The Politics of Food* (Toronto 1975); Wallace Clement, *The Canadian Corporate Elite* (Ottawa 1975). For an older study in this field, which has recently been published, see Gustavus Myers, *A History of Canadian Wealth* (Toronto 1972).

30 A.B. Atkinson, *The Economics of Inequality* (Oxford 1975), 82

31 M. Friedman and S. Kuznets, *Income From Independent Professional Practice* (New York 1945), 84

32 J. Mincer, 'The Distribution of Labour Incomes: A Survey with Special Reference to the Human Capital Approach,' *Journal of Economic Literature*, VIII, 1 (March 1970), 1-26. Barry Chiswick, *Income Inequality* (New York 1974), 9

33 Mincer, ibid.; J. Mincer, *Schooling, Experience and Earnings* (New York 1974)

34 S. Bowles, 'Schooling and Inequality from Generation to Generation,' *Journal of Political Economy*, LXXX, 3, Part II (May-June 1972)

35 S. Bowles and H. Gintis, 'I.Q. in the U.S. Class Structure,' *Social Policy*, III, 4 and 5 (Nov.-Dec. 1972, Jan.-Feb. 1973)

36 H. Gintis, 'Education, Technology and the Characteristics of Worker Productivity,' *American Economic Review*, LXI, 2 (May 1971), 266-79

37 Karl Polanyi, *The Great Transformation* (Boston 1965)

38 Ibid., chaps. 3-6

39 Ibid., chap. 7

40 Frances Piven and Richard Cloward, *Regulating the Poor* (New York 1971)

41 J. Wilczynski, *The Economics of Socialism* (London 1970), 109

42 Ibid., 105

43 For references to Libermanism, see J. Wilczynski, *Profit, Risk and Incentives Under Socialist Economic Planning* (London 1973), chap. 1; Robert Bernardo, *The Theory of Moral Incentives in Cuba* (Alabama, 1971), 28-9. On self-management, see Broekmeyer, *Self-Management*.

44 Oskar Lange and F.M. Taylor, *On the Economic Theory of Socialism* (Minnesota 1964), 99

45 Wilczynski, *Economics of Socialism*, 97
46 For discussion of labour theory of value, see Karl Marx, *Capital* (New York 1975), I, chaps. 7-17; Paul Sweezy, *The Theory of Capitalist Development* (New York 1970), chaps. 2-4; Ernest Mandel, *Marxist Economic Theory* (New York 1970), I, chaps. 1-3.
47 For a discussion of this, see Radivoj Davidovic, 'Distribution in the Socialist Economy: Some Principles and Methods,' in Radmila Stojanovic, ed., *Yugoslav Economists on Problems of a Socialist Economy* (New York 1964), 158-65.
48 Marx, *Gotha Programme*, 29 f.
49 Davidovic, 'Distribution,' 162 f.
50 J. Wilczynski, *Socialist Economic Development and Reforms* (New York 1972), 108
51 Wilczynski, *Profit, Risk and Incentives*, 127
52 Marx, *Gotha Programme*, 30
53 See Leo Huberman and Paul Sweezy, 'The Peaceful Transition from Socialism to Capitalism,' *Monthly Review*, XVI (March 1964), cited in Bernardo, *Moral Incentives*, 9.
54 Charles Hoffman, *The Chinese Worker* (Albany 1974), 1
55 Ibid., 93
56 E.L. Wheelwright and Bruce McFarlane, *The Chinese Road to Socialism* (New York 1970), 148
57 Bernardo, *Moral Incentives*, 30
58 Ibid., 53; see also notes 43 and 53.
59 Castro, cited in David Barkin, 'The Redistribution of Consumption in Socialist Cuba,' *Review of Radical Political Economics*, IV, 5 (1972), 95
60 Wilczynski, *Economics of Socialism*, 136
61 Ibid., 137
62 Lange and Taylor, *Economic Theory*, 72-98
63 For a discussion of Lange and adaptations of his basic ideas, see Howard Wachtel, *Workers' Management and Workers' Wages in Yugoslavia* (Ithaca 1973), chap. 3. See also Benjamin Ward, *The Socialist Economy* (New York 1967), chaps. 2, 9, and 10.
64 E.S. Kirschen, ed., *Economic Policies Compared: West and East* (Amsterdam 1974), I; Walter Connor, *Socialism, Politics and Equality* (New York 1979)
65 P.J.D. Wiles and S. Markowski, 'Income Distribution Under Communism and Capitalism,' *Soviet Studies*, XXII, 3 (Jan. 1971); 344, 369, and ibid., XXII, 4 (April 1971), 487-511. In a later book on income distribution Wiles reports that the range of wage distribution in the Soviet Union was wider than in the United Kingdom. Unlike Western studies, however, Wiles does not report on income distribution after taxation and government expenditures.

When a high percentage of goods and services is distributed through the public sector, as appears to be the case in Eastern countries, the net effect is likely to be greater equality. See Peter Wiles, *Distribution of Income: East and West* (Amsterdam 1974), and 'Recent Data on Soviet Income Distribution,' *Survey 21*, III (1975), 28-41.

66 Wilczynski, *Economics of Socialism*, 136

67 Bernardo, *Moral Incentives*, 68-73; Hoffman, *Chinese Worker*, chap. 4 and appendices; Carmelo Mesa-Lago, *The Labor Sector and Socialist Distribution in Cuba* (New York 1971), chap. 4

68 This seems to be particularly true of China and Cuba, but in Eastern Socialist countries, public services are structured to provide more egalitarian opportunities than in the West. See Frank Parkin, *Class Inequality and Political Order* (London 1972).

69 Lars Erik Karlsson, 'Industrial Democracy in Sweden,' in G. Hunnius et al., eds., *Workers' Control* (New York 1973), 185

70 For discussion of the negative income tax, see C. Green, *Negative Taxes and the Poverty Problem* (Washington 1967), and 'Implementing Income Supplements: The Case for a Tax Credit Approach,' *Canadian Tax Journal*, XXI, 5 (Sept.-Oct. 1973), 426-40.

71 National Council of Welfare, *Guide to the Guaranteed Income* (Ottawa 1976), 5

72 Miller and Rein, 'Income Transformation,' 22

73 Tinbergen, 'Self-Management,' 125

74 Jan Tinbergen, *Income Distribution* (Amsterdam 1975), 8 f.

75 Ibid., 8

76 Miller and Rein, 'Income Transformation,' 5

77 Tinbergen, *Income Distribution*, 156

78 Arthur Lewis, *Socialism and Economic Growth* (London 1971)

79 For example, Hunnius et al., *Workers' Control*; H.B. Wilson, *Democracy and the Work Place* (Montreal 1974)

80 Gillespie, 'Redistribution of Income,' 419-43

7
Taxation and the capitalist state

BERT YOUNG

> In general, the art of government consists in taking as much money as possible from one class of citizens to give to the other. *Voltaire*

A central question in regard to the fiscal activities of the capitalist state is the effectiveness of the tax system in reducing inequality. The analysis here focuses on the reforms and changes in recent federal government policies as to their impact on redistribution and the economy. This examination will show not only that these policies have failed, but that Voltaire's statement is as true today as it was in the eighteenth century. The difficulty in accepting such a statement is that the government of Voltaire's period provided few, if any, programs designed to redistribute income. The modern welfare state, by contrast, is a top-heavy bureaucratic system of tax benefits, welfare benefits, medicare programs, family allowances, and unemployment insurance schemes.

Nevertheless, Gillespie could report that 'the poor are those 21.7% with incomes less than $3,200 in 1969 and roughly $5,300 in 1975, and the highest-income families are those 5% with incomes in excess of $17,500 in 1969 and roughly $32,000 in 1975.'[1] The question is a simple one: with all these state programs why has the level of inequality remained stagnant? Our analysis suggests a simple answer. The programs of the federal government since the Second World War have consistently promoted the concentration of wealth in the hands of a minority at the expense of the majority. The evidence presented here will show that, rather than having as its objective the humanitarian principle of equality, the Canadian government has perfected the art of taking as much money as possible from the dominated classes to give to the dominant classes.

This paper is divided into three main sections. The first describes the particular perspective adopted in the paper. The second section discusses the various policies the Canadian state has employed to benefit the dominant classes in the corporate sector and the degree of effectiveness of these policies. The third section discusses the impact of government tax policies and welfare programs on the dominated classes and the subsequent degree of effectiveness.

TAXATION AND THE STATE

The notion that the state simply collects a portion of income from individuals and corporate bodies to pay for goods and services does not take us very far. Equally important are the huge amounts of revenue the state spends to pump-prime the economy, bail out and/or take over failing firms, offer tax incentives to foreign firms to set up business in Canada, foster corporate profit, and maintain basic inequalities in the distribution of wealth.

However, the explanation of these expenditures and taxation schemes has tended to confound public finance analysts up to the present day. As late as 1970, a leading analyst of the Canadian Tax Foundation, Richard Bird, had to admit, after studying the past one hundred years of public finance in Canada, that 'empirical analysis suggests that "political" variables have no discernible influence on the outcome of the eminently political public expenditure process. But theoretical analysis is unable to explain how the *economic* determinants which *do* seem to matter empirically, become incorporated into policy.'[2] Bird notes that a theory of public expenditures ultimately depends on an adequate theory of politics; however, he contends that Canada does not possess the latter. Like many liberals he is convinced that one of the reasons behind the state's social expenditures is the egalitarian objective of redistribution. Bird believes that the logic of the welfare state is based on this objective rather than the prevention of a potentially disastrous social problem. He does not appear to be interested in developing a theory which would help explain the political economy of the modern capitalist state.

Contrary to a strictly economic interpretation of taxation, there are political and economic factors which, when combined, explain the expenditure process and public policy of the state. This explanation has been pursued by political economists, but the most interesting development to date has been the work of Clause Offe.[3] Offe has argued that the state in late capitalism has become interwoven with the accumulation process of capitalist development such that the latter becomes a function of bureaucratic state activity and organized political conflict. In stressing the integrative functions of capital and state, Offe suggests the need to analytically distinguish between the 'allocative' and 'productive' state policies.

Allocative policies include those state attempts to maintain conditions for profitable accumulation through the allocation of resources of 'state' property (taxes, tariffs, Crown lands, etc.). These resources are usually distributed according to power struggles within and without the state itself. On the other hand, productive policies strive to bolster sagging supplies of both variable and constant capital, where such capital either is not provided or provided in inadequate supply by private market decisions. In this sense they are crisis-avoidance strategies designed to maintain the flow of the accumulation process. The best example here would be the serious commitment of the state in supporting research and development in the monopoly sector in order to ensure the competitive edge and to raise the rate of surplus value.[4]

Offe also argues that these imperatives of late capitalism necessarily force the state to discriminate selectively in favour of organized labour and oligopoly capital. This results in benefits to privileged groups at the expense of disadvantaged groups and regions (those on welfare and pensions, immigrants, low-skilled and unorganized labour in the competitive sector). Moreover, there is a tendency for the level of state expenditures to outrun state revenues, and the state more frequently finds itself cutting back those many services and goods which these latter groups and regions have come to rely on.[5]

THE CANADIAN EXAMPLE

Employing these explanations to fit the Canadian case is not difficult. In fact, the basic cause of our inequality can be directly traced to the maintenance role of the state in reducing the risks and consequences of major recessions in the post-war period. This function has been further complicated by the spiralling of wages and prices, by labour's attempt to raise its share of the national income, and by capital's attempt to raise prices so that its net losses may be offset. As David Wolfe has argued, 'in order to perform its accumulation function successfully, the state must be prepared to counter persistent inflationary wage demands with counter-cyclical budgetary policies designed to relieve the upward pressure on corporate profits. Yet at the same time, in order to adequately perform its legitimation function, the state must ensure a high and stable level of employment and income.'[6]

The other major complication for a national economy is the degree to which it is dependent on foreign or multinational capital. This is especially relevant to the special constraints imposed by the high degree of foreign ownership of Canadian industry and resources. These constraints naturally curtail policy options of the state in areas of social policy. As Wolfe notes, international competition plays a crucial role in setting limits on the ability of domestic firms to raise their prices. If firms competing with foreign rivals cannot raise their prices when their costs go up, the result is that their profit margins are squeezed. This, of course, may lead to lower levels of both investment and economic growth, and eventually to economic stagnation. Canada's high rate of inflation, unemployment, and foreign and public debt all indicate an ailing economy with little promise of business confidence in the future.

The state, however, can and has used budgetary policies to encourage investment, increase consumer demand, protect Canadian businesses, and control wage and price increases. In fact, one might argue that the capitalist state has done everything it could to prevent economic stagnation. As our analysis will show, however, these tax policies and concessions have not been successful in reducing inequality. They have been successful in holding up profit levels and encouraging mergers and concentrations among foreign corporations, and to some degree, Canadian firms. They have also been successful in increasing Canada's foreign and public debt. But as measures designed to redistribute income, they have failed to radically alter the position of low-income earners. They have, however, been very successful in providing tax shelters and tax benefits to the middle- and high-income earners, who already enjoy a better standard of living.

THE PUBLIC PURSE AND THE PRIVATE BENEFIT

The *Report* of the Royal Commission on Taxation in Canada (known as the Carter Commission), published in 1966, was hailed by some as the most progressive report on taxation to date. It argued that to achieve an equitable distribution of income the government should impose progressive marginal tax rates on all sources of income, using the ability-to-pay principle. As to incentives for increasing business income, it recommended that subsidies should be used, rather than tax concessions. The Carter Commission argued that tax concessions are always inequitable, are frequently inefficient, and tend to distort the allocation of resources and erode the tax base. If such special concessions are to be given, the commission noted, they should be in a form that will make it possible to assess their costs so that an appraisal can be made. The commission also noted that, besides providing avenues for tax avoidance and tax postponement, the present corporate income tax is riddled with special concessions.[7]

Table 1
Major tax concessions for investment in non-resource sector in Canada, 1970-75

Year	Tax incentive	Benefit in $ millions*
1970	Capital cost allowance supplement	25
1971	Removal of 3% surtax on corporate income tax	80
1972	Corporate profit tax reduction to 40% and two-year depreciation write-off of machinery and equipment for manufacturing and processing firms	500
1974	Reduced taxes on corporations with taxable income less than $500,000	95
1975	5% investment tax credit for new buildings, machinery, and equipment in manufacturing, minerals, logging, etc.	200
Total 1970-75		900

* Measured on a full-year basis. Benefits will vary from year to year.
Source: W. Irwin Gillespie, *In Search of Robin Hood* (Montreal 1978)

A careful glance at the list of the tax incentives established after 1966 in table 1 and the benefit accrued to business indicates how carefully Ottawa listened to the business lobby and ignored the recommendations of the Carter Commission. Three years after the recommendations had been ignored, capital cost allowances saved manufacturers $339 million; the mining industry benefited from another $350 million; and $640 million in capital gains income was not taxed. In 1969, corporations also reported $1,296 million in non-taxable dividends.[8]

This total of $900 million in revenue losses was precisely what the Carter Commission could not justify under an equitable system of sharing the tax load. By contrast, the Carter Commission estimated that if its proposals had been introduced by 1964, two years before the commission *Report*, corporate tax would have increased and personal income tax would have been reduced. As table 2 shows, this would have saved the majority of the people $310 million and gained $222 million for the treasury. Little wonder, then, that Bay Street breathed a collective sigh of relief when the draft of the tax reform bill was introduced in Parliament in June of 1971. Instead of corporate income tax increasing and personal income decreasing, the inverse took place.

Table 2
Estimated effects of Carter Commission
proposals for 1966

	$ millions
Personal income tax	−42
Gift and estate tax	−143
Sales and excise tax	−125
Corporate income tax	+532
Change	+222

Source: Royal Commission on Taxation,
Report, vi (Ottawa 1966), 420

Table 3
Corporate tax deductions for manufacturing and mining industries in Canada, 1970-79
(in $ millions)

Tax concessions	1970	1971	1972	1973	1974	1975	1979
Capital cost allowances							
Manufacturing			2,483.9	3,165.2	4,067.0	4,089.9	
Mining			543.8	795.0	1,107.5	1,342.0	
Accelerated capital cost allowances for machinery and equipment				987.4	1,856.8	1,975.7	1,150.0
Accelerated capital cost allowances for processing assets	145.9	160.1	137.1	102.8	152.8	73.8	
Accelerated capital cost allowances							
Water pollution	32.2	54.1	70.9	82.8	81.0	72.2	
Air pollution			47.4	50.4	62.1	67.1	
Exploration and development expenses for mining			1,127.9	1,478.1	1,829.7	1,409.0	1,250.0
Net capital gains			1,101.4	1,086.0	1,133.0	1,376.0	505.0
Total	178.1	214.2	5,512.3	7,670.3	10,270.2	10,405.7	2,905.0

Sources: Statistics Canada, *Corporation Taxation Statistics* (1970-75); *Government of Canada Tax Expenditure Account* (Ottawa 1979)

The relief felt by the corporate boards increased when the savings from tax concessions were added up for the 1970s. The $900 million noted in table 1 was only an estimate contained in the budgets. However, when the actual deductions reported are taken into account, the total is over $3.4 billion, as shown in table 3. These deductions, and especially the capital cost allowances and accelerated cost allowances, continued to rise significantly from 1972 to 1975. Deductions for explorations and development in mining showed the same increases over the three-year period, as did the net capital gains benefits. These tax deductions were designed to encourage corporations to invest in new machinery and processing, in the hope that the economy would grow and that employment would increase.

There is, however, serious doubt that these tax-saving devices actually produce the desired effect of increasing investments or that corporations seriously consider them in their investment decision making. Mendelsohn and Beigie argue that in and of themselves, tax concessions are unlikely to be the major determinant of investment decisions; rather, business perceptions of the economy's future prospects are likely to be the critical factor.[9] The authors report that results of studies in the United States and Great Britain also indicate that in many cases investment decisions are made with little regard for specific tax incentives. They also note that concessions such as accelerated depreciation allowances reduce the effective cost of employing capital, thereby creating an incentive to use more capital-intensive means of production and less labour-intensive means. Moreover, if the economy is experiencing high unemployment (such as Canada's is) these types of concessions make the problem worse and do not encourage upgrading of skills in the labour force; they simply encourage the replacement of skilled workers.

Tax concessions tend to favour existing firms over potential entrants to an industry to the extent that they provide existing firms with an increased cash flow. One of the main objectives of tax concessions is to generate greater sources of internal funding, but most new firms cannot do this because they have yet to build up their liquidity. Since these concessions are usually fixed at a particular rate of investment, they have the effect of favouring the growth of large capital-intensive firms in relation to smaller firms. Since the farmers' investment outlays are greater, they derive greater benefits from tax concessions.

More importantly, a large proportion of any tax concession granted in manufacturing and mining will accrue to foreign firms. The increased cash flows may not be available for investment in Canada; instead, they may flow out of the country in the form of dividends to foreign residents. There is also a further problem related to the tax rates foreign corporations pay as a result of tax concessions. Under current U.S. law, American firms operating abroad are permitted to deduct foreign taxes on repatriated profits against U.S. taxes due on these foreign earnings. If foreign taxes paid exceed U.S. taxes payable, no further payment is due. In the event that foreign taxes are less than U.S. taxes, the parent firm is required to pay the difference to the U.S. treasury.[10]

Although Mendelsohn and Beigie believe that the present tax concessions do not serve the Canadian economy, they recommend that tax rate decreases are more desirable because they reduce the bias of the tax concessions. This conclusion says little to the income earner who sees his tax bill rising and that of the corporation continuing to fall. Of course, Mendelsohn and Beigie simply ignore the Carter Commission recommendations; their desire is to find a better way to help the capitalist enterprise. Recent studies, however, of the effectiveness of tax concessions in encouraging investment in Canada only confirm Mendelsohn and Beigie's suspicions.

Taking the increases and decreases in corporate tax rates between 1970 and 1977, Gillespie's data show a net benefit to corporate coffers of $1.6 billion.[11] This includes investment tax credits, dividend tax credits, depreciation write-offs of machinery and equipment for manufacturing and processing plants, and corporate tax boosts to petroleum and mining corporations. Hyndman estimated that the combined effect of the 1972 tax reduction and the accelerated capital cost allowance scheme alone was equivalent to a reduction in the tax rate from 52 per cent to 28.6 per cent.[12] From a similar study Harman and Johnson argue that although the state lost $419.7 million between 1963 and 1967, it recovered almost all of this by 1975.[13] However, since the accelerated capital allowance deduction is a permanent change, the cost to the government in revenue lost is approximately $500 million yearly. As we have already seen from table 3, this increased every year and by 1975 stood at $1,975.7 million. The authors also point out that even if the government does regain some of this loss, the timing is costly to the general public. In a period of high inflation, a deferral of taxes involves a decrease in the real value of these receipts. It also means that alternative sources of funds are required if the level of government expenditures is to remain unchanged. In this case it has necessitated large-scale borrowing on the money-markets, which drives up our public debt. At the present time the government is having to spend $1 for every $6 it borrows for interest payments.

More importantly, however, is the conclusion reached by Harman and Johnson. They argue that it is far from certain that tax incentives actually induce investment expenditures, a conclusion which contradicts the rationale for the policies introduced. The policies were designed to shift investment expenditures from a period of relatively full employment to a period of otherwise low investment and high unemployment. The evidence suggests

Table 4
Unemployment and lay-off rates in Canada, 1975-78

	Total unemployed	Lay-offs	Percentage of unemployed due to lay-offs
1975	697,000	317,000	45.5
1976	736,000	381,000	51.8
1977	862,000	473,000	54.9
1978*	972,000	554,000	57.0

* Jan.-July
Source: *Canadian Dimension*, XIII, 5 (1979), 5

that firms do not significantly change their investment patterns to take advantage of the incentive schemes of short duration. In the case of Canadian manufacturing, most of the changes in investment took place three years or more after each of the policies was introduced.

In terms of the actual impact of the policies, although the 1970 increase in the tax loss cost the state $72.3 million, the increase in investment by firms was doubled to $145.3 million. By contrast, the 1972 tax cuts and the acceleration of cost allowances meant a loss of $568.2 million and only $313.3 million in additional investment.[14] The net gain of induced investment by corporations is not what one could call significant. The question is whether we can afford to hand out these grants without a firm commitment that corporations will invest at the time the policies are instituted and to a degree which will justify the amounts of the grants. Given the rates of inflation and unemployment throughout the 1970s, one can only conclude that these policies have been a dismal failure. As table 4 indicates, the rates of unemployment and lay-offs suggest that we have been throwing away windfall profits to corporations.

Table 5 indicates that in the period between 1971 and 1974, precisely the period when the tax concessions were in force, corporate profits increased 110.3 per cent, while labour had to fight an uphill battle to regain its losses in 1975. Even if one were to argue that we would have been in a much worse state if the tax policies had not been introduced, the real effect of the policies was to provide the needed accumulative push which corporate capital desired. In other words, these tax concessions were introduced when the just demands of workers' wage increases in the mid-seventies began to pull down corporate profits. The effect of the government tax policies was that the

Table 5
Who benefits from inflation? (in billions of current dollars)

	1971	1974	Percentage increase	1975	Percentage increase
Corporate profits	8.7	18.3	110.3	17.0	−7.3
Wages, salaries, and supplementary labour income	51.4	76.0	47.8	84.9	11.7

Source: Cy Gonick, *Inflation and Wage Controls* (1976), 116-17

inflationary spiral remained, placing the workers' income back on the tread-mill again and, in the end, pump-priming not the economy, but corporate profits. The recent record high profits for the last quarter of 1978 are further proof of this effect.

It is evident that most of these profits went to the large capital-intensive firms, and that the tax policies benefited these types of firms over the small and medium ones. Although Statistics Canada does not usually break down the concentration of firms into different sectors and the actual tax rates they pay, it did so for 1971.[15] As Kierans reports:

Of all categories in the manufacturing sector, the 83 firms with assets in excess of $100 million paid the lowest effective rate of corporate income tax in 1971, 30.8%. The next lowest rate was paid by firms with assets of more than $25 million but less than $100 million; the effective rate for 197 firms in this category was 35.6%. The remaining 21,718 firms with assets less than $25 million paid an effective rate of 45.3% on their profits. Similarly, in the resource sector the largest 106 firms with assets over $25 million provided $68 million for current income taxes in 1971 on profits of $961.8 million for an effective corporate tax rate of 7.1%. The two hundred firms with assets between $5 million and $25 million paid an effective rate of 38.2%. The 83 largest manufacturing firms were able to defer the payment of $1.3 billion in taxes out of a total deferral of $1.9 billion for the 21,998 corporations engaged in manufacturing at the end of 1971.[16]

Given the degree of corporate concentration at the present time, as shown in table 6, there is little likelihood that these tax rates have changed in the last eight years. It should also be noted, if not already evident, that almost two-thirds of manufacturing and about three-quarters of the mining industry were foreign controlled by 1970. It follows that not only are these low rates

Table 6
Percentage of assets, sales, equity, and profits accounted for by 500 leading enterprises
ranked in terms of sales, by control, 1975

	Sales	Assets	Profits	Equity
220 Canadian	21.2	30.4	24.2	31.1
280 foreign	30.0	28.7	39.2	34.3
500 total	51.2	59.2	63.4	65.4

Source: Statistics Canada, *Corporations and Labour Unions Returns Act*, Report for 1975, part I –
(Corporations) 1978 April 12

Table 7
Dividends paid to non-residents, 1970-76 (U.S. residents) (in $ millions)

1970	1971	1972	1973	1974	1975	1976
555.3	634.5	658.6	751.1	950.7	1,046.9	1,034.7

Source: Statistics Canada, *Corporations and Labour Unions Returns Act*, Reports for 1971-76

Table 8
Selected taxes as a source of federal government revenues, 1961-76

	1961 (%)	1976 (%)	Percentage of change 1961-76
Corporation tax	22.7	15.7	−30.8
Income tax	30.5	43.5	+42.6

Source: Allan Moscovitch, 'Income Tax and Working People,' *This Magazine*,
XI, 1 (Jan. 1977), 21

and deductions mostly going to U.S. multinational firms, but much of non-taxable unearned income is transferred to the United States. As table 7 shows, there was an increased flow of dividends to non-residents throughout the early part of the seventies. In fact, between 1971 and 1973 foreign firms with assets exceeding $5 million paid out between 27 per cent and 34 per cent of the after-tax earnings in the form of dividends.[17] In short, a substantial portion of any increase in net income arising from tax concessions would flow out of Canada. Finally, as tables 8 and 9 demonstrate, the increased

Table 9
Selected taxes as a source of provincial government revenues, 1962/63-1974/75

	1962-63 (%)	1974-75 (%)	Percentage of change 1962-63 to 1974-75
Corporation tax	9.4	5.5	−41.5
Income tax	8.5	21.1	+148.2

Source: Same as table 8, p. 2

shifting of the burden of taxation from the corporate sector to the individual income earner forced the worker to continue to demand higher wages to offset his losses in net earnings, while the corporations could regain their losses by raising prices and enjoying a lower tax rate.

ALLOCATIVE POLICIES – A REGIONAL PERSPECTIVE

In an attempt to use its tax dollars more effectively, the federal government in the seventies designed programs to encourage investments in those regions which were lacking in industrial development. The DREE (Department of Regional Economic Expansion) program is the most visible and the most dramatic failure of these programs. By 1975 a total of over $1.5 billion was given to corporations under the DREE program. As table 10 illustrates, the questionable effectiveness of seven major grants suggests that the program had no controls and no limitations on the corporations which received grants or on what they actually did with the money.

Not surprisingly none of the independent studies published on the effects of this program has concluded that it is a success. Usher, Woodward, and Phillips have all stated that profits rather than jobs have resulted from the program.[18] This is because most of the grants go to capital-intensive, rather than labour-intensive, industry. Phillips reports that grants are not of much use in attracting investments.[19] Furthermore, 85 per cent of the firms in the Maritimes (the Atlantic region accounts for 45 per cent of all grants) which received grants were foreign owned and, therefore, not responsive to Canadian needs and policies. All of the studies also conclude that the money spent could have been much more effective if it had gone to the support of poor people. At least, they argue, there would have been an obvious effect one way or the other. At present, there are few controls put on corporations

Table 10
Effects of selected grants under the DREE program for selected years

---

1 Aerovox Canada Ltd. got an industrial incentives grant of $253,950 from the federal government to start a new factory in Amherst, NS, so it closed its Hamilton, Ont., plant. In Hamilton, 68 jobs were lost; in Amherst, 90 new ones will be created. The company paid an average of $3.23 an hour in Hamilton; it will pay $2 in Nova Scotia.
2 Celanese Canada Ltd. got four federal grants, totalling $278,628, for modernization and expansion in Drummondville, Montmagny, and Coaticook, Que., so it shut down its Montmagny plant and laid off 450 workers. Then Ottawa handed $2,477,600 to two other companies to create 412 new jobs in the old Celanese plant.
3 Bruck Mills Ltd. got a grant of $843,105 to create 140 jobs in Sherbrooke and Cowansville, Que., so it laid off 95 workers in Sherbrooke – a net gain of 45 jobs.
4 Rayonier Quebec Inc., a subsidiary of International Telegram and Telephone of New York, got $13.8 million from Ottawa to create 459 jobs in the pulp industry in Quebec, while Canadian International Paper was laying off 550 workers also in the pulp industry in Quebec.
5 In 1971 Noranda Mines Ltd. got a grant of $3,522,000. Gaspé Copper Mines, a wholly owned subsidiary of Noranda, was offered a $3,267,000 grant. In 1977 Noranda reported that 2,000 workers were eliminated through attrition. In 1978 Noranda Mines was given substantial tax concessions and massive government-financed infrastructure (including a 15-mile spur line built by CNR) in New Brunswick. Noranda received exclusive rights for a ten-year period to smelt lead and zinc concentrates in New Brunswick. DREE provided 'incentive' grants of $2.5 million, along with $750,000 of non-interest repayable loans. DREE's predecessors gave $3.5 million to the chemical fertilizer plant at Belledene, New Brunswick, and $3 million to the particleboard plant at Chatham, New Brunswick, shortly before Noranda's take-over of these firms. Noranda recently invested $350 million to develop rich copper deposits at Andacolla, Chile.
6 International Nickel Company laid off 3,450 workers in Sudbury, Ontario and Thompson, Manitoba, while it received a $77 million loan from the Canadian Export Development Corporation to build a nickel industry in Indonesia.
7 A $68 million grant was given to Ford Motor Company in 1979 by the federal ($40 million) and Ontario ($28 million) governments to build an engine plant at Windsor, Ontario. The new plant is supposed to create 2,750 jobs. Two months later, Budd Automotive of Canada in Kitchener, Ontario, laid off more than 45 per cent of its workers, 1,175 jobs. The result is a net benefit of 1,575 new jobs at the cost of $43,175 per job.

Source: Wallace Clement, 'A Political Economy of Regionalism in Canada,' in D. Glenday, ed., *Modernization and the Canadian State* (1978), 104; *Canadian Dimension*, III, 4 (Dec. 1978), 5-6; *Gazette*, 19 Jan. 1979; and *Globe and Mail*, 2 Feb. 1978

which receive the grants, no prosecutions of those which misuse them, and no legal sanctions for corporations to pay back that part of the grant which did not produce jobs or to pay back to the state the amount owing on the number of workers laid off.

We might have been better off if we had spent all this money in research and development; at least there would have been a long-term effect on our competitive market and sales potential. As Gonick points out, the investment tax credits and grants designed to spur employment are used to buy labour-saving machinery and not to create employment for the region.[20] Public funds are used to build new plants in one region of the country, allowing the company to close down its existing, and probably outmoded, machinery facilities in another region. Moreover, as we have seen, companies invest public monies abroad while phasing out operations at home. As long as economic policies such as these require no limitations or conditions, they are nothing more than windfall benefits to monopoly capital at the majority of the tax-payers' expense.

STATE ENTERPRISES AND SUBSTITUTE CAPITAL

When the state is not performing its accumulation function for capital through direct allocative and productive policies, it provides services for capitalist production by employing Crown corporations to take up the slack. This has led to a proliferation of state enterprises that distinguishes the capitalist state in Canada from others. So extensive is their reach that public firms and their subsidiaries at all levels of government account for about one-third of Canada's economic activity. Federally, there is a mélange of 380 corporations, and provincially, there are more than 100 Crown corporations. In addition, Ottawa is a minority shareholder in an uknown number of companies owned by federal-provincial development corporations set up in the past ten years. Given what has been stated earlier in this paper, it should be no surprise that almost half of the federally owned or controlled enterprises and three-quarters of their subsidiaries and associates were set up or acquired between 1970 and 1975. This is precisely the period when business confidence was low, and investment in the private sector was cautious. The state was therefore bailing out firms and/or investing in areas where private capital feared to tread.

Although the state maintains that it rarely bails out the private sector, it acquired De Havilland of Canada in 1974, Canadair in 1976, and (through Air Canada) Nordair (for $28.4 million) in 1978. Petro-Canada, a federal Crown corporation, also successfully acquired 48 per cent of Pacific Petroleum for $671 million in November of 1978. In the same period, the state doubled its payments to Canadian Pacific in 1974 from $49.7 million to $88 million. Most of these take-overs were predicated on the eventual return of these firms to the private sector; we are still waiting for this to take place.

However, if the New Brunswick government is any example of what happens when firms like these are turned over to the private sector, we are likely to be in trouble. In 1977 the New Brunswick government sold a paper-mill it bought for $4.75 million in 1976 for $1 million to Consolidated Bathurst. This loss of $3.75 million will result in jobs for about fifty people when the mill is in full operation.[21]

TAKING FROM ONE AND GIVING TO THE OTHER

By the time the Economic Council of Canada got around to looking at the tax system in Canada, there was only one conclusion it could come to: 'While government expenditure programs may contribute to the redistribution of income ... the tax system as a whole does nothing to contribute to this goal. Indeed, over the lower portion of the income scale, the system tends to contradict the ability-to-pay principle by taxing the poor at a higher rate than those who are better off. The effect of the few taxes ... that are progressive is completely offset by the remainder of the taxes in the system.'[22] This study by Allan Maslove for the Economic Council of Canada was published in 1973 and was based on the tax system as it existed in 1969. It showed that federal taxes were mildly progressive (the percentage of income collected in tax increased as income rose), except for the lowest-income group. Where progressivity did exist, Maslove found, was in the personal income tax. All other federal taxes were either proportional (they collected the same percentage of income from everyone) or regressive (they levied a heavier burden on the poor than on anyone else). Provincial taxes imposed their heaviest burden on the lowest-income group and were basically proportional for all other groups. Personal income tax was the only consistently progressive aspect of the provincial tax system. Other taxes were either proportional or regressive. Municipal taxes, mainly property taxes, were highly regressive.[23]

These findings may not be too surprising since the 1966 Carter Commission had already argued that unless the ability-to-pay principle was introduced, the tax system in Canada would continue to produce inequality. Yet both the Carter Commission *Report* and the Maslove study failed to impress civil servants or politicians. Nevertheless, there is hardly a minister in the cabinet who in the seventies has not dedicated his party and his government to removing the terrible plight of inequality in Canada. However, as will become evident, almost every tax reform introduced by these ministers had the effect of increasing the amount of regressivity in the tax system.

Not surprisingly, there is hardly a study on the effects of taxation on inequality published in the seventies which has not concluded that this dedi-

Table 11
Average tax savings from selected tax deductions, 1976 (in dollars)

Deduction	Under $5,000	$5,000–$9,999	$10,000–$14,999	$15,000–$19,999	$20,000+
Interest income	–	39.06	56.39	174.05	216.01*
RPP and RRSP†	2.88	31.10	111.68	260.77	777.38
RHOSP†	203.18	269.93	309.93	365.80	571.06
Family allowance	529.92	689.15	719.46	779.01	848.28
Unemployment insurance	–	38.88	56.61	67.39	75.48
Average benefit‡	243.75	484.65	788.06	1,177.46	1,786.93

* For $50,000 and over, the average saving would be $339.40.
† RPP – Registered Pension Plan; RRSP – Registered Retirement Savings Plan; RHOSP – Registered Home Ownership Savings Plan
‡ Average estimated benefits per taxpayer in 1974 from the 17 subsidies, which include the basic exemptions and deductions found in the TP1 tax form.
Source: National Council of Welfare, *The Hidden Welfare System* (1976), and *Bearing the Burden, Sharing the Benefits* (1978)

cation has done nothing to change previous levels of inequality and, in some cases, has increased it. Two of the publications of the National Council of Welfare, *The Hidden Welfare System* (1976) and *Bearing the Burden, Sharing the benefits* (1978), indicate that tax-related schemes, such as pension plans, health insurance, retirement and home ownership saving plans, child care deduction, and unemployment insurance, have had the effect of benefiting the higher-income earner, redistributing some increases to middle-income earners, and doing nothing for low-income earners. Table 11 shows that even such social security schemes as family allowances and unemployment insurance benefit the higher-income group at the expense of the low-income group. As the National Council of Welfare states: 'These tax subsidies are institutionalized inequality and because the tax subsidies are phrased in technical language, hidden in the tax act and not subject to annual Parliamentary review, the public is largely unaware of their nature and extent.'[24]

This 'hidden welfare system' occurs not because there exists an ability-to-pay principle, but the very opposite: a deduction always gives a greater benefit to a person with a higher income and a lesser benefit to a person with a lower income. This occurs because deductions always take money out of a person's highest tax bracket – the bracket which is taxed at the highest rate applicable to his or her income. This is certainly evident in the deductions and subsequent savings as illustrated in table 11. The interest income deductions on such investments as Canada Savings Bonds, bank interests, etc., mostly accrue to the higher-income earner who can afford such investments. The purpose of the registered home ownership plan was to assist young people in saving for a down payment on a house. However, not only are the benefits greatest for the over $20,000 earner, but in 1974 among persons making between $5,000 and $10,000 a year, only one in 32 opened up a plan, but in the $50,000 bracket the ratio was one in 16.

The RPP and the RRSP cost the federal government $1.4 billion in 1976 and $2.1 billion in 1979, while the RHOSP allowed deductions totalling $105 million in 1976 and $115 million in 1979. It should also be noted that the tax rate at the time of withdrawal in these programs is generally less than at the time of contribution. Thus while tax is deferred, some tax is in fact never paid. The Department of Finance estimates that on the basis of assets in the plans in 1976 some $6.2 billion of the deferred tax of $15.2 billion will in fact not be paid. By 1979 this amount is estimated to have grown to $8.5 billion.[25]

While you are getting older and paying into your Canada Pension Plan, your benefits are still based on the same criteria; a worker earning $8,000 a year is only entitled to about three-quarters of a full retirement pension, while workers earning $12,000 a year pay $3 less and get a full credit pension. The same applies if you are unemployed; an $8,000 earner pays $120 in net unemployment insurance premiums to buy coverage which guarantees him or her $103 a week, but the $25,000 a year earner pays an extra $9 to buy coverage worth $160 a week.[26]

These programs cost the federal government over $2.6 billion a year, and a large percentage goes to those who least need a supplement to their income. The principal recommendations of the Carter Commission did not become part of our tax system for the simple reason that they would have hurt the 50 per cent in table 12 who share 93 per cent of the wealth of Canada.

However, the most significant study to date on the effects of federal budgetary policies during the 1970s on the distribution of income is Gillespie's *In Search of Robin Hood* (1978), published by the C.D. Howe Institute. Some of the effects are shown in table 13. These policies have not been redistributive towards the poor, rather they have provided larger benefits for the highest-income families. They have provided modest benefits for lower-middle income families relative to the poor and to the highest-income families. Although table 13 shows the effect of budgets for selected years, the aggregate budgetary effects cover the entire period of 1970-77 and leave no doubt as to the impact on inequality.

Table 12
Distribution of wealth in Canada, 1970

Share of total assets* held by:	All family units (%)
The richest 1%	12.0
The richest 2%	17.4
The richest 5%	28.6
The richest 10%	41.8
The richest 20%	60.8
The richest 50%	93.3

* Total assets include cash on hand, bank deposits, government of Canada bonds, other bonds, publicly traded stocks, shares in investment clubs, market value of home, investment in other real estate, and value of automobiles.
Source: Statistics Canada, *Perspective Canada* (1974), table 7.18

Table 13
Effect of federal budgetary policies on the distribution of income for selected years in Canada

	Family-money-income class					
	$2,000–2,999	$4,000–4,999	$6,000–6,999	$7,000–9,999	$10,000–14,999	$15,000+
June 1971 budget, benefit per family unit*	25.08	89.23	31.85	40.99	68.66	193.10
Feb. 1973 budget, benefit per family unit	245.77	408.70	506.95	547.96	671.73	1,822.57
Nov. 1974 budget, benefit per family unit	57.02	187.59	251.75	288.26	316.48	394.64
May 1976 budget, benefit per family unit	40.90	−99.60	−100.20	−89.10	−82.30	−35.10
March 1977 budget, benefit per family unit	4.61	55.49	111.91	78.46	79.18	617.83
Aggregate budgetary effects, benefit per family unit	450.14	834.82	967.53	1,010.71	1,234.56	3,709.77

* Benefit per family unit is expressed in dollars per family unit.
Source: W. Irwin Gillespie, *In Search of Robin Hood* (Montreal 1978), 50-5

The tax reforms of the 1970s clearly show that the more equitable Carter Commission recommendations for reform of the income tax system were ignored. Instead, the main thrust of the reform legislation was towards substantial increases in personal exemptions, the introduction of a child care allowance deduction, and an employment expense deduction. These measures provide relatively larger tax benefits for those with higher incomes who are paying higher marginal tax rates; they provide no tax benefits for those with incomes too low to be taxable, i.e., the poor. The unemployment insurance revisions of 1972 also provided virtually no fiscal benefits for the poorest families, although they did redistribute fiscal benefits from upper-income families and the highest-income families to lower-middle income families. As noted in table 13, the most substantial gains for the average highest-income family resulted from Mr Turner's budget; it received a benefit of $1,823, compared with $134 for an average poor family. In fact, the budgets of the 1970s benefited the rich eight times more than the poor and needy. Although the impact is evident, the inclusion of certain budgetary factors would suggest even greater inequality than appears in Gillespie's study.

Contrary to popular belief and the intentions of the Liberal party in power, more radical policies must be introduced if any substantial change is to occur in the distribution of income and wealth among Canadians. Nevertheless, the recently announced Refundable Child Tax Credit program may contradict this sober conclusion. This program will provide low-income families with an extra $264 per year. The effect of the new measure will be to establish a mechanism for distributing social benefits on a geared-to-income basis. Although it will not significantly reduce inequality, it is the *most* radical step taken so far.

As to the effects of state expenditures and tax concessions in terms of allocative and productive policies, these too have not been impressive. The allocative policies simply reflect the long history of subsidized capitalism in Canada from railroads to oil extraction. If the recent Science Council of Canada report is taken seriously, we will increasingly see more Canadian corporations in select industries which are more heavily subsidized. Likewise, productive policies – especially the planned provision of scientific and technological support for the accumulation process – have not fared well. In fact this is precisely the area in which increased expenditures could be considered justified. The Canadian state, however, has continued to spend as little as possible on research and development while Canadian corporations have continued to decline in competitiveness in many fields. As an Ontario government report, recently submitted to the federal government, has noted,

Canada spends only 1.1 per cent of its GNP on research and development, compared to 2.4 per cent in the United States, 2.3 per cent in West Germany, and 1.7 per cent in Japan.[27] Comparing industry investment, Ford, General Motors, and IBM each spend more on research and development than Canadian industry as a whole, and U.S. industrial firms undertake 70 per cent of all research and development, compared with only 30 per cent in Canada. The Ontario report also quotes a recent Organization for Economic Cooperation and Development (OECD) study on the scale and range of technological innovation in developed countries. It states that 'Canada ranked last among ten Western countries.' It is, the report adds, hardly a coincidence that the countries beating Canada in both domestic as well as international markets are those very countries which place great emphasis on technological development and product design. A further result of this poor performance is the increasing imbalance in Canada's labour force. Since 1972, manufacturing has produced 78,000 jobs, or 6 per cent of all new jobs, while the service sector has produced 1.14 million jobs, or about 88 per cent of all new jobs. So much for the $3.4 billion give-away to the manufacturing and mining industries for the purpose of increasing their investments. If this de-industrialization continues, we will end up not only a nation of hewers of wood and drawers of water, but a nation of filers of paper and producers of memoranda!

The proposals contained in the Science Council's study would, if implemented, alter this trend through the pouring of massive amounts of public funds into select Canadian corporations. These expenditures would be used in reorganization, research and development, government assistance in world marketing, and a favourable government purchasing policy.[28] The recent federal grant of $235 million to the Canadian forest industry is the first indication that the Science Council's recommendations are being taken seriously in Ottawa. The November 1978 budget also included a 25 per cent tax credit increase for research and development to small Canadian businesses. If they do nothing else, these grants *might* create more jobs.

On the surface, these recent incentives should help revitalize our sagging economy as they are in the spirit of the Carter Commission and they should provide a better return on tax dollars being spent. However, the logic of such incentives is inescapable. The state must provide a favourable investment climate for capital. This also means that the state has no bargaining power; corporations can be bribed, but, in the end, the state either pays the price or finds itself faced with a lot of unemployed people. Corporations can always exert their freedom not to reinvest their capital or to invest it in some other country. In the end, these policies, no matter what their content, put off today what tomorrow will bring.

We are left with the Carter Commission's general recommendations which argued that we have to make the ability-to-pay principle work if we want to end taxation-induced inequality. We also have to stop giving tax concessions to foreign corporations so they may grow larger, and give only to Canadian corporations who will agree to signing a contract stipulating the conditions of the commission. These conditions must include equity in the corporation that receives either a grant or a tax advantage, as a prelude to, and a basis for, the extension of social ownership and planning of the Canadian economy. The Carter Commission also thought that the best way to help our economy was by providing people with enough net income to purchase our goods and services. In other words, we have to start taking from the class that is getting, and start helping the class that is giving.

NOTES

1 W. Irwin Gillespie, *In Search of Robin Hood: The Effects of Federal Budgetary Policies During the 1970s on the Distribution of Income in Canada* (Montreal 1978), 5
2 R.M. Bird, *The Growth of Government Spending in Canada* (Toronto 1970), 114 (emphasis in original)
3 The most recent critical review of Offe's work can be found in John Keane, 'The Legacy of Political Economy: Thinking With and Against Claus Offe,' *Canadian Journal of Political and Social Theory*, II, 3 (Fall 1978), 49-92.
4 Ibid., 57
5 Ibid., 58
6 David Wolfe, 'The State and Recent Economic Policy in Canada, 1968-1975,' paper presented to the Annual Meeting of the Canadian Political Science Association, Quebec City, May 1976, p.6. This excellent article can also be found in L. Panitch, ed., *The Canadian State: Political Economy and Political Power* (Toronto 1977), 251-88.
7 Canada, The Royal Commission on Taxation, *Report*, II (Ottawa 1966), 18
8 David Lewis, *Louder Voices: The Corporate Welfare Bums* (Toronto 1972) 115
9 Joshua Mendelsohn and Carl E. Beigie, *Tax Concessions to Boost Investment: A Perspective*, C.D. Howe Research Institute, Observations, no. 13 (Montreal 1976), 31
10 Ibid.
11 Gillespie, *Robin Hood*
12 R.M. Hyndman, 'The Efficacy of Recent Corporate Income Tax Reductions for Manufacturing,' *Canadian Tax Journal*, XXII, 1 (Jan.-Feb. 1974), 89
13 F.J. Harman and J.A. Johnson, 'An Examination of Government Tax Incentives for Business Investment in Canada,' *Canadian Tax Journal*, XXVI, 6 (Nov.-Dec. 1978), table 3, p. 701

14 Ibid., table 3, p.701
15 Statistics Canada argues that they have stopped making these breakdowns because of costs.
16 E. Kierans, 'Foreward' to T. Naylor, *The History of Canadian Business* (Toronto 1975), xii
17 Mendelsohn and Beigie, *Tax Concessions*, 33
18 Dan Usher, 'Some Questions About the Regional Development Incentive Act,' *Canadian Public Policy*, I, 4 (Autumn 1975), 557-75; R.S. Woodward, 'The Capital Bias of DREE Incentives,' *Canadian Journal of Economics*, VII, 2 (May 1974), 161-73; R.S. Woodward, 'The Effectiveness of DREE's New Location Subsidies,' *Canadian Public Policy*, I, 2 (Spring 1975), 219-30; Paul Phillips, *Regional Disparities* (Toronto 1978)
19 Phillips, ibid., chaps. 4 and 5
20 Cy Gonick, 'Strategy, Strategy, Who Has the New Industrial Strategy?' *Canadian Dimension*, XIII, 3 (Nov.-Dec. 1978), 6-11, 19
21 *Globe and Mail*, 3 October 1977
22 Allan M. Maslove, *The Pattern of Taxation in Canada* (Ottawa 1973), 64
23 Ibid., 78
24 National Council of Welfare, *The Hidden Welfare System* (Ottawa 1976), 15
25 Ibid., 27. See also Government of Canada, *Tax Expenditure Accounts* (Ottawa 1979), 78.
26 National Council of Welfare, *Bearing the Burden, Sharing the Benefits* (Ottawa 1978), 10
27 Queen's Park Report. A summary can be found in *Ontario Report*, III, 4 (Feb. 1979), 16.
28 Ibid., 16

8
Social expenses and regional underdevelopment

NILS KUUSISTO, RICK WILLIAMS

In Canada the problem of social inequality is inextricably intertwined with that of regional disparities. Indeed, the inability of particular local or regional economies to provide adequate levels of employment and other supports, and regional variations in wage levels are primary structural causes of lower incomes and more limited life chances.[1]

As with social inequality in general, regional disparities have been held at 'manageable' levels over the past few decades through massive expenditures by the state. Prior to the initiation of such redistribution measures in the post–Second World War period, the poorer provinces were experiencing severe economic decline and depopulation. Through transfers to persons and to provincial and municipal governments, the federal government has brought about a redistribution of incomes and fiscal resources on a national scale. This has stabilized social conditions in the poorer regions and has controlled the historic tendency for the economy to progressively collapse inwards toward the centre.

The current period is one of serious questioning with regard to the long-term efficacy of these approaches to regional disparities. First of all, it is increasingly apparent that regional development and equalization programs have not stopped or reversed the process of regional economic decline but have merely controlled it at socially and politically acceptable levels. (The same issue is raised about income redistribution or medicare relative to the particular problems they are intended to 'solve.') Consequently, some critics are calling for renewed efforts and new approaches while others suggest that the task is impossible and might better be abandoned.

Secondly, following from this basic failure, the levels of expenditure for regional equalization have had to expand continually merely to maintain the status quo. As a result, regional development programs are being subjected to severe pressure in the current atmosphere of fiscal restraint and cut-backs. Again, in parallel with redistributive programs in social welfare and health, it is being seriously proposed that continuing support for dependent populations is a luxury that Canada cannot afford.

While arguments about the viability and affordability of regional development efforts are much in the public view, there is a regrettable absence of debate about basic causes. Why have regional disparities been such an entrenched element in the Canadian political economy, and why have massive redistribution expenditures failed to dislodge the problem? Why has it suddenly become an unacceptable expense to maintain the economic structures and population bases of the poorer regions? In the following essay we will attempt to deal with such basic questions on both a theoretical and an analytical level.

UNEVEN DEVELOPMENT AND FISCAL CRISIS

Two major concerns in current Marxist political economy provide, we believe, an effective theoretical base for the analysis of regional disparities in Canada. The first is the theory of uneven development, and the second is the fiscal crisis of the state. These theories treat regional disparities, social inequality, and other basic social problems in an integrated manner, and we will follow this approach in developing the theoretical framework before focusing specifically on the regional development issue.

The theory of uneven development[2] has its base in the de facto recognition that capitalist economic growth is, by its very nature, a process which concentrates both the location and the control of the factors of production. Firms compete for resources and markets by realizing economies of scale, by investing in more capital-intensive modes of production, and by consolidating infrastructural development. It is also within the logic of capitalist growth that the labour force be massed in urban centres so that the costs of its maintenance can be rationalized and so that it constitutes a readily accessible mass market.

Over time, competition results in the evolution of monopoly structures. While the so-called competitive sector of small independent businesses remains in existence, it is increasingly restricted to the secondary and marginal labour and commodity markets. Monopoly-controlled production centralized in the most developed metropolitan regions (except in the cases of primary production enclaves) establishes firm and uncontested control over the most remunerative markets nationally and internationally.

In short, the basic characteristics of advanced capitalism are automation, high technology, mass production and mass marketing, the growth of metropolitan cities, and the emergence of the multinational corporation as the dominant economic institution. These very terms are strongly associated with positive images of dynamism, scientific advancement, human progress, and expansion.

Orthodox economic and social theory accepts the most advanced or modernized sector or region as the standard by which to measure the progress and development of all others. If groups, industries, or areas fail to share in the dynamism and benefits of growth, it is due to some failure on their own part to adapt to, integrate, or conform to, dominant modes.

Marxist analysis (in particular, the theory of uneven development) strives to make evident the 'shadow side' of capitalist growth. It points out that development at one pole inevitably implies, and indeed requires, underdevelopment at another. The major negative consequences of capitalist accumulation can be summarized as follows:

1 The creation of national capital markets (through such national institutions as the federal government, banks, trusts, conglomerates, etc.) 'liberates' capital from local control so that it can freely pursue the highest rates of return in boom industries in growth areas.[3] Less profitable, but nevertheless viable, enterprises find it increasingly difficult to raise capital for renewal and expansion. Smaller industries geared to local markets find it impossible to survive the competition of large-scale producers. The consequent collapse of small businesses, local industries, and local marketing structures generates over time in less populated regions the entrenched social and economic stagnation that is termed underdevelopment.

2 Capitalist growth by its nature throws off surplus labour. It destroys skilled trades and replaces workers with machines.[4] It closes out small businesses and local production for local needs. When it serves its manifold purposes, it shifts production from one region to another and even out of the country in pursuit of cheaper labour power. In advanced capitalism, the labour-market is highly unstable with a basic tendency towards the generation of permanent unemployment and underemployment and towards the general 'degradation of work.' Surplus labour tends, of course, to get concentrated geographically because of the underdevelopment process described above.[5]

3 Capitalist economic growth generates greater social inequality in the very process of creating more and more wealth. Regional economic decline and unemployment themselves contribute directly to social inequality. In addi-

tion, the maldistribution of wealth is exacerbated by inflation, by changes in the industrial base which downgrade the exchange value of labour power, and by the general tendencies under monopoly capital conditions for the rich to progressively get richer as they further consolidate their social and economic power.

There are a wide range of social problems which can be attributed to capitalist growth, and increasingly this viewpoint is being developed by political economists in specific fields such as public health, mental health, urban planning, environmental protection, and so on.[6] But for our purposes we will concentrate on the three primary elements described above. Because they are so closely interrelated, these elements are often tautologically defined as causes of each other. In fact, they are each a form or expression of the same phenomenon – the essential unevenness of capitalist development – and their common causation is to be found in the dynamics of the accumulation process.

This perspective would suggest that capitalism is a highly unstable, self-destructive system. The problem which we arrive at, then, is to explain how the economic instability and the socially and politically disintegrative impacts of capitalist growth can be counteracted or compensated. A major contribution towards the understanding of this problem has been made by the American political economist, James O'Connor. In two seminal works, *The Fiscal Crisis of the State* and *The Corporations and the State*,[7] he analyses the growth of the modern state in the context of the demands and consequences of capitalist growth. For our purposes here, we will briefly summarize the core concept of the 'fiscal crisis of the state.'

O'Connor develops the Marxist view of the state in capitalist society as an institution controlled by, and operating in, the general interests of the capitalist class as a whole.[8] As such, 'the capitalist state must try to fulfill two basic and mutually contradictory functions – *accumulation* and *legitimization*. This means that the state must try to maintain or create the conditions in which profitable capital accumulation is possible. However, the state must also try to maintain or create the conditions for social harmony.[9] The state must maintain both its own legitimacy as an institution which appears to mediate between classes and interests, and the legitimacy of the social and economic status quo as 'the best of all possible worlds.' At the same time, its primary role is to implement fiscal policies, to monitor and encourage international relations conducive to trade, to develop, educate, and organize the labour force, and to perform a host of other functions so that a 'healthy' growth rate is maintained. Indeed, expansion of its own institutional power is derived from its share of a larger social surplus produced by capitalist growth. O'Connor carries through the dual functions of the capitalist state into two basic types of state expenditures: '*Social Capital* is expenditures required for profitable private accumulation; it is indirectly productive ... *Social expenses* consist of projects or services which are required to maintain social harmony – to fulfill the state's "legitimization" function. They are not even indirectly productive. The best example is the welfare system, which is designed chiefly to keep social peace among unemployed workers.'[10]

O'Connor does not present these as neat distinctions, but as consistent expressions of the complex and contradictory nature of the capitalist state. (For example, unemployment insurance is a social expense when it is used to mollify workers displaced by a technical advance. However, it may function as a social capital expenditure when it is used to maintain a work-force in place for a seasonal low-paying industry.)

With respect to the three primary dimensions of uneven development described above, we can identify the major social and capital expenses undertaken by the state in Canada:

1 In relation to the general tendency towards intensifying regional disparities (i.e., towards the deepening underdevelopment of semi-autonomous economic and social sub-units), the state generates a wide range of offsetting and controlling measures. The national government makes use of equalization payments, transfers for shared cost programs, incentives to private sector relocations, services to encourage labour mobility, and even public ownership of key local industries with marginal profitability. At the provincial level, the state undertakes parallel programs with an even greater commitment to stimulation of the local economy.[11]

2 In relation to the expanding dilemma of unemployment and underemployment, the major responses of the state have been to absorb surplus labour directly through expansion of public sector employment, and indirectly through growth of government expenditures on goods and services. Unemployment insurance, manpower services, vocational training and higher education, and other such programs constantly adapt and organize the labour force for the shifting demands of the market, and compensate for the market's destructive fluctuations.

3 In relation to social inequality, state expenditures have grown prodigiously. Between 1965 and 1975, for example, government transfer payments to persons increased by 400 per cent in Canada. The Canada Assistance Plan, the Canada Pension Plan, the system of 'progressive' income tax, and unemployment insurance are all means by which the state continually blunts the impact

and visibility of growing income disparities. The state also undertakes massive expenditures to equalize the quality and accessibility of education, health care, recreation, care for the aged, and other aspects of what has been termed the 'social wage.'[12]

Reflection upon the post-war era in Canada leads us to an appreciation of the contradictory nature of the state's accumulation and legitimization functions. In the process of economic transformation and dramatic growth, tendencies to unemployment, inequality, and regional decline have been kept under control, but only at massive cost to the economy as a whole. In fulfilling its legitimization functions, the state withdraws social surpluses from private control, seriously intervenes in the operations of the 'free' labour-market, and implements fiscal measures which stimulate inflation and national debt. Obscuring the basic nature of capitalist accumulation, politicians, economists, and business leaders attack 'big government' and welfare as the causes of high wage demands, unemployment, runaway inflation, and a spate of other limitations on health, profits, and growth rates.

The fiscal crisis of the state evolves as legitimization expenditures grow more rapidly than state revenues. The crisis hits municipal governments first, most dramatically in the overpopulated metropolitan regions, because of their dependence on inadequate property taxes as a revenue base. Income tax revenues are more remunerative and adjust automatically to inflation and economic growth, but the poorer provinces suffer as population and personal incomes grow more slowly. The central government has the strongest revenue base but is eventually forced to compensate for the growing weaknesses of local and provincial governments. Fiscal crisis is like a cancer that takes root in the smallest and poorest jurisdictions and grows towards the strong centre.

If the state is indeed a capitalist state, as our theoretical framework asserts, its response to the crisis will be to sacrifice 'social wage' expenditures in favour of the revitalization of accumulation. It will thus sacrifice other national goals such as social equity, Canadian ownership and control, diversification of industry and the greater domestic processing of natural resources, and environmental protection. In cutting back on existing services, and in compromising basic social priorities, the state inexorably escalates the growth/stability contradiction. This, of course, must eventually result in some degree of 'delegitimization' of the economic, social, and political status quo. Allegiances to national institutions and interests will weaken, while regional, sectoral, and class conflicts will intensify, and basic social order will be threatened. These tendencies are much in evidence today in such instances as the middle-class tax revolts, increasing crime rates, the strong regionalist trends in politics, and the accelerated flow of investment dollars out of the country. Clearly, people who are adversely affected by fiscal crisis have numerous options as to how to express and act upon their frustrations. Whether or not they focus upon capitalist accumulation as the root problem will depend to a very large extent on the level of development of their consciousness with regard to basic social problems. This, in turn, is a reflection of the availability and quality of critical analysis and public debate.

We have summarized this theoretical framework at some length because we believe it provides the basis for a much more developed understanding of the regional disparities problem. In the following sections we will employ the framework in the analysis of changes in the economy of the Atlantic region, and then we will draw out implications for the overall Canadian perspective.

REGIONAL DISPARITIES VERSUS REGIONAL UNDERDEVELOPMENT

In this section we will examine the role of legitimization expenditures in stabilizing the process of regional decline in the Atlantic region. What will be made clear is that, while intergovernmental transfers and transfers to provinces have protected personal incomes and have maintained adequate levels of services and employment, they have not prevented the structural collapse of the regional economy from continuing apace. Thus while regional disparities – the comparable relationship to the rest of Canada – may have been held constant or even reduced, the underdevelopment of the region has been allowed to proceed and, indeed, has been stimulated.[13] The result and the measure of this effect is the profound dependence of the region on the federal government and on fiscal transfers. This, in turn, produces a very serious vulnerability with regard to the current economic stagnation at the national level. Cut-backs in legitimization expenditures represent not only a temporary discomfort for a marginal social sector but a fundamental threat to the economic and social survival of the region.[14]

One of the most publicized measures of disparities is the level of incomes per capita in the Atlantic region compared with the rest of Canada. As table 1 shows, the period from 1957 to 1977 indicates some progress in this direction, but the progress has been slow. Per capita income includes all forms of income received by persons in the provinces of the region; e.g., earned income, rents, interest, as well as transfers from government such as pensions, UIC payments, and welfare.

But it is crucial for our thesis to show the relative growth of forms of income. What is clear is that such income growth as has taken place has been

Table 1
Per capita personal income in the Atlantic provinces as
a percentage of the rest of Canada, selected years, 1957-77

Year	Nfld.	PEI	NS	NB	Atlantic region as percentage of rest of Canada
1957	52.4	49.4	71.1	62.8	62.8
1962	54.0	58.3	73.0	64.0	64.8
1967	59.1	60.2	74.4	67.3	67.6
1972	62.0	64.4	77.8	71.4	71.2
1977	66.2	68.0	77.4	73.5	72.7

Sources: calculated from Canada, Department of Finance, *Economic Review* (April 1978), 134-5; and Atlantic Development Council, *The Atlantic Region of Canada: Economic Development Strategies for the 80s*, 3

largely the result of government transfers rather than the expansion of earnings from productive work.[15] One of the key areas of income transfer growth in this period was unemployment insurance. UIC as a source of income increased at a rate much faster than per capita income in general.[16] In the Atlantic provinces increases were between 626 per cent (Nova Scotia) and 812 per cent (Prince Edward Island) in the 1970-77 period, compared with 424 per cent in the other provinces of Canada combined.

Another form in which transfers have affected income distribution has been equalization grants, which, among other things, have allowed government employment and wages to expand much faster than would have been the case had it been necessary to pay for it out of the provincial tax base. The Atlantic region's combined gross provincial product increased by 117 per cent, but equalization transfers increased by 181 per cent in the same period.[17]

Without going into great detail, it is possible to give clear indications of the degree to which regional income has become dependent on transfer payments from regions of surplus generation. The excess of central government spending over tax revenues in the Atlantic provinces gives a gross measure of the importance of the federal government's role in redistributing income (see table 2). The data clearly show that since 1961 the proportion of gross provincial expenditures supported by federal deficit financing (excess of spending over revenues) has increased in importance for all the Atlantic provinces. This trend is much stronger in Newfoundland and Prince Edward Island – the lower-income provinces of the region. It appears too, despite the

Table 2
Federal deficit* spending in the Atlantic region and other selected provinces as
a percentage of gross provincial expenditures, selected years, 1961-76

Year	Nfld.	PEI	NS	NB	Que	Ont	Alta.	BC, Yukon, NWT
1961	19.4	28.9	24.2	17.5	−4.5	−2.9	2.2	−2.4
1966	18.7	33.7	22.9	15.9	−3.6	−4.7	0.1	−1.2
1971	25.5	38.5	21.0	18.2	−1.0	−4.4	−1.3	−2.4
1976	31.2	46.5	25.4	23.5	3.3	−1.9	−10.2	−1.2

* 'Deficit' refers to the surplus of federal spending of all sorts over federal revenues from
the taxes raised in the province in question.
Source: calculated from Statistics Canada, *Provincial Economic Accounts, Experimental Data,
1961-1976* (cat. no. 13-213), 2-23 and 28-71

experimental nature of the data, that 1975 was the peak year of subsidization
of the provincial economies, and that there was a significant downturn in this
trend in 1976 for all four provinces. In other words, in the 1961-76 period
the federal transfusion of funds to the four Atlantic provinces increased at a
significantly faster rate than their economies, despite the fact that the economies were stimulated by the excess of federal government spending.

By 1976, gross expenditures (which include transfers to individuals, governments, and business, plus spending on goods and services, the military,
and other federal employment) accounted for $3.096 billion in the region, or
over 27 per cent of the regional economy. This surplus of money was transferred from the wealthier provinces, particularly through federal excesses of
revenue over expenditure in Ontario, Alberta, and British Columbia. In fact,
it has increasingly been Alberta in the years since the 1973 oil price increases
which has provided the transferable surpluses.

Some additional indicators of the dependence of the economy and society
of the Atlantic region can be identified from existing official data. According
to a recent Atlantic Development Council publication, *The Atlantic Region:
Economic Development Strategies for the 80s*,[18] the following comparison
shows the per capita *earned* income of the Atlantic region as compared with
Canada (see table 3). The level of earned income in the Atlantic region per
capita increased only 1.2 percentage points on the level for the rest of Canada
between 1970 and 1976, but decreased as a proportion of regional per capita
income from 83.8 per cent to 79.4 per cent. On the other hand, transfer
income increased by 14.2 per cent to a level of 26.2 per cent above the

Table 3
Categories* of per capita personal income for the Atlantic provinces and the rest of Canada, 1970 and 1976

	1970						1976					
	Atlantic provinces		Rest of Canada		Atlantic provinces as percentage of rest of Canada		Atlantic provinces		Rest of Canada		Atlantic provinces as percentage of rest of Canada	
	($)	% of total	($)	% of total			($)	% of total	($)	% of total		
Earned income category*	1,877	83.8	2,902	90.0	64.7		4,013	79.4	6,091	88.1	65.9	
Transfer payment-category*	363	16.2	324	10.0	112.0		1,041	20.6	825	11.9	126.2	
Total	2,240	100.0	3,226	100.0	69.4		5,054	100.0	6,916	100.0	73.1	

* Components of each of the two categories are as defined for the purposes of the Statistics Canada document (cat. no. 13-201).
Sources: Statistics Canada, *National Income and Expenditure Accounts* (cat. no. 13-201); and Atlantic Development Council, *The Atlantic Region of Canada: Economic Development Strategies for the 80s*

Canadian average; it also increased as a percentage of personal income (in the region) from 16.2 per cent in 1970 to 20.6 per cent in 1976. In terms of personal income the seventies have not seen increasing earned income in the region but the reverse. It should also be remembered that much of the increase in earned income is derived from the expansion of the government sector, itself dependent on transfers.

Some indication of the distorting effects of the trend to increased dependence can be seen in the structure of employment by sector in the region. Data from the same Atlantic Development Council report show that the only sector in which the region exceeded the national average growth rate of employment between 1970 and 1977 was the service sector. In other words, the regional economy is burdened with service and support sectors which are seriously overdeveloped relative to the wealth-producing industrial base. While regional employment increased by 20.3 per cent from 1970 to 1977, service sector employment increased by 31.2 per cent, and employment in the public services increased by 42.6 per cent in the same period.[19]

Further indication of the importance of the government sector in the growth of employment is seen in two further tables. The first gives the proportion of government expenditures as a percentage of gross provincial product. The second shows the proportion of capital formation in the provinces financed by government (see tables 4 and 5). The four Atlantic provinces show rates of government spending (all levels) on goods and services markedly higher than the Canadian average and even higher for provinces (Alberta and Ontario) wherein national surpluses are gathered (table 4). The range is from 23.7 per cent of all spending in Newfoundland to 34.9 per cent in Prince Edward Island in 1976, compared with 19.9 per cent for all Canadian provinces and only 13.8 per cent in Alberta. The data are even more dramatic when one considers the degree of reliance (in the region) on government for fixed capital formation – a crucial factor in maintaining and expanding the infrastructure and to some degree the actual means of production (table 5). Government finances ranged between 20 per cent (New Brunswick) and 26.6 per cent (Prince Edward Island) of all fixed capital in the region in 1976, compared with 14.6 per cent for all Canadian provinces and only 10.6 percent in Alberta. If marginal regional economies are drained of capital through low prices for products and high prices for imports – a central thrust of uneven development – the data show the degree of redistribution required just to keep the regional economy from collapsing. It is clear that the government sector is the growth sector of the regional economy, and that this growth is dependent on federal transfers of surpluses to the region.

Table 4
Government spending (all levels) on goods and services as
a percentage of gross provincial product, selected provinces and for Canada

Year	Nfld.	PEI	NS	NB	Ont.	Alta.	Canadian avg.
1970	18.7	31.0	33.1	23.6	18.8	17.5	19.0
1971	20.3	35.3	33.4	27.9	18.8	17.6	19.1
1972	20.1	36.1	32.3	27.1	18.4	17.0	18.9
1973	19.4	33.7	30.4	24.0	17.8	15.7	18.2
1974	21.4	39.3	33.5	24.3	17.8	13.5	18.3
1975	23.5	36.0	34.5	26.1	19.5	13.9	19.7
1976	23.7	34.9	34.3	27.1	19.4	13.8	19.9

Source: calculated from Statistics Canada, *Provincial Economic Accounts, Experimental Data, 1961-1976* (cat. no. 13-213), 2-23 and 28-71

Table 5
Government-financed fixed capital formation as a percentage of
total fixed capital formation, Atlantic provinces and selected other provinces, 1970-76

Year	Nfld.	PEI	NS	NB	Ont.	Alta.	BC, Yukon, NWT	Canadian avg.
1970	14.9	37.4	16.3	24.6	16.8	13.1	13.4	17.6
1971	16.9	34.7	19.2	19.9	16.9	12.3	13.1	18.1
1972	20.1	24.7	22.6	19.4	15.7	11.8	15.5	17.2
1973	22.0	19.7	24.7	20.8	13.5	10.9	13.2	15.5
1974	25.5	17.0	28.3	20.9	14.2	12.3	14.3	15.9
1975	30.6	30.7	26.6	19.4	13.6	13.1	14.7	15.8
1976	23.8	26.6	26.0	20.0	13.1	10.6	14.7	14.6

Source: calculated from Statistics Canada, *Provincial Economic Accounts, Experimental Data, 1961-1976* (cat. no. 13-213), 2-23

What these data argue is that the effort to compensate the region (in pursuit of legitimization) has not produced a greater capacity to support its population. Instead, there is indicated a strong and growing need for transfer
income to ensure that the Atlantic provinces do not fall further behind the
national standard of living. In addition, the data reveal the continuing failure
of government to resuscitate the private sector as a basis for making a living

in the region. Instead of generating balanced social and economic growth, federal support programs have reinforced the function of the Atlantic region as a reserve army of labour. This function is to provide a supply of mobile workers who can be called upon as the economy demands reallocation of labour power to areas of growth. It also helps to control wage demands by ensuring a surplus of available workers.

The Atlantic region has been providing a continuous flow of surplus labour to elsewhere in Canada and to the northeastern United States for generations, as Veltmeyer points out.[20] Only wartime and booms or depressions have restrained this flow in the twentieth century. In the 1960s, during a period of dramatic national economic growth, more than 150,000 people left the Atlantic region. The effect of redistributive policies after the mid-sixties was to momentarily restrain this flow. For the first time during a period of peace or non-depression, there was a net gain of population in the region from migration. This gain was not, however, based on any substantial growth of opportunities for productive work, but rather on a growth of government employment and subsidies, which shielded people from the forces which had required emigration in the past. Recent figures (for 1975-76) show that the pressure to emigrate may be increasing.[21]

The regional labour force, therefore, has been maintained as a reserve army. An indication of this is the low rates of participation in the labour force, compared with the national rate: 53.8 per cent of those over 15 years of age in the Atlantic region compared with 61.5 per cent nationally.[22] Seasonal unemployment is also more prevalent in this region than in the rest of Canada, averaging 33 per cent from 1966 to 1976, compared with 24 per cent in Canada generally.[23] The regional labour force is more likely to become mobile as employment opportunities and UIC eligibility are tightened. In 1970 the regional unemployment rate was only 0.5 per cent higher than the national average of 5.7 per cent of the labour force. By 1977 the regional unemployment rate was 12.7 per cent compared with 7.7 per cent nationally (table 6). This differential of 5 per cent, plus the hidden reserve of those not in the labour force or only in seasonally, indicate the potential for mobilization.

In summary, the data on regional disparities in the Atlantic region suggest that changes in income levels are misleading. Such changes reflect, more than anything else, a higher level of transfer payments. Another major factor in reducing income disparities has been the creation of government employment directly through federal government deficit spending in the region and indirectly through the increasing dependence of the provinces on revenues from

Table 6
Unemployment rates for the Atlantic provinces and the rest of Canada, 1970-77*

Year	Nfld.	PEI	NS	NB	Atlantic provinces	Rest of Canada
1970	7.3	6.7	5.4	6.3	6.2	5.7
1971	8.5	7.2	7.0	6.1	7.1	6.2
1972	9.2	11.1	7.1	7.0	7.8	6.1
1973	10.1	7.2	6.7	7.8	8.0	5.4
1974	13.3	7.4	6.8	7.3	8.5	5.1
1975	14.2	7.7	7.8	9.9	9.9	6.7
1976	13.6	9.8	9.6	11.1	11.0	6.8
1977	15.9	10.0	10.7	13.4	12.7	7.7

* Rates shown for 1970-75 have been converted to the new labour force surveys base introduced by Statistics Canada in 1976.
Sources: Statistics Canada, *Labour Force Survey* (cat. no. 10-001); and Atlantic Development Council, *Economic Development Strategies for the 80s*, 15

equalization. Slightly reduced income disparities, therefore, are the result primarily of a very large and expanding government sector presence in the region.

THE FISCAL SQUEEZE ON LEGITIMIZATION EXPENDITURES

The development of the social services in the Atlantic region in the seventies has been supported both by Canada Assistance Plan (CAP) cost sharing and by equalization revenue to the provinces which, although not tied to specific provincial activities, have served to allow the provinces to maintain levels of activity not supportable from their own tax bases. These transfers to support provincial governments in the region have been supplemented by the federal government's central role in providing direct income maintenance to individuals.

Motivated by the apprehended fiscal crisis, the federal government has taken initiatives in regard to both types of transfers in order to reduce the draw on state resources necessary to cover them. The social services block-funding proposal to replace the 50-50 cost-shared Canada Assistance Plan is the most direct attack on the social expenses of the state. This proposal has been shelved for the moment, but it illustrates the pressures on central government to reduce the priority of social equity in policies. Under the proposed block-funding formula the rapid growth of social services since CAP was introduced in 1967 would have a ceiling put on it. This would be done by removing funding from any relation to demand for services in the region – which under CAP could be translated into cost-shared funds by the provinces by meeting CAP eligibility criteria. This was easy enough for the Atlantic provinces to do considering the social conditions in the region. The only real restraint was the unwillingness of provinces to allocate some of their own funds to these programs. With block funding there would be no requirement of meeting eligibility criteria for social services, but the funding formula was to be restrained in aggregate by the rate of growth of the GNP. The base rate, moreover, was to be determined by a national average of per capita spending on social services, with the objective that after a five- or ten-year period of adjustment, all provinces would be getting an equal per capita grant for social services. For some provinces in the Atlantic region – particularly Prince Edward Island and Newfoundland – since per capita social services spending was considerably above the national average (because of need, one must assume), the block-funding adjustment would be particularly harsh. In the Atlantic region, only Nova Scotia was clearly in the position of benefitting on the basis of the per capita formula. There were, as part of these negotiations, short-term incentives offered during the period of adjustment. But, basically, block-funding would have reduced the growth of the funding provided by the federal government for social services to a level where it would not exceed national economic growth, i.e., regardless of national needs for social services. And, by equalizing funding on a per capita basis, it would have removed in the long term the consideration of special regional needs which reflect national uneven development.

The unemployment insurance program is an area in which the central government has been able to move unilaterally. The 1978 cut-back of 10 per cent maximum benefits and the raising of eligibility requirements to eliminate the seasonally employed workers and students will particularly affect the Atlantic region. While there are lesser eligibility requirements for labour force regions with more than 11.5 per cent unemployment, the effect in the Atlantic region will still be pronounced.

In fact, in the seventies, one of the pronounced factors relieving the social expense burden on the provinces was the extension of unemployment insurance coverage following the 1971 changes of the act.[24] Table 7 shows social assistance recipients for the provinces in the seventies. There was a notable levelling in the size of welfare rolls after 1972-73 for a couple of years, particularly noticeable in New Brunswick. This allowed an extension of social assistance benefits and eligibility as UIC reduced, the demand for provincial welfare without undue strain on provincial resources. The rising levels of unemployment in the region since 1973-74 appear to have had a delayed but

Table 7
Social assistance recipients in the Atlantic provinces, 1970-77

Year	Nfld.	PEI	NS*	NB
1970	24,581	2,563	12,503	15,679
1971	24,755	3,150	13,920	18,430
1972	22,723	2,939	14,235	18,801
1973	20,956	2,616	15,129	18,348
1974	20,990	2,817	16,475	18,926
1975	19,950	2,855	17,059	21,918
1976	–	3,265	17,728	23,648
1977	–	3,617	18,366	26,069
1978	–	3,702	–	25,728

* Nova Scotia figures are for provincial assistance only; municipal assistance case-loads have not been available, and generally this is a short-term case-load.
Sources: calculated from the *Annual Reports* of the departments of social services in the Atlantic provinces.

consistent effect in expanding the numbers of social assistance recipients. Multiplied by increased rates of assistance, this basic income maintenance service has reimposed a strong growth in demand for funds at the very time when restraint of funding is taking place. This situation is one which will be crucial to the future direction of policy in the provincial social service structures of the region.

On the provincial level the squeeze on fiscal resources for social services has been intensifying since the early 1970s. The provinces of Prince Edward Island and Newfoundland have in fact held social services spending to a lesser growth rate than total provincial government expenditure for most of the seventies. In Newfoundland this effort has been quite dramatic in reducing the social services spending from 15.2 per cent to 10.4 per cent of provincial spending between 1970-71 and 1977-78 (see table 8). In New Brunswick and Nova Scotia there has been an increase in the proportion of provincial spending on social services in this period. But in the last two to three years there has been a freeze on employment in welfare offices as a policy to restrain the rate of increase of expenditure. In addition, guide-lines on overall provincial budgetary increases have been imposed, accompanied by increasing control from treasury boards.[25] The New Brunswick Department of Social Services exhibited the fastest rate of growth of expenditure of the Atlantic provinces in the seventies and has had severe cut-backs imposed on

Table 8
Comparative social service expenditure,* fiscal years 1970/71–1978/79
(as a percentage of provincial government spending)

	70-71	71-72	72-73	73-74	74-75	75-76	76-77	77-78	78-79
New Brunswick	8.3	9.5	9.5	9.7	11.6	12.3	12.0	12.3	12.4
Newfoundland	15.2	14.3	13.3	12.0	12.0	11.6	11.0	10.4	9.9
Nova Scotia	7.3	8.3	7.7	8.7	8.6	8.8	9.2	9.7	9.3
Prince Edward Island	12.1	10.7	10.2	9.7	10.5	10.3	10.1	10.2	9.8

* Does not include expenditure on social services from municipal level
Sources: calculated from provincial public accounts for the years cited

it since 1975-76. Since then it has levelled off at about 12.4 per cent of the provincial budget after accepting cut-backs of community work projects and senior citizen shelter supplements. In 1978-79, policy changes were applied to reduce the numbers of social assistance recipients by 3,000, or about 10 per cent.[26] We shall get into this further in discussing the specific impacts of fiscal restraint on the social services. It is clear, nevertheless, from the expenditure figures that the fiscal resources available from the provincial level in the region are under severe restraint despite equalization payments and cost sharing under the Canada Assistance Plan. In Prince Edward Island and Newfoundland this restraint has been in place virtually throughout the seventies, perhaps because these provinces with the weakest tax bases and most acute problems of unemployment have set their priorities on economic development. New Brunswick and Nova Scotia, on the other hand, have been perhaps less burdened with this problem (relatively speaking), and starting from a lower level of social service expenditure have increased it more rapidly in the period. But these relatively better off provinces have therefore had to put more effort into the turning down of the expanding costs of social services in recent years.

RESTRAINTS ON ACCUMULATION

At the same time that the squeeze is on government functions directed at legitimization, efforts to revive capitalism are diminishing too. Government efforts at trying to make the regional economy perform as a capitalist economy have been intense in the last twenty years. A major agency in this has been the Department of Regional Economic Expansion (DREE). The department's expenditures in the region, however, peaked in 1971-72 and have been declining in real (constant dollar) terms since then (from a high of $184 million in 1970-71 to $108 million in 1977-78 in 1971 dollars).[27]

The other major federal effort at sustaining capitalism in the region has been DEVCO – the Cape Breton Development Corporation.[28] DEVCO was a self-consciously political pacification project intended to facilitate the phasing out of major coal and steel industries. In parallel with DREE, the most concerted action was taken in reaction to crisis points in the collapse of capitalism in the region. Concentrated effort in 1969-71 brought about a peak of capital investment in Cape Breton, particularly in the Canso Strait area. Since then, like DREE, DEVCO's efforts have been of marginal importance, compared with the overriding impacts of national capitalist development. The renewal of interest in coal has taken away some of this pressure but has not meant that there has been any success in reducing one of the highest localized rates of unemployment in Canada.

Again, on Cape Breton Island, SYSCO – the Sydney Steel Corporation – came into being in response to the same crisis. Under provincial auspices the investment necessary to make it a viable state-owned steel producer has been put off for ten years. The central requirement – a new furnace complex – would have cost approximately $80 million in 1970, and today its cost is estimated at $400 million. Meanwhile, operating debts have accumulated to the point that federal government assistance has been necessary to reduce the heavy burden on the province.

Cape Breton reveals in high relief what has happened to the regional economy in general. Adventures in subsidizing private capital have created a history of disasters – Bricklin, Deuterium Ltd., Clairtone, the Come-by-Chance Refinery, the Stephenville Linerboard Mill, etc. – costing hundreds of millions of dollars.[29] These all represent attempts to revive the private sector through direct grants, loan guarantees, tax breaks, infrastructure costs, utility subsidies, and other commitments. One of the results of this process was that by 1976 the provincial governments of the region were much more burdened with debt than generally was the case for other provincial governments in Canada. By 1976 the proportion of provincial spending on debt servicing ranged from 1.8 per cent (Nova Scotia and New Brunswick) to 4.8 per cent (Newfoundland), as against 1.2 per cent for all Canadian provinces.[30]

In general terms this decline of the private sector can be seen in the trends of private capital investment in the region (see table 9). By 1977 the region had returned to the level of the early sixties (at about 60 per cent of the national per capita private investment after the brief boom during 1970-71), when per capita private investment equalled the national average. What is apparent now is that the efforts to revive capitalism in the Atlantic

Table 9
Per capita private investment (excluding housing) in the Atlantic region as
a percentage of Canada (current and constant* dollars), selected years, 1961-77

Year	Atlantic region Current	Constant	Canada Current	Constant	Atlantic region as percentage of Canada
1961	177.5	244.2	265.4	365.1	66.9
1966	355.2	413.5	488.7	568.9	72.7
1971	576.1	576.1	556.8	556.8	103.5
1976	757.6	457.8	1,141.7	689.8	66.4
1977	735.6	414.4	1,217.5	685.9	60.4

* 'Constant dollars' are current dollars deflated by the Implicit Price Index for Business
Gross Fixed Capital Formation, 1971 = 100 (*Economic Review* [April 1978], 172).
Source: *Economic Review* (April 1978), 134-5

region have failed. The withdrawal of the federal life support system, which
is now taking place, will reveal the vulnerability of the regional economy, a
weakness that has been disguised by the massive transfers of resources
through the period before the crisis.

INCREASING DEMANDS FOR SERVICES

At the same time as the fiscal squeeze is imposed from the centre, the impact
of the general economic crisis is generating increased demand for social welfare services. In the Atlantic region, because of its feeble and dependent
economy, the exercise in restraint hits doubly hard. There are few areas, if
any, in which there is enough strength in the economy to be able to stand
without the transfusion of funds from the rest of the country. This has been
seen above in the rapid rise of unemployment in the region (see table 6).
The impact of unemployment on the full range of social problems is not
directly traceable, but there is little doubt about its potential for generating
poverty and family stress.

Social assistance recipients have increased in the last four years despite the
prevalence of categorical eligibility barriers[31] (table 7). In New Brunswick,
categorical eligibility was liberalized in 1973 and then reintroduced to the
extent of cutting off 3,000 cases in 1978. The other provinces have not had
to do this because they did not liberalize their eligibility requirements to the
same degree. So, in Nova Scotia the effects on the numbers of social assistance recipients of increased eligibility barriers for unemployment insurance

will be minimal because of rigid provincial eligibility requirements. In Prince Edward Island and particularly in Newfoundland, the numbers of social assistance recipients have been severely restrained throughout the period by narrow eligibility. Newfoundland's experience of falling numbers of recipients since 1973 reflects extraordinary measures to exclude people who are in any way employable from social assistance – these cases are reviewed monthly and even if people qualify, the employable single or childless married person gets one-third of the rate.[32]

Despite these barriers the welfare rolls are expanding as the severity of unemployment increases continually. The indicator of this is in the flood of single parent families seeking social assistance. Social service administrators see the welfare rolls as being out of control; that is, there are demands that cannot be easily deterred by barriers of eligibility. Moreover, the lack of resources for day-care and homemaker services, and the lack of plausibility of employment training programs do not allow for any optimism about their being able to control this situation.

The demand for other services is not diminishing either. The boom in nursing home care in the seventies – despite the effort to restrain the provision of more facilities – will demand more resources as costs escalate. Ceilings on old-age security and guaranteed income supplement will reduce the client's fees as a factor in covering costs – as much as 20 per cent in the nursing home program in Prince Edward Island. Efforts to restrain spending in day-care and homemaker services – small though these programs have been to date – will only compound dependence on social assistance.

One conclusion can be drawn about such restraint policies across Canada: it is the poor and the service dependent people who generate the public savings by absorbing lower real incomes and reduced access to material and personal supports. It is a process of impoverishment. In the Atlantic region there is the added problem that these populations are relatively poorer (nationally speaking) to start with, and have fewer, if any, alternative sources of support. Restraint policies are thus an additional pressure for the young and mobile to leave, which in turn further isolates and ghettoizes the old, the handicapped, and other state dependents.

CONCLUSION

Based on the theoretical framework and empirical analysis presented above, it is possible to propose or affirm general answers to the questions posed at the outset. Regional disparities have persisted in spite of dramatic economic growth on a national scale because that growth, qua capitalist accumulation, engenders regional decline via the continuous concentration of capital.

Equalization expenditures and regional development strategies have been primarily utilized for *legitimization* purposes. As private capital and initiative retreats from less populated, non-central areas, the state fills the vacuum not with viable economic activities but with non-productive supports and social expenses. The result is the deepening *dependency* of both regional economic and social structures. Substantial capital expenditures by the state have been aimed at attracting and facilitating private investment, *not at controlling it or replacing it.*

State expenditures on regional stabilization are under attack because the costs of maintaining poorer regions and populations have grown to the point where they inhibit continued capital accumulation on a national scale. Having created dependent sub-economies and sub-societies, the capitalist state, acting on behalf of the capitalist class (and not, as is often asserted in the media, on behalf of the wealthier regions per se), now acts decisively to cut them off and punish them for their lack of autonomy and vitality.

In a major paper prepared for government policy makers, Professor T.J. Courchene of the University of Western Ontario articulates this current tendency.[33] In a brilliantly confusing attack on Keynesian economic planning principles, he blames the regional disparities problem on the very measures taken by the capitalist state to counter or control regional disparities – minimum wage legislation, liberal unemployment insurance qualifications, financial aid to declining industries, the DREE program, and other inter-governmental transfers:

The thrust of this paper is that the level of, and incentives embodied in, the current system of transfers both between governments and from governments to persons is not at all conducive to eliminating regional economic differentials in this country. Indeed, I shall argue that the current pattern of transfers is serving to rigidify and perhaps even exacerbate provincial and regional disparities.

... the problem of regional disparities is essentially a problem of economic adjustment ... the presence of the large and growing network of transfers lessens both the necessity for and the desires on the part of the have-not regions to make the adjustments required to remain economically viable. As a consequence, their relative economic position has deteriorated vis-à-vis the have provinces to the point where several of the provinces are in danger of being reduced to the level of 'dependencies' of the federal government.[34]

Courchene's solution to the regional disparities problem is to remove barriers to factor mobility – basically, to allow wages to drop to their 'real' level relative to local market conditions. As a result, many people will emigrate, 'backward' industries (such as inshore fishing, farming, etc.) will collapse, and thus problems of poverty and structural backwardness will be 'solved' within the particular region. He asserts that lower wages will attract capital investment, without reference to the fact that historically lower wage levels in the Atlantic region have not attracted significant private investment. The exception to this pattern has been marginal or super-exploitation industries ('runaway shops') that have contributed little or nothing to regional economic stabilization. He does not examine transportation or marketing structures or economies of scale factors in explaining why investment doesn't come to peripheral regions. In short, when all the mystifications about the equilibrating capacities of the free market are removed, what Courchene is in fact proposing is that the regional disparities problem be solved by cutting back on social expenses and by depopulating the societies of the poorer regions. While his attack on the transfer system accurately identifies its negative dependency-creating aspects, he misrepresents legitimization mechanisms as being the source of the problem rather than a false and intellectual antidote. It is a sobering thought that, in the absence of substantial opposition, his line of thinking may well become dominant in the public policy formation process.

Keynesian and liberal economic thinking is somewhat on the defensive at present due to its identification with uncontrolled growth in government expenditure. In *Living Together: A Study of Regional Disparities* the Economic Council of Canada reviewed the successes and failures of regional development efforts and came up with a patchwork series of policy recommendations.[35] The theory section of the report reviews a series of approaches, all of which locate the problem in weaknesses *within* regional economic and social structures. There is no consideration of national economic trends and structures, and no critical reflection on dominant growth patterns. Despite rhetoric about stabilization and social equity, the general drift of the policy proposals is again towards increased factor mobility.

In a recent publication entitled *Regional Disparities*, Paul Phillips has taken a refreshingly positive approach to the policy question.[36] He sees the need for a national economic planning and industrial development strategy which would reallocate economic surpluses from energy and resource industries towards manufacturing and secondary development on a national scale. Greater Canadian control of the economy and the more widespread and creative use of public ownership are key elements in his conception of a more *even* process of development.

While Phillips' proposals make economic sense as far as they go, they leave unanswered the essential political question as to the conditions under which more progressive social and economic policies might be implemented.

This is particularly a problem given the much vaunted 'shift to the right' in public attitudes, and the preponderance of conservative politicians in public office at the moment. Our own concluding comment would be that the reduction of state legitimization efforts in response to fiscal crisis may perhaps represent a growing weakness in the ideological hegemony of capitalism. There is, therefore, a critically important *educational* task to be undertaken in presenting the realities of regional decline and social inequality to affected constituencies. The demystification of the sources of social problems and the delineation of clear and positive alternative policies and programs are prerequisite to the emergence of a political climate conducive to structural reform and transformation.

NOTES

1 See the Economic Council of Canada publication, *Living Together: A Study in Regional Disparities* (Ottawa 1977), chap. 4.

2 For a comprehensive review of current work on uneven development, see *The Review of Radical Political Economics*, x, 3 (Fall 1978), especially John Lovering, 'The Theory of the "Internal Colony" and the Political Economy of Wales'; Kenneth Fox, 'Uneven Regional Development in the United States'; Henry Veltmeyer, 'The Underdevelopment of Atlantic Canada'; and James Overton, 'Uneven Regional Development in Canada: the Case of Newfoundland.'

3 For an excellent analysis of this process operating in the Maritimes, see T.W. Acheson, 'The National Policy and the Industrialization of the Maritimes, 1880-1910,' *Acadiensis*, I, 2 (1972).

4 See Harry Braverman, 'Work and Unemployment', *Monthly Review*, XXVII, 2 (June 1975).

5 See Veltmeyer, 'Underdevelopment of Atlantic Canada.'

6 Useful examples of such analysis are to be found in the *International Review of Health Services* e.g., J. Eyer, 'Hypertension as a Disease of Modern Society,' x, 4 (1975), and W.K. Tabb and L. Sawers, eds., *Marxism and the Metropolis* (London 1978).

7 James O'Connor, *The Fiscal Crisis of the State* (New York 1973), *The Corporation and the State* (New York 1974).

8 O'Connor sees this as a complex and dynamic situation which cannot be oversimplified with 'conspiracy' or 'executive committee of the ruling class' kinds of conceptions. For an excellent review of orthodox and Marxist theories of the modern state as they apply to Canada, see Leo Panitch, 'The Role and Nature of the Canadian State,' in Leo Panitch, ed., *The Canadian State: Political Economy and Political Power* (Toronto 1977). See also D. Gold,

C. Lo, and E. Wright, 'Recent Developments in Marxist Theories of the Capitalist State,' *Monthly Review*, XXVII, 5 and 6 (Oct.-Nov. 1975).

9 O'Connor, *Fiscal Crisis of the State*, 6 (emphasis in original)

10 Ibid., 6-7 (emphasis in original)

11 For a valuable treatment of the relationships between different levels of government in the evolution of the welfare state, see Garth Stevenson, 'Federalism and the Political Economy of the Canadian State,' in Panitch, *Canadian State*. Also, for an historical analysis, see Alvin Finkel, 'The Origins of the Welfare State in Canada,' ibid.

12 Rick Deaton, 'The Fiscal Crisis of the State in Canada,' in D. Roussopoulos, ed., *The Political Economy of the State* (Montreal 1973), 18-58

13 'Regional disparities' are used here to denote the aggregate indices of relative economic well-being commonly used in doing interprovincial comparisons. These are one measure of inequality. We wish to contrast this with comparisons of other indices which more directly reflect the infrastructure of inequality. These are measures of degrees of development/underdevelopment which point in the Atlantic region to the lack of productive capacity, of slow rates of fixed capital formation, and the structure of employment reflecting accelerating underdevelopment. The contrast is of disparities remaining despite a spate of transfer payments, but this nevertheless disguises a much more fundamental process, the increasing underdevelopment of the region.

14 See Atlantic Development Council, *The Atlantic Region of Canada: Economic Development Strategies for the 80s* (n.p. 1978), 31-4. This recent report is used extensively in this paper because its data parallels that which we have been developing, and it shows that even to official agencies the failure of regional development policy is becoming plain – hereafter *Atlantic Region*.

15 Atlantic Provinces Economic Council, 'National Unity and Regional Disparity,' from Atlantic Provinces Economic Council *Newsletter*, XXII, 2 (Feb. 1978). The following table is from this source.

Transfers as percentage additions to net provincial income*

	Newfoundland	Prince Edward Island	Nova Scotia	New Brunswick
1961	45.0	57.0	45.0	38.4
1966	46.9	72.5	43.1	34.9
1971	55.9	69.8	38.9	38.3
1973	64.1	60.3	42.4	37.6
1974	66.8	119.1[†]	47.2	43.8

* The table may be interpreted as saying that for each dollar earned in a province in a given year, the federal government transferred so many extra cents.

† This figure is unusually large because the losses on the CN ferries to Prince Edward Island were all attributed to the province as a transfer payment as of 1974.

16 Statistics Canada, *Statistical Report on the Operation of the Unemployment Insurance Act* (Ottawa 1974-77, cat. no. 73-001), cited in *Atlantic Region*; and Statistics Canada, *Social Security, National Programs* (Ottawa 1978, cat. no. 86-201). By 1976 UIC benefits had risen to 5.0 per cent of personal income in the Atlantic region from 2.1 per cent in 1971. In Canada as a whole, the parallel increase was to 2.2 per cent from 1.2 per cent of personal income. See also T. Bailey and N. Naemark, 'A Note on the Transfer Payment Implications of Benefit and Contribution Operations under the Unemployment Insurance Act,' *Canadian Statistical Review* (Nov. 1977), Reference Paper 73-001. The authors note that in 1975 the contributions of employees in the Atlantic Provinces ranged from one-third of their benefits (Newfoundland), to half for Prince Edward Island and New Brunswick, and approximately three-quarters for Nova Scotia. The benefits paid therefore constitute a significant transfer of income to the Atlantic region from regions of lesser unemployment in Canada.

17 Gross provincial product from *Atlantic Region*, 8; and equalization revenue from Public Accounts of Provinces, 1970-71 to 1976-77

18 *Atlantic Region*, 6

19 Ibid., 13 and 160

20 Veltmyer, 'Underdevelopment of Atlantic Canada,' 95-105: 'Forced to migrate for productive employment, at least 300,000 Maritimers abandoned the region over the first three decades of the twentieth century. Significantly, nearly half of this emigration which, it has been estimated, involved half of the region's most productive workers, occurred between 1921 and 1931. Although there are no exact data on the direction and volume of this movement, it clearly corresponds to periods of economic expansion at the Centre. This massive exodus of people out of the region has continued apace, but assumed alarming proportions in the 1960's. It has been estimated that between 1961 and 1969 more than 150,000 persons (almost two thirds of whom were between the ages of 15 and 34) left the region. Over the same period, employment in the region increased by 113,000. The various studies that have been conducted suggest that the major provincial recipient of the endemic out-migration from the Maritime region has been Ontario. In a period (1956-61) for which data on internal and external migration are broken down, Ontario received 46.9% of emigrants from Newfoundland and Nova Scotia, 42.2% of those from New Brunswick, and 40.7% of those from P.E.I.'

21 *Atlantic Region*, Table 7, p.11

22 Canada, Department of Finance, *Economic Review* (April 1978), 156

23 Economic Council of Canada, *Living Together* (Ottawa 1977), 53

24 It could be said that the extension of UIC and the higher rates of payment after 1971 were a substantial subsidy to the provincial social services and enabled them to allocate more funds to expand their revenue from cost shar-

ing under CAP. New Brunswick and Nova Scotia, at least, seem to have gone this route in expanding eligibility for welfare (with reduced demand for just income maintenance) and in increasing spending on new programing, particularly homes for the aged, and day-care in Nova Scotia. Prince Edward Island and Newfoundland, particularly the latter, seem to have taken this relief from demand for income maintenance as a way of reducing or stabilizing expenditure. The evidence of this is in the fact that the social assistance case-loads actually declined up until 1975 (the last figure we have). The heavy emphasis on employment creation in Newfoundland indicates that there is a strategy of requalifying employable clients for UIC payments to reduce the burden on the provincial treasury for social assistance.

25 From interviews with personnel administrators of social services.

26 From interviews with social services administrators in New Brunswick

27 Department of Regional and Economic Expansion, Moncton; also *Atlantic Region*, 30

28 DEVCO was created to cope with the economic disaster of Industrial Breton when the coal mines and the steel plant all faced closure in the mid-sixties. Its mandate was to close the coal mines, which had been sustained by increasing subsidies since the thirties. This was to be accomplished through early retirement for some miners and through development of alternative industries to employ others. After the usual mediocre performance in creating other industries, the economics of coal mining have swung back in DEVCO's favour due to the oil crisis. Still, the federal funds available in grants for alternative industries and for coal development have not been adequate to the tasks either of stabilizing old industries or of generating substantial new ones. In 1976-77, DEVCO's budget was cut in half by a restraint measure.

29 See Phillip Matthias, *Forced Growth* (Toronto 1971).

30 Statistics Canada, *Provincial Economic Accounts: Experimental Data* (Ottawa 1978, cat. no. 13-213)

31 'Categorical eligibility' denotes criteria of eligibility for financial or social assistance depending on specific characteristics of applicants, such as disability or social dysfunction. This implies a narrow range of eligibility for social services rather than qualification by a degree of need, such as low income or extra financial burdens faced by some families and individuals.

32 From an interview with a social services administrator in Newfoundland

33 T.J. Courchene, 'The Transfer System and Regional Disparities: A Critique of the Status-quo,' Annual Public Lecture Series, School of Public Administration, Carleton University, Ottawa, 1978

34 Ibid., 1

35 *Living Together*

36 Paul Phillips, *Regional Disparities* (Toronto 1978)

9
Education and inequality: some strategic considerations

STEPHEN SCHECTER

Schools contribute to inequality by reproducing, via a hidden curriculum and social structure, the class structure of contemporary capitalism. This paper focuses on the legitimation or ideological functions of the school as a social institution which maintains political order in the widest sense and provides a properly qualified labour force for the owners of capital. It then discusses the need to situate reform movements within this overall framework, in the hope that an insight into the history and contradictions of school reform will open up the possibilities for strategies of change that will help undermine, rather than reinforce, inequality in Canada. The latter half of this paper addresses some of the issues involved in realizing such strategies.

SCHOOLING, SCHOOL REFORM, AND INEQUALITY

Out of the long debate over the relationship between schooling and inequality has emerged the understanding that schools do not so much produce as reproduce the class structure of capitalism.[1] Their crucial role lies not in determining future school attainment or economic success – the constellation of class forces do that – but in legitimating the inequality and alienation that are characteristic of the wider social order. This distinction may seem a fine one, but its implications for strategies of school reform are serious.

The dominant discourse surrounding school reform in the past decade and a half focused on giving more schooling to a greater number of people. Schools were seen as the major social institution determining the eventual allocation of resources in Western industrial countries. This viewpoint was buttressed by the statistics which indicated a strong association between higher incomes, post-secondary education and higher status occupations, an association which was explained in terms of the sophisticated technology required by citizens in those societies. People were poor, therefore, because they lacked the skills necessary for succeeding in modern times. If we want to reduce inequality, so the argument ran, we will have to supply more of these skills to these people, which means giving them more schooling. To the extent that there exists financial or cultural barriers to doing so, we will have to devise programs to overcome them.

The use of education as a means to overcome inequality has proved to be false on nearly all counts. Despite the association between education, income, and occupation, very little of future economic success is actually explained by school attainment; and very little of what schools do seems to affect the latter. More money, smaller classes, and a host of other panaceas might make politicians or parents feel better, but they do not seem to make students stay in school longer.

In their now famous study of the relationship between schooling and inequality,[2] Jencks et al found that education accounts independently for only about 10 per cent of the variation in income and 42 per cent of the variation in occupations when other factors, such as income, are held constant. The correlation between achievement on test scores and schooling obtained is higher than the correlation between socio-economic status of parents and schooling obtained; but even at that, the correlation only comes to 60 per cent. Only half of the effect of cognitive aptitude is really due to aptitude, which means that IQ genotype explains only about 2 to 9 per cent of the variation in schooling obtained. Streaming does not determine future schooling options for more than 20 per cent of the student population, and the figure is more likely to be around 12 per cent. Money is not a significant differentiating factor either, even though there are wide discrepancies between schools in terms of resources and programs: 'Our 91 Project Talent high schools reported their expenditures per pupil in the entire school system, the average salary of their teachers, and the number of teachers per student. If we compare ninth graders with similar aspirations, best scores, and economic backgrounds, we find that those who got the most education attended high schools which spent less money than average, had worse-paid teachers, and had larger classes.'[3]

Not only were assumptions about school policy erroneous, so were assumptions about the processes at work in the wider society. The subordination of technological development to capitalist rationality resulted in the replacement of skilled labour with routinized jobs that required increasingly less training. The subordination of the Canadian economy to American corporate interests ensured that even at the post-graduate level, available jobs would not match prospective candidates since most research and technology in the private sector is carried out in the parent country. Success, then, in educational terms, does not necessarily mean a top job in good times.

As in earlier periods, the key to understanding current school reforms lies in the role schools play in legitimating the changing class structure of capitalism.[4] On the one hand, schools instil those values which justify the workings of the general social order and especially the subordinate position in which members of the working class eventually find themselves. Schools must provide workers in the different strata of the capitalist work hierarchy with those attitudes and behaviour patterns commensurate with their occupational destinies. As economic growth continuously transforms the organization of work, the socialization tasks imposed on schools change accordingly. In the period since the end of the Second World War, the principal transformations in the work structure of Canadian capitalism have been the massive integration of women into the work-force, a generalized deskilling of jobs in the monopoly sector, and an increase in the new middle classes or petite bourgeoisie. The expansion of post-secondary education, especially at the community college level, must be seen as an attempt to prepare those individuals slotted to occupy the middle management posts of both the public and private sectors with the necessary combined attributes of personal initiative and corporate or state loyalty. At the same time the content of ideological legitimation for the subordinate members of the occupational hierarchy also changes. Technology and democratization woven around the idea of upward social mobility became the main themes of school reform, resulting in the ideology and practice of progressive education at the elementary and secondary levels. In actual practice, special classes, refined streaming, and polyvalent high schools were new techniques to prepare those youngsters headed for dead-end positions in the workplace to acquiesce to their own subordination.

A study of BC community colleges indicates that the higher up the academic ladder one goes, the less one is likely to find students of working-class origin: 43 per cent of the population of British Columbia earned $10,000 and over in 1971; 47 per cent of technical institute students came from families who did so; 59 per cent of university students and 51 per cent of college students came from such families. Within the college student population, those of lower-income backgrounds were more readily found in the vocational and career technical streams.[5]

This pattern is accentuated in the lower echelons of the school system. Martell has vividly explained what schooling means for the vast majority of high school students who do not go on to college. Their reading levels are drastically below the average. One study showed that only 7 per cent of vocational school graduates make any use of their acquired technical skills in the job market. Only those females headed for clerical and sales jobs in the expanding service sector of the economy learned anything of relevance. As Martell points out, the middle-class definition of technical education as giving students a reasonable feeling of self-confidence in the face of technology is 'just plain crazy' to working-class people, who 'understand very fast that there is a big difference in this society between having a usable skill and feeling good about not having a skill.'[6]

The process of school reform is not, however, a linear one, as pressures in favour of changes in education preceded actual implementation by thirty years. These pressures stemmed in part from the logic of earlier school reforms, which paved the way for individualized programs, streaming, and psychological testing. The reforms acquired their force, however, only when material conditions had changed to render them imperative.

The most important change was the restructuring of the work-force as monopoly capital expanded to all sectors of the economy following the Second World War. Braverman has made it very clear what this meant for most working people. On the one hand, the increasing mechanization of industry and the intensification of work that this entailed required new functions of surveillance and control. These functions themselves are stratified in a hierarchy of occupations running from top management to foreman and to supervisory personnel in a steno pool. On the other hand, blue-collar jobs require less skill; the expansion of office work and its separation from production require a vast army of clerical workers, also with little skill, as the organization of work pioneered in automobile production lines is extended to offices; and the incorporation of services into the commodity market has vastly increased those active in sales, but again at fairly low level jobs. Finally, there is the burgeoning number of cleaning jobs that are required to service the corporate institutions which this expansion of monopoly capital has entailed. It was this transformation in the class structure which underlay the school reforms of the sixties.[7]

The expansion of state expenditures in areas of social reproduction, such as education, brings about its own contradictions, most notably an increasing fiscal crisis of the state as expenditures outstrip revenues. One way out of this crisis, as O'Connor has suggested, is through the growth of the so-called social-industrial complex. This involves closer co-ordination between the state and monopoly capital in order to plan investment of state expenditures in such a way that they provide an outlet for surplus capital. Much of the new technology that went along with the educational reforms of the sixties can be seen in this way. Software was increasingly being used in the schools. Systems building is being tried out in construction, as in the case of a school design agency which received the backing of the Metro Toronto School Board despite its increased cost of school construction, on the grounds that discontinuation of funds would jeopardize the development of systems building in North America. At the same time, the school reforms of the sixties provided an occasion for the state apparatus to restructure itself, centralizing fiscal control at the provincial level so that funds could be shifted from one area to another as occasion and limited revenues required.

It is evident in the seventies that schools have ceased to be a prime area of government investment. Urban problems have become a more salient area of social contradictions – pollution, rapid transit, day-care centres. At the same time, capital is experiencing an accumulation crisis and looking to the state to underwrite more of its accumulation needs. The problem, of course, is that the shift away from education coincided with the contradictions coming home to roost from these same much-heralded reforms of the sixties. The promise of upward mobility held out by the school expansion of the sixties is proving to be a sham. As Lockhart pointed out, the state was incapable of keeping up its end of the implicit bargain in providing appropriate jobs for all those who 'agreed to accept a narrow, sometimes irrelevant, often alienating and increasingly prolonged education confinement as the price paid in youth for privilege in later life.'[8]

In the division of powers within the state, local school boards and commissions have been transmitted the more overt policing functions, while professional expertise exercises planning and fiscal control from centralized provincial departments of education. Progressive education seems only to have produced students with fewer real skills. At the same time, the expansion of the sixties has escalated state expenditures even more, leading to attempts at cut-backs in the public sector, with teachers being one of the prime targets. Government attacks on teachers' corporate interests have been fuelled by disenchantment with the school reforms, which has itself unleashed a back-to-basics movement on the part of the educational establishment and large numbers of parents. The radical critique of schooling which emerged in the sixties is being blamed for the current ills, while at the same time more sophisticated elements of the educational establishment are attempting to incorporate parts of this critique in a new set of practices designed to rationalize the prevailing contradictions.

Part of this process involves continuing the reorganization started in the sixties, which would favour an even greater rationalization of resources and provincial fiscal control, thus permitting the state to shift priorities and funds from one area of state legitimation activity to another. Such freedom necessarily entails revamping the dominant ideology to remove its expectational framework.

Thus the back-to-basics movement, to the extent that it is endorsed by the dominant educational elites, represents the thin edge which will divide the theme of upward mobility from school ideology and prepare the ground for the new conservatism inherent in the bourgeoisie's appropriation of the ecological critique. One has only to look at the Quebec government's recent green paper on educational reform, which advocates increased homework in primary grades and reminds us that 'education presumes, today as yesterday, work that is patient, structured, often repetitive, and at times austere.'[9]

Whether such a strategy will work depends ultimately on the balance of class forces in society and on the capability of contesting forces to develop a counter strategy, programmatically and organizationally, one that will give school reform a liberating and revolutionary dynamic. Although the response to this question will only emerge from praxis, the theoretical consideration of many of the issues posed by this practice may help alter the odds somewhat in the favour of revolutionary forces.

NON-REFORMIST REFORM

Any attempt to develop strategies around the issue of schooling that will push society in the direction of greater equality must first unburden itself of the myths that have hitherto informed school reform efforts. The most important myth is that which locates the source of our society's inequality in the structure of our schools instead of in the institutional fabric of capitalism. The second myth is that egalitarianism, as opposed to simple meritocracy, is not only desirable but also possible. The meritocratic conception of equality was the premise upon which progressive schooling relied; yet the kind of equality it presaged only meant ensuring equal access to inequality. Class divisions were accepted as the inevitable functional concomitant of the division of labour in a technologically complex society. This premise has had incredible legitimating force, for it builds structured inequality into its very conception of equality in terms of a seeming social determinism, obscuring the possibility of altering existent social relations.[10]

The use of ability to explain social success reinforces individual conceptions about the natural order of things and the position each person occupies. Schools play a key role in this process since they have claimed a monopoly on defining ability and have elaborated a series of practices to measure it. The fact that IQ does not have a determinant effect on future life chances for most people does not diminish the belief that intelligence explains class position. On the contrary, not only does IQ provide a legitimizing rationale which has the advantage of not being amenable to social change; it also turns people's subordinate position in the class structure into a weapon, which they then turn on themselves. Not only are people thrown the question: 'If you're so smart, why aren't you so rich?'; they are also given the converse explanation: 'If you're not rich, you're obviously not so smart.'

The Jencks study, as mentioned earlier, has pointed out the limited explanatory power of IQ for school or economic success. Sennett and Cobb have vividly sketched its legitimating power as it turns ability into a badge of individual worth and, hence, into an instrument of subordination:

The early IQ testers believed in a bell-shaped curve of ability, with fewer and fewer people having more and more ability. Let us not worry about the scientific shakiness of this idea. The image is important because on the most intimately personal level it appears to people as a way to decide who can wear the badge. In these struggles for worth there are two classes, the many and the few; the selves of the many are in limbo, the selves of the few who have performed win respect ...

... Now a badge of ability seems the perfect tool to legitimatize power. The concept of human potential says that the few are more richly endowed than the many and that only the few can know themselves – i.e., recognize themselves as distinctive individuals. Having gained 'more' dignity by virtue of greater personal power, it is logical that they ought to rule the many. Apply to that simple meritocratic argument the tentative rule proposed above about legitimized power: the more inclined are the many, the masses, to a belief that dignity exists in these terms, and the more they surrender their own freedom to the few, the less chance they have of respecting themselves as people with any countervailing rights.

If, however, the people we encountered in the course of writing this book taught us anything, it is that this set of notions is all wrong, because the people who are subject to limits on their freedom do not take dignity away from themselves that they accord to higher classes – as though dignity were a commodity. They react to power in a much more complicated way: look at Frank Rissarro's attitude toward 'educated' work, for example. Educated men can control themselves and stand out from the mass of people ruled by passions at the bottom of society; that badge of ability earns the educated dignity in Rissarro's eyes. Yet the content of their power – their ability considered in essence rather than in relation to his personal background and memories – this he finds a shame, and repugnant. Still, the power of the educated to judge him, and more generally, to rule, he does not dispute. He accepts as legitimate what he believes is undignified in itself, and in accepting the power of educated people he feels more inadequate, vulnerable, and undignified.[11]

A movement for school reform which seeks to address the problem of inequality in our society must therefore recognize at the outset that the problem is rooted in the very nature of capitalism and will only be overcome with the overthrow of capitalism by a workers' movement committed to socialist democracy. Furthermore, the key articulation between contemporary schooling and inequality lies in the legitimation role which schools assume under capitalism. This legitimating role is assured not only by the formal content of schooling but also by its hidden curriculum.

It is true that much of the formal curriculum is class based, sexist, and discriminatory towards non-dominant peoples, such that students from socially subordinate groups find school even more alienating than the general student body. It is also true, however, that the more subtle legitimating mechanisms of schools are even more effective. Grading, streaming, standardized tests, obligatory attendance, hierarchical social relations, credentials, uniform and irrelevant curricula are all means of making school unpalatable and boring to most, while simultaneously fostering the myth that schooling is essential to economic success. Thus students who decide not to proceed to post-secondary levels are resigned to a subordinate position in the class structure and are made to feel that the fault is their own. The division between manual and intellectual labour, which monopoly capitalism has deepened, is further reinforced, thereby depriving working-class people of those tools which would enable them to pierce the ideological domination of capital.

Bowles and Gintis have described the means by which schools carry out these legitimation functions in terms of the correspondence principle: each level of the school hierarchy is governed by a certain behaviour and set of values corresponding to the comportment and attitudes that will be required of workers at the corresponding level of the job hierarchy. Such characteristics as autonomy, self-direction, outspokenness, and critical judgment are highly prized by teachers at the upper end of the school ladder (community colleges, universities), while passivity, conformity to norms, and internalization of externally imposed rules are more rewarded at the bottom rungs of the school system (elementary and secondary grades). It is not surprising then that high school graduates are destined to perform routine, deadening jobs in the corporate and state apparatuses. These are jobs that require little initiative and an already instilled inclination to accept an organization of work, in both its technical and social aspects, giving these workers little room for creativity and control.

The graduates of community colleges and universities, on the other hand, are slotted to fill the gamut of control and surveillance jobs in our society, tasks which require the capacity for initiative and rule determination without, of course, challenging the wider system on which the entire hierarchy rests. Hence the almost brutal rupture in the passage from high school to community college which many students experience. Hence, too, the maintenance throughout the educational system of an underlying social structure that is hierarchical and authoritarian, even if the relations of authority become progressively masked as one ascends the scale.

In this sense, the social structure of the school corresponds to the social structure of the wider society, and through its own social structure of hierarchy and control reproduces those social relations which reinforce the system of inequality outside it. Within the class-room, students at any level remain subordinate to the teachers, and within the educational system itself, teachers remain subordinate to a whole battery of surveillance and control personnel, running from principals to district superintendents, to school commissioners, ministry of education officials, and government ministers.

It is this elaborate system of social control which accounts for much of that bureaucratic interference and red tape which seems to so many teachers and parents as simply rules-for-rules'-sake. Yet that red tape serves a very functional purpose. It ensures that the socialization tasks of schools get carried out, while alternatives become difficult to imagine and even harder to execute. Teachers learn that they are not allowed to experiment without first getting the approval of their superiors, just as workers are not allowed to use equipment without the authorization of foremen or introduce technological changes into factories without the approval of industrial engineers. Young children learn that they are not allowed to go to the bathroom without asking the teacher's permission, just as workers cannot go to the toilet except during designated breaks.[12] High school students learn that they are free to the extent that they conform to the often unstated, but nonetheless omnipresent, lines of control, much as young workers learn that they are free to the extent that they submit to the hard and soft discipline imposed in the social and industrial factories of contemporary capitalism.

A radical school reform movement in Canada must therefore hit out at both the hidden and overt curricula and combine an alternative school structure with a relevant curriculum that is linked to a class-based analysis of that society. One of the major weaknesses of the free school movement lay precisely in its failure to develop a class-based strategy. The absence of the class dimension isolated the free school movement and left it as an enriching experience for the sons and daughters of the professional middle class but without an impact on the working class, whose daily life and future prospects made such experiences seem remote and irrelevant.

In the last analysis, the experience was not totally irrelevant, for the challenge posed by the free school movement struck at the very heart of the legitimating functions of contemporary education. A non-hierarchical, truly individualized, student-oriented learning process makes for autonomous, critical human beings, the very opposite of what is required by corporate capitalism and of what is elicited by dominant school practices. In offering non-repressive learning environments, free schools indicated that an alternative to the existing system was possible, and also affirmed that the kind of alternative social order envisaged was libertarian, in contrast to the authoritarian character of existing socialist societies.

Important as these contributions were, however, they remained partial, for in the absence of a class perspective, relevant education in the free school movement too often reflected the relatively privileged class position of the students and their parents. The oppression of the dominant social order and the need for collective action to counter it tended to get submerged in the emphasis on individual growth, as though schools could be liberated in a society that remained repressive.[13]

The recognition that the liberation of schools, like the liberation of individuals, requires the transformation of society must underlie an effective radical movement of social reform. Thus demands formed within a perspective that linked school reform to change would focus on changing the social relations of schooling and on providing a content that addressed itself to the class nature of the prevailing reality. The explosive power of such a program can be seen from the reaction of the educational establishment to the *May First Manual*, prepared by the political action committee of the Centrale de l'enseignement du Québec (CEQ). The document used the format of the daily lesson plan to introduce subjects that are rarely talked about, in spite of the fact that they make up the reality of most people's lives – the nature of work under capitalism, strikes, industrial safety, pollution, and sexism. The minister of education denounced it quite appropriately as a revolutionary act and forbade its use. The reason for his judgment can be evaluated by the following introduction and sample lessons taken from the manual:

TO ALL WORKERS EMPLOYED AS TEACHERS

This manual for a special study day on the working class is a collection of suggestions on courses and activities to do with students of all levels to celebrate May Day. It has been prepared by active members of the Teachers' Union from all parts of Quebec.

The manual is one of the consequences of action by CEQ militants, who in the last three years have produced the analysis of the school, which can be found in L'école au service de la class dominante (The School at the Service of the Dominant Class) and was further developed in Ecole et luttes de classes au Québec (The School and Class Struggle in Québec).

WHY THIS PROJECT?

BECAUSE   the majority of students are children of workers.

BECAUSE   the capitalist schools, by the values they transmit, do not serve the interests of workers' children, but those of a minority.

BECAUSE   as workers our interests are tied to the working class.

BECAUSE   we want our profession to serve as much as possible the interests of workers.

BECAUSE   we want to develop a pedagogy of 'conscientization' which encourages the majority of students, who are the children of workers, to be conscious of the interests of the working class and to understand the necessity for organizing themselves.

BECAUSE   we believe that it is possible, in a school, to promote action which makes the school less discriminatory for workers' children and at the same time encourages the development of conditions which will bring about a new organization of society which doesn't rest on the exploitation of workers.

NOTES

You can adapt projects which take into account local needs and resources ...

Several projects prepared for one subject or level can be modified to be used for another subject or level, or can be extended to last longer than a day.

The projects will have more effect if they are related to real problems experienced by workers in their own setting.

In cases where May 1st is celebrated by a work stoppage or holiday, we suggest that you hold a study day before May 1st so that you can explain the origins of May Day, the interest of workers and of employers, etc ...

SAMPLE PROJECT No. 3
Subject: French Language – Art
Level: Elementary school
Topic: Workers

TEACHING OBJECTIVES
Oral and artistic expression. Manual dexterity.

'CONSCIENTIZATION' OBJECTIVE
To sensitize children to the fact that everything we need to live is produced by workers.

METHOD AND CONTENT
The teacher uses questions to elicit discussion.

First Stage: What do I need to live? The children reply verbally. The teacher notes on the blackboard what they say (i.e., housing, clothing, food, transportation, etc.) The teacher could also ask the children to draw or to look for pictures to cut out, or even to talk about or explain these needs.

Second Stage: Who makes the things I need to live? Verbally the children are encouraged to list the different types of workers necessary to construct these items. For example, to construct a house: carpenters, painters, bricklayers, truck drivers, manual labourers, etc. The teacher writes the list on the blackboard. The children are asked to draw or cut out pictures of these workers. The teacher can hang this work up in the classroom.

Third Stage: How do the workers who make these items live? How do their bosses live? The children are asked to compare the living conditions of workers and their bosses using drawings and cut-out pictures.

MATERIALS
Crayons, felt pens, scrapbooks, scissors. The exercise can lead to subsequent studies.

TEACHING NOTES
Teachers should avoid ranking skilled workers in relation to each other, or in relation to unskilled workers.

SAMPLE PROJECT No. 4
Subject: Language – Observation
Level: Kindergarten, elementary school
Topic: The Family (sex role differentiation)

TEACHING OBJECTIVES
Observation and verbalization. Learning to listen. Learning to speak.

'CONSCIENTIZATION' OBJECTIVE
To break down traditional sex role distinctions.

METHOD AND CONTENT
The students paste-up pictures representing different family jobs (e.g.: dishes, baby, cars, sports equipment, lawn mower, sewing machines, dolls).

The children make up models of men and women in cardboard.

After discussion, the children pin pictures which they think appropriate to the model men and women.

Discussion: Find out why certain jobs are identified with men and some with women, since all tasks can be undertaken by both.

TEACHING MATERIALS NECESSARY

Cardboard, periodicals, glue, pins.

NOTES

The same task can be undertaken by kindergarten or nursery school children in the form of a game ...

That only 5 per cent of teachers did use the manual owed less to the minister's threats than to the fact that the document lacked a sufficiently wide political base among the teachers – a state of affairs that poses a number of lessons and questions for the strategy of school reform.[14] The manual indicates in the first place that programmatic content is insufficient without an organizational base to carry it through. To develop and implement a pedagogy of the oppressed, teachers must find allies both within their own ranks and within the community. The demands presented must therefore be of such a nature both to raise political consciousness and to win support from students, parents, and teachers. This is important if the parents, students, or teachers raising these demands are not to be isolated by the dominant political forces.

Therefore, the more collective an action, the better it is – though this does not necessarily mean that the school board level is the place to start. Teachers may start at the class-room level in devising learning projects that make students reflect critically on the class structure of their community and thereby may enlist the sympathy, if not the support, of working-class parents. At the same time, teachers could work on the establishment of political networks within their unions in order to widen political consciousness and to build the support necessary to withstand reprisals from principals, school board members, and ministry officials. Parents could raise demands that give them greater control over school practices, such as the hiring of personnel, the determination of curricula, participation in the class-rooms, access to their children's test scores and related data. Teachers could support parent initiatives for community control of schools, while parents in turn could support teachers in their union struggles for better pay and working conditions.

Such a parent-teacher alliance based on school issues would be the working-class response to the bourgeoisie's attempt to manage the fiscal crisis of the state. This response is the only logical one, as workers and clients in the state sector link their immediate economic interests to non-reformist demands on monopoly capital and the state.[15] Teachers could only expect parent support to the extent that they link their demands for improved working conditions to improved education and carry out that link in daily practice. At the same time, parent demands for community control would only win teacher support to the extent that greater autonomy for teachers is implied. In the absence of such a united front, the state at various levels will continue trying to divide the working class by cutting back on teachers' salaries or on school services. Nonetheless, serious obstacles still remain that make it difficult for the different sectors of the working class to transcend their corporatist interests. These are obstacles that characterize other areas of social life and, therefore, bear some scrutiny.

OBSTACLES TO CHANGE

The first obstacle to change is the wearing effect of daily life under capitalism, which tends to grind most people down and reinforce a sense of powerlessness. This situation is in turn reinforced by their ideological subordination to the dominant value system, whose hold is many faceted: an acceptance of the inevitability of the given social order; submission to the expertise of authorities; family relations which tend to reproduce the authoritarian and repressive nature of capitalist work relations and, hence, those of school relations as well; and attempts to find individual ways out within a psychological dynamic that tears people apart. Such ideological subordination not only makes working-class people prey to the counter-attack of the dominant class, for example, by branding teachers' strikes as narrow and selfish, or attempts at school reform as revolutionary; it also makes the political mobilization of the working class difficult.

As well, there are all the tactical considerations. Where, for example, does an individual, especially a working-class parent, start? What issues does he or she raise first, and with whom, even within a revolutionary strategy of school reform? Does not the separation of manual and intellectual labour make it likely that the leadership of these movements will initially fall into the hands of the new petite bourgeoisie, thus reproducing within the reform organizations the very relations which the movement aims to abolish? The predominance of the professional middle classes which seems to characterize struggles outside the workplace also opens up these struggles to eventual reformist or social democratic practice.[16] The state itself has already undertaken measures to encourage this tendency through decentralization programs, which result in the appointment of powerless consultative bodies designed to contain potential protest. School-parent committees and community health clinics are two such examples.[17]

The class position of teachers is equally problematic. Attempts to link teachers' struggles with struggles of other workers and with working-class parents in the community have been characterized by considerable corporatist ideology and by practices which reflect the ambiguous class position of teachers. On the one hand, teachers perform the dirty work of the education system, and their position within the organization thus resembles that of workers within corporations – relatively little autonomy and increasing pressures towards proletarianization. On the other hand, they carry out important political control functions, internalize many aspects of the dominant ideology, and receive relatively higher wages in recognition of their role.[18]

These obstacles are not an exhaustive list of the pitfalls confronting revolutionary attempts to organize around the issue of schooling. They are indicative of some of the general strategic problems facing a revolutionary strategy based on non-reformist reforms.

Despite these obstacles, such a strategy seems to offer the only viable alternative under today's conditions that at the same time attempts to implement in daily practice those principles of socialist democracy which render it a counter-model to capitalism: the critique of capitalism as an alienating ensemble of social relations; the redefinition of the democratic transformation of the social relations of production and reproduction; the abolition of the social and sexist division of labour; the creation of autonomous worker organizations that would subsequently become the sovereign political institutions of the emerging socialist society; and the recognition, in practice, of the independent contribution to the revolutionary struggle made by diverse attempts to organize around the multiple contradictions of capitalism. Massive democratic mobilization is at the very core of such a strategy and gives it the character of historical necessity, in the multiple sense of that term. Only such a strategy recognizes that the contemporary political situation of the Western working class requires working through and transcending bourgeois political institutions, that the political strength to push through these reforms and strengthen workers' autonomous organizations demands mass mobilization, and that such strategic principles are alone compatible with the revolutionary project.[19]

Between the possibility and the realization of this historical necessity lie a number of obstacles, such as those already described, which are only insurmountable to the extent that one forgets the dialectical and contradictory nature of capitalism and, indeed, of all social life. In the first place, movements with a revolutionary thrust, organized both around the workplace and outside it, have emerged in the past, and though they have suffered defeat, one can learn from past mistakes; the future need not be a repetition of the past.[20] Theory is important here as is the creation of political networks which would help people working in and around schools to continue to evaluate collectively their experiences. In the second place, capitalism is itself in crisis, rent with contradictions. Social democratic reformism is one possible outcome to this crisis, but not the only one. The unity between state workers and clients, though far from realized, is proceeding to some extent. The very fiscal crisis which produced increased state confrontation with teachers has also made an alliance between teachers and parents a practical possibility. The class position of teachers is not a static relationship but a dynamic one which responds to the social pressures around it. The very real constraints on the political radicalization of certain social strata, such as teachers, should not blind one to possible alternatives.[21]

Discussion of strategy questions always seems to end on a note of dissatisfaction or of 'unfinished business' suspended in the air. This quality reflects the very nature of revolutionary struggle. It reflects, too, the fact that theory is only effective when linked to political practice, and that the analysis of struggle, though necessary and long overdue, can serve only as a guide-line to the tactics required by specific, concrete situations. In these hard times, perhaps beginning to discuss these issues is sufficient and signals the existence of an alternative to the misery and inequities of daily life under capitalism. Schools are especially important in this regard because they deal with the very real lives of people who are our inheritors and, thus, pose both the hope and the necessity of making that alternative a reality.[22] Just as important, they are central to any effort which seeks to overcome the basic inequalities of our society.

NOTES

1 The two major works in this debate were C. Jencks et al., *Inequality* (New York 1973), and S. Bowles and H. Gintis, *Schooling in Capitalist America* (New York 1976)

2 Jencks et al., ibid., 149 and rest of book for other figures

3 For an elaboration of the relationship between technology, capitalism, and the organization of work, see H. Braverman, *Labor and Monopoly Capital* (New York 1974). For the comments on the relationship between Canadian education and the American control of research and development, see A. Lockhart, 'Future Failure,' in E. Zureik and R. Pike, eds., *Socialization and Values in Canadian Society* (Toronto 1975), II.

4 See S. Schecter, 'Capitalism, Class, and Educational Reform in Canada,' in L. Panitch, ed., *The Canadian State* (Toronto 1977), for a more detailed and documented elaboration of the argument that follows.

5 J.D. Dennison et al., *The Impact of Community Colleges* (Vancouver 1975), 39

6 G. Martell, *The Politics of the Canadian Public School* (Toronto 1974), 13

7 Braverman, *Labor and Monopoly Capital*, especially part IV, chaps. 15 and 16

8 Lockhart, 'Future Failure,' 195-9

9 Quebec Ministry of Education, *The Green Paper on Primary and Secondary Education in Quebec* (Quebec 1978), 6

10 Schecter, 'Capitalism, Class, and Educational Reform,' especially 373-80

11 For an insightful treatment of the way ability is turned into a badge under capitalism, see R. Sennett and J. Cobb, *The Hidden Injuries of Class* (New York 1973), 67, 77-8.

12 I am indebted to Charles Ungerleider of the Foundations of Education Department at the University of British Columbia for this particular example, which I have always found highly illustrative and which I have taken the liberty to embellish in order to try and explain the difference between socialism and capitalism. Under capitalism, body functions are organized around the dictates of work; under socialism, work will be organized around the needs of the body.

13 For a discussion of some of these themes, see Bowles and Gintis, *Schooling*, chaps. 10 and 11; J. Kozol, *Free Schools* (New York 1972); and G. Dennison, *The Lives of Children* (New York 1969).

14 See the document prepared by the Centrale de l'enseignement du Québec (CEQ) *Pour une journée d'école au service de la classe ouvrière* – manuel du 1er mai, Québec, 1975, and the reaction it provoked. Interviews with certain militants in the CEQ provided some of the information. The translation was made by the editors.

15 Such are the general implications suggested by J. O'Connor, *The Fiscal Crisis of the State* (New York 1973).

16 For evidence on contemporary urban struggles, see, for example, E. Cherki and D. Mehl, 'Quelles luttes? quels acteurs? quels résultats?' *Autrement*, VI (Sept. 1976), 6-9.

17 This has clearly been part of the Quebec government's logic underlying the creation of comités de parents in the schools and the Centres locaux de service communautaires.

18 For a discussion of the class identification and practice of teachers, see G. Carchedi, 'On the Economic Identification of the New Middle Class,' *Economy and Society*, IV, 1 (Feb. 1975), 1-86, 'The Economic Identification of the State Employees,' *Social Praxis*, III, 1-2 (1975), 93-120; C. Baudelot and R. Estabelet, *L'école capitaliste en France* (Paris 1971), especially chap. 4; C. Baudelot, R. Estabelet, and J. Malemart, *La petite bourgeoisie en France* (Paris 1975); R. Deaton, 'The Fiscal Crisis of the State,' in D. Roussopoulos, ed., *The Political Economy of the State* (Montreal 1973); G. Martell, *The Politics of the Canadian*

Public Schools (Toronto 1974), especially part III; D. Ethier, J.M. Piotte and J. Reynolds, *Les travailleurs contre l'etat bourgeois* (Montreal 1975).

19 See 'Italy, Social Democracy, and Revolution in the West: An Interview with Lucio Magri,' *Socialist Revolution*, 36 (Nov.-Dec. 1977).

20 Recent historical experiences in Chile and Czechoslovakia, as well as contemporary events in southern Europe, offer concrete examples.

21 For a timely warning to see classes not as 'fixed entities but rather ongoing processes,' see Braverman, *Labor and Monopoly Capital*, 409. The work of Ethier, Piotte and Reynolds, *Travailleurs*, suffers in this regard from a rather static conception, which prevents one from learning from strategic errors. The relatively strong support given to teachers by the public in the 1976 Common Front strike is indicative of the initial gropings toward some kind of intra-class solidarity.

22 For a beautiful cinematographic portrayal of this problem, see the recent film, *Jonah Who Will be 25 in the Year 2000*, screenplay by John Berger and Alain Tanner. For a good discussion of the themes, see R. Kazis, 'Berger-Tanner and the "New Narcissism,"' *Socialist Revolution*, 35 (Sept.-Oct. 1977).

10
Inequality in the media:
public broadcasting and private constraints

LIORA SALTER

Problems of inequality run throughout all aspects of the media system. They are readily apparent in the loss of diversity in information and entertainment, resulting from an increased concentration of ownership and control in media industries. They are evident in the overwhelming domination of Canadian airwaves by American-produced or American-styled programing. In some circles it is now heresy to talk of a Canadian cultural style or content. Class relations have been obscured, and stereotypical images of women and minorities are regular nightly television fare. If media have an inherent capacity to reflect and examine the conditions of daily life, they are failing in their task. Anyone with a television knows something about the problems.

Inequality in the media is, however, rooted more deeply than in television's failure to report or account for reality. Media also set a political agenda, an agenda which establishes a sense of what can and should be done to address problems of inequality. To the extent that these problems are ignored, or that the full range of human emotions and needs are capsulized into a consumer-oriented perspective, then the media play an active role in constraining political life. The critical documentary is contained, then, in a sea of programing that contradicts every intention of its producers. All of this is widely recognized as well. In fact, many have argued that the media form a closed system, manipulating public consciousness under the constraints of advertiser sponsorship and the compelling corporate need for consumerism.

Still, there are problems in the latter approach. Since the emphasis in this analysis is on the dynamics in the media system that generate inequality, any talk of alternatives seems futile. The hard-hitting public affairs show represents only an incidental opportunity in the system. The efforts of journalists are co-opted by the inevitable pressures and dynamics of the system as a whole. Thus unless the discussion of problems of inequality in the media is widened, the most radical critique may also constrain any political possibilities by its very pessimism. At the very least, any analysis of the media should include public broadcasting and the work of an increasing number of people who are providing the basis for an increasingly sophisticated and insightful analysis of what might be called media politics. This is of particular importance in Canada since public broadcasting is a significant part of the media picture and since the tradition of media politics is also well established.

In this paper, then, I want to begin by examining the prevailing analyses of the media in Canada, drawing on these to outline some dimensions of inequality but also indicating why they fail to take into account the full range of media inequality. Then, I will outline some prerequisites for a more comprehensive theory, drawing on the work of sociologist Dorothy Smith and of Canadian economic historian Harold Innis. Finally, I want to explore the role of public media within the media system and to argue that they play an important, relatively unconstrained role by providing alternative sources of information, based on a different relationship between producer, audience, and public issue.

Community media as a form of public media, however, are constrained in the context of their own development. While they do expand the possibilities for political life, they also act to consolidate the boundaries of the media system. Community and mass media, I will argue, are in a dialectical relationship. A simple analysis of co-optation will not serve to indicate the dynamic of the relationship between mass and public media systems; nor will it indicate the potential for, or limitations of, equality in the media. Both the mass system and the public system need to be examined in their own right and, in turn, in relation to each other.

THE NATURE OF THE PROBLEM: INEQUALITY IN MASS MEDIA

It is generally granted that there are problems of ownership and control of the media. These were clearly noted in the *Report* of the Special Senate Committee on Mass Media (also known as the *Davey Report*): 'Within Canada, ownership or control of one medium by another is equally a concern if it tends to develop into a monopoly. There is a growing number of cases where either ownership or control extends to both local newspapers and local radio or television facilities.'[1] In the *Report*, Senator Keith Davey argued that such capital concentration in the media could not contribute to the public interest. Judy LaMarsh sought the roots of the problem in her 1975 *Report of the Ontario Royal Commission on Violence in the Communication Industry*, which concluded that 'the objective of television networks and stations is not to produce programmes but to produce audiences. These are sold to advertisers who seek mass audiences ... the object is to reach and maximize that segment of the audience which may have an interest in his product.'[2]

Even established commentators, then, can agree that the media systems in Canada are highly integrated and that integration is increasing to the detriment of the public interest. Thus it is easy for a critical analyst like Clement to demonstrate the significant deterioration of programmatic diversity that is a result of the close integration between media and political elites.[3] If Judy LaMarsh can state that a system based on advertising imposes constraints on programing, and that the resultant programing is therefore dominated by the more violent (anxiety producing) of the American series, the mainstream press has co-opted the argument and Clement supplies only further detail.

In fact, anyone who watches television knows that programing reflects problems of inequality, whether these problems are explained as being due to media ownership, American dominance, the quality and content of programing, or the nature of broadcast policy. To be specific, 98 per cent of all American prime time television is available to the vast majority of Canadians with cable television, and Canadians seem to prefer the American material. Although the state-supported CBC has been ordered to decrease its reliance on advertising, CBC management depends increasingly on the same ratings used by commercial broadcasters to make programing decisions; thus the CBC – the public system – is often indistinguishable from its American commercial counterparts. Recent cancellation of the CBC radio 'National News' (by all accounts one of the CBC's most competent productions) for lack of a large audience is a good case in point.

Similarly, inequality extends into the content of programing. Several women's welfare, minority, and native organizations have appeared before the Canadian broadcast regulatory agency – the Canadian Radio-Television and Telecommunications Commission (CRTC) – to argue that their aspirations are not adequately reflected in the hiring or programing policies of broadcast/cable stations. A task force report completed in 1975 found strong evidence of 'systemic bias' in CBC hiring policies.[4] Although community programing is a condition of licence for all FM stations, native groups in northern Manitoba pay high 'airtime charges' for an hour-long weekly program; yet native people constitute more than half of the population in the communities served. The CRTC claims that it is powerless to act in such situations.

An American study, which could have been completed equally well in any Canadian city with cablevision, found a lack of coverage of women's issues, or of items mentioning women in any significant role, and found few women newscasters reporting 'hard news.' The study concluded that individuals who become visible through television are worthy of attention and concern; those who are ignored remain invisible.[5] The study has been replicated by students in the Vancouver area. Neither CBC National News nor local radio and television stations were found to employ women in significant roles or provide equal coverage of 'women's issues.'[6]

Regulation, which might monitor and mitigate the more deleterious effects of inequality, has failed to produce significant changes in the media system. There are few indications that the CRTC, which many claim is the most publicly minded regulatory agency in Canada, has either the ability or the will to change the situation. Although the CRTC *Annual Report* in 1975-76 did state that the agency would 'ensure that people served by broadcasting undertakings [would] be more directly involved in the communication process through local ownership and participation,'[7] the trend toward acceptance of concentration in ownership is firmly established. Between 1968 and 1975 the agency received 515 applications for transfer of ownership and denied 20 per cent of them. It denied less than 10 per cent on the basis of increasing concentration. The approval of a sale of Toronto's CITY-TV – first to Multiple Access of Montreal and then to the CHUM conglomerate – is an excellent case in point. The CRTC lacks an ownership policy and has tended to consider each application on its merits. Thus it rejects an application only 'if no net benefit to the community can be found.'[8] Since 1968, cross ownership between broadcast and cable systems has been actively discouraged, but that 'policy' is currently under re-examination as it has been argued on numerous occasions that cross ownership might benefit the Canadian production industry. When the CRTC did attempt to control the integration of Canadian broadcasting into the American system in 1975 by refusing permission for the development of pay television, the federal cabinet ordered a rehearing of the issue. When the agency *did* veto a proposed consortium between satellite and telephone companies with the intention of keeping maximum possible accountability in regulation, the decision was overturned by the minister of communications.

The CRTC has little control over programing, of course, but it can call stations to account through its licence renewal system. Between 1968 and 1976, however, only four licences were revoked (two for performance), and the agency still lacks a licence challenge procedure that might open existing stations to competition or community pressure. A licence challenge procedure in the American system, for example, has acted as an important pressure point for minority and ethnic groups. The CRTC does require a promise of performance from all stations and must approve all programing format changes, including such changes by the CBC. But although the CBC's proposed plan to provide 'cultural programming' to the urban dweller and mass programing to the remote regions was rejected by the CRTC in 1974, an examination of current program schedules indicates that the CBC may have proceeded with the plan in any case.[9] Many commercial stations have changed formats in response to market conditions without submitting a new promise of performance and, of course, without losing their licence. All this is widely known; the limitations of the CRTC are recognized by public media and agencies alike.

THE DYNAMICS OF INEQUALITY

To recognize or even document the extent of inequality in the media is not enough. Clearly there are structural constraints that render the media immune from criticism and resistant to change. Several Canadian authors have addressed the more fundamental questions. Two such authors, Clement and Smythe, provide persuasive analyses of media as a factor of production, and Clement adds a discussion of the impact of intra-class relations to explain part of the ideological consistency in programs. Nonetheless, both Smythe and Clement fail in one important sense. By concentrating on the production of consciousness, they neglect the role which media play in generating a critical political consciousness. Neither discusses the CBC at any length; neither considers to any depth the active role of producers and audience in the construction of meaning from the images presented through the media. The impact of the technology itself or the factors that mediate the relationship between the ownership and the content of media are also ignored.

Recent work by Dorothy Smith helps fill in some of the gaps in analysis by accounting for the practices within media organizations that shape news and information. The long-neglected communications analysis of Harold Innis, too, is critical to the understanding of the dynamics of inequality in the media system. Unlike more recent media analysts, Innis provides a theoretical framework that can incorporate the relationship between media technologies and the content of programing, and the relationship between the ownership of media industries and the simultaneous development of mass appeal programing and political movements.

To understand the contribution of Innis, it makes sense to begin with a review of Clement and Smythe. Clement's work centres on the integration of media and political elites, on increasing trends toward corporate concentration, and on the shared ideological orientation of elite members. He views media elites as functionally different from other elites: 'They are partially like the economic sector primarily as corporations but they are more. They are also organizations whose major activity is the dissemination and reinforcement of ideology and values.'[10] He argues that the media are 'conductors of ideas of the ruling class par excellence.' Like John Porter (*The Vertical Mosaic*), Clement suggests that the media legitimate a series of explanations. He draws heavily on C. Wright Mills, in suggesting that the media function to homogenize the public into a single mass audience and to reduce the number of sources of information. Media workers in his view, are the gatekeepers of information and ideas.

The selection of media industry employees is reinforced by a professional ethic 'in the media, by peer group pressures, by socialization and by pressure on those who wish to be promoted.' Although in his recent book Clement emphasizes the differences between elites, in his article published in 1977, distinctions between media elites and political elites, or the divisions within the media elite, were not stressed. Social integration of elites accounts for ideological consistencies.

Clement's data are limited. He updates Porter with material drawn from the *Davey Report* (1970). In general, the trends toward corporate concentration noted are irrefutable. Nonetheless, in a study of local BC newspapers conducted in 1975, although Dorothy Smith found some indication of cross ownership, she could locate no necessary relationship between ownership and content.[11]

A background study prepared for the Royal Commission on Corporate Concentration found ownership linkages between the *Vancouver Sun* and MacMillan Bloedel, but its authors admit to the methodological difficulty of determining the relationship between ownership and content.[12] Had they examined other major corporations in British Columbia, they might have found no ownership linkages, but equally favourable *Sun* coverage. Clement (or those who draw heavily on his analysis) accounts for the consistency between ownership and content with a sociological analysis of class, but he has not demonstrated the ways in which class inequality is written into content. There is little question of whether it is or not; what we need to know is how this occurs.

Smythe goes further than Clement in exploring the structural constraints of the media system. He encounters many of the same problems as Clement; however, he builds his argument by placing Canadian media development in the context of continentalist media expansion and concludes, in part, that the media functions as an intermediate state in the support (legitimation) and sale of American foreign policy. His early work pioneered the concept of audience as commodity. In a recent article he restates that position: 'The prime object on the agenda of the consciousness industry with media content is to produce people in markets motivated to buy "new models" of consumer goods and motivated to pay taxes which support the swelling budgets for military sales.'[13]

Advertising and programing are, Smythe argues, an integrated product. Programing functions as a kind of 'free lunch' designed to attract a particular kind of audience. While media and other cultural forms express a consistency of approach, media are a specialized institution. Their development presupposes advertising (brand names) and is concomitant with the development of monopoly capitalism. Media represent a use of technology which creates cheaper and more effective control mechanisms for demand management. Media replace the door-to-door salesmen.

Production takes place, Smythe argues, at three interrelated levels in the media system. First, of course, the media produce spectacles to attract audiences (making individuals into spectators of reality, while distorting that reality).[14] Second, media produce audiences as a form of demand management in the production of commodities-in-general. Third, media produce labour power.

This last point requires amplification. Using work by Livant – which develops a distinction between production of commodities-in-general and production of labour power under monopoly capitalism – Smythe suggests that the media produce labour power by commoditizing the non-work time of the labourer. In a society characterized by a high degree of media participation, leisure ceases to be rest from work and becomes itself part of the production process. Specifically, by watching television the worker learns skills necessary for functioning as a consumer in a brand-dominated market. The worker/consumer learns to distinguish among the multitude of almost indistinguishable products. The worker/consumer as television audience learns brand loyalty. Moreover, the worker/consumer begins to orient him/herself around a perceived insatiability of need. Programing (or advertising) which stresses 'newness,' immediacy, a fast-changing environment, and the rapid growth of information engenders this sense of insatiability. That media can produce specific needs is widely recognized (as it forms the basis for an advertising industry); that media produce insatiability of need goes beyond the simple analysis of media as manipulator.

Smythe, more than Clement, places emphasis on inconsistency in media content. He allows that the relationship between content and control is complex, arguing that 'media allow for dissent as an hegemonic filter, as a means of co-opting structural conflicts.'[15] Furthermore, 'in this way, and in token respects through media content individual and ethnic alienation is kept within limits tolerable to the system.'[16]

Both Clement and Smythe treat media only as a system of production, although clearly their analyses differ markedly. Both would argue that media industries bear close resemblance to other industries, although they would disagree on the nature and significance of the integration of a Canadian bourgeoisie into continental capitalism. Both argue mainly from a perspective on capitalist development; both integrate the Canadian material into the larger picture. The media analysis, in the Smythe case at least, is metropolitan.

There are certain problems in the debate, as preliminary as it is. Media are viewed only in their role in supporting capitalist economic structures. To a large extent the analyses are instrumental in the emphasis on functions and effects. But the dynamics of the complex relationships between class and ideology, between media as institution and as industry, and between public and private media systems are all underemphasized. Because the emphasis is on the nature of production, there is little discussion of the means through which content and control are linked and of the impact of distribution technologies on what can and will be produced. Patterns of media development within Canada (as a hinterland) have received relatively little attention. And finally, the roles of audience as listener, of media producer as worker, of public as organizer of alternative media efforts or protest, and of media worker as critic are all dramatically underrated.

Smith takes a direction which is more promising to an understanding of inequality in the media. She argues that practices and organization of work in media industries constrain media content.[17] She makes the point (and it will be discussed again in an examination of Innis' communications theory) that most 'news' *comes to* the newspaper. She suggests that events conducive to being reported in a standard news format tend to get defined as 'news,' while events and processes not easily accessible to the news collection process are likely to be eliminated from news coverage. Decision-making processes, she states, can be separated from 'decision announcing' or 'staging' processes. The press conference is a decision-staging process, accessible to the press; the decision to rezone a neighbourhood is not. News presented in an event-centred format is particularized and expert centred; it may well present a range of ideas, or public debate on local issues, and often will include public input as a resource and source of information. At the same time it structures out information that might facilitate an understanding of why a decison was made. When news is particularized or event centred, it eliminates most of the potential for effective participation and control of events being reported.

An example would be useful. The decision to rezone a city neighbourhood is reported on television with commentary from opposing local citizen groups. The city council meeting functions as the 'decision-announcing' event; information is made accessible through the meeting to the media. Yet a decision to rezone a city neighbourhood usually has a long history, one extending back years before the city council 'decision' was made. Little media coverage accompanies the purchase of housing by a major urban development company, or the deterioration of local housing stock, or the relocation of local stores, or the deterioration of local public services – all of which limit choices available to the city council at the point of decision making. In all probability, the council responds to an application generated in the private sector. It responds when neighbourhood change is irreversible and, therefore, when public opinion is segmented. Media coverage is concentrated at the end point of the process in part because what happens at the end point can be easily translated into 'news,' while much of what has gone before cannot.

Smith's work provides more of a methodology than a theory. By exploring aspects of the business structure and practice, some complexities in the relationship between control and content become apparent: 'The term "business structure" serves merely to recognize at this stage that a newspaper is organized as part of an economic process and must function within and by commercial practices. We do not know exactly how different types of business structures, such as types of corporate organization, corporate affiliation, managerial and ownership structure, etc. are tied into the typical differences in form and content of the news relation.'[18] By documenting work practices, which are shared (but usually implicit) within any organization, she can trace some of the underlying constraints: 'The concept of ideology as I am developing its use here, identified a *practice* or *method* in the use of ideas and images which is ideological rather than a determinate object or type of object. I want to be able to recognize the ideological aspects of methods.'[19] While allowing for the critical consciousness of many media workers, and the daily range of opinion in the press, she notes, nonetheless, an underpinning of bias: 'Images, vocabularies, concepts, knowledge and methods of knowing the world are integral to the practice of power. The work of creating the concepts and categories, developing the knowledge, and the skills transform the actualities of the empirical into forms in which they may be governed; the work of producing the social forms of consciousness in art and literature, in news, in TV shows, plays, soap operas and etcetera – these are built into institutions which are themselves an integral part of this ruling structure.'[20] If dissenting media workers can be seen as co-opted, they are co-opted in the sense that they share the same working conditions, practices, informal patterns of sociability, and prevailing explanations of the work organization. It is the practices within media as work organizations that mediate co-optation.

If practices within media organizations mediate co-optation and engender an inegalitarian bias in media content, they do so in concert with technological form. Recently much has been written about the impact of technological form, most of it, however, with a technologically determinist cast. Only the communications analysis of Canadian historian Harold Innis explores the relation between media content, work process, and technological form and manages to escape fully from the heavy grip of determinism. It is worth serious consideration here (and much more consideration than it has been given to date in the literature).

Innis is better known, of course, for his studies on Canadian political economy. Interestingly, his communications analysis is remarkably similar to his political economy work, although it is written in a somewhat different vein. Essentially, Innis has developed a political economy of communications. Communication technologies are viewed as variants of distribution technologies. Their impact on society is like that of the railway or the canoe. They facilitate access to, or production of, some kinds of staples, biasing development options in the process. For Innis information and ideas can be seen as a form of staple. Like staples of fish and fur, ideas leave their stamp upon both political and social relations. The nature and process of their production and distribution (again, like fish or fur) facilitate certain forms of economic life but are themselves the product of the interplay of political and economic interests, as such interests combine to foster particular forms of development and consolidate systems of power.

All distributive technologies, whether communication media or railways, act to extend, maintain, or solidify systems of power. At the same time, however, they also engender the conditions necessary for the dissolution of those same systems by provoking activity at the margins of society that challenge the control of those at the centre. Centre and margins are terms which have either spatial or temporal referents; they refer to the nature of power in operation, whether over geographic space or throughout any period of history. Distributive technologies have been instrumental, Innis argues, in the consolidation and the disintegration of the church-based empires of the Middle Ages and the expansionist (or imperialist) empires of our own era.

Distributive technologies also shape the nature and form of what can or will be distributed. They facilitate the transmission of some staples, but not others. They indicate some forms of linkage, but not all. Staples, whether grain or information, cast a heavy shadow on all aspects of social and political life by virtue, in part at least, of their means of production and distribution. They sustain but also mediate interests by shaping both access to and content of staple production. The production and distribution of staples, and thus the staples themselves, engender particular forms of dependency relations.

Mass communication systems are a form of distributive technology. Such systems, Innis argues, produce and distribute information and ideas to facilitate control of geographically distant regions under a centralized authority. Mass systems generate dependence of the margins on the centre. In the Canadian case, they tie the East and West to the centre, to Toronto, and then, in turn, to the major production centres in the United States. In the process, information and its dissemination is shaped to the needs of the metropolitan centres. Computer data transmission establishes a centre-controlled system of linkage. Television technical standards in Canada have been matched to the American system, allowing non-mediated cultural penetration of all regions on the continent.

Mass communication systems also shape the content of the information made available for the understanding and interpretation of experience. They tend to reduce the significance of locality and the autonomy of regions, even as they increase the scope and coverage of information. The impact of technological form is felt directly in media content. The significance of class, region, or national experience, the complexity of on-the-spot data, and the richness of complex human relationships and experience are reduced to that which can be expressed in broad general categories, common to all locations and having no specific ties to workplace or neighbourhood. The ability, through mass systems, to speak to everyone at once engenders communication which is tied directly to no particular experience. Only those ideas that can be transmitted in a common language through the new technological forms are in fact transmitted. As Innis put it: 'The radio appealed to a vast area, overcame the division between classes in its escape from literacy, and centralization and bureaucracy. A single individual could appeal at one time to vast numbers of people speaking the same language and indirectly, though with less effect, through interpreters speaking other languages.'[21]

Expressive language does not travel well through mass communication systems, but masses of data do. Although both satellites and television were developed after Innis' death, they are good examples of how technological form shapes content. Had he known their capabilities, Innis might well have forecast their link to the expansion of American capitalism, noted their power in the extension of colonialism, noted the increasing flatness and consistency of the information transmitted, and commented upon their inability to encompass the richness and wealth of local experience. As he put it then: 'Superficiality became essential to meet the various demands of larger numbers of people and was developed as an art by those compelled to meet the demands.'[22]

Access to, and expertise in the use of, technology are critical since they introduce a separation between producer and receiver, and between the programmer and audience. Through this separation, increased with the growing limitations on access to technology, the viewer loses the right to the interpretation of his/her own experience. What is viewed as 'knowledge,' even knowledge about everyday events, is that which is generated in, and defined by, the process of its own production. News is considered 'news,' for example, because it is collected and disseminated through news gathering associations and, as well, because it is prepared by those with access to, and expertise in, news gathering communication systems. The wire service, increasingly controlled by the metropolis, defines what will be available as an explanation of events to an increasing proportion of the world's population. 'News' is what has been transmitted through the appropriate technological system; in turn, the technological system used has a direct biasing impact upon the content of the 'news' being transmitted. The technological development of the wire service news system cannot be separated from a discussion of the content of 'news.'

The inegalitarian underpinnings of media, in other words, extend beyond the practices within media as work organizations; they are mediated by the distributive technologies being used. Shared experience, class, region, and collective interpretation – all so critical in the development of political life – are made irrelevant with mass rapid information transmission to the extent that authority comes to rest, as it does in time with all distribution technologies, in the process of its own production. Thus those who control the process of production of distributive technologies and access to, or expertise in, their use hold authority that biases media to sustain the existing and unequal social relations of production. Through work practice and through the development of technological form, inequalities are structured at the core of the media system. As such, the media system can and does operate within extensive political constraints, even when those who practice the journalistic craft do so honestly and without overt censorship.

PUBLIC MEDIA IN THE MEDIA SYSTEM

The existence of public broadcasting as a significant sector of the media system often has been ignored by those proffering media analyses. The neglect has serious implications for an understanding of inequality in the media. The sector is large and commands a major commitment of financial and programmatic resources. The amenability of the media system to challenge and change, the usefulness of media to political groups, and the ability of the media to constitute a force for equality all hinge upon the public aspects of the media system. Too many political struggles have been fought in order to establish and maintain a public system to warrant such neglect. Any analysis ignoring the potential of public media only 'legitimates' and promotes the interests of the most powerful segments of society. It eliminates media praxis from a more general discussion of praxis. For those whose goal is simply good scholarship – as traditionally defined – the neglect of a major portion of the media system is serious. For those who share a commitment to the promotion of equality, the oversight is inexcusable.

Public media are often viewed as state-supported systems of broadcasting. This definition of 'public' is too narrow. In Canada, as in other countries, a significant development of non-commercial public media has occurred outside the state-supported system. Media have also been used to powerful effect as tools of community organizing. They are often viewed as critical instruments in the development of political movements, or as a forum through which public campaigns can be launched. In fact, in several cities in Canada, those with little interest in either the commercial or the state-supported system control a major media outlet. The resulting stations are technically indistinguishable from other stations on the dial; they are accessible on the same basis to the same audiences as commercial broadcasting. The sound of these stations and the content of their programing, however, stand in stark contrast to both state-supported and commercial media.

A more substantive definition of public media from the point of view of inequality would hinge on an analysis of the central dynamic of advertiser sponsorship within the media system as a whole. Following Clement and Smythe, public media can be viewed as those not responsive to pressures from advertising or ratings. Activists in public media have freedom to relate to their audience as more than consumers of the media product. They can assume that programs, producers, and audience interact actively in the creation of a system of meanings and consciousness. Public media are those media capable, in theory at least, of responding to, or generating, the full range of human needs and aspirations. They are media that have the capacity to promote the expansion of political practice and social life.

It may be useful to indicate where public media exist in Canada. Obviously, as public media have been defined, the state-supported media are not necessarily public media, nor are all aspects of commercial media non-public.

The Canadian Broadcasting Corporation rating system and panel evaluations determine much of its programing; some commercial stations sponsor programs that do not increase the size of their market or sales. Public media include only that part of CBC programing not covered by the ratings system – the experimental radio and cable community stations, the occasional program on commercial television, and the community media used in organizing.

Even limiting what might be called public media in this way, they constitute a major portion of broadcast activity in Canada. Some examples will be useful. All cable systems serving more than 2,500 subscribers must allocate a channel and a proportion of their gross revenues to public media production. Although cable systems are controlled by some of the largest media conglomerates, such channels operate without censorship and have programs that more or less successfully challenge both established institutions and the media system itself. The Canadian cable experiment is unique. In other countries, those wishing access to television are often faced with costly court challenges and, if successful, win only an hour or two a week for programing that reflects the needs and aspirations of the constituent groups within the audience. In Canada, prospective programmers on the public channel debate about the amount of money, the kind of regulatory support, or the kind of equipment that will be made available.

The CBC is still a repository of public media, although many programs are now responsive to ratings. With funds estimated at one-fifth those of the American PBS, the CBC manages to generate political action on issues like lead poisoning, the building of the Garrison Dam, and the War Measures Act. That the CBC has become enmeshed in ratings considerations, in bureaucratic entanglements, or has become the object of derision of artists and conservatives alike should not mask its contribution to public broadcasting.

Canada has also a long tradition of supporting media experiments connected with community organizing projects. One of the first, 'Radio Farm Forum,' involved farmers in weekly discussion groups debating critical issues in agricultural policy and regional development. Until recently, the National Film Board has sponsored a film production unit, *Challenge for Change*, that produced films on tenant organizing, labour politics, women's issues, and nuclear proliferation. Although the government was often criticized, the films were produced and, for the most part, distributed without interference from the funding agencies.

Finally, in the last ten years a number of community radio stations have been established in Canada. In Vancouver, one such station broadcasts programing that ranges from the wildly experimental to the frankly political.

Like other community radio facilities, the station draws no revenue from corporations or even government grants. It is funded through donations and the voluntary labour of its staff. Little attempt is made to gauge the size of the audience for such stations. Alternatively, programs reach small pockets of listeners and fulfil the need for adequate news analysis for a city wide audience. Programs have included live music, remote coverage of public meetings, a legal aid soap opera, and Chilean music; producers include any member of the community with something to say and the inclination to say it on radio. Programmers in BC have included the Federation of Labour, tenants groups, native organizations, and classical music buffs.

CONSTRAINTS ON EQUALITY IN PUBLIC MEDIA

To argue that public media exist and form an influence in promoting equality in Canada is not to fall prey to some naïve, pluralist notion of a media system that is at once public and mass based. However significant the development of public media may be, it operates within a network of constraints imposed by pressures within the media system as a whole. In spite of the apparent success of public media, certain facts must be accounted for. Only a few community radio stations are flourishing; only a few films produced by the social animators working with the National Film Board have generated either national or local controversy. Several community cable facilities have attracted enthusiastic volunteers, but no community or public media in Canada command the same loyal audience as the PBS service in the United States. Although some CBC national radio programs have shown the capacity to generate public debate, community stations – which, by definition, should be closer to local needs and aspirations – have not. Participation in 'town hall democracy' types of experiments has not been incorporated into the public process in Canada or the United States. Most community media experiments have not been incorporated into social service funding priorities at the end of the experimental period. Even the fact that after fifteen years of well-funded experimentation, the literature on community or public media retains a descriptive or prescriptive flavour may be significant. Simply put, the limitations of community or public media are surprising, given what ought to be the strength of their appeal, the level of funding and regulatory support they receive, and Innis' hypothesized need for a 'balance of time and space.'

Two short case examples will illustrate something of the relationships involved. In 1970 the National Film Board conducted a major experimental project using film and video as a tool of social animation in the Newfoundland outport community of Fogo Island. Without doubt, video tapes of local meetings trained some people in group participation skills, and films helped in the articulation and presentation of issues. The project was used as a model for similar experiments in Tanzania, Algeria, and the United States. Partly as a result of the efforts of the Film Board, local residents put forward a plan for a co-operative fish-processing plant. Nonetheless, the Film Board project receives little comment in the studies of relocation effects conducted by the Institute for Social and Economic Studies at Memorial University. The Film Board project came towards the end of a process of redevelopment in Newfoundland – a process which included the massive importation of resource extraction technology, extensive labour mobility and retraining programs geared to industrialization, and relocation of outporters to more industrialized settlements. The amount of money made available to the Film Board project was an insignificant proportion of the total funds spent in social and economic redevelopment. The goals of the Film Board 'animators' stood in direct contrast to, if not in conflict with, the goals of the redevelopment project as a whole. The redevelopment project emphasized industrialization and urbanization, while the Film Board explored community integration and 'intermediate technology.' If the literature available today on the Film Board project tends to emphasize only group process effects, it may be because of the context in which the experiment took place.

The Anik satellite was hailed as the harbinger of a new communications era for the North, but in its initial installation Anik made no provision for facilities which would have linked northern communities to each other. Early Anik stations were often located near resource and military bases, and the first television programing most northerners saw was 'All in the Family.' There was a good deal of protest about the dislocating effects of this south-to-north communications link. Four major studies were conducted, partly in conjunction with the federal Department of Communications. All reached a similar conclusion: 'Emphasis should be given to those systems which promote intra and interpersonal communications rather than to systems which increase the already considerable flow of information to the south.'[23]

Some community media experiments were established between 1971 and 1977, and in 1973-74 the CBC and several native communications societies began serious production of local programing. The latest of the experiments is of particular interest. Using the CTS experimental satellite, the Department of Communications sponsored a number of short-term efforts in educational and community broadcasting. One experiment in Alberta made provision for the transmission of video programs from an originating centre in Edmonton (with some video tapes produced in remote areas) to four northern Alberta communities. The communities made a television set and microphone connection available in the local community centre, and sent an audio response back to the originating centre. No funds were made available for production in remote communities or for program research. No funds were made available for animators or community development workers. No funds were made available for cable transmission so that programing would be available in the homes of most of the northern residents who had access to regular television. Most of the cost of the experiment was borne by the community group, in this case, the Alberta Native Communications Society.

Similar experiments were sponsored through provincial governments and major educational institutions as, generally, only governments could allocate sufficient financial resources to implement the projects. While the experiments were considered as a means of using a satellite for 'two way interactive television,' the amount of capital demanded, the lack of community support work, and the cost of the distribution technology in the receiving communities made their impact more technological than social. The experiments will be continued through Anik B, but the fundamental problems in design from the CTS experiment remain. In any case, all experimentation follows the explorations of resource development companies, a series of proposals which would ship export resources south to American markets, and the commercial development of satellites as accessory to business expansion. While the satellite experiments are considered community or educational media by their sponsors, in no sense are they tied to local needs and aspirations.

In general, media experimentation tends to come at the end of a development process, at a point when the impact of large-scale technological systems may be irreversible. The emphasis is on process. The experimenters may reject high technology models of development as they did in Fogo Island or the Department of Communications-sponsored projects. They may argue for self-sufficient economies as people did before the Berger hearings. The literature may emphasize interaction as it does in the CTS experiments. The strength of an Innis analysis may be recognized by the government and by local people as it was in the Berger report. But the dynamics of the distribution process, and the practices of both corporate and government organizations, which support these experiments, contribute to an underpinning of bias, irregardless of the perceptions or actions of the experimenters.

While the picture is somewhat different in the urban media experiments, Innis' work is again useful. To go back: Innis emphasized that it was in the separation between production and viewing that monopolies of knowledge were created. He was talking primarily of mass communication systems, but he might just as well have been commenting on similar propensities in current attempts at public media communications. In the development of urban experiments, the viewer becomes a producer, but the process of production is again separated from viewing. Specifically, while the audience can learn the skills of media production, the process of media production becomes an end in itself. How something is produced, its technological form, and the group process override consideration of the audience relation.

Community cable programing, for example, is often produced without any reference to its audience. Professional staff are encouraged to facilitate amateur production not in addition to, but to the exclusion of, professionalism. Policy guidelines for community programing stress process and the role such programing can have in helping 'the community find or define itself.' Much of the programing centres on information to the exclusion of entertainment. A CRTC *Annual Report* states: 'Cable television systems in particular have responded positively to the Commission's suggestion that they develop community identity through locally produced programming. Community channels can serve as a forum for concerned citizens and groups. It is hoped that both cable operators and communities will realize the potential of local programming and utilize the facilities fully so that the community can be helped to both see and solve its own problems.'[24]

Regulatory guidelines make it clear that community programing should not be competitive with commercial broadcasting. Community stations are expected to be 'broadly representative of the community as a whole.' Cable owners have argued that they should have no role in programing, and community groups have offered to take responsibility for community programing. Nonetheless, the CRTC insists that the responsibility and control of community programing remain with the owner-licensees instead of separately licensed citizen groups. All of the above conditions often combine to ensure that local controversy is reduced to a panel discussion, and that public or community stations display none of the characteristics of a journalistic medium.

For the most part, public media are not integrated into the broadcast system except as an outlet for local production energies. It is not accidental that the development of public program outlets is concomitant with the growing strength of a cable industry whose main function is the importation of American signals. In the early attempts to regulate broadcasting in Canada, the demands of the public service were assumed to take precedence over the needs of the private sector. At one time, the CBC functioned both as the national service and as the regulator of private broadcasting, while the private system was assigned the limited and well-defined role of 'filling the gaps' in the public service. In the last two decades – but particularly since the establishment of the CRTC in 1968 – the relation between public and private systems has been reversed. Now the public service is expected to fill the gaps left by a fully developed private system. The orientation of regulation has shifted so that now the primary function of the agency is the control of the private sector. In moving towards a more traditional concept of regulation, the CRTC increasingly assumes the role of traffic police. Extension of service, and socially oriented programing goals are seen to be a 'tax' on the regulated profits of a monopolistic industry. The CRTC proposes that the cable systems allocate 10 per cent of their gross revenues to community programing. The 'tax' is voluntary and cable systems are left to work out their own accounting procedures through which the 10 per cent will be allocated. A CRTC report puts the issue clearly: 'The 10% minimum will not be enforced but is regarded as a useful standard of expenditure for community programming.'[25] If the cable licensees fail to provide resources for community programing, the CRTC – which has given them a rough hearing during the renewal process – would be the first to accept that the system has been open to abuse.

Community programing, first instituted in 1970, has become a duty of the licensee, an adjunct to the basic service. Community programing fills the gaps left by an insufficiently funded, nationally oriented CBC by the development of a commercially oriented private sector, and by the massive importation of American signals through cable. In the process, community or public programing gets defined as 'special interest' programing and as a minority interest. The understanding of community or public programing as minority or special interest programing permeates the approach of the experimenters.

The CBC is equally affected. Programing that lacks mass appeal, or fails to draw high ratings, is often considered an adjunct to the basic CBC service. Currently it is included in the programing schedule as a means of meeting what CBC staff often call the special interest groups needs within its audience. If planners within the CBC have their way, programing that is not designed to garner high ratings will be siphoned off into a separate network, made available as a second service to those living in major urban areas. Thus the preoccupation with ratings, even when divorced from the imperatives of advertiser sponsorship, again creates a situation in which public media are pushed out of the mainstream and become those media designed to serve the needs of specialized minorities.

Individual programs on radio and television may have a political impact, but the development of a media politics or the use of media in the development of a more comprehensive political life demands more than a one-time effort on the part of individual producers. If the relationship between program and audience is an active one, and if the full range of individuals' needs and aspirations are to be addressed, then programing which is produced as an adjunct to the basic service or to meet the needs of special interest groups is not sufficient to create or sustain political consciousness.

In accepting the constraints imposed by the mass system, both the CBC and the community broadcasters have opted out of the discussion of equality in the media, reducing that discussion to questions of hiring practices in media industries or stereotypes on television. Unfortunately, even if women constitute half the staff in every television station and Chinese drink Tang in every commercial, the problems of inequality in the media remain.

This paper began with an argument for an understanding of the structure of inequality in the media, one which took into account the means through which a correspondence was achieved between content and control. Working with some new research insights and with the extensive writings of Canadian communications theorist H.A. Innis, some new directions for an analysis of the structure of inequality were suggested. The focus was on public media, in part because they represent some potential for the promotion of equality, in part because so much of the analysis of the structure of inequality rests on the central importance of advertiser sponsorship. Nevertheless, there are real limitations in any analysis that focuses only on the constraints and dynamics of the existing system. Without doubt, the technology, the contextual factors, and even the perceptions of the programmers have their impact; the media do legitimate a system of explanations that precludes most aspects of political life. But, however much it permeates consciousness, the media system does not exclude the possibility of response, reaction, or protest.

NOTES

1 Special Senate Committee on Mass Media, *Report* (also known as the *Davey Report*), II, *Words, Music and Dollars* (Ottawa 1970), 3

2 *Report of the Royal Commission on Violence in the Communication Industry*, VII (Ottawa 1975), p. 26 – also known as the *LaMarsh Report*

3 W. Clement, *The Canadian Corporate Elite* (Toronto 1975), 270-82

4 Task Force on the Status of Women, *Women in the* CBC (Ottawa 1975)

5 Gaye Tuchman, *Window Dressing on the Set*, United States Commission on Human Rights (Washington 1977), 55

6 The study of the CBC 'National News' coverage was conducted by Mary Hill in October 1977. The study of news departments and news coverage in local media outlets in Vancouver was completed in 1976 by Karin Konstanty-nowicz, Wanda Horan, and Kathryn Wilburn.

7 Robert Babe, 'The Regulation of Private Television,' *Canadian Public Administration*, XIX, 4 (Winter 1976), 570-1

8 *Broadcaster*, XXXVII, 1 (Jan. 1978), 10

9 The plan was called 'CBC 1 + 11.' It was rejected in a lengthy decision by the CRTC in 1974. See *Globe and Mail*, 10 January 1978, for data on the CBC current programing schedule and its relation to 'CBC 1 + 11.'

10 Clement, *Canadian Corporate Elite*, 270

11 D. Smith et al., 'BC Community News Project,' a report prepared for the BC Department of Labour, Vancouver, mimeo., 1975, 3

12 R. Schwindt, 'The Existence and Exercise of Corporate Power: A Case Study of MacMillan Bloedel Ltd.,' background report for the Royal Commission on Corporate Concentration (Ottawa 1977), 232

13 D. Smythe, 'The Role of Mass Media in Defining Development,' a paper prepared for the International Scientific Conference on Mass Communication, Leipzig, mimeo., 1974, p. 5

14 D. Smythe, 'Communications: Blind Spot of Western Marxism,' mimeo., 38; now in print in *Canadian Journal of Political and Social Theory* (Winter 1977)

15 Smythe, 'Role of Mass Media,' 8

16 Ibid.

17 The argument emerges from the work of an ongoing research group. Several papers explore different aspects: Dorothy E. Smith, 'An Analysis of Ideological Structures and How Women are Excluded,' presented at the conference on The Economics of Sex Roles, University of Alberta, May 1975; Smith et al., 'BC Community News.' See also Gaye Tuchman, 'Objectivity as a Strategic Ritual,' *American Journal of Sociology*, LXXVII (Jan. 1972); E. Epstein, *News From Nowhere* (New York 1973).

18 Smith et al., 'BC Community News,' 3

19 Smith, 'Analysis of Ideological Structures,' 7

20 Ibid., 1 (emphasis in original)

21 H.A. Innis, *Essays in Canadian Economic History* (Toronto 1956), 383

22 H.A. Innis, *Bias of Communication* (Toronto 1964), 4

23 Heather E. Hudson, *The Northern Pilot Project: An Evaluation* (Ottawa 1974), 22

24 CRTC Annual Report (1975-76), 3

25 Ibid., 2-4

11
Housing: who pays? who profits?

ALLAN MOSCOVITCH

Inequalities are pervasive in capitalist societies. They are nowhere more evident than with respect to housing. Since the latter years of the nineteenth century, the unequal distribution of private sector housing has been recognized as a characteristic of capitalist cities. Most recently the problem has been described in such government reports as the Hellyer Task Force on Housing, as well as in the Dennis and Fish study on low-income housing.[1] Both reports conclude on the one hand, that vast inequities remain in the use and distribution of Canadian housing stock. On the other hand, both reports also suggest a role for the state in righting this wrong and in acting as an equalizer of housing opportunities. As will be seen later in this article, the state, and particularly its agent, the Canada Mortgage and Housing Corporation (CMHC), have taken action which has only marginally offset the basic inequalities resulting from private production. In reality, public investment in housing works in concert with finance capital in promoting private profit. The forms of state assistance most frequently used are tax relief, guaranteed profits, and the socialization of the risks involved in the production of housing, rather than direct production and protection for users of housing.

The basic reason why inequalities exist in housing, however, is that they are integral to the capitalist mode of production. Inequalities are not only consistent with low risk, high profit opportunities but essential to them. Instead of isolating individual causes of the housing crisis for the poor, such as rising land prices, the unavailability of mortgage credit, shifts in demand, or land speculation, the position taken in this paper is that such factors are important because they are reflections of problems rooted in the system of housing production, which perpetuates inequality. This system is based upon the profitability of finance capital, such that the amount of money invested in housing by finance institutions is determined by how profitable the housing sector is, compared to other sectors of the economy. It is a system in which developers determine, according to the potential profits, whether housing will be built at all and, if so, what type it will be and where it will be located. Housing, as a result, has become a commodity produced for a market in which inequalities of income and of consumption are the norm. In the housing market, as in other markets, those with the lowest income get the worst deal, or they get no deal at all.

THE UNEQUAL CONSUMPTION OF HOUSING

It is conventional wisdom that if the average standards of housing have increased, then people are better housed. This is the conclusion of the 1971 federal government study *Housing in Canada*:

(1) to the extent that our nation is better housed than ever in terms of number and basic facilities, there is no immediate housing problem;

(2) to the extent that our construction industry has averaged approximately 200,000 dwelling starts per year for the last two years (the Economic Council of Canada's target) and can provide numerically sufficient dwellings for our population, there is no housing crisis;

(3) to the extent that shelter costs are not outpacing and are probably lagging income increases so that housing accommodations are generally more affordable, there is no housing problem;

(4) to the extent that there are few doubled families (180,000 or 4% of all families in Canada in 1966) and considerable numbers of non-family households, there is probably no housing problem;

(5) to the extent that there is likely a group of low-income families living or previously living in soon-to-be demolished or previously demolished core dwellings who cannot or will not be able to find satisfactory alternative accommodations, there is a housing problem – or more properly an income or poverty problem;

(6) to the extent that our transportation, servicing, zoning, taxing, and building code policies remain unmodified, unenlightened, or non-existent, we will most certainly have a future housing crisis. We are not in such a crisis yet, however, and rational and concerted policy can prevent it.[2]

Conventional wisdom on housing propagates the view that as long as average housing standards are rising, there is more and better housing available to be bought or rented. Witness the virtual media obsession with numbers of annual housing 'starts.' Who buys or rents which housing is not generally of concern. What occurs is deemed to be simply the result of the operation of the 'housing market.' It is the 'job' of the housing market to distribute housing. Since the result depends on income, poor housing – according to this view – is simply a problem of income.

There are several assumptions contained in this conventional wisdom. The first is that a rising standard affects everyone in the same way. The report of the CMHC Low-Income Housing Task Force, the Dennis-Fish report,[3] took up this question by examining the housing of households with different incomes. The report argued that the conventional wisdom which focuses attention on housing standards alone disregards the real conditions of people who have low incomes. The latter share unequally in rising standards. It is they who are consigned to the housing in the worst physical condition, with the fewest facilities in the worst location. It is their housing which is the most crowded because the units are small, and it is the least secure because people with low incomes are more likely to be renters. Their housing is relatively less secure because, whether rented or owned, it is more likely to be in an inner city area, where it is subject to the continuous risk that the demands for profit will result in eviction or compulsory public purchase, making way for high-rises, town houses, and renovations of roads and airports, which are all publicly heralded as marks of progress.

This is also the conclusion which must be drawn from an examination of the data on the relationship between the incomes of working people and occupancy, adequacy, and tenure of housing which appear in the Statistics Canada survey of *Household Facilities by Income and Other Characteristics*.[4] The survey results link 1975 data on incomes to 1976 data on housing. In 1975 the average household income was $14,983. Income group 7 contains the average household income in its range of $12,000 to $14,999. In order to obtain an indication of the relative inequality in housing, we compare income groups above and below the average, according to measures of housing standards. The distribution over the range of income groups according to these measures can also be examined. The income groups are set out in table 1.

The number of persons per room is one measure of the rate of occupancy available in the survey. Households with average and below average incomes have the same or a higher incidence of crowding (defined here as more than one person per room) than households in income groups above the average income. For example, households in income groups 6 and 7 have the highest incidence of crowding. Those with the lowest income in groups 1 and 2 have the lowest incidence of crowding. This is contrary to what we might expect, but it can be explained by the large numbers of single individuals (primarily over 65 years) with low income. There is some disparity in crowding, but

Table 1
Percentage distribution of all Canadian households by household income groups, occupancy rate, and number of rooms, 1976

Group	Income class, 1975 (in dollars)	Distribution of households with more than one person per room, 1976 (%)	Distribution of households with 1-4 rooms, 1976 (%)	Average size of household, 1976	Distribution of households in the survey, 1976 (%)
1	under 2,000	2.5	60.9	1.8	3.2
2	2,000–3,999	1.5	61.1	1.6	8.4
3	4,000–5,999	3.1	49.9	2.2	8.4
4	6,000–7,999	4.8	49.3	2.5	7.7
5	8,000–9,999	4.7	40.4	2.7	7.6
6	10,000–11,999	5.2	37.6	3.0	8.5
7	12,000–14,999	5.1	30.9	3.2	13.2
8	15,000–24,999	4.5	19.0	3.6	30.3
9	25,000+	4.8	8.2	4.0	13.0
Average all income groups		4.3	32.1	3.0	–
Average household income	$14,983	$16,184	$10,014	–	–

Source: Statistics Canada, *Household Facilities by Income and Other Characteristics*, cat. no. 13-567, tables 1A and 2A

Table 2
Percentage distribution of all households within income quintiles by
number of persons per room

| | More than 1 person per room | |
	1967	1975
Lowest quintile	6.3	2.4
Second quintile	12.6	4.9
Middle quintile	13.7	5.0
Fourth quintile	12.1	4.4
Highest quintile	10.6	4.7

Source: Statistics Canada, *Household Facilities by Income and Other
Characteristics*, cat. no. 13-567, table 11

using the measure adopted here, it is not large.[5] An examination of historical changes in this crowding index reveals that, due to demographic change, the continuing decline of the extended family, and to the expansion of the housing stock, crowding has been significantly reduced. The distribution in table 2 of crowding by quintiles from 1967 to 1975 shows considerable change in the recent period.

The data do reveal that there are still 4.3 per cent of individuals and families living in crowded conditions, on this measure. What the data do not reveal is the range of inequality in crowding (by income) among the 95.7 per cent of households which have met the basic minimum standard of one person per room or less. Nor do they reveal the relative size or quality of housing conditions of different income groups.

The number of rooms as an indication of the amount of housing available to people with differing incomes shows a considerable disparity. Referring to table 1, the percentage of people living in housing with four or less rooms rises continuously from 8.2 per cent for those with $25,000-plus income to 60.9 per cent for those with $2,000 or less. Of those living in housing with four or less rooms, 62 per cent have incomes below average. Poorer households have relatively less space. This is confirmed by the numbers of those who have seven or more rooms, of whom 72.0 per cent had incomes above group 7. The conclusion, which is not surprising, is that there is a wide disparity in access to housing space. It is a conclusion, however, which must be tempered by the data on household size and household distribution. The average size of household rises from the lowest-income category at 1.8 persons to the highest at 4.0 persons. Further, 43.3 per cent of households are in

Table 3
Percentage distribution of all Canadian households
by dwelling characteristics

Income group, 1975	Without bath, 1976 (%)	Without flush toilet, 1976 (%)
1	7.9	7.2
2	7.3	5.5
3	5.6	4.4
4	4.3	3.4
5	3.7	3.0
6	2.3	2.0
7	1.2	1.1
8	0.7	0.6
9	0.6	0.3

Source: Statistics Canada, *Household Facilities by Income and Other Characteristics*, cat. no. 13-567, table 2A

the two income categories above the category containing average income. In other words, since as many individuals and families in the survey have incomes in the higher categories, we would expect to find a higher percentage of households with relatively more space.

There are still a relatively large number of low-income households without a bath or flush toilet (see table 3). The statistics again reveal a range of inequality in the condition of housing. The incidence of households lacking a bath and a flush toilet is highest in the lowest-income groups – 7.9 per cent and 7.2 percent for those with incomes below $2,000, and 7.7 percent and 5.5 per cent for those between $2,000 and $3,999. The incidence of lack of facilities falls as income rises, such that those in the highest-income group have a very low incidence of lack of facilities.

Two further indications of housing quality available in the survey of *Household Facilities by Income and Other Characteristics* are period of construction and housing type. The period of construction provides a rough indication of housing quality, on the grounds that older housing, in general, is still not modernized. Older housing tends to have poorer facilities and to have more design and structural faults.[6] Table 4 shows the percentage distribution of housing constructed before 1940, by income groups. The lower the income, the higher the percentage of housing that was built before 1940. Similarly, housing type provides a rough indication of quality. The single

Table 4
Percentage distribution of all Canadian households by income group,
period of construction, type of housing, and tenure

Income group	Period of construction before 1940	Type of housing single detached	Tenure Owned	Rented
1	42.3	43.8	45.6	54.4
2	40.2	43.2	46.2	53.8
3	40.7	46.8	49.3	50.7
4	37.8	45.5	47.6	52.4
5	33.0	47.3	51.1	48.9
6	29.7	51.4	54.6	45.4
7	25.7	52.0	58.6	41.4
8	19.7	63.0	72.3	27.7
9	17.2	75.1	83.7	16.3
Average			$17,103	$11,518

Source: Statistics Canada, *Household Facilities by Income and Other Characteristics*, cat. no. 13-567, table 2A

detached house tends to be larger, to have better facilities and more amenities. It remains the 'ideal' type of housing. Table 4 shows that access to single detached housing is directly related to income. Seventy-five per cent of households with $5,000-plus income have single detached housing, falling to a low of 43.2 per cent for households with $2,000-$3,999.

The statistics on tenure for Canada provide the same story. Almost 84 per cent of households in the $25,000-plus group owned their own home, while 45.6 per cent were home owners in the below $2,000 group. Of all renters, 70.3 per cent had incomes in group 7 or below, 5.8 per cent had $25,000-plus incomes, and 29.7 per cent had incomes above group 7.

The statistics are spare and bloodless; they do not convey the daily meaning of poor housing, the present and future economic and social implications of continuing inequality which are reinforced by the daily outpouring of the latest in modern homes. What is more, the conventional wisdom envisages a housing market which treats everyone the same – money in, housing out. However, several studies and reports[7] have provided evidence that people with low income pay relatively more for the same products. In addition, they have much more difficulty than the rich in obtaining credit or service, and do not have the funds to pay for advice when they need it. They are less informed of their rights because it is neither their business nor their way of life to know them. The same is true of housing.

The conventional wisdom sees poor housing as a problem for a minority of people.[8] It is only a short distance from the establishment of low minimum standards and the operation of a just, perfect market to the conclusion that it is a minority of families and individuals with low incomes that are the problem. These are the people on welfare or the people living in public housing or in housing which is described as being part of a slum. This view of housing ignores, however, that inequality is more than simply the difference between being above or below some arbitrary standard. It is the difference between the best and the worst, the distance from any particular level to the average, whether above or below. In today's society it is also the difference between moving up and being moved out, between a high or a low level of municipal services and educational facilities for children, between quiet or noisy streets, pavement or parks, crumbling plaster or bright, clean walls. Housing isn't simply some commodity like oranges or ball-point pens. It is the place in which people live and work, in which children grow up and adults grow old. It is the place for which the measures of quantity and price cannot tell the whole of the story.

PRICES, WAGES, AND SALARIES

Prices and wages do, however, have an important story to tell. Recently, working people have been faced by a situation in which house prices have been rising more rapidly than wages.

A rough indication of the relation between wages and salaries and house prices can be derived from a comparison of average weekly earnings with selected price data. In order to make this comparison, indices of average weekly earnings and of prices, using 1971 as the base year, have been developed (see table 5). A comparison of the indices reveals that between 1971 and 1978 the industrial composite average weekly earnings rose by considerably less than house prices, as given by the index of new single detached housing financed under the National Housing Act, by the index of sales through the Multiple Listing Service of real estate boards across Canada, and by the Home Ownership Shelter Component of the Consumer Price Indix. Indices of earnings data from the commerce and service sectors have been included since these sectors tend to have a higher proportion of low wage workers. Between 1971 and 1976, average weekly earnings in both of these sectors rose by less than average weekly earnings in all sectors.[9]

Table 5
Indices of average weekly earnings, and housing prices, 1966-78 (1971 = 100)

	Index* of average wk. earnings			New† housing under NHA 1971 = 100 all single detached dwellings	MLS‡ sale price 1971 = 100	Home§ ownership shelter component CPI
	Industrial composite	Commerce	Services			
1966	69.9	70.9	71.2	87.3	71.3	68.9
1967	74.7	74.9	76.5	88.8	77.7	72.8
1968	79.8	80.1	80.1	90.1	86.5	78.1
1969	85.5	86.5	85.5	98.9	94.5	85.1
1970	92.1	92.7	92.0	96.6	95.1	92.5
1971	100.0	100.0	100.0	100.0	100	100.0
1972	108.4	108.4	108.9	106.3	108.2	108.0
1973	116.5	116.63	116.2	115.5	131.4	118.8
1974	129.4	129.0	127.9	134.9	167.0	130.3
1975	147.7	146.7	145.8	160.6	186.7	143.6
1976	165.7	162.8	162.8	180.5	209.0	163.4
1977	181.6	176.1	173.8	190.7	219.2	181.2
1978	192.8	186.1	182.6	203.1	231.0	196.1

Sources:
* Statistics Canada, *Average Weekly Earnings*, Bulletin no. 72-002, table 11 (March 1967); table 15 (Jan. 1975); table 12 (June 1979). Own calculation of index data based on unadjusted large firm national averages
† Central Mortgage and Housing Corporation, *Canadian Housing Statistics*, table 90 (1976); table 93 (1978)
‡ Canadian Real Estate Association, *Multiple Listing Service Annual Report, 1976*. Own calculation of index from average annual housing sales prices
§ Central Mortgage and Housing Corporation, *Housing Statistics*, table 106 (1976); table 108 (1978)

The recent period of housing crisis is not unique in Canadian history. The periods 1911-13, 1918-22, 1940-41, 1946-51, and 1957-59 were also described as times of crisis. These were periods of rapidly increasing prices and rents, decline in construction, and, consequently, increasing shortage of housing.[10] However, the recent period is different, in that construction has continued to expand during a period of price increase. It is similar, however, in that it is the product of the same basic economic system of production and distribution.

Finally, the key question in regard to prices (as with housing standards) is: who gets which housing and relatively how much do they pay for it? The

Table 6

Housing expenditures as a percentage of income for urban families
in eight Canadian cities, 1976: income groups

No.	Family income ($)	Shelter/ income (%)	Rented housing/ income (%)	Owned housing/ income (%)
1	Under 4,000	34.6	24.7	4.3
2	4,000–4,999	30.4	20.2	5.1
3	5,000–5,999	27.1	17.5	4.2
4	6,000–7,999	24.8	15.0	5.3
5	8,000–9,999	21.5	15.1	3.2
6	10,000–11,999	18.6	11.0	4.3
7	12,000–14,999	17.1	9.9	4.2
8	15,000–17,999	16.5	6.4	6.8
9	20,000–24,999	15.3	4.4	7.9
10	25,000–29,999	14.1	3.1	7.7
11	30,000–34,999	13.1	2.3	7.7
12	35,000+	11.4	1.3	7.0
13	Average all groups $18,494.90	15.7	5.8	6.7

Source: Statistics Canada, *Urban Family Expenditure, 1976*, cat. no. 62-547, table 1

most recent data on household expenditures are available in Statistics Canada's *Urban Family Expenditure, 1976*. The income groups used do not, unfortunately, correspond directly to those in the Statistics Canada survey of *Household Facilities by Income and Other Characteristics*. Nonetheless, the data allow us to form a picture of how much it costs people with low incomes for the relatively poorer housing which they have.

Table 6 indicates that for the poorest housing, those families and individuals with under $4,000 income pay an average of 34.6 per cent of gross family income on housing. Those who rent pay 24.7 per cent of income on rent. These figures compare with the average of all income groups of 15.7 per cent of income on housing costs and 5.8 per cent on rent. The expenditures of those in the $35,000-plus group are 11.4 per cent of income on housing and 1.3 per cent on rent. The extent of this inequality is not fully revealed by these figures, however. The average shelter cost of the richest individuals and families is 11.4 per cent of their income, leaving an average gross income of $32,415 after tax to spend on other things such as food, clothing, entertainment, and transportation. Shelter costs of individuals and families

Table 7
Housing expenditures as a percentage of income for urban families
in eight Canadian cities, 1976: quintile groups

	Shelter/ income (%)	Average income ($)	Rented housing/ income (%)	Owned/ income (%)
1st quintile	27.0	5,388.30	17.3	4.9
2nd quintile	18.3	11,668.20	11.5	3.8
3rd quintile	16.6	16,876.90	6.8	6.7
4th quintile	15.2	22,563.10	4.3	7.7
5th quintile	12.5	35,978.10	2.0	7.4
Average	15.7	18,494.90	5.8	6.7

Source: Statistics Canada, *Urban Family Expenditure, 1976*, cat. no. 62-547, table 33

with incomes in the lowest-income group are 34.6 per cent of their average income, leaving them an average of $1,898 income (after tax) to spend on other things. Accounting for differences in family size would make this comparison $7,906 *per person* in the highest-income group and $1,650 per person in the lowest.

The quintile distribution (table 7) provides a clearer indication of the range of inequality. The income groupings do not necessarily refer to an equal number of families. The quintile distribution for 1976 shows that the 20 per cent of families and individuals in the lowest quintile of income pay more than double the percentage of income on housing that those in the highest quintile pay. In addition, the figures indicate that between 1969 and 1976 the cost of housing as a percentage of income has risen for those in the first quintile and fallen for those in the fifth. Rising prices and rents tend to hurt those with the lowest incomes relatively more than the rich.

Yet, the data here do not confer the full meaning of inequality of housing. First, those families and individuals with relatively low incomes also have a relatively small amount of income which is left over for spending on other essentials of life. Second, they are too often paying much more than the 27.0 per cent of income which is the average for people with incomes in the lowest quintile. Third, the housing they live in, for the relatively high price they pay, is also in the poorest condition and the smallest. Standards of housing have risen and with them the standard of housing of people with low incomes. But when standards rise, those with relatively high incomes continue to benefit far more.

HOW HOUSING IS PRODUCED AND DISTRIBUTED

While the standard of housing has increased over time, the use, or the consumption, of housing remains relatively unequal. The question to consider is: why has this been the case? Conventional economics explains inequality by using what is called the market model. In this view, there are two basic reasons for inequality of housing.

The first is that people live in the housing that they choose. In other words, if people live in bad housing it is because they choose to live there rather than spending more of their income on housing. Similarly, some people live in luxurious housing simply because they are prepared to pay more money for housing than others. While individual choice might be the reason that a family lives in one apartment building rather than another (with a slightly different rent), it cannot explain the major inequalities in housing which exist in Canada at present.

Second, it is said that many people live in low quality, poorly located, or crowded housing because they simply do not have enough income to get something better. While this is undoubtedly true, it is also obvious that the argument can go no further because of two crucial assumptions which underlie it: (a) Everyone, regardless of income and wealth, is treated the same way when they go to buy or rent. (2) The system of finance, production and distribution is simply a technical system having nothing to do with the inequality that results.

This conventional wisdom is, consequently, inadequate for two reasons. First, its explanation of the market for housing does not express the real powerlessness of those at the bottom. Conventional wisdom is based on a formal and stylized textbook housing market, which not only does not exist, but never existed. In it the only specific difference between rich and poor is income. Such a simplification may appeal to theorists with their heads in the clouds, but it does not tell the story of the disadvantages, the difficulties, and the frustration of trying to buy or rent housing with low income, little cash, insecure employment, and little access to credit except of the most expensive sort. Second, the conventional wisdom is inadequate because it is concerned mainly with the price and rent of housing in the market. In doing so, it fails to explain the way in which the economic system of finance, production, and distribution operates to create and perpetuate inequality in housing.

While for the person or persons living in it, housing represents their home, to corporations it represents potential or actual profits. In other words, the drive for profits is in direct conflict with the needs of ordinary people for housing. This conflict between corporate profit and housing need is affected by what happens in the rest of the economy since, in general, in order to help keep profits high, corporations of all sorts attempt to keep wages and salaries low. But the lower the salaries and wages, the less there is available for rents and mortgage payments, and for the fees and commissions involved in buying and selling. If housing rents and prices continue to rise when workers haven't the money to pay, one of two things can happen: (a) prices and rents rise less quickly or even fall, finance capital moves to other sectors where profits are better, and construction slows, creating shortages; or (2) the state steps in to ensure that housing continues to be available.

In both cases, the result is the reinforcement and extension of inequality in housing. This may occur because, at times of housing shortage, lower incomes mean that access even to poor housing is made more difficult. When policies such as CMHC's Assisted Home Ownership Program (AHOP) are introduced, the state operates to ensure that developers are able to sell at high prices. The subsidy which allows people to buy is a subsidy to corporate profits, not to families who need housing. The consequence is that the need of working Canadians for housing – a need which is itself socially defined – remains largely unmet. The poorest are inevitably forced to accept the housing which is below societal standards, while the richest own, or can pay for, luxury housing which is well beyond the standard. It is not sufficient simply to state that the poorest people have the lowest incomes and cannot buy better housing. Inequality in housing is not simply the result of inequality in income; it is the inevitable result of the primacy of profits over need, in the production and distribution of housing.

The drive for profits makes the construction of new housing at prices which can be afforded by individuals and families with low incomes an unlikely possibility. The drive for profits in general and in development itself has continuously made impossible the private construction of housing at relatively low prices. Priority is determined by the demands of finance corporations for profits at low risk. (The demands of other corporations for finance, materials, land, and labour are higher profit areas of the economy.) Priority, as a consequence, can only be given to housing which is likely to return a higher profit. And with an increasing cost structure it is not cheap housing.

FINANCE

Finance capital holds the key to housing production, both sale and rental. Developers and construction corporations are dependent on the finance institutions (including CMHC), which supply much of the capital with which they can carry on their activities. Landlords, large and small, require finance to buy rental housing. For those looking to buy housing for their own use or to sell housing in order to move, finance capital – in the form of a mortgage – is also crucial. Without it a sale is unlikely since few people have the cash for an outright purchase. Finance capital – whether in the form of mortgages, bonds, loans, or shares – also holds the key to other forms of production and sale. As a consequence, there is a line-up for capital at the doors of the finance institutions: only what they favour receives funds, and only what they favour receives capital at relatively favourable terms.

The key factors in any loan are the risks involved, the cost of administration, the terms, and, consequently, the rate of return on a loan in a given period of time. In the past, finance institutions have considered housing loans as risky and costly, with unfavourable terms, and have put their funds elsewhere. Banks were barred from holding mortgages for these reasons. Mortgage funding for many other financial institutions was a residual activity. Since the Second World War the situation has gradually changed in combination with changes in the structure of the housing industry, in the finance industry, and in the laws regulating them both. The changes were brought about not without the efforts of the federal government to ensure a more stable flow of funds and to ensure that these funds came from private sources.

Between 1951 and 1976 lending institutions expanded their holdings of mortgage loans from 10.2 per cent to 23.2 per cent of their assets. Non-bank institutions, in particular, expanded their holdings of mortgages while banks until the late 1960s had relatively small holdings of mortgages.

In an effort to prop up a sagging private enterprise mortgage market in Canada, banks were allowed into the field in 1954 for the first time since 1841. The federal government, through CMHC, also tried to up the amount of finance capital by establishing a market in already existing mortgages and by selling off large numbers of mortgages (between 1961 and 1965) that CMHC had accumulated between 1957 and 1959, when CMHC lent out large amounts of funds which the finance institutions would not lend. Similarly, other changes were brought about in 1954 with the establishment of the CMHC loan guarantee of private finance capital, in 1967 with the Bank Act, and in 1969 with the abandonment of the fixed National Housing Act (NHA) mortgage rate. All these changes were effected in order to establish and develop private finance institutions as sources of housing finance.[12]

Why did this situation occur? First, in the line-up for capital, housing did not stand high on the list. Despite the profits to be made, there were other

Table 8
Mortgages as a percentage of the total assets of financial institutions

| | Percentage of assets in mortgages | |
	1951	1976
1 Life insurance companies	25.5	43.1
2. Chartered banks	–	7.2
3 Trust companies	28.7	73.3
4 Loan companies	68.3	83.2
5 Other	8.2	48.9
6 Total	10.2	23.1

Source: J.V. Poapst, *Developing the Residential Mortgage Market*
(Ottawa 1973), III, 124, table A-8, and CMHC, *Canadian Housing Statistics* 1978, table 79

places even more profitable. After the war, state involvement in housing grew, despite CMHC's unsuccessful efforts to curtail its own direct intervention in the housing sector. CMHC was forced to lend out more and more funds under the National Housing Act because of corporate inability and reluctance. The changes in the NHA enacted in 1954 were designed to encourage private enterprise to increase, and to allow CMHC to significantly reduce, mortgage funding.[13] After 1954, although private finance increased, housing still went begging for funds. In addition, when the government changed in 1957 to the Conservatives, there was a decision taken to expand housing construction in order to expand the economy. Since that time the federal government has used a variety of methods to reduce involvement, to leave the profits to private finance institutions, and, at the same time, to guarantee their profits in a variety of ways. Despite its efforts, CMHC has had to remain a major financier of housing.

There are several important aspects of the current state of housing finance to note here. First, development corporations could not have developed without the growing interest of Canadian banks and other finance institutions, such as insurance, trust, and savings and loan companies, in urban development and redevelopment. Large-scale downtown commercial/office complexes have been their priority since such developments offer the chance at gigantic profits with low risk. They allow the financial institutions to make one large loan instead of several smaller ones, which are more expensive and less secure. Such loans require large corporations to plan and execute these projects, and such has been the case. The result has been the destruction of older core city areas, which through deterioration – often encouraged by purposeful corporate neglect – had become areas of housing inhabited by those with lower incomes.

The second preference among finance institutions, particularly in the 1960s with the increased need for housing as a result of the children of the post-war baby boom reaching maturity, has been for high-rises in the downtown areas of major cities. High-rise apartments also had the virtues, from the point of view of finance, of largeness of scale, high density, and 'good returns' when rented.

A third preference was for integrated subdivision development, including high-rise, low-rise, and row housing (rental and owner-occupied), as well as shopping centres. The result has been that finance institutions, with the assistance of CMHC, have had the dominant role in the direction of development, ensuring the destruction of neighbourhoods, the construction of even more expensive high-rise housing on expensive land, and the continued development of new suburban single detached housing. The only funds available for the financing of cheaper housing are those which come either directly from CMHC or from finance institutions and are guaranteed by CMHC. In the latter case, the profits which private finance could not otherwise obtain on its own are paid for by the state.[14]

Housing like other commodities, is not financed such that corporations can build the housing that people need. It is financed to make a profit, if and only if the profit is sufficiently high. The resulting system of finance is one in which the banks finance large-scale development, while the smaller-scale development, as well as individual mortgages are financed by the insurance, trust, and savings and loan companies. Profits are guaranteed by the nature of the project itself or by CMHC. Further, CMHC makes available the financing necessary to ensure that the housing industry remains profitable; in doing so, CMHC also helps in dealing with economic crises generated elsewhere in the economy. CMHC's role is not hard to understand as soon as it is made clear that it is primarily a bank for banks and developers. At CMHC, as in the finance business, profits come first, needs second. The result is the financing of the inequality which is the dominant feature of the Canadian economy and Canadian housing.

LAND

In order to produce new buildings it is necessary to have the land to put it on, the materials with which to construct it, and the workers who will put it up.

For land, as for finance, there is a line-up based on the potential profits to be derived from particular uses. Housing must take its place in that line-up, along with offices, shops, shopping centres, and factories. In addition, particular types of housing are of more interest than others because of what they will produce at the bottom line of the income statement.

Both finance and land are crucial to housing, but in the end it is the money men who decide, according to their assessment of profitability. The line-up for land, as for capital, perpetuates the same inequality in housing in Canadian society. This occurs in several ways. The construction industry has come to be dominated by large-scale development corporations, which by their nature have come to control a larger and larger share of land for potential development. Of this land, there are two types – land on the fringes of the major urban areas, and land in the central areas. A recently published study on land development[14] showed a startlingly high degree of control over the production of new 'lots' for housing (on fringe or core city land) by a relatively small number of corporations. The absolute numbers do not necessarily reflect the real power which these corporations exert because they are regionally based. Many corporations had most or all of their land holdings in one locale. Campeau Corporation held 97 per cent of its listed development land in Ottawa, where its holdings constituted 73.8 per cent of development land holdings. Similarly, St. Lawrence Corporation held 100 per cent of its land in the Montreal area, where it held 41.2 per cent of development land, and Allarco, which had the biggest holding in Edmonton, 43.97 per cent, held all its land in the region of that city.[15]

One implication of this control is the effect on the price of housing that corporations can have through increases in the price of land. While significant control of land by a relatively small group of major corporations is hardly the full explanation for increases, it is an important part. Such increases are a possibility because of the price leader effect and the key role that the price of new housing plays in housing prices in general. Since corporations 'produce' land (with zoning and services) both for internal use as well as for sale to other corporations, they can influence the price of land both directly and indirectly.[16] According to CMHC statistics, land costs for new single detached housing financed under the National Housing Act rose by 139 per cent between 1971 and 1978, considerably faster than construction costs (per square metre), which rose by 99 per cent in the same period. Much of this increase was concentrated in the 1974-76 period when land costs rose by 90 per cent while construction costs rose by 21 per cent. A similar increase in land costs took from 1961 to 1974 to be generated.[17] In the same 1974-76 period, land costs rose from 16.3 per cent to 23.1 per cent of costs of production of new single detached National Housing Act-financed housing (see table 9). Clearly, development corporations could not of their own accord initiate increases in land costs or housing prices. However, major development corporations were in a much better position, with extensive land banks, to profit from demographic and social changes which occurred.

The historical data show that land costs have become an increasing proportion of the cost of construction of new single detached dwellings financed under the National Housing Act since 1951 (see table 9). These data also indicate that the 1970s boom resulted in rapidly increasing land costs as a proportion of new construction costs, while in the 1974-76 period in particular, construction costs as a proportion of total costs of new housing constructions actually fell by almost 10 per cent. The data suggest that, in their pursuit of profit, the corporations which dominate the control of urban development are able to increase the cost of development land to some degree.

The *Land and Urban Development* study also showed that a sizeable stock of empty lots ready for construction has existed over the years 1965-73 in major cities.[18] The implication of data on the large stock of raw and undeveloped land is that the problem is not that the land is not there or cannot be developed; it is a question of timing and profits. Undoubtedly, reform of many municipal and regional planning systems would cut down on some of the time taken in moving land from a raw to a developed stage, as the construction actually fell by almost 10 per cent. The data suggest that, in their end it is the developers who determine the timing of development, not without close friends in city halls all across the country who still conceive of city government as simply being in place to serve the interests of major corporations. Even in cities which have elected reform governments, the elected friends of the developer still have their place, and while reform governments have curbed the most blatant of developer-serving excesses, they have not effected fundamental change either at the municipal or the regional level.[20] Control of land still brings with it the power to determine, in large part, the pattern, scale, nature, and timing of development, as well as the power to have a strong influence on price. The result of the land system, as of the finance system, is the structuring of inequality of housing by insuring that disposition of land is determined according to the most profitable uses – meaning first, commercial, then industrial, and lastly residential. It also helps ensure that the prices will be high and that housing itself will be unequally distributed.

Table 9
Percentage distribution of major cost items. All new single detached dwellings, financed under the National Housing Act, Canada, 1951-78

	1951	1956	1961	1966	1971	1972	1973	1974	1975	1976	1977	1978
Land costs	9.6	14.6	17.5	18.0	20.8	20.8	13.8	16.3	20.9	23.1	24.4	24.4
Construction costs	87.4	83.5	80.9	80.1	77.2	77.0	79.8	81.8	77.1	73.7	72.8	72.4
Other costs	3.0	1.9	1.6	1.9	2.0	2.0	1.9	1.9	2.5	3.2	2.8	3.1
Total	100	100	100	100	100	100	100	100	100	100	100	100

Sources: Central Mortgage and Housing Corporation, *Canadian Housing Statistics*, table 93 (1978); table 89 (1973); table 85 (1970)

PRODUCTION: THE GROWTH OF THE DEVELOPMENT CORPORATION

The contradictory forces involved in the system of finance production, sale, and rental of housing are both cause and effect of the growth of the development corporations, which are fast coming to dominate housing production. As a result, development corporations are a major part of the generation and maintenance of inequality in housing. Such corporations are, however, a relatively recent phenomenon in Canada.

It was not until the years after the Second World War that the residential construction industry began to expand after the devastating effects of the depression. In 1928, housing completions hit a peak of 59,000 units, a level which was not exceeded until 1946. In fact, completions fell to a low of 21,000 in 1933, and by 1940 had struggled up to 49,000. The residential construction industry consisted largely of small companies constructing a modest number of houses per year and was dependent on the savings and loan, insurance, and trust companies for much of the necessary mortgage finance.[21]

As a consequence, the federal government made a decision to establish its own development corporation in the form of the Wartime Housing Limited (WHL). The industry was not capable of responding sufficiently to build the war-related housing which it was anticipated should be built. WHL established a national organization to finance, plan, construct, manage, and sell housing. In retrospect, it could be seen as one of Canada's earliest development corporations.

In the post-war period there were a number of factors which led not only to the expansion of production but to the concentration of housing production into the larger-scale companies which we now know as development corporations. The depression had provided evidence of the fragility of the industry and of the finance sector on which it was dependent. The Dominion Housing Act of 1935 was introduced to assist the needed restructuring of residential mortgage financing. After the war, the Central Mortgage and Housing Corporation was founded as the means by which the federal government was to play a crucial role in expanding the availability and flow of residential finance capital to industry, in particular by reducing the risk of investment in housing on the part of finance institutions. Special tax concessions to corporations building housing were also introduced.

At the same time, the deterioration of housing before and during the war, the increase in crowding, and the post-war influx of returning soldiers and immigrants all contributed to an enormous demand for housing. The conditions were ripe for the realization of large-scale profits. Data compiled in

Table 10
Date of entry into development industry of 100 largest public corporations in Canada, 1971

Date of entry	1900-09	1910-19	1920-39	1930-39	1940-49	1950-59	1960-69	1900-69
No. of corporations	2	6	0	0	4	31	57	100

Source: G. Barker, J. Penney, and W. Seccombe, *Highrise and Superprofit* (Kitchener, Ont. 1973), 17 (compiled from *Canadian Real Estate Annual*, 1971)

Highrise and Superprofits[22] show that of the 100 largest public development corporations in 1971, 31 began operations between 1950 and 1959. An additional 57 began operations between 1960 and 1969. Developers who had earlier concentrated largely on expansion of the fringe of urban areas began to look increasingly at the profits to be made from the redevelopment of city centres. The high cost of land, and the increasing scale of the operations in general, required ever greater pools of capital and productive capacity. The necessary concentration of capital, which was generally assisted by federal government tax policy, was given a boost by the tendency of municipal governments to demand that developers provide or pay for needed municipal services and by the increased popularity of core city urban renewal schemes promoted by CMHC.

The result has been a growing number of large-scale corporations in residential housing construction. Data compiled in an Economic Council of Canada study on the construction industry showed that in 1970 there were 7,518 incorporated companies involved in all types of building construction. Of these, 0.6 per cent had assets in excess of $10 million, and these 45 corporations controlled 19.5 per cent of *all* sales. Ninety firms (1.2 per cent) had assets of $5 million or more, accounting for 25.8 per cent of sales. With subsequent mergers and expansions, several development corporations now exceed $1 billion in assets.[23]

The significance of this growth is that major corporations, both foreign and Canadian, are coming to dominate the housing industry. These corporations have tended to concentrate their activities in particular urban areas such that there are significantly large corporations based in most regions in the country. The development corporation is, however, not simply a large construction company. In order to reduce costs and instability, the corporations have moved to ensure the availability of the materials, the land, and the skilled labour necessary to ensure their own growth and profit. The integration of many aspects of production and of distribution into a vertically integrated corporation also occurred in housing. A detailed investigation of Genstar by Donald Gutstein illustrates what this means. Genstar now has an integrated set of subsidiaries which buy and assemble land; develop subdivisions; supply materials; build houses; and sell land, lots, materials, and houses.[24]

Genstar operations also illustrate the close ties which exist between the large development corporations and their sources of finance capital. A study of the ten largest development corporations in 1971 revealed a large number of interlocking directorships between these corporations and major financial institutions, one indication of these ties.[25]

REAL ESTATE TRANSACTIONS

The housing market is largely run by, and in the interests of, a growing number of middlemen of all sorts – real-estate agents, lawyers, brokers, finance managers, appraisers and surveyors, rental agents, and housing managers. When it comes to sales, the more times a house or an apartment block sells and the higher the price, the more profitable is it for the professionals who handle the transaction. In the past, renting was a far more simple affair since there were few middlemen, if any, and few papers – tenants had few rights even on paper anyway. Now here, too, the middlemen are growing, in the form of agents offering to find rental accommodation, management representatives for one or several large buildings, and lawyers who run the appropriate papers through the appropriate court in order to evict tenants.

The middlemen have several things in common. They have an interest in ensuring that the public view of their work is that it is difficult and essential. One way this is done is through public organizations which group different types of professionals together – the Canadian Real Estate Association and the Appraisal Institute of Canada are two such examples. They also have provincial and regional organizations which attempt to operate in much the same way that the national and provincial associations of doctors and lawyers do. The middlemen are self-policing to give the public the sense of weeding out the fast buck artists; they standardize fees to eliminate competition; and they commission 'studies and reports' which explain the virtues of owning property. They also regularly advise governments at all levels of what is good for housing, meaning, in effect, what they believe will secure greater profit. Among other things, it means that they advise more private ownership of housing, and restricted funding for public housing because public housing is not where the money is. They also help to ensure that the system of property and finance remains a needlessly complicated one so that it can support the many thousands of professionals who live off it. For example, a book of advice on how to buy and sell housing in Ontario had this to say: 'This is not a "do-it-yourself" book. We are not attempting here to provide a kit through which you can avoid the lawyer's office ... To attempt to handle a real estate deal without a lawyer is almost the same as to attempt to perform a complicated medical operation on one's self without a doctor.'[26]

The purchase and sale of housing is the base upon which many thousands of salespersons, lawyers, appraisers, and surveyors are supported. In 1976 there were 417,989 MLS listings of houses for sale, an increase of almost 200 per cent since 1971, of which 34 per cent resulted in sales, down from a high of 54.8 per cent in 1973. In 1976 MLS accounted for 142,272 sales at an average price of $51,380. Estimating a conservative 5 per cent commission, those sales generate $365.5 million annually on MLS listings alone. Lawyers' fees on those houses would probably add another $146.2 million.[27] When other commissions and fees are considered, housing professionals are involved in a billion-dollar business.

The housing market operates to reinforce the inequality on which it is based. High income means more cash, steady employment, good credit risk (and consequently the better housing), easier credit on better terms, the cash to cover the expenses of buying, and the income to keep up the payments. Middlemen in the housing market exact a large-scale profit essentially by keeping buyers and sellers from meeting directly. In this way they help to keep up the price (and their commission) on each sale. They operate to increase expectations of price increases, which are in their interest since they gain from higher prices. They also work to reinforce the desirability of home ownership and work actively to oppose government funding of public or third sector (non-profit co-operative) housing. They can, of course, and in practice some do, oppose third sector housing by refusing to deal with non-profit and/or co-operative corporations. None of their activities are, of course, in the interest of people with lower incomes trying to obtain housing.

Renting housing is also big business for the middleman. There are a growing group of so-called home-finders who charge the individual a fee for the privilege of receiving a list of rental housing which may or may not be either available or suitable. These agencies function as the more crass of profit-making activities, often providing no more than the average newspaper would offer at a considerably lower cost to the potential renter. However, after finding a suitable apartment or house to rent, the process is far from over. Many major and minor corporations require an application to rent to be filled out by a prospective tenant. The key is whether you can pay regularly, so the signing of the form is like an application for credit; i.e., the lower the income, the less the chance. Although landlord tenant acts have been changed in many provinces, and many provinces have enacted some form of continuing rent review, the major effect of these acts is to increase the number of middlemen involved. Both types of legislation are normally complicated and cumbersome, but when you're in the business it's your business to know them or to hire the expertise. Extensive reviews of landlord tenant cases in Ontario, after major changes in the legislation, have shown that landlords rarely lose and that there is a specialized group of lawyers who handle these cases on a regular basis. Most cases are taken by landlords against tenants for failure to pay rent. But since poverty is not an acceptable reason for failure to pay, the courts act as a legitimate and fail-safe means of putting people with low incomes onto the street. But, then, that is what property law is all about.[28]

GOVERNMENT POLICY

The financing, production, and distribution of housing in Canada have been conducted within an economy of private enterprise. A private enterprise economy is one in which housing is built for profit, and sold or rented for profit. A large number of corporations and individuals benefit from this system. Government policy towards housing has developed in order to ensure the continued existence of this system; at the same time, many of these policies have been explained as helping those who are especially ill-housed. Government policy at all levels has been predicated on, and has acted to perpetuate, the same system which generates inequality. This is neither an accident nor a conspiracy. Almost all governments, at all levels, have been dedicated to private enterprise. Those to whom they would most logically turn for advice would be those very people who could explain what was in the interests of the industry, meaning capital and profits. Similarly, many members of government have been involved in one way or another in private enterprise. Naturally, they would support policies, where necessary, which would support the industry. This isn't to say that there would always be agreement on what exactly to do – only on what not to do. Not all people have always seen what are called the virtues of private enterprise, particularly when large numbers of people are without good housing. Governments, like the industry, have worked hard to keep up the image of the industry, to support the myth of the necessity of home ownership, and to oppose public housing and non-profit or co-operative (third sector) housing. They have brought in policies on increasing funding to support public housing or third sector housing only when pushed. Similarly, they have brought in regulations to curb industry abuses only when necessary.

The rule in government, as in the industry, has been profit first, needs second. In 1918, when the dominion government brought in, briefly, the first national housing legislation, it was to deal with political pressure – the threat of signficant political unrest as a result of high rents and shortages – as well as the need to stimulate production generally in the economy. The program was presented as a major contribution to bettering housing conditions, but it is clear from the commitment of funds, the amounts spent, and the number of houses built, that it was of minor significance. Nonetheless, this was Canada's first piece of federal housing legislation. The program was abandoned in 1924; housing policies did not reappear federally until 1935, in the years of the depression.[29]

The Dominion Housing Act (DHA) was enacted by the Bennett government before the 1935 election. The essence of this act was the joint loan under which mortgages for new residential housing would be jointly financed by the government and a finance institution. However, the government portion of the mortgage was provided at below market rates in order to ensure an above market return to the finance institution. The act introduced several changes in the form of mortgage financing such as a twenty-year term, higher valuation, and the now common blended payments of principal, interest, and taxes. These changes were necessary for the finance institutions and the industry but, in fact, little funding was supplied under the act. The final important feature was the introduction of a partial government guarantee of the loans of the private lending institutions. The DHA was superseded in 1938 by the National Housing Act (NHA), which reiterated the terms of the 1935 act but added a clause specifying the terms of mortgage loans to local housing authorities and limited dividend housing companies.[30]

In 1918, 1935, and 1938, legislation was introduced – despite the constitutional questions surrounding federal level housing policy – in order to deal with an economic and, consequently, political crisis. The legislation provided funds to encourage private lending and/or construction but were largely insignificant. In each case, they were represented as providing a political response to deal with the housing of the poor, with unemployment, and with economic downturn. Housing policy in peacetime was conceived of as a means of bolstering, in certain of its parts, a sagging private industry. It was presented as a means of helping the poor obtain better houses. Nothing in the presentation or use of legislation has changed since that time. Policy is still a question of aiding, assisting, and nursing a private industry that takes no risks since NHA funds are guaranteed. It takes only profits, when it wants, on its own terms. It leaves the federal government to ensure that the industry will be patched up when it has holes.

The war period forced significant changes in the nature of federal government involvement in housing. It moved from being a minor supplier of finance capital to involvement in all phases of housing production and distribution. During the depression the construction industry had been particularly hard hit. At the beginning of the war, there was little confidence that the private industry could actually produce the houses that would be required by the government effort to run the war. The federal government established a Crown corporation, Wartime Housing Limited, to build war workers' housing in 1941. To be sure, however, housing built directly by Wartime Housing Limited was to be temporary in nature so that it could be demolished and rebuilt by private industry after the war. In addition, many of the houses built were constructed by private corporations. In fact, profits from house building rose dramatically during the war. After the war, Wartime Housing Limited continued to produce veteran's housing until 1949. A total of 45,930 houses were produced by Wartime Housing Limited between 1941 and 1949. Despite government objectives, many of these houses remain in existence today.

There was a second strand of development of government action in housing during the war – regulation. War conditions successively forced the establishment and tightening of materials, rent, price, and profit controls. In fact, the federal government during the war had a hand, mainly through Wartime Housing Limited and the Wartime Prices and Trade Board, as well as other organizations, in most aspects of the system of financing, production, and distribution of housing. But the commitment to profits ensured on the one hand, that from 1944 onward, every effort was made to disengage, and on the other, to build up a private industry despite the continuing lack of interest of private finance capital in housing.

A 1944 government report prepared by the Advisory Committee on Reconstruction[31] called for a large-scale program of construction of low rent housing to meet the backlog of need caused by the fall-off in construction over the fifteen years since 1928. This too was resisted in the interests of avoiding the implementation of any form of public housing. Instead, post-war government policy consisted of (1) gradual removal of all controls; (2) re-enactment of the National Housing Act in 1944; (3) the establishment of the Central Mortgage and Housing Corporation as a mortgage bank for the industry; and (4) a variety of tax write-offs to bolster the profits of the private industry. This was the origin of the present housing policy for the industry, in which government as well as industry put profits before needs. C.D.

Howe, minister for reconstruction in 1946, put it this way: 'It is the policy to ensure that as large a portion as possible of housing be built by private initiative. The Dominion Government will lend every facility to provide private enterprise to build as many houses as are needed ... if, however, with all the assistance we can provide for financing, materials and labour supply, the houses required to substantially improve the housing standard of the Canadian people are not forthcoming, then the Dominion Government will take a direct position in the housing field.'[32]

Government policy was to be 'residual' to the industry on a continuing basis. To ensure this, Howe refused to authorize any funds under the NHA for public housing. The first project, established in 1947 after a municipal referendum in Toronto, was required to incorporate as a limited dividend company until 1949, when the legislation was altered.[33] In addition, the stock of low rent public housing already in existence which had been constructed by WHL was systematically sold. In 1949 CMHC was the largest landlord in the country, with 41,348 houses, most in urban areas, of which 38,364 were single units and 6,434 had already been sold. By 1958, CMHC's holdings had been reduced to 13,000.[34]

From the point of view of the government, the task was largely accomplished successfully. From the point of view of the industry, the task was accomplished successfully. What was accomplished was the re-establishment of the same system of finance, production, and distribution which remains the basis of inequality in housing today. Successive changes in the federal legislation have served to give the industry every possible assistance, but, nonetheless, CMHC has run the risk on a number of occasions of taking over the majority of industry financing. As a consequence, CMHC has been involved in a continual process of building up a reluctant private industry; it could, of course, have done otherwise.

The rest of current federal policy was set in place during the post-war years. In 1949, public housing legislation was altered to a capital cost-sharing arrangement between two levels of government. There were few funds and little public housing was produced until 1964 when the act was changed to allow the provinces to borrow federal money to build public housing. While public housing construction grew considerably after 1964, it still remains a marginal source of low rent housing. It has been and remains largely cheap housing as well. However, even this source of public housing is currently in danger of disappearing. The province producing the largest amount of public housing (Ontario) is pulling back from production, in favour of rent supplements and other industry assistance programs.

Successive Liberal and Conservative governments have been completely unwilling to assist co-operative housing, resisting demands to make NHA available to continuing co-operatives. This has been consistent with their position of supporting the myths of private enterprise, including owner occupation of housing. Only since 1974 has federal funding become available. Although there has since been a rapid expansion of co-operative housing, it still remains a highly marginal source of lower cost housing. Recently this source of funds has been curtailed.

What has been promoted is private development at public expense. Rapid expansion of NHA joint loans after the war led to changes in the act in 1954 to guarantee private finance institution loans, to eliminate joint loans, to bring in more private capital, to establish a secondary mortgage market, and to make CMHC once again residual. It didn't quite work out that way since CMHC mortgage funds, as we have seen, were used to expand the economy in 1957-59, 1961-62, and the mid-1960s as well, while finance institutions continued to place housing low in the line-up for capital. Changes in the Bank Act in 1967 and in CMHC policy in 1969 have encouraged the chartered banks to consider mortgages as being sufficiently profitable to put funds into. Since 1971, CMHC has been gradually shifting funds into more selective types of spending, such as the Assisted Home Ownership Program;[35] at the same time, the banks have been entering the finance market.

A program which for several years was of major importance was the funding of urban renewal in major urban areas. The strength of political reaction to urban redevelopment forced the effective curtailment of CMHC funding for urban renewal in 1968. Federal funding required that development plans be undertaken. The plans encouraged consideration of redevelopment and provided an impetus to corporations to engage in the destruction and reconstruction of urban areas. Land assembly funds, funds to encourage modernization of municipal sewage treatment facilities, and funds for the development of rental housing, including so-called limited dividend housing, all contributed to the climate in which large-scale corporations emerged which, while rapidly expanding the stock of housing, reaped large-scale profits at public expense. Housing policy has been founded on developing and encouraging a large-scale private enterprise system of housing, a system which increases the quantity and the standard of housing while perpetuating inequality. The inequality which results is neither accidental nor conspiratorial. It is the result of conscious policy tuned to profits first, needs second. It is a policy which has been consciously promoted by government and industry alike. Programs such as public housing are kept small and the housing unattractive thereby promoting the problems which are the basis of attacks on their efficacy.[36] In addition, until recently the poorest were barred from public housing[37] because of minimum income bars. Programs such as assisted home ownership have promoted the myth of private ownership to those who can't really afford to buy. Grants and loans reduce the initial cost of home ownership payments, spreading the cost over more years and moving the weight of payments from the early years. What they do not do is lower the price. Such programs become a means by which the profits from high house prices are assured by the state. Assisted rental housing programs have done the same. There is simply no evidence that relative inequality in the distribution of housing has changed at all due to these and other CMHC programs. They are not significantly different from past policies which funded private ownership and large-scale high-rise rental housing. Over the years, a large number of studies[38] have shown that because policies were geared to industry profit, or because so-called social housing programs were as well, or were not funded, which amounts to the same thing, federal housing policy has not meant any change in the continuing unequal distribution of housing. In fact, CMHC's role has been to fund inequality, to guarantee it, and to encourage its perpetuation.

CMHC, of course, administers only a part of what should be seen as housing policy. Programs administered by other federal government departments and corporations also have an impact on housing. The most important of these are the policies regarding the regulation and control of finance capital, and the taxation of profits. Write-offs of the cost of holding land and housing, including interest and taxes, depreciation of assets at high rates for tax purposes less than full taxation of capital gains, write-offs of book losses against other profits, and low rates of corporate tax have all in the past contributed to high rates of profit. Post-war Canadian tax policies have been a key ingredient in the growth of large-scale corporations and large-scale profits in housing, as in other sectors of industry.[39]

Provincial and municipal governments have also had their part to play in the development and perpetuation of the system of inequality in housing. In the division of powers which has emerged, the provinces have legislated property and landlord tenant laws, planning, property tax assessment, and housing and public health standards. They have also legislated to borrow federal funds. The municipal governments and the courts have been the agents of administration. As a result, municipal governments, until the recent reaction against development, have been the preserve of the construction and real-estate business. The business of the city halls of Canada has been in ensuring that developers' interests come first. Tighter zoning and planning restrictions are a very recent development. As David Lewis Stein's book on Toronto shows, these restrictions can be and were circumvented by aldermen dedicated to the interests of such large Toronto developers as Meridian and Marathon.[40] It is arguable that the advent of reform municipal governments has curbed little more than the worst examples of special treatment.

Financial support of municipal government has been an issue which affects development in a number of ways. In the 1950s, with the advance of larger-scale subdivisions, municipal governments lacking the funds to pay for services turned to the corporations to provide the services or financing. The costs and the economies of scale involved required the development of large corporations to carry out such projects on an increasing scale. Municipal governments remain short of revenue and dependent in most provinces on property tax for at least a third of their revenue. Tax incidence studies have repeatedly shown the property tax to be the most regressive of taxes, further reinforcing housing inequality.[41]

Provincial policies in housing have been of three types: (1) tied to CMHC policy directly; (2) independent provincial programs usually in land or mortgages; and (3) regulation and administration of property and planning law. Only the NDP government of British Columbia, of the years 1972-75, tried to innovate by bringing restrictions on the turnover of agricultural land for development and by buying up a large BC-based development corporation, Dunhill, as a base of operations. There was a debate within the government as to what to do with Dunhill, but the government was defeated shortly after, before the debate was resolved.[42]

If there is a conclusion on housing and the state in Canada it would be that the principles of protection of private property and profit have dominated the policies of successive governments at all levels. State and private industry have walked hand in hand promoting, supporting, nourishing, and enforcing the predominance of profit over need and at public expense. If inequality in housing is to be changed, it will require a reorientation of policy towards the provision of housing in much the same way that primary and secondary education are provided – as a public service. It will also require a housing policy and a co-ordinated series of state actions rather than an ad hoc collection of programs developed to meet each succeeding economic and political crisis. Housing is too important for it to remain as a means of stabilizing the economy or as a residual state activity. The government funding exists with which to create a truly innovative and large-scale public sector oriented to housing needs, at costs in relation to income which would leave those housed enough income for the purchase of other necessities as well.

NOTES

1 Michael Dennis and Susan Fish, *Programs in Search of a Policy* (Toronto 1972); Government of Canada, Task Force on Housing and Urban Development, *Report* (Ottawa 1969)

2 Lawrence Smith, *Housing in Canada: Market Structure and Policy Performance*, Research Monograph no. 2 in the series *Labour Urban Canada: Problems and Prospects* (Ottawa 1971), 19

3 Dennis and Fish, *Programs in Search of a Policy*, chaps. 1, 2, and 4

4 Statistics Canada, *Survey of Household Facilities by Income and Other Characteristics*, Bulletin no. 13-567 (Ottawa 1978)

5 See Economic Council of Canada, *Economic Targets and Social Indicators*, 11th Annual Review of the Economic Council of Canada (Ottawa 1974), chap. 4, pp. 73-87, for a more extensive review of indicators of crowding in Canada; See also John S. Kirkland, *Patterns of Housing Quality* (Ottawa 1972), chap. 2; A. Maslove, *Towards The Measurement of Housing Quality*, Economic Council of Canada, Discussion Paper no. 75 (Ottawa 1977).

6 Kirkland, ibid., 26

7 See, for example, National Council of Welfare, *Prices and the Poor* (Ottawa 1974).

8 See, for example, I. Silver, *Housing and the Poor*, Ministry of State for Urban Affairs, Working Paper no. A.71.2 (Ottawa 1971).

9 For a consideration of the reliability of the housing price data, see S.W. Hamilton, 'House Price Indices: Theory and Practice,' in *Housing: It's Your Move*, a report prepared by a study team in the Urban Land Division, Faculty of Commerce and Business Administration, University of British Columbia, (Vancouver 1976), 383-418; and David Baxter, 'Published Housing Data: Trends and Evaluation,' ibid., 419-48.

10 See A. Moscovitch, 'The Political Economy of Housing Policy. Origins to 1948,' unpublished, 1977.

11 Some of these differences in approach are brought out in a self-examination by L.S. Bourne, 'Choose Your Villain: Five Ways to Oversimplify the Price of Housing and Urban Land,' *Urban Forum*, III, 1 (Spring 1977), 16-23.

12 On the changes in legislation, see 'Banking Legislation, 1822 to 1944,' in E.P. Neufeld, ed., *Money and Banking in Canada* (Toronto 1967), 360-9. See also in the same volume, R.M. MacIntosh, 'The Bank Act Revisions of 1954,'

304-5. Historical treatment of the points raised here may also be found in
A.D. Wilson, 'Canadian Housing Legislation,' *Canadian Public Administration*,
II, 2 (Dec. 1959), 215-28; James Gillies, 'Some Financial Aspects of the Cana-
dian Government Housing Program: History and Prospective Developments,'
Journal of Finance, VIII, 1 (March 1953), 22-33; Albert Rose, 'Canadian
Housing Policies,' in M. Wheeler, ed., *The Right to Housing* (Montreal 1978),
63-128; A. Moscovitch, 'Canadian Federal Government Housing Policies,'
unpublished, 1976.

13 These points have been brought out by many authors. See, for example,
Donald Gutstein, *Vancouver Ltd.* (Toronto 1975); G. Barker, J. Penney, and
W. Seccombe, *Highrise and Superprofit* (Kitchener 1973); John Sewell, 'The
Suburbs,' *City Magazine*, II, 6 (Jan. 1977), 19-55; F. Lamarche, 'Property
Development and the Economic Foundations of the Urban Question,' in C.G.
Pickvance, ed., *Urban Sociology* (London 1976), 85-118.

14 P. Spurr, *Land and Urban Development* (Toronto 1976), table 4.7, pp. 203;
table 4.8, p. 208

15 Ibid., see also Federal-Provincial Task Force on the Supply and Price of Serviced Residential Land, *Report*, I (Ottawa 1977), table 5A, 69.

16 The effect of private and public land banking on house prices, and in particu-
lar of increasing land prices on the final price of new housing, has been the
subject of considerable recent controversy. The major pieces in the debate are
Basil A. Kalymon, *Profits in the Real Estate Industry* (Vancouver 1978); James
Lorimer, *The Developers* (Toronto 1978); J.R. Markusen and D.T. Scheffman,
*Speculation and Monopoly in Urban Development: Analytic Foundation with Evi-
dence for Toronto* (Toronto 1977); P. Spurr, *Land and Urban Development*;
Federal-Provincial Task Force on the Supply and Price of Serviced Residential
Land, *Report* (Ottawa 1978) – also known as the *Greenspan Report*; *Housing:
It's Your Move*; Royal Commission Corporate Concentration, *The Cadillac
Fairview Corporation Limited*, Study no. 3 (Ottawa 1977); R.A. Muller, *The
Market for New Housing in The Metropolitan Toronto Area* (Toronto 1978);
Winnipeg Land Prices Inquiry Commission, *Report* (Winnipeg 1977). The
Greenspan Report is a case in point in the debate. The *Report* sets out to
refute so-called monopoly-developer conspiracy theories. The staff of the Task
Force was largely made up of the authors of the books and articles dedicated
to the same purpose. Their conclusion is that price and cost changes seen in
the 1970s are really just examples of market forces at work. Presenting their
arguments they have set up a strawman to knock down and this they do, dis-
missing entirely the effects of land holdings on prices: 'The land and house
price explosion was not caused by either high profits or monopolistic developers' (p. 79). This seems as much to overstate the case as those who argue

that changes in the housing sector in the 1970s can be explained only by reference to land developers' holdings or to bureaucratic red tape.

17 Central Mortgage and Housing Corporation, *Canadian Housing Statistics, 1978* (Ottawa 1979), table 93. Calculations are my own.

18 Ibid., table 2.14

19 See, for example, Urban Development Institute, *Lowering the Cost of New Housing* (Toronto 1976).

20 There are now several books and articles which provide a critical perspective on municipal reform governments; see, for example, Jon Caulfield, *The Tiny Perfect Mayor* (Toronto 1974); Donald Gutstein, 'The Developers' Team: Vancouver's "Reform" Party in Power,' *City Magazine*, I, 2 (Dec.-Jan. 1975), 13-28; Michael Goldrick, 'The Anatomy of Urban Reform in Toronto,' *City Magazine*, III, 4 and 5 (May-June 1978), 29-39. The pages of *City Magazine* contain many case studies which illustrate that after reform politics, it is still the case that 'plus ça change.'

21 Moscovitch, 'Political Economy of Housing Policy'; data are drawn from O.J. Firestone, *Residential Real Estate in Canada* (Toronto 1951). The analysis which follows here draws on my unpublished paper; calculations are my own.

22 Barker, et al., *Highrise and Superprofit*, chap. 2

23 Economic Council of Canada, *Toward More Stable Growth in Construction* (Ottawa 1974), tables 1 and 2, p. 15

24 Gutstein, *Vancouver Ltd.*, 135

25 Barker et al., *Highrise and Superprofit*, 66

26 M. Green, *Buying or Selling Real Estate in Ontario* (Toronto 1975), 7

27 The Canadian Real Estate Association, *Multiple Listing Service Annual Report, 1976* (Toronto 1977) – lawyers' fees calculated at 2 per cent of sales

28 Simon Fodden, 'The Landlord Tenant Act Since 1970,' *Osgoode Hall Law Journal*, XII, 2 (Nov. 1974), 441-74; M. McGraw, 'An Examination of the Landlord and Tenant Act in Ottawa-Carleton from 1970-1976,' MSW research paper, Carleton University, 1979

29 Andrew Jones, 'The Beginnings of Canadian Government Housing Policy, 1918-24,' Centre for Social Welfare Studies, Carleton University, 1978

30 Moscovitch, 'Political Economy of Housing Policy'

31 Advisory Committee on Reconstruction, *Housing and Community Planning* (Ottawa 1944), chap. 9

32 C.D. Howe, Minister of Reconstruction, Government of Canada, House of Commons, *Hansard* (1946), 367

33 A. Rose, *Regent Park* (Toronto 1958), chap. 6, especially pp. 85-6

34 Data drawn from Firestone, *Residential Real Estate in Canada*

35 This program has since been discontinued.

36 Dennis and Fish, *Programs in Search of a Policy*, 174

37 P. Streich, 'A Review of the Rent to Income Scale for Public Housing Units,' Central Mortgage and Housing Corporation (Ottawa 1972)

38 Dennis and Fish, *Programs in Search of a Policy*; Social Planning Council of Metro Toronto, *The Rent Race* (Toronto 1974); M. Wheeler, *The Housing Conditions of Social Assistance Recipients* (Ottawa 1971); Davis C. Neave, *Housing Survey of Social Assistance Recipients in Calgary* (Calgary 1973); J. Patterson, and P. Streich, *A Review of Canadian Social Housing Policy* (Ottawa 1977)

39 Donald Gutstein in *Vancouver Ltd.* uses the example of Daon Development Corporation to illustrate how development corporations take advantage of tax advantages to reduce tax payable. He argues, using 1973 data, that Daon's reported 20 per cent profit was more like 165 per cent, when account is taken of favourable tax treatment claimed by Daon (132-3).

40 David Lewis Stein, *Toronto for Sale* (Toronto 1972). Many other books and articles have been published illustrating the relationship between city hall and the developers in areas across Canada. See note 20 for references.

41 A. Maslove, *The Pattern of Taxation in Canada* (Ottawa 1972)

42 For a review of the two BC government reports on rent control – one by K. Jaffery and the other by D. Runge, E. Achtenburg, P. Larmour, and P. Streich – see A. Moscovitch, *Housing and People* VI, 3 and 4 (Fall-Winter 1975-76), 24-6.

12
Inequality and the social services

HOWARD BUCHBINDER

The social service system in Canada functions as a means of supporting inequality. It serves as an agent of the capitalist state apparatus at the same moment that it produces programs and services 'responsive' to need. Although the major focus here is on contemporary analysis and illustrations, it should be clear that the production, and the state response to the existence, of need and inequality have a past as long as the history of class relations.

HISTORICAL ANTECEDENTS OF SOCIAL WELFARE SERVICES

The historical antecedents of present-day social services and policy extend to pre-capitalist times. The dramatic events which shifted the nature and scope of the ruling order's response to need are to be found in the tremendous upheaval which wrenched apart the fabric of European feudal society as the new era of capitalism emerged. Much of the population was dislocated. Peasants, uprooted from the land, wandered through town and country searching for some form of sustenance and subsistence. This was a time of transition from an economy in which production was tied to the land (fiefdom), to one in which production was dependent on a mobile labour force (wage-labour). The social unrest posed a threat to the ruling order; the English Poor Law of Queen Elizabeth (1601) was one response to this situation. This law provided a right to relief payments for those who could not find work. While it was innovative in recognizing that 'right,' it was also defensive in its attempt to protect the ruling order from the anger and desperation of the masses. At the same time, the Poor Law was a device to integrate this new class into the state since the feudal bonds had broken.

This period of transition was also a period of struggle between remnants of the old order, and emerging structures and forces of the new order. For example, the creation of a labour-market supplied by landless, rootless, mobile workers with only their labour to sell meant the final destruction of the traditional society. One response of the old land-based classes was the introduction of the Speenhamland decrees, filling that vacuum between the old society and the newly developed market in labour: 'The justices of Berkshire, meeting at the Pelikan Inn, in Speenhamland, near Newbury, on May 6, 1795, in a time of great distress, decided that subsidies in aid of wages should be granted in accordance with a scale dependent upon the price of bread, so that a minimum income should be assured to the poor *irrespective of their earnings.*'[1]

Whereas the earlier Elizabethan Poor Law had provided relief only for those who could not find work, the Speenhamland decrees represented a subsidy in addition to wages. The rules of parish serfdom, which were relaxed in 1795, would have allowed for the setting up of a national labour-market. The Speenhamland decrees interfered with that process. These decrees drove wages down and forced people onto the 'rates,' as they were called. It was only with the Reform of the Poor Law of 1834 that the transition to a market economy was completed. 'Under Speenhamland society was rent by two opposing influences, the one emanating from paternalism and protecting labour from the dangers of the market system; the other organizing the elements of production, including land, under a market system, and thus divesting the common people of their former status, compelling them to gain a living while offering their labour for sale, while at the same time depriving their labour of its market value.'[2]

Both the Elizabethan Poor Law and the Speenhamland decrees represented a collective provision for certain needs. The former legitimized the right to relief and the latter was ancestor to the guaranteed annual income proposals of today. Nevertheless, in both instances the services, while relating to need, were inspired by the social and historical conditions of the time. They were responses to both the social effects and the productive demands of the new order. In one case they mediated; in the other they obstructed. The Poor Law attempted to mediate its effects. The Speenhamland decrees obstructed the development of a mobile market in labour (in one section of the country) by tying workers to one location after the parish rules – which had previously restricted mobility – had been relaxed.

The Poor Law Amendment Act of 1834 substituted the workhouse for what had been known as the outdoor relief system. It instituted the categories of the deserving and undeserving poor. In the former category were the sick and the old, who continued to receive outdoor relief, and the able-bodied who could and would work for relief. In the latter category, were those whose relief was indoors – in the workhouse. Consequently, the social service system engendered by the new poor law was cruel in the extreme. It was quite simply a deterrent against idleness, and as such it served to consolidate the development of the labour-market and the working class at one and the same time.

Thus the role of social services both as a response to need and as a mediating influence of the state was established early in the development of the capitalist era. With the establishment of the market in labour, and a rapidly developing industrial economy, people were buffeted about by the market and exposed to the inhuman conditions suffered by those 'lucky' enough to find employment.

The impact of Social Darwinism was to reinforce the 'sink or swim' philosophy, and those who sank were condemned for their failure to succeed at swimming. However, with the rise of the socialist movement, born out of the cruelty, exploitation, and inequality suffered by the new working classes, there was rising pressure on the ruling class for mediation to soften the process.

These were the beginnings of the modern day British social service system. Although the policies they reflected were ostensibly geared to need, they always served other objectives as well and often had results which aggravated the needs they had set out to satisfy. The Speenhamland decrees pauperized many by forcing down wages and limiting the mobility demanded by a market society. In fact, they blocked the development of a market in labour. The Poor Law Amendment Act created a system of workhouses indistinguishable from prisons and forced unemployed workers into the inhuman conditions of the nineteenth-century workplace.

The process of industrialization – with its attendant new luxury for the few and degradation of the many – and the state's response to it engendered, anticipated, and influenced – both directly and indirectly – the conditions of the New World. In the colonies of British North America in the early seventeenth century, only in Nova Scotia and New Brunswick was there a system of relief based directly on the English Poor Law.[3] The Constitutional Act of 1791, establishing the system of government for Upper Canada, specifically excluded the Poor Law from application in that province. Such poor relief was established on a permissive, but not compulsory, basis.[4] Similarly, the poor of Quebec existed in a social and legal system largely outside of British influence, and provisions for poor relief were made largely through church-organized, private, and charitable institutions. Legislation permissive of municipal poor relief was only established in the Municipal Code of 1871.[5]

Neither Confederation of the provinces nor the addition of new provinces to Canada had any effect on provisions for social assistance. Poor relief remained in the exclusive jurisdiction of the provinces until the late nineteenth and early twentieth centuries. Urbanization, immigration, and industrialization combined to create in Canadian cities conditions similar to those in Britain and Europe. Only then were there demands for the institution of reform. The urbanization accompanying industrial development subjected workers to horrific living conditions. Charles Dickens' 'Coketown' presented an image of such a place:

It was a town of red brick, or of brick that would have been red if the smoke and ashes had allowed it; but as matters stood it was a town of unnatural red and black like the painted face of a savage. It was a town of machinery and tall chimneys, out of which interminable serpents of smoke trailed themselves forever and ever, and never got uncoiled. It had a black canal in it, and a river that ran purple with ill-smelling dye, and vast piles of building full of windows where there was a rattling and a trembling all day long, and where the piston of the steam engine worked monotonously up and down like the head of an elephant in a state of melancholy madness.[6]

Engels described the reality of those times even more dramatically than Dickens' fiction:

The way in which the vast mass of the poor are treated by modern society is truly scandalous. They are herded into great cities where they breathe a fouler air than in the countryside which they have left. They are housed in the worst ventilated districts of the towns; they are deprived of all means of keeping clean. They are deprived of water because this is only brought to their houses if someone is prepared to defray the cost of laying the pipes. River water is so dirty as to be useless for cleansing purposes. The poor are deprived of all proper means of refuse disposal and so they are forced to pollute the very districts they inhabit.[7]

The proletarianization of the new working class was accomplished within the walls of the factory having a new set of working conditions and relationships. Engels describes some of these conditions:

In most branches of industry the task of the worker is limited to insignificant and purely repetitive tasks which continue minute by minute for every day of the year. How much human feeling can a man of thirty expect to retain if since childhood he has spent twelve hours or more daily making pin heads or filing cogwheels, and in addition has dragged out the normal existence of a number of the English proletariat? The introduction of steam power and machinery has had the same results. The physical labour of the worker has been lightened, he is spared some of his former exertion, but the task itself is trifling and extremely monotonous.[8]

In Canada the conditions of working classes were investigated in the 1880s by the Royal Commission on the Relations Between Labour and Capital. In an appendix to the commission report, J.A. Clark describes the impact of industrialization on children:

Boys and girls, not more than ten years of age, were found in these places in considerable numbers, and some witnesses not older than fourteen had finished their apprenticeship at cigar-making and were working as journeymen. The evil in these instances was accentuated by the evident fact that the tobacco had stunted the growth of the witnesses and poisoned their blood. They were undersized, sallow and listless, wholly without the bright vivacity and rosy hue of health which should animate and adorn children.'[9]

The process of proletarianization and urbanization produced a population which was alienated and atomized. The breakdown of family life, the decreasing influence of institutions, such as the church, and the lack of any clear definition of community provided all sorts of dislocations: physical, social, and emotional. With the decline of these stabilizing institutions there was a need for some sort of intervention to replace them. In capitalist countries it was first the voluntary charity societies and later the state that attempted to fulfil this role. The expansion of these human or social service activities into the state sector served to meet several demands. There was a need for maintaining some sort of 'stability' in the face of the alienation and atomization (referred to above), which were generating an increase in social antagonisms. At the same time, there was a growing pressure for actual services to meet emotional, health, educational, and other needs created by this process. Most importantly, the expansion of state sector activities, following on the heels of the Great Depression, was both a cause and effect of the expansion of monopoly capital.

What then are the results of the advance of industry and of the state policies, which taken together have caused many modern capitalist states to acquire the term welfare state? More specifically, how has the development of a complex system of social services ameliorated the nature and extent of social inequality? In order to assess the social services it will be necessary to consider the following: (1) a theoretical basis for understanding the operation and function of state social policy and services, and (2) the actual functioning of some of these programs.

THEORETICAL PERSPECTIVES

The growth of monopoly capitalism, while producing periods of high employment and economic growth, also creates poverty, unemployment, and economic stagnation. These results have been rationalized to some extent by the operation of the capitalist state. Contrary to the prevailing liberal view that the state sector grows at the expense of private industry, I would argue that the state sector is and has been indispensable to the maintenance and expansion of private production and accumulation. While the costs of such public intervention and support are socialized, the profits realized are made private.[10] Socialized support via the tax system means that welfare state expenditures represent a redistribution of income *within* the working class rather than a redistribution from the ruling class to the working class.[11]

James O'Connor writes of two major functions of the capitalist state: those of accumulation and legitimization. These functions, while basic, are also contradictory:

The state must try to maintain or create the conditions in which profitable capital accumulation is possible. However, the state also must try to maintain or create the conditions for social harmony. A capitalist state that openly uses its coercive forces to help one class accumulate capital at the expense of other classes loses its legitimacy and hence undermines the basis of its loyalty and support. But a state that ignores the necessity of assisting the process of capital accumulation risks drying up the source of its own power, the economy's surplus production capacity and the taxes drawn from this surplus (and other forms of capital) ... The state must involve itself in the accumulation process, but it must either mystify its policies by calling them something that they are not, or it must try to conceal them.[12]

Accumulation describes the basic economic goal of capitalist organization, a goal which is supported and enhanced by the operation of the state. Legitimization refers to the maintenance of an atmosphere of consent and support. Outlays for social programs can be associated with both these functions. Projects and services that lower the reproductive costs of labour also, thereby, increase rates of profit. The costs are socialized. These would include such social insurance schemes as workmen's compensation, Canada/Quebec pension plans, and unemployment insurance. The responsibility and costs of these programs are accepted and supported by the working class, primarily via the apparatus of the state rather than by private industry, even though unemployment, industrial accidents and illness, and vulnerability of workers at retirement are not determined by the working class but result from the production process and state policies. Program costs are socialized through public revenues. The incidence of such work-associated trauma is high. A study of occupational disease and accidents by the Canadian Labour Congress 'concluded that 70 million working days were lost in 1977 due to occupational disease, illness and injuries ... Between 20 and 38 per cent of fatalities from cancer can be traced to the effects of chemicals and other products used on the job ... As many as 16,000 Canadian workers die each year from cancer induced by working conditions.'[13]

The Canadian Labour Congress study is indicative of the role that medical care can play in contributing to the maintenance of a 'productive' work-force. It also reveals the need for medical programs to pick up the tab for the very serious injuries to health suffered on the job. The operation of state-sponsored medicare represents a social cost of production. Such care is provided at little or no cost to private business, but at great cost to the public.

Other social service programs support the legitimization function as well. Welfare programs are social expenses that provide a measure of social control and also socialize the costs of the upkeep of people victimized by the economic and social system in various ways. A study by Piven and Cloward refers to the function of welfare as 'Regulating the Poor.'[14] Discussion of the theory of the capitalist state and these functions is treated extensively elsewhere.[15] Suffice it to point out that the types of social expenditures referred to here fulfil several functions:

1 They respond to the threat of working-class militancy by building social control devices into the administration of social service programs. These are implemented by social service workers at the point of production of these services.
2 They socialize the costs of providing a fit work-force and thereby subsidize the private sector at public expense.
3 They influence demand levels through the mechanism of transfer payments. Such devices keep up consumer purchasing for the benefit of the corporate sector. The way in which workers benefit from this supports the overall process.

O'Connor further argues that in responding to economic recessions, the state spends more and at a faster rate, leading expenditures to outstrip revenues. This resultant fiscal crisis of the state leads to cut-backs in the public sector as a logical imperative of accumulation – a way of continuing to protect the private sector in the face of growing contradictions, and to once again shortstop potential working-class militancy.

The social work literature, while often critical of the profession, falls short of any class analysis. Much of the literature on public welfare and relief policy and services describes social programs as efforts by one secton of the population to collectively aid another more disadvantaged sector. The institution of such programs is seen as a progressive and humanitarian advance from the harsher and crueler fate of the poor in the early days of capitalist development, when they were left to the whims of charity or the confines of the workhouse.

Piven and Cloward's study provides a more jaundiced view that 'much of the literature on relief – whether the arid moralisms and pieties of nineteenth century writers or the ostensibly value neutral analyses of twentieth century professionals and technicians – merely serves to obscure the control role of relief agencies in the regulation of marginal labour and in the maintenance of civil order.'[16]

Their study further discusses the role of relief giving as follows:

[Relief giving] ... goes far toward defining and enforcing the terms on which different classes of men are made to do different kinds of work; relief arrangements, in other words, have a great deal to do with maintaining social and economic inequities. The indignities and cruelties of the dole are no deterrent to indolence among the rich, but for the poor man, the specter of ending up on the 'welfare' or in the 'poorhouse' makes any job at any wage a preferable alternative and so the issue is not the relative merit of work itself; it is rather how some men are made to do the harshest work for the least reward.[17]

There is a social stigma attached to those who receive relief of any kind. The media publish articles about those who receive 'handouts.' Low-paid workers rail against the 'laziness' of public welfare recipients who receive financial assistance and other benefits thereby affording them a position of somewhat more security than these marginally employed workers. The loathing of reliefers is not accidental as 'it has deep roots in two main tenets of market ideology: the economic system is open, and economic success is a matter of individual merit (and sometimes luck); those who fail – the very poor – are therefore morally or personally defective.'[18]

This Social Darwinist attitude focuses the stigma of and blame for poverty on those who are victimized, and thereby deflects criticism from the social order in general, particularly from that class which most enriches itself through this process of victimization. The welfare system mediates this process and at the same time controls the victims. Piven and Cloward describe it in this way:

Capitalist societies control people and work tasks precisely as they control goods and capital – through a market system; yet this is a simplification since the maintenance of a surplus of unemployed workers is not simply a by-product of market fluidity, but a deliberately contrived condition, designed to ease the flow of labour and to lessen the bargaining power of workers in market transactions. The periodic intervention of government to increase the pool of unemployed by slowing the rate of economic growth and the use of government power to force men to work for any bidder lend credence to these views.[19]

The functions of such social service not only perpetuate inequality, but serve as a control over the resultant social unrest. The Piven and Cloward study links up the influence of rising and declining rates of relief payments to periods of social unrest and stability. Certainly the welfare system ties a sector of the underclass to the bureaucracy of the state apparatus. Underclass involvement in the rules and regulations of welfare assistance serves as a control factor and, ironically, the very goals of many welfare rights groups, if realized, would have the effect of enlarging the very apparatus which dominates them.

Although there are critical studies of this system (Piven and Cloward, for example), even these do not deal with the role of social service programs as supports to profitable capital accumulation. The social control aspects of the programs and the control of labour by capital are perceived, but not their relevance to the primary process of accumulation. So, even the seemingly radical literature falls short of any explicit analysis of class and/or the role of the state in the accumulation process.[20]

SOCIAL SERVICES AND CAPITAL ACCUMULATION

Let us now take a closer look at how some of these programs operate to support capitalist accumulation, exacerbate inequality, and increase the burden on the working class. The workings of the unemployment insurance system are a case in point. The principle involved is the assumption of social responsibility for unemployment. The worker in 1978 paid a pay-roll deduction (tax) amounting to 1.5 per cent of earnings up to a limit of $240 per week. The employer contributed 1.4 times the amount of the employee contribution. The cost of these premiums is deducted from taxable income. The program is stacked in favour of higher-income earners in several ways: 'The contribution of the maximum insurable earnings and the ability to deduct contributions from income operate to provide higher benefit levels to higher income contributors at less cost – While everyone making over the maximum insurable earnings contributes the same amounts, the net contribution for higher income earners is lower as income rises because they derive a bigger tax saving from their exemptions.'[21] So, those who earn less pay more: 'It costs $1.17 annually for a person making $6,000 a year to purchase $1.00 of weekly benefits while it costs the person making $50,000 a year only $0.56 for the same one dollar entitlement. Although it may be argued that low income people are a greater risk, and should pay more for the entitlement, in effect such a policy implies that unemployment is the responsibility of the unemployed.'[22]

In recent years the Canadian state has utilized a policy direction fostering increased unemployment. The government, via the Unemployment Insurance Benefits Act, assumes some responsibility for this unemployment. At the same time, as unemployment increases, the state blames the unemployed for this 'dilemma' and pursues policies to cut back on benefits and make access much more difficult. These and other cut-back proposals insert themselves in the relationship between the agencies of the state and unemployed workers. The corporate sector is protected from the assumption of any responsibility, either moral or financial. It pays the standard rate contribution to the unemployment insurance fund and thereby fulfils its 'responsibility' to the working class. The state apparatus jumps into the breach, and as the employment crisis escalates, workers are made to face declining benefits and the unemployment insurance service system is utilized in a more punitive fashion.[23] This makes eligibility determination more difficult for the unemployed and confronts them with constant bureaucratic policing once they are in receipt of benefits.

Thus the unemployment insurance program lowers the reproductive costs of labour to a minimum for the corporate sector by shifting a good part of the cost to the workers, and is used as a means of enforcing social control. Both accumulation and legitimization functions are present.

The 1978 National Council of Welfare report on taxation and the distribution of income further illustrates the inequality fostered by the welfare state.[24] Income inequality remains a constant in the twenty-five years that the government has been gathering such data. This inequality is reinforced through the operation of the tax system and of the social assistance, insurance, and pension plans. 'In 1951, the bottom fifth of Canadians received 4.4% of the national income and the top fifth got 42.8%. In 1976 the counterpart figures were 3.9% for the group at the bottom and 44% for those at the top.'[25] In actual dollars, the gap has been 'multiplied by over two and one-half times,' even though the respective proportions of income share have remained more or less constant:[26] 'That the income gap between rich and poor Canadians has grown so dramatically over the same years in which Canada was constructing an elaborate multi-billion dollar income security system may come as a surprise. However, it isn't hard to explain in light of the fact that so much of this welfare system consists of programmes providing equal benefits to rich and poor alike ... And these "universal" programmes account for more than 80% of all expenditures for the income security programmes administered by the federal Health and Welfare department.'[27]

In addition to these programs, it is the tax system which is also a supposed mechanism for reducing income inequality. Personal income tax represents 40 per cent of all federal and provincial revenues. This is the part of the system which is somewhat progressive in favour of lower-income earners. The rest of the system, accounting for 60 per cent, is a regressive system in which the less one earns, the higher proportion of income one pays. In 1972 the Economic Council of Canada found that, 'while government expenditure programmes may contribute to the redistribution of income ... the tax system as a whole does nothing to contribute to this goal. Indeed, over the lower portion of the income scale, the system tends to contradict the ability-to-pay principle by taxing the poor at a higher rate than those who are better off. The effect of the few taxes ... that are progressive is completely offset by the remainder of taxes in the system.'[28] This sort of inequality is part and parcel of all the social service/welfare programs. If one considers provincial health insurance premiums, premiums for unemployment insurance, and contributions to the Canada/Quebec pension plans as taxes, then the total picture is one of exacerbating inequality among workers through the social welfare and taxation programs, which socialize the costs of production and the reproduction of labour; subsidize the process of private accumulation from the public trough; and present the bill to those exploited and victimized by the process.

SOCIAL SERVICES AND SOCIAL CONTROL

There are other sorts of inequality packaged in social service programs: (1) the treatment of women, (2) the labelling of deviants; and (3) the personal adjustment services.

A study by Janet Barnsley is quite revealing of the relationship of social services to women. The levels of payment which women receive, either from estranged husbands or in welfare payments from the state, are not 'based on the worth of the work done in the home but rather are based on the belief that women are dependent and that it is the responsibility of society to see that they are provided for. Such provision often takes the form of minimal maintenance or welfare payments which makes it impossible for women to save enough to provide for security in old age.'[29]

There is no valuation of work in the home. Maintenance or welfare payments are based on subsistence requirements. Thus women are dependent when they are married and in the face of marriage breakdown and financial need. The system of social services serves to continue that dependence. Rather than providing equal access to the labour-market, the policies and services prevent it. The older the person, the more difficult such access becomes. Although this is true for men, it is even more applicable to women. Canada Manpower training, for example, tends to favour younger workers: 'Between 1967-72 only 9 to 11 percent of those undergoing full-time manpower retraining were 45 years or older, and the majority of these were men. Thus technological advance and fluctuations in demand for labour (e.g. from goods producing to service producing industries) take place at the expense of older workers who are less likely to be included in government and industrial retraining programmes. As a result, older individuals whose skills have become obsolete may be forced to take jobs considered undesirable by younger workers due to low wages and poor working conditions.'[30]

Barnsley's study points out that the Canada Pension Plan discriminates against women. It thereby exacerbates an already inequitable situation for women within a situation of inequality for all workers, and 'thus reinforces their financial dependence on a male or the state.'[31] The discrimination occurs in three areas: (1) 'formulas used to calculate benefits are based on male work patterns making it difficult for female workers to realize maximum benefits after retirement,' (2) 'spouses' pensions are dependent on marriage prior to retirement and the continuance of that marriage,' (3) 'housewives and women employed by their husbands are totally excluded from independent CPP coverage.'[32]

The structure of the plan provides a specific financial aid, meets a need, and at the same time exercises a control function in maintaining and perpetuating the structure of inequality which prevails between working men and women.

Another way social control is exercised through the social services is by using deviance as a concept which allows for categorizing behaviours that violate the norms of the ruling interests. Cloward and Ohlin suggest that 'every deviant act involves the violation of social rules that regulate the behaviour of participants in a social system ... The principal feature of a deviant act ... is that it is not consistent with the behaviour which the victim has been led to expect from others on the basis of the social position he occupies. The deviant does not abide by the accepted rules of the game that the victim is playing. In effect, his act challenges the legitimacy and authority of these rules.'[33]

This can apply to a variety of behaviours and interactions. The response of some students to the authoritarian nature of the school setting can be perceived as deviant if that behaviour does not conform to the rules of the school game. There is the example of a student at a school of social work who had a field practice placement in an inner city school. In many ways the school resembled a correctional institution rather than a school. There was much more emphasis on control than on education. This social work trainee was assigned to work with a group of teen-age girl students who were engaged in what is often labelled as 'acting-out' behaviour. They would skip classes, talk back to teachers, and generally create disturbances. The goal of the group work was to help the girls arrive at some understanding of the feelings and conflicts within them that were causing such 'deviant' behaviour.

Each time the group met and the social worker attempted to get the girls to look at their feelings, they would disrupt the process and leave. The social worker became quite frustrated and consulted someone about this. It was suggested that perhaps there was nothing 'pathological' about these girls, that their behaviour was healthier than that of most of the students since they were fighting back against intolerable conditions. Perceiving their behaviour as deviant lended support to 'treating' them through group counselling so that they would conform. This is pointed out by Cohen, who suggests that 'one way of classifying human actions is in terms of their conformity or nonconformity to rules. There are many ways of classifying human actions, but insofar as we clasify them THIS way and try to develop a theory to explain why actions fall in the one class or the other, we are concerned with a theory of deviant behaviour, which is also a theory of conformity.'[34]

The thrust of social services aimed at the rehabilitation of deviants is in fact a social control geared to conformity. They do this by utilizing therapeutic processes to encourage conformity. When such services do not succeed, the client groups are classified as even more deviant. The issue of drug abuse policy illustrates this: 'Those ... who expect a powerful addictive drug like methadone to cure heroin addiction have failed to see that at the root of ... attitudes toward drug abuse, transcending politics and even race, as the animus against deviant behaviour ... from being regarded as a deviant, the user became a criminal, then a diseased person, and now a criminally diseased deviant.'[35]

The class roots of much behaviour that is, or could be, labelled as deviant are well described by Alan Sillitoe in *The Loneliness of the Long Distance Runner*.[36] Smith, the main character, is sent to the Borstal. As soon as he gets there he is made a long distance cross-country runner. The governor of the Borstal wants Smith to win the 'Borstal Blue Ribbon Prize Cup for Long Distance Cross Country Running (All England).'[37] Smith's view of society is a class view, which is expressed as a division between the 'In-law blokes,' like those who manage the Borstal, and 'outlaws' like himself. The In-Laws are 'waiting to 'phone for the coppers as soon as we make a false move.'[38] When the governor expresses his confidence that Smith will win them the cup, Smith says to himself: '"Like boggery, I will." No. I won't get them that cup, even though the stupid task-twitching bastard has all his hopes on me ... and I'll lose that race, because I'm not a race horse at all.'[39] Smith is true to his word. He runs a good race, is leading, and then stops just at the finish line and waits for the other runners to pass him. So Smith refuses to be a 'racehorse' for the governor of the Borstal. More than that, he refuses to play by the rules of the 'In-law Blokes.' They are his class enemy. Yet such a response is 'deviant' in their terms; an act of non-conformity. For this he is punished. It is clear that the process of legitimization operates at all levels of the system; it is integrated within the 'helping process' through the determination of deviance and pathology.

Thus the expansion of state services reinforces the inequalities it sets out to treat. Women suffer from the impact of programs ostensibly geared to help them. Social services oriented to rehabilitating 'deviant' behaviour (e.g., addiction, delinquency, etc.) exercise social control by reinforcing conformity. They offer adaptation or further exclusion. Involvement with such service systems presents clients with a double bind. They need the services to cope with the impossible realities they face; yet the services encourage further dependence and in fact tie them even more strongly to the very social order which has victimized them.

SOCIAL WORK AND INEQUALITY

The development of social legislation in the years following the Great Depression heralded a corresponding shift of focus by the 'private' (nongovernmental) social service sector toward problems of personal adjustment; economic need was left to the new public programs: 'A new conception of private casework began to emerge, one heavily dominated by psychological conceptions of family problems. It tended to eschew the importance of environmental approaches ... leaving responsibility for them to public agencies despite an awareness that public programmes were inadequate to the task.'[40] The service pie was divided up. The poor were 'regulated' through the public welfare system, social insurance programs, etc. The privately funded expanded services were geared to personal and family adjustment problems and began to serve more of a middle-class clientele.

This shift from concrete services to personal adjustment was accompanied by an 'increasing tendency of private agencies to define client-problem priorities in heavy psychological terms.'[41] The influence of psychoanalytic theory and the medical model on the profession of social work produced a psychologically oriented treatment methodology called casework. Casework, in contradictory fashion, rationalized its legitimacy as a separate form of personality treatment by its emphasis on the socially oriented aspects of personality. Its adherents did not choose to practice a form of psychotherapy based on the direct utilization of transference, as in orthodox psychoanalytic models. The new casework technology which developed became 'class bound': 'The private agency field, having developed a new conception of casework, seeks out a clientele who can make use of it. Hence it moves towards those whose socialization is compatible with the new technology – the middle class.'[42]

This treatment-oriented private agency sector served two purposes. It absorbed and reinforced the development of social work professionalization. The social workers who received graduate degrees in social work tended to be absorbed more readily into this part of the service sector where salaries were higher and where the nature of casework treatment allowed for the practice of 'therapy.' This seemed to be a more desirable goal than the low-paid, financially oriented public welfare service sector. The focus on personal adjustment defined social problems as 'resulting, not from institutional inadequacies but from the presumed moral, social or psychological defects of the people implicated in those problems. To the extent that these definitions are successfully imposed, criticism is deflected from the social order and support is mobilized for the existing system of social arrangements.'[43]

The impact of these developments served to deflect social service workers away from basic social issues and supported a process whereby economic and social problems were defined in emotional terms. Social work took on the colouration of psychology and psychiatry, and with some few deviations, operated within a psychoanalytic framework. The separation of the public and the private sectors disengaged most of the social work profession from the poor. Christopher Lasch suggests that 'social questions inevitably present themselves as personal ones.'[44] The development of casework did not deal with this. It focused on personal questions as reflections of intrapsychic conflict. Just as the poor assumed responsibility for their poverty, the clients of private agencies assumed responsibility for the alienating effects of capitalism. Family breakdown, marriage breakdown, child guidance, and the like were treated as individual and group forms of psychopathology, and although some lip-service was given to social conditions, the treatment process which evolved revealed the emptiness of any social concerns. This is not to suggest that emotional problems or problems of social adjustment do not justify a response. It is to suggest that 'through the intermediary of the family social patterns reproduce themselves in personality. Social arrangements live on in the individual, buried in the mind, below the level of consciousness ... The ethic of self-preservation and psychic survival is rooted ... not merely in objective conditions of economic warfare, rising rates of crime and social chaos, but in the subjective experience of emptiness and isolation.'[45] In ignoring this, the family social services employed their efforts in mediating the internalized effects of inequality, exploitation, and alienation.

The preceding provides some illustrations of how the social services (or human services, as they are sometimes called) embody elements of both service and control. More needs to be written about the linkage between a capitalist social order and the resultant patterns of domination which are integrated into personality. How to formulate a treatment process of personal and interpersonal response which is not adaptive to the prevailing system of class oppression should be a major focus of concern and study. Gad Horowitz, with reference to Herbert Marcuse, begins his study of repression with the following comments:

Radical thought has for decades been faced with the challenge of taking fully into account the implications of Sigmund Freud's discovery that the 'laws of slavery' are not only socioeconomic but also bio-psychological, that domination consists not only in conscious and external but also in unconscious and internal 'processes of restraint, constraint and suppression' (Marcuse – *Eros and Civilization*). These processes unfold for the first time, and have their greatest effects, during the first five or six years of life. Through unconscious internal repression the dominated and exploited themselves reproduce and sustain their own oppression.[46]

The service system which developed parallel to the welfare state did not embark on such a road. The system of social treatment for individuals, groups, and even communities reinforced the role of the public sector programs and services, in rationalizing the irrationality of monopoly capitalism. The social service system, in mediating the effects of inequality, expanded its purview from the economic to the psycho-social level. It thereby played a key role in containing the effects of the social relations of production. There have been occasions, such as those during the 1960s, when groups directly involved as clients in these programs, both 'public' and 'private,' resisted their style, if not their substance. But, except for minor modifications, the system carries on as usual and in the present climate of cut-backs and unemployment becomes more punitive and coercive.

There are two major contradictions faced by social service workers at the point of production and consumption of social services. The first contradiction is between the service function and the social control function, both of which are present in the form, content, and process of social service delivery. The second major contradiction resides in the job title of social service worker. The worker is both the oppressed (rooted in capitalist social relations of production) and the oppressor (rooted in the social relations of production and consumption present in the social services).[47]

The social relations of production and consumption are different in the social services than in the goods-producing industries.[48] The specific nature of these relations bears on the contradictions cited above. In the social services, production and consumption are not separated in time and space; they occur simultaneously. The results of production are not a tangible product but an intangible service delivered within an 'interaction between two or more people.'[49] Thus the service is not produced unless it is consumed. Automobiles are produced without the act of consumption taking place at the point of production or at the moment of production. However, if the patient does not arrive for the appointment, the physician does not produce the service. If the prospective client does not make application for assistance, no service is produced. 'Therefore nothing is produced unless it is consumed ... Only for human service workers do there also exist social relations with the human object of their labors ... direct and immediate social relations with the consumer.'[50] This adds a dimension for service workers not present for workers in material production – the relations with the consumer of the service produced. In goods production, consumption is not as closely and directly related to production. Social service workers, 'like workers in other industries, enter into certain social relations of production with their peers ... and into quite different social relations of production with those above them in the hierarchy such as administrators [and supervisors for social service workers] ... owners or their representatives for manufacturing or extractive workers. But only for human service workers do there also exist social relations with the human object of their labours.'[51]

The function of social control which is exercised in the production and consumption of social services is expressed in the relationship between worker and client. The flow of available resources, whether financial or emotional, is channelled through an authority relationship – the patient or client abiding by the rules of the game. These relations are oppressive and controlling for the consumer, regardless of the intentions or motivations of the worker. They involve determination of eligibility, 'management' of the client through various rules, regulations, and just plain administrative fiat. Oppression and control are also accomplished through the treatment processes which deflect criticism from the social order by interpreting social pathology (effects of work, alienation, atomization, etc.) as personal pathology, with the responsibility placed on the victim. It is between the subjective attitudes and dedication of the social service worker and the social relations of production and consumption that the second contradiction stands.

What the client gets is incidental and is itself not provided essentially in his/her interest. The client's interest does not lie with any continuation of the arrangements which produced his/her plight. The inequality resulting from the production of poverty, along with the accumulation of capital and profits, creates needs and demands which are dealt with by means of the social welfare network. The social service worker stands at the interface, at the wicket in the welfare office, and faces the victim. The nature of the service is oppressive, in that it rationalizes the process of victimization. The rules and regulations provide a framework for defining the service and controlling the client. This is an onerous task for the worker who comes to the job believing in such concepts as client self-determination. In fact, the worker is a 'dirty worker.'[52]

STRATEGY FOR CHANGE IN THE SOCIAL SERVICES

Recent trends among social service workers provide some insight into where we go from here. There is a growing problem of funding as the fiscal crisis of the state deepens. Privately supported agencies need to turn more and more to public funding sources. Organizing efforts among social service workers in Canada are fragmented and of limited success. Even when such organizing efforts 'succeed,' they do not deal with the service/control contradictions. There are no easy answers. The functions which the social services carry out in a corporate capitalist society are clear, as are the contradictions which emerge. It is necessary to move the task of organizing such workers forward, a difficult task indeed. Gelvin Stevenson poses the following view:

In the immediate capitalist future, deepening economic crises will lead to increased structural unemployment, more diseases of civilization (diabetes, cancer, stress, etc.), and heightened social antagonisms. These in turn will cause a continued increase in the numbers of students, unemployed, patients, counsellors, and other consumers of services. And this phenomenon will tend to increase the numbers and the significance of human service workers ... This is a particularly significant trend because ... they have a unique and expanding role to play in either radicalizing or oppressing consumers.[53]

This view suggests that the significance of social service workers will increase as their numbers increase. Their significance will be felt either as a radicalizing or as an oppressing force. The determination of which role they might play will be dependent on the sort of consciousness held by these workers. There is no reason to assume that the increasing size of the service sector suggested by Stevenson will necessarily affect the role of social service workers in one direction or another. One variable which might be crucial in this determination is the economics of the service sector. How difficult will it be to support this sector? If the fiscal crisis of the state intensifies, there will be increased pressures on workers, clients, and administration alike. Will this create a more progressive or a more reactionary cadre of service workers?; will it produce a more militant or a more passive client group?; will more money or less money be diverted to this sector in the interests of 'stability,' in spite of the fiscal squeeze? These questions are not easily answered; yet it is important that they are asked. By posing such questions, we chart the terrain for continuing the work of organizing in this sector – work which is still only in its beginning stage. By asking these questions we can formulate the content of organizing, in the hope that social service workers will ally themselves with consumers on the progressive side of the contradictions, and in a joint struggle along class lines. Whether social service workers accept the challenge remains to be seen.

NOTES

1 Karl Polanyi, *The Great Transformation* (Boston 1944), 78 (emphasis in original). Much of this discussion is based on Polanyi's treatment of this period.
2 Ibid., 82

3 Nova Scotia, General Assembly. An Act for the regulating and maintaining of a House of Correction or Work-House within the Town of Halifax, and for Binding out Poor Children, 42 Geo. 2 chap. 1 Halifax 1759. An Act to enable the Inhabitants of the several Townships within this Province to Maintain their Poor, 3 Geo. 3 chap. 7 Halifax 1763.
4 R.B. Splane, *Social Welfare in Ontario, 1771-1893* (Toronto 1965), 21-116
5 E. Minville, *Labour Legislation and Social Services in the Province of Quebec*, a study prepared for the Royal Commission on Dominion-Provincial Relations (Ottawa 1939)
6 Charles Dickens, *Hard Times* (New York 1961), 30
7 Frederick Engels, *The Condition of the Working Class in England* (London 1952), 110
8 Ibid., 333-4
9 Cited in Greg Kealey, ed., *Canada Investigates Industrialism* (Toronto 1973), 22
10 For a much more comprehensive treatment of the brief theoretical statement in this article, see James O'Connor, *The Fiscal Crisis of the State* (New York 1973); and Leo Panitch, ed., *The Canadian State: Political Economy and Political Power* (Toronto 1977), especially the following articles: Leo Panitch, 'The Role and Nature of the Canadian State,' 3; Alvin Finkel, 'Origins of the Welfare State in Canada,' 344.
11 Jack Lewis, 'British Capitalism, the Welfare State and the First Radicalisation of State Employees,' in John Cowley et al., eds., *Community or Class Struggles?* (Boston 1977)
12 O'Connor, *Fiscal Crisis*, 6
13 Ed. Finn, 'Ontario's Bill 70 a Major Step in Workplace Safety: Unionist,' *Toronto Star*, 19 Feb. 1979
14 Frances Piven and Richard Cloward, *Regulating the Poor* (New York 1971)
15 It is not necessary to elaborate a theory of the capitalist state and its functions in this article. In addition to references in note 10, see Ralph Miliband, *The State in Capitalist Society* (London 1969).
16 Piven and Cloward, *Regulating the Poor*, xvi
17 Ibid., xvii
18 Ibid., 148
19 Ibid., 4
20 This refers to the social work literature. There is a literature which develops a class critique of the welfare state, some of which is referred to in these notes. My analysis departs somewhat from James O'Connor's, which situates welfare as a legitimization function and not as a support for the accumulation process. Transfer payments influence aggregate demand, which affects the market.

21 Social Planning Council of Metropolitan Toronto, 'The Problem is Jobs ... Not People,' *Policy Statement* (Oct. 1978), 27

22 Ibid., 28

23 Cut-backs in unemployment insurance benefits (Jan. 1979) and revisions in eligibility requirements illustrate this. Lower benefit floors are part of the state's struggle to lower wage floors and wage demands; cf. ibid.

24 National Council of Welfare, *Bearing the Burden, Sharing the Benefits* (Ottawa 1978)

25 Ibid., 1

26 Ibid.

27 Ibid., 2

28 Allan V. Maslove, *The Pattern of Taxation in Canada* (Ottawa 1973), 64, quoted in ibid., 4

29 Janet M. Barnsley, 'An Analysis of Income Maintenance Policy in Relation to Elderly Women,' unpublished manuscript, York University, 1976, p. 8. Barnsley's findings are supported by two more recent studies: Kevin Collins, *Women and Pensions*, Canadian Council on Social Development (Ottawa 1978); Louise Dulude, *Women and Aging: A Report on the Rest of Our Lives*, Canadian Advisory Council on the Status of Women (Ottawa 1978).

30 Barnsley, ibid., 29

31 Ibid., 71

32 Ibid.

33 Richard A. Cloward and Lloyd E. Ohlin, *Delinquency and Opportunity* (New York 1960), 2

34 Albert K. Cohen, *Deviance and Control* (Englewood Cliffs, NJ 1966), 1 (emphasis in original)

35 David L. Lewis, 'Color it Black: The Failure of Drug Abuse Policy,' *Social Policy*, VI, 5 (March-April 1976), 32

36 Alan Sillitoe, *The Loneliness of the Long Distance Runner* (London 1959)

37 Ibid., 12

38 Ibid., 10

39 Ibid., 13

40 Richard A. Cloward and Irwin Epstein, 'Private Social Welfare's Disengagement from the Poor: The Case of Family Adjustment Agencies,' in Mayer Zald, ed., *Social Welfare Institutions* (New York 1965) 624. Privately funded services refer to those supported by 'voluntary' giving, channelled through agencies such as the United Community Funds. Ironically, these 'community' contributions are realized in great part from a working-class constituency through pay-roll deduction plans. This fund-raising effort is given a 'push' by management and the trade union bureaucracy – the workers paying once again.

41 Ibid., 627

42 Ibid., 636

43 Ibid., 637

44 Christopher Lasch, 'The Narcissistic Society,' *The New York Review of Books*, 30 Sept. 1976

45 Ibid., 12

46 Gad Horowitz, *Repression – Basic and Surplus Repression in Psychoanalytic Theory: Freud, Reich and Marcuse* (Toronto 1977), 1

47 This discussion of the social relations of production and consumption is based on Gelvin Stevenson, 'Social Relations of Production and Consumption in the Human Service Occupations,' *Monthly Review*, XXVIII, 3 (July-Aug. 1976), 78-87.

48 Note that I am not dealing with the service industries but am contrasting the goods-producing sector with the human services sector. See Stevenson, ibid., 78.

49 Ibid., 82

50 Ibid.

51 Ibid.

52 E.C. Hughes first used this term in relation to Nazi Germany. Lee Rainwater wrote an article about school teachers and social service workers, who do the 'dirty work' for the rest of society; see L. Rainwater, 'The Revolt of the Dirty Workers,' *Trans-action*, V, 1 (Nov. 1967). Also quoted by Rick Deaton, 'The Fiscal Crisis and the Public Employee,' *Our Generation*, VIII, 4 (Oct. 1972), 11-51

53 Stevenson, 'Social Relations,' 81

EPILOGUE

13
A future for equality in Canada?

STANLEY B. RYERSON

When I was asked to write on 'the future of equality in Canada,' my immediate reaction was modestly to disclaim the gift of tongues and prophecy. I don't know, and I suspect most of us don't, what the future of equality *is* in Canada. In some areas we are so humbly unaware of inequalities that exist and run deep, and in even more areas find ourselves without answers of a kind that compel consensus, that if one did want to prophesy (which one doesn't), it could only be more than a trifle precarious.

One could take the title and ask, *what* Canada? – since there is a rather large debate over the 'two nations' and the very nature of the country. One could ask, *what* equality? – and that is what I shall try to say a word about. Or one could ask, *what* future? – because as never before in the history of the world, a terrifying question mark hangs over the future of a species which seems singularly bent on extinguishing itself, a prospect in relation to which we have some responsibilities.

I think first of all one could usefully emphasize that the problem of equality doesn't simply exist 'in general.' Although the concept of equality is respectably ancient, going back to and beyond the *Politics* of Aristotle and the *Ethics*, the actual ways in which people have been bothered about the question of equality and inequality, the urgent issues around which people have grouped themselves, and organized and fought and died, and sometimes won, make up in large part the tissue of history. The question of equality did not stand two hundred years ago in just the way it does today. Yet the question of equality as the Jacksonian democrats saw it in the 1830s – Thomas Hart Benton put the matter this way – was 'whether People, or Property, shall govern. Democracy implies a government by the people. Aristocracy implies a government of the rich.'[1]

In the context of the transition from a society of small property and agrarian community to a society of immense concentrated property – that of the corporate business of the twentieth century (the industrial society that is very far from being 'post-industrial') – the issue was indeed that of 'democracy' and 'equality' ('liberté,' 'égalité,' 'fraternité').

Such was the context of 1776 and 1789, of Thomas Paine's writing of the Declaration of the Rights of Man and the Citizen.

For Alexis de Tocqueville, what was fundamental in the revolutions against privilege and arbitrary rule was the achievement of equality. Clearly, the author of *Democracy in America* vastly underestimated both the existing class cleavage and the extent of the oncoming industrialization. Yet he sensed a looming challenge, asking, 'Can it be believed that the democracy which has overthrown the feudal system and vanquished kings, will retreat before tradesmen and capitalism?'[2] And in a chapter headed 'How aristocracy may be engendered by manufactures,' he remarked that, 'if ever a permanent inequality of conditions and aristocracy again penetrate into the world – this is the gate by which they will enter.'[3]

At the very time when de Tocqueville was pondering these matters, in the Canadas the leaders of popular democratic movements, William Lyon Mackenzie and Louis-Joseph Papineau, were voicing their distrust of monopolies and the mercantile empire. The independent democracies they envisioned – of mechanics and yeomen, small farmers, and professionals – had their place in the general context of the bourgeois democratic movements of their time. But the egalitarian democracy for which those rebels fought was not to be.

For already under way was the implanting of the new relationship between capital and labour, between the owners of industry and 'their' wage-workers. In place of the promised agrarian democracy of small producers there loomed an urban-based industrial autocracy. 'Liberté' was freedom for private entrepreneurs to pursue profit without let or hindrance, and for dispossessed peasants and artisans ('liberated' from the encumbrance of property) to see their power to work, their muscle and nerve as 'hands' on the free market for wage-labour. 'Egalité' underwent a sea change, to emerge as the common denominator underlying 'equal' exchanges in terms of exchange value, social labour crystallized in commodities: a social relation wherein informally equal buyer and seller enter freely into a contract that turns out to be one between master and servant.

Thus the evolution of market economy, built on the 'law of value' sensed by Smith and Ricardo (and William Petty before them) and worked out in theoretical explication by Engels and Marx, led to a formal 'equality' and a factual subjection. 'Hands for hire' on the free labour-market, free competition among formally equal competitors – this was to lead to the massive dispossession of yesterday's small independent producers scattered across the countryside, and the concurrent buildup of a structure of industrial power – a structure of great property that is ever more concentrated – that of the great corporations and ultimately the twentieth-century transnational, multinational corporate oligarchs.

So it turns out that 'equality before the law' – equality in relation to a political structure such as parliamentary electoral democracy – is metamorphosed by the fundamental relationships of capitalist society into a non-equality, non-democracy, at the heart of which is the exploitation of wage-labour by capital. On the scale of a society, the rule of capital over labour is a system of minority rule. In this context one is reminded of the dictum expressed by Sir John A. Macdonald when the purpose of an upper chamber or senate was under consideration in the pre-Confederation discussions. It was to fulfil the function of protection of minorities (regional and other). As Sir Joseph Pope recalls it in his memoirs, the Father of Confederation was heard to remark in the privacy of the 1864 Quebec Conference: 'We must protect the interests of minorities, and the rich are always fewer in number than the poor!'[4] This is, after all, but the basic premise of all bourgeois democracy.

The historic tradition of struggle for 'responsible government' in the Canadas had to do with colonial/imperial relationships, self-government, and 'home rule' for Canadians. Its implications for internal, domestic structures pointed toward some boarder base of democratization, transcending Family Compact and Clique du Chateau oligarchy. What actually emerged was a 'liberal-conservative,' quasi-federal, partly self-governing dominion of the Empire. As the political framework for a unified domestic market and for an expanding rule of private capital over social labour, the new state set-up has turned out to be something less than the responsible government to which our forbears aspired. The formal structure of a freedom that is exercised intermittently and with variable impotence serves as a screen behind which operate the day-to-day transactions of business – those of property and power of a kind having no answerability, and held accountable to no ther higher body than the boards of directors of the private corporations. In other words, we are confronted with a *social structure* as the real context within which questions of equality arise for us. Underlying its multitude of complex manifestations are patterns of relationships between people and people's relations with things, as expressions of relations among *people at work* and the holders of property and, hence, of power. All of which, increasingly, calls forth question marks.

What, then, is this preoccupation of ours with equality? Is it the thought that in some way or other everyone is or ought to be the same? That, of course, is the prejudice with which the anti-equalitarians put the issue, saying 'what you want is total uniformity – everyone in uniforms and in barracks and eating out of a common trough.' Well, equality as sameness – one = one, or four = four – is one of the components of identity. But it is surely not in that sense that people have battled under the banners of 'liberté,' 'egalité' – the sense that 'all men are equal by virtue of the fact that they are men' – a sense that includes solidarity, 'fraternité.' Were there no differences among individual persons, universal sameness would never engender the issue of equality. Nor are we bothered by diversity, non-sameness, as it is manifested in a difference of talent or creativity; nor in the differences between old and young, in a likely remoteness or a certain propinquity of death (however much those who have less time left to them may envy those with more). What we rightly quarrel with are the impediments to fulfilment of the human potential such as are derived from a certain societal *arrangement* of things and of persons: serfdom and other servitudes. *Equality* becomes a watchword of struggle where *inequality* is entrenched, yet is subject to abolition. It arises as an issue in sytemic terms, with those 'arrangements' that provide for a built-in subordination of serf to overlord, servant to master, wage worker to capitalist, woman to man.

Consider this last relationship, which the early socialist, Charles Fournier, cited as being the yardstick of any society's advance. 'All men are born equal' – and all women? 'The rights of man and the citizen' – males only? Is this peculiarity (of Western languages at least) merely a lexical, semantic oddity: 'man' meaning at one and the same time (or at different times) 'mankind' and 'male'? Or have we here just one more expression of the blighting distortions born of male dominance in class societies? God the Father, or Zeus, replicates in the sky the pattern of the patriarch holding sway from ancient times: the Mother-god being sent into exile as the pagan deity Astarte, or demoted to second place as Queen of the Christian heaven. In slave-owning antiquity, in the feudal Middle Ages, in the modern and contemporary capitalist epoch, male dominance has been interwoven with each of the social class structures.

In a paper that I found extraordinarily moving and lucid, Helen Levine has written 'On Women and on One Woman as Provider and Consumer of

Health and Social Services.' Her point is that what is involved in the situation of women is a dimension of exploitation: the fact of the assignment of a service or subordinate capacity to women, a society- and economy-designated service role. 'We're slotted into a particularly deadly responsibility in the current nuclear family. There women not only have been trained to exchange domestic and sexual services for economic support in various subtle and not so subtle ways ... It is the double oppression of women, within the family and within the work force, that creates our second-class minority position.'[5] She tells of her experience not only as a social worker, but on the other side of the relationship, as a patient-consumer in hospital. After noting that 'hospitals are really not designed for sick people,'[6] she mentions a doctor practising in that hospital who had published a work in which he asserts: 'equality in marriage is destructive, as it is in any "management."'[7] The doctor is 'le grand patron,' the repository of power and authority in that situation. The social institutions of alms-giving and social service, what Lenin called the work of 'social welfare police,' are one dimension of the relation between the state and the operation of 'welfare,' in a society founded on exploitation. Attitudes of superiority are ingrained in our society: you are a man so you are superior, and you are a woman so you are inferior, in some way or another; alternatively, you feel that you are, or are *made* to feel that you are – and it's hard to say which is worse, whom it disfigures more, the dominated or the dominator.

What of our attitude to 'natives,' to those who were here first, by perhaps two hundred centuries before we came, and whom we have ousted and reduced to appalling penury and near extinction? It is no accident that part of the real awakening of a social conscience in Canada in the last ten years or so has expressed itself not only in the emergence and action of the women's movement but in the fact that the Amerindian and Inuit peoples are stirred to struggle in a new way. We are witnessing the replacement of a seemingly passive resignation (seen from outside as apathy, which can perhaps be one way to offer resistance), by initiative, militancy, demonstrations, and action. The movement has developed in ways that registered and rang bells across the country, starting in the 'Brantford Uprising' in the late 1950s (of which Edmund Wilson has written, in *Apologies to the Iroquois*[8]) and going on to the fight over land claims and constitutional status in the issues of James Bay and the Mackenzie. The impact has been far out of proportion to the numbers of the native peoples in the country. The resonance and reverberation have resulted from the fact that a raw nerve of inequality was being touched at a time of deepening of doubt, of questioning, and uncertainty about the legitimacy of our power structure of private business.

A rather old but beautiful work on our theme is R.H. Tawney's *Equality*, written in the 1920s. Tawney wrote: 'To criticize inequality and to desire equality is not to cherish the romantic illusion that men are equal in character and in intelligence. It is to hold that, while their natural endowments differ profoundly, it is the mark of a civilized society to aim at eliminating such inequalities as have their source, not in individual differences but in its own organization; and that individual differences, which are a source of social energy, are more likely to ripen and find expression if social inequalities are, as far as practicable, diminished.'[9] This involves, then, 'economic equality, not necessarily in the sense of an identical level of pecuniary incomes, but of equality of environment, of access to education and the means of civilization, of security and independence.'[10] It is here that the dimension of health and the affirmation of physical being and spiritual existence come up against the confining bulwark of great property for the few and the relations of inferiority and dependence that such great property entails for the rest. It is 'the rule for the rich to be rewarded, not only with riches, but with a preferential share of health and life ... the penalty for the poor to be not only poverty, but ignorance, sickness and premature death.'

The Jeffersonian ideal of a society of small, individual, independent, agrarian producers has faded with the onset of an order based on large-scale, collective, machine-powered industry. Fundamental to it is the structure of property and power based on the social relationship of wage-labour and capital. Jean-Jacques Rousseau had written,[12] that 'no citizen shall ever be wealthy enough to buy another and none poor enough to be forced to sell himself,' but *that* precisely is the relationship expressed in the labour-market, as it was in the relation of the slave market in antiquity. It is the essential feature of the labour-market in modern business society that some are rich enough to buy not only 'another,' but thousands of them.

Take the company formed through a merger between Consolidated Edison and Montecassini in Italy. Montedison, with its 150,000 employees, is one of the great chemical conglomerates of the world. It has been busy dumping titanium bioxide into the Mediterranean at the rate of hundreds of tons per day per kilometer of coastal waters, thereby polluting the sea with the toxic red mud that swept up on the shores of Corsica.[13] This outrage has led to a mass movement of protest in Corsica, of a kind that is overdue in response to Union Carbide Ltd. at Valleyfield (on the St. Lawrence west of Montreal). It is overdue in response to all those corporations whose poisoning of the air and waters is in the realm of mercury and the Minimata disease. All of which bespeaks the singular inequality existing between the owners of the multinationals and their victims. Awareness of it helps to explain the questioning of the legitimacy and desirability of a continuance of the relationship of exploitation of labour by capital; at the same time it rends the decorous drapery that enfolds the real relationship of mastery and subordination that is the free-world, formal democracy of corporate business society.

'Liberty is thwarted,' Tawney writes, 'by the pressure of an economic system which vests in a minority of property owners, the control of the plant and equipment without access to which the majority cannot live, and thus enables the former to impose its will on the latter, without physical compulsion, by economic duress.'[14] As Lord Beveridge noted in his *Full Employment in a Free Society*, 'the private ownership of the means of production, to be operated by others, is not an essential citizen liberty in Britain, because it is not and never has been enjoyed by more than a very small proportion of the British people ... The list of essential liberties ... does not include liberty of a private citizen to own means of production and to employ other citizens in operating at a wage'.[15] It isn't a 'citizen liberty,' but it is the *structure of our society*. As John Maynard Keynes, writing in 1919, perceived the essential character of his social world, 'the principle of accumulation based on inequality was a vital part of the pre-war order of Society and of progress as we then understood it.' Moreover, 'this remarkable system depended for its growth on a double bluff or deception.' Deprivation, 'the laboring classes accepted from ignorance or powerlessness,' while for 'the capitalist classes ... the duty of "saving" became nine-tenths of virtue': a mind-set fostered by self-deception. 'The war has disclosed the possibility of consumption to all and the vanity of abstinence to many. Thus the bluff is discovered.'[16] Keynes was writing about the 'good old days' before the First World War. But at issue was not so much psychological conditions as it was the socio-economic conditions of capitalist ownership and production.

The principle of an 'accumulation based on inequality' is no stranger to us; it is at the heart of the self-expansion of capital. Examples are to be found in any issue of the *Canada Year Book* or *L'Annuaire du Québec*, in the data on manufacturing industries, under the heading 'Value Added.'[17] Thus for one year in Quebec, the workers employed in 'production and related activities' produced a 'value added' (new value, over and above that of raw material, wear and tear of machinery) amounting to $3.6 billion. This covered the cost of wages – $1.2 billion – and left in the hands of the deserving employers a tidy surplus of $2.4 billion. Such is the extraction of the unearned surplus of capital, the involuntary philanthropy of the proletariat. Wage earner and employer ('equals' in the eyes of the law) stand in fact in a relation of utter inequality: the propertyless versus great property.

There is, finally, one other dimension of inequality which rends the British North American dominion at the moment. We are told that it is the 'crisis of Canada,' but before we panic, as we are invited to do, we might perhaps pause to consider very carefully whether the issue *is* Canada or perhaps rather one particular structure of the big business state – one arrangement of power among others. We have known in our history five different constitutions – 1763, 1774, 1791, 1840, and 1867; we should hardly be scared stiff now at the very idea of facing up to the possibility and opportunity of inventing something else. What is involved is the relationship between what are called 'the two founding peoples' – 'an equal partnership' (as projected by Lester Pearson, in launching the Royal Commission on Bilingualism and Biculturalism) between French-speaking and English-speaking Canadians.[18] The structure of the state established in 1867 made such an equality of partnership highly questionable, as there was no provision whatever in it for the recognition of the dualism of a two-nation political community. The structure of the state is such that it contains no mechanism whereby the relationship between French and English can be democratically discussed. You can't do it at a federal-provincial conference where you have one versus ten or eleven. You can't do it in Parliament on any footing of equality, where you already have a prefabricated Anglo-majority. A new framework has got to be invented, and to invent it is probably seditious. But it is going to have to be done if ever we are to edge in the direction of something more than a papering over of our past hypocrisies. Because what is involved is going beyond one particular pattern of state structure embodying a relationship between peoples, founded on an historical inequality – on an historical injustice. Actually we are perhaps on the threshold of a real chance to rectify an ancient injury, to put equality in the place of an ancient, demoralizing, debilitating inequality. In that case the panic mongering is simply part of one more attempt at obstruction by the beneficiaries of a highly profitable status quo who fear nothing quite so much as change itself.

Lester Pearson, in an unguarded moment, once said that Quebec is in a sense 'the homeland of a people.'[19] It was part of his view of a certain Canadian dualism, a view that Professor Donald Creighton and others have blasted as the unspeakable heresy that was out to wreck Canada. Because unless one insisted on the one-nation Canada which thinks of itself, in fact, as English and rejects the idea of a partnership and a duality, then there is likely to be the kind of trouble that attends on democratization. It is no accident that the work of the B. & B. commissioners came to a premature end before they could draw conclusions about the implications of their research at the level of political equality. They themselves, in the 'General Introduction,' referred to cultural inequality and social and economic inequality. (In the blood-curdling Book 3 on the 'World of Work,' they extended and deepened this area. If ever one wanted a vivid picture of the social inequality, institutionalized and entrenched, that goes back to the British conquest and the British Industrial Revolution, this is where to find it.) In sections 81-83 of their 'Introduction,' the B. & B. commissioners propose to consider one other dimension of equality as between the two communities – the *political* dimension. This latter covers the possibility for each of the two societies (each 'nation-community') to choose its own political institutions or at least to have the full opportunity to participate on an equal footing in making the decisions that define the state framework shared by the two communities. 'The collective aspect of equality is here still more evident. It is not cultural growth and development at the individual level that is at stake, but the degree of self-determination which one *society* can exercise in relation to another.' That is the right of national self-determination which has been and remains such a heresy on Parliament Hill. (It is at this point that Monsieur Trudeau must have begun to have the shakes.) It is the selfsame principle which had been at issue when in 1832, in an article on the front page of the Patriote paper, *La Minerve*, an anonymous correspondent predicted that there was going to be a revolution in Lower Canada: 'Nulle nation ne veut obéir à une autre par la raison toute simple qu'aucune nation ne saurait commander à une autre.' (No nation can be expected to obey another nation for the quite simple reason that no nation can command another.)[20] *That* is the principle of national equality and of national self-determination. This was written fifteen years before a German exile in London got up at a public meeting of solidarity with the Polish Independence Movement, a meeting commemorating the Polish insurrection for the Polish right to nationhood, and made the point that 'a nation that oppresses other nations cannot itself be free.'[21] The speaker was Frederick Engels; it was the year before the *Communist Manifesto* was written. But in 1832 it was in *La Minerve* in Lower Canada. The theme runs through the fabric of history since the eighteenth century and the beginning of the epoch of the bourgeois revolutions, and is linked with the posing of the issue of social property and ultimately of social revolution.

It is worthy of note that Jean-Jacques Rousseau inscribed on the title page of the *Contrat Social* the motto: 'Foederis aequas dicamus leges,' a quotation from Virgil's *Aeneid*: 'Let us establish fair conditions for a treaty,' or if you will, 'an equal union.' (The words are drawn from a speech of the King of Latium in relation to the Trojans at the end of the war): 'Let this whole tract with the high mountainous district of the pines pass to the Trojans in friendship. Let us prescribe fair conditions for a treaty and invite them into our realm as allies. If however they prefer to approach some other nation, there is no reason why they should not, if they so wish, withdraw from our own soil.'[22] It is curious that Virgil speaks here of the relationship of friendship between peoples and the problem of 'aequas leges foederis,' fair laws for an equal union, or a fair covenant or pact between two peoples. Rousseau, of course, goes on to speak of the problem of *inequality in terms of property as the impediment* (cf. his 'Origine de l'inégalité parmi les Hommes').

Engels has a chapter on equality in his *Anti-Dühring* that bears on the historical context:

> From the moment when, like a butterfly from the chrysalis, the bourgeoisie arose out of the burghers of the feudal period, when this 'estate' of the Middle Ages developed into a class of modern society, it was always and inevitably accompanied by its shadow, the proletariat. And in the same way the bourgeois demand for equality was accompanied by the proletarian demand for equality. From the moment when the bourgeois demand for the abolition of class *privileges* was put forward, alongside it appeared the proletarian demand for the abolition of the *classes themselves* ...
>
> The demand for equality in the mouth of the proletariat has therefore a double meaning. It is either – as was especially the case at the very start, for example in the peasants' war – the spontaneous reaction against crying social inequalities, against the contrast of rich and poor, the feudal lords and their serfs, surfeit and starvation ... Or, on the other hand, the proletarian demand for equality has arisen as the reaction against the bourgeois demand for equality, drawing more or less correct and more far-reaching demands from this bourgeois demand, and serving as an agitational means in order to rouse the workers against the capitalists on the basis of the capitalists' own assertions ... In both cases the real content of the proletarian demand for equality is the demand for the *abolition of classes*. Any demand for equality that goes beyond that, of necessity passes into absurdity.[23]

Engels makes the point that if modern society itself is not to be destroyed, the deep-rooted contradictions within the structure of business society must transcended.[24] The fact that he makes the passing reference, 'if society itself is not to be destroyed,' could remind us of a point that is made in the *Communist Manifesto*, where Marx and Engels assert that the struggle within society between social classes leads to the conquest of power by one class and the dislodgement and the overthrow of the other. Historically, the authors assert, this struggle has 'each time ended either in a revolutionary re-constitution of society at large, or in the common ruin of the contending classes.'[25] There have been cases when there were insoluble contradictions that simply blocked, resulting in disintegration and regression (the Thirty Years' War in the seventeenth century in some of its aspects had that character). But never before has it been possible for the struggle – such as that between the multinational rulers of the world and all those who question the legitimacy of their power – to result in such an ending on a world scale. Never before has there been such a possibility as this, that out of the red mud of Scalino – of Montedison – out of the poisonous pollution of industrial wastes, and the total irresponsibility of elected governments in relationship to the self-intoxication of urban and rural communities would come the possibility that there may *not be a future*.

Recently there have been a number of studies released on the pollution of the oceans, with one authority making the more or less informed guess that perhaps in twenty-five years the oceans will be dead. Perhaps the plankton will by then have disappeared and organic living beings in the seas of the world, which cover the greater part of the surface of the globe, will have become extinct. That home from which we originally came, in the days of which the vestigial gills of the human foetus are the persisting reminiscence – perhaps that source of life will become the watery grave of life. Perhaps we as a species will do ourselves in for lack of consciousness, lack of realization, lack of organization, and of struggle. Pitted against that possibility stands whatever there is left of human sense and decency, ranging through the innumerable areas where equality is an issue because there is subordination, exploitation, and oppression. Where, out of the interweave of innumerable issues and challenges there will grow a measure of social conscience and political consciousness that will tackle the national question, the sexist question, and the class question, in terms of the structure of the economy, the social, economic, political, military, and cultural institutions in which we have our being. That isn't the most cheerful note on which to end, but it's the nearest I can come to what we must have in mind as we tackle the problems of responsibility, action, happiness, and freedom – to the extent that those things can still be snatched from a threatening Last Judgement on ourselves and on our species.

NOTES

1 Cited in Irving M. Zeitlin, *Liberty, Equality and Revolution in Alexis de Tocqueville* (Boston 1971), 7
2 Ibid., 12
3 Alexis de Tocqueville, *Democracy in America* (New York 1948), II, 161
4 Cited in Research Committee of the League for Social Reconstruction, *Social Planning for Canada* (Toronto 1935, 1975), 500
5 Helen Levine, 'On Women and on One Woman as Provider and Consumer of Health and Social Services,' Carleton University, Ottawa, mimeo., 1975, pp. 5-6

6 Ibid., 15

7 Ibid., 18

8 (New York 1959)

9 R.H. Tawney, *Equality* (London 1931), 49

10 Ibid., 32

11 Ibid., 163

12 Jean Jacques Rousseau, *The Social Contract and Discourses* (London 1913), 42

13 C. Huglo and R. Cessni, *La société de pollution* (Paris 1977), 26 and passim. The recent Harrisburg, Pa., Three Mile Island near-disaster occurred at a Metropolitan Edison nuclear plant.

14 Tawney, *Equality*, 214-15

15 W.H. Beveridge, *Full Employment in a Free Society* (London 1945), 23

16 J.M. Keynes, *The Economic Consequences of the Peace* (New York 1920), 19-22

17 *Annuaire du Québec 1973* (Québec 1973), 604 ff.

18 Royal Commission on Bilingualism and Biculturalism, *Report*, Book I, Terms of Reference, P-C.1963-1106, p. 173. The Term 'founding races' (sic) is used, which is a Victorian pre-scientific absurdity. The French version reads 'peuples fondateurs.'

19 In Peter Stursberg, *Lester Pearson and the Dream of Unity* (Toronto 1978), 198

20 Cited in S.B. Ryerson, *Capitalisme et Confédération* (Montréal 1978), 320

21 'Reden über Polen,' K. Marx and F. Engels, *Werke*, Bd. 4 (Berlin 1959), 417 (my translation)

22 Virgil, *Aeneid*, trans. W.F.S. Knight (Baltimore, Md. 1956), xi and 289

23 F. Engels, *Anti-Düring: Herr Eugen Dühring's Revolution in Science* (New York 1976), 117-18 (emphasis in original)

24 Ibid., 174

25 K. Marx and F. Engels, *Selected Works*, I, Communist Manifesto (Moscow 1962), 34

Contributors

WARWICK ARMSTRONG teaches geography at McGill University. His current project is a comparative study of industrialization in Canada, Australia, and Argentina. His recent publications include 'Land, Class, Colonialism: The Origins of Dominion Capitalism,' in W.E. Willmott, ed., *New Zealand and the World: Essays in Honour of Wolfgang Rosenberg* (1980).

HOWARD BUCKBINDER teaches social science at Atkinson College, York University. For many years he has been a social worker and community activist. His publications include 'The Just Society Movement,' in Brian Wharf, ed., *Community Work in Canada* (1979).

GLENN DROVER is an associate professor and director of the School of Social Work, Carleton University. He has published articles on social welfare and urban development. A recent article on 'Urban Struggle and Organizing Strategies' (with E. Shragge) appeared in *Our Generation* (1979).

PHILIP EHRENSAFT teaches sociology at the Université du Québec à Montréal. His most recent article, 'Les longues vagues dans le developpement agricole en Amerique du Nord,' is forthcoming in *Sociologie et Société* (1981). His current research is in agriculture and argibusiness.

PATRICK KERANS is an associate professor of social work at Dalhousie University. His previous writings include 'Punishment Versus Reconciliation in Canada,' in Peter Slater, ed., *Religion and Culture in Canada* (1977). He has recently been a Maritime area commissioner for the Peoples' Food Commission, conducting an enquiry into food production and distribution in Canada. He was one of three writers who prepared the Commission report, *The Land of Milk and Honey* (1980).

NILS KUUSISTO is a research consultant in the field of regional development. He has served as a consultant on policy analysis to the Maritime School of Social Work's Manpower Project, a three-year study of social welfare in the Atlantic region.

ALLAN MOSCOVITCH teaches political economy in the School of Social Work, Carleton University. He has experience as a trade union and community activist. He is the compiler (with the assistance of Peter Findlay and Theresa Jennissen) of *The Welfare State in Canada: A Select Bibliography*, which will be published by the Wilfrid Laurier University Press in 1981.

STANLEY RYERSON is a professor of history at the Université du Québec à Montréal. His works include *Unequal Union* (1968), *The Founding of Canada: Beginnings to 1815* (1963), *French Canada: A Study in Canadian Democracy* (1943) (study to be revised), and co-author of *Bethune: The Montreal Years* (1978). For many years he has been a leading Marxist theoretician and activist, taking a particular interest in the social history and politics of Quebec.

LIORA SALTER teaches in the Department of Communication, Simon Fraser University. She has had extensive experience in community organizing and in community media. She is the co-editor with William Melody and Paul Heyer of *Culture, Communication, and Dependency* (1980) and the author of *Public Inquiries in Canada*, which will be published by the Science Council of Canada in 1981.

STEPHEN SCHECTER teaches sociology at the Université du Québec à Montréal. His book on *The Politics of Urban Liberation* was published by Black Rose Press (1978). Recently he has written on problems of self-management for several French and Italian anarchist journals.

DOROTHY SMITH is a professor of sociology at the Ontario Institute for Studies in Education. She is the co-editor with Sarah J. David of *Women Look at Psychiatry* (1975) and the author of *Feminism and Marxism* (1977) and several articles on aspects of the sociology of women in Canadian society. She has been a leading activist in the women's movement.

RICK WILLIAMS teaches political economy in the Maritime School of Social Work, Dalhousie University. He has worked extensively in labour education and organization in the Maritimes. He has written on the organization of inshore fishermen and on the structure of the fishing industry.

BERT YOUNG teaches sociology at John Abbott College in Montreal. He is a member of the editorial board of *Our Generation* magazine and has contributed several articles on economic and social affairs.